The Disenchantment of the Orient

The Disenchantment of the Orient

Expertise in Arab Affairs
and the Israeli State

GIL EYAL

Stanford University Press
Stanford, California
2006

Stanford University Press
Stanford, California
© 2006 by the Board of Trustees
of the Leland Stanford Junior University

Printed in the United States of America
on acid-free, archival-quality paper

Library of Congress Cataloging-in-Publication Data

Eyal, Gil.
    The disenchantment of the Orient : expertise in Arab affairs and the Israeli state / Gil Eyal.
        p.   cm.
    Includes bibliographical references and index.
    ISBN 0-8047-5403-9 (cloth : alk. paper)
    1. Palestine—History—1917–1948—Historiography.   2. Israel—Historiography.
3. Jewish-Arab relations—Historiography.   4. Orientalism—Israel.   5. Middle East
specialists—Israel.   6. Palestinian Arabs—Israel—Historiography.   I. Title.

DS115.5.E93 2006
956.940501'9—dc22

2005031347

Original Printing 2006
Last figure below indicates year of this printing:
15 14 13 12 11 10 09 08 07 06
Typeset at TechBooks, New Delhi, in 10.5/12 Bembo

For Johanna

Contents

Tables, Figures and Photos

Acknowledgments

THIS BOOK HAS BEEN LONG in the making. It began as master's thesis that I wrote under the supervision of Professors Abraham Cordova and Haim Hazan at the Department of Sociology and Anthropology at Tel-Aviv University. The year was 1989. The wall came down in Berlin, horrible pictures from Tiananmen were on the television screens, and in Israel the first intifada had just shaken Israelis out of their complacency regarding the occupation, or so it seemed. Yet, this was also a period of formative intellectual experience for me, under the guidance of my two sage mentors. Even after more than fifteen years, this book still evinces the deepest intellectual debt to them. They were the critical spirits, hovering behind my shoulders as I was writing, forcing me to reject facile solutions and empty phrases.

Once at UCLA, I had the greatest fortune to work under the tutelage of Professor Ivan Szelenyi. Together, we explored the exciting new developments that were unfolding in postcommunist Central Europe at the time, but Ivan also found the time to read and counsel me about this project – he may have never visited Israel, but he knew intellectuals and experts inside out, and at certain critical junctures he gave me invaluable advice that steered the project clear of blind alleys and hidden pitfalls.

Portions of this book have been previously published in an Israeli journal – *Teoria u-Bikoret* (Theory and Criticism), and an abridged Hebrew version was published by the Van-Leer Institute. The editors of the journal and the book series – Yehouda Shenhav, Adi Ophir, and Hanna Herzog – have treated me with utmost indulgence. Patiently and delicately, they helped me distinguish the core of my argument from the excess baggage and the youthful posturing. My debt to Yehouda Shenhav is especially great. Over the years, he has read countless versions of this manuscript, and his fingerprints can be found on every page of this book. More importantly, the chief ideas of this book were developed and crystallized in the course of conversations with him and also as I tried to come to terms with the critical and intellectual endeavor he began with his book *The Arab-Jews*. My debt to Hanna Herzog is only slightly less. Hanna read the whole manuscript several times, made invaluable comments, and enlightened me about obscure or difficult points. This book would have been much poorer had I not been able to draw on her vast knowledge of the history of Zionism and of Israeli politics.

Many other individuals have read portions of this manuscript and made insightful comments. I also spoke about this project with many knowledgeable individuals, and oftentimes I learned through these conversations important items of information or discovered that my materials could be viewed from a different and possibly more profitable perspective. Without these conversations, my work might have ended a long time ago, but the end product would not have been as good. I would like to thank Gideon Aran, Karen Barkey, Michael Burawoy, Haya Bambaji-Sasportas, Uri Ben-Eliezer, Irit Dosh, Dani Eshet, Adriana Kemp, Aziza Khazoomm, Shai Lavie, Emmanuel Marx, Hagai Ram, Julia Resnick, and Yuval Yonay. Daniel Bauer, Ruth Doron, Irit Keynan, Alec Mishori, and Gioia Perugia Sztulman were generous with their time and knowledge and helped me at crucial points to locate and reproduce the photos and artwork that appear in this book.

Kate Wahl and Kirsten Oster at Stanford University Press have been my sure guides throughout the whole process of manuscript preparation. I was impressed with their professionalism and with the speed and perfection with which they solved any problems, big or small. My thanks also to Christian Milord, who copyedited the whole text with utmost care and sagacity. The readers should be grateful to him as well. In many places, I incorporated suggestions of his that make the argument clearer and easier to follow. I am also indebted to John Feneron and Harold Moorehead at Stanford University Press and Vageesh Sharma at TechBooks for their professionalism and speed in coordinating the technical and administrative aspects of producing the book.

As I started by saying, this book has been long in the making. When it was no larger than a couple chapters, I met Johanna Shih. She has been with me ever since, through the happy moments and the difficult times. While the book grew and took shape, she gave birth to our two sons. If I could write this book and bring it to completion, if I could navigate the dire and narrow straits that are the age of disenchantment, it is only due to her indomitable spirit, her reasoned judgment, and her kind and generous love. This book is dedicated to her.

The Disenchantment of the Orient

At the end of every Hebrew sentence that you utter,
There sits an Arab, smoking his hookah,
Even if it begun in Siberia,
Or in Hollywood, with *Hava Nagilah.*
—Me'ir Ariel

THE SCENE IS PLAYED OVER and over again in the novels of the First Aliya:[1] Jewish travelers on the road recently arrived in Palestine. Evening is drawing near and the shadows are lengthening. From a distance they spy the figure of an armed horseman approaching, who seems to them to be an Arab, possibly a robber. They are afraid, and in their fear there is a hint of the Diaspora from which they have just arrived, the "old Jewish" fear of the Cossack, the Gentile. But how surprised and relieved they are, and how overjoyed (and yet somewhat ashamed), when the approaching stranger, dressed in *Abaya* (robe) and *Kafia* (headdress) in the manner of the Bedouin, addresses them in Hebrew. He turns out to have been a *Shomer* (literally "guard"), a new Jew mistaken for an old enemy.[2] The scene opens with the old Jew, marked by the Diaspora, and ends with the appearance of the new Jew, the *Shomer*, the farmer-fighter. And in between these two, in the liminal space marked by the road trip in the Orient, where identities dissolve into one another and are postponed, the figure of the Arab mediates between the opposites. It is the face reflected in the mirror, permitting an internal transformation – the bridge upon which past and future could meet.

Almost three-quarters of a century later, a Jewish traveler is again threatened by an ambiguous figure, possibly an Arab. Me'ir, the protagonist of Jacob Shabtai's *Past Perfect*, goes to Amsterdam for a holiday, but at his hotel he encounters "a burly man ... black-haired and with a black mustache, his skin of a white-greenish-olive hue, in a fancy suit ... and with the same glance he told himself that this man was an Arab ... in his hard-set dark face there was the clear expression of a bitter, arrogant enmity, and violence." The muted encounter between them is repeated over and over in Amsterdam's streets but does not lead to any resolution. It serves only to evoke Meir's submerged fears, which in the context of the novel function as a premonition of his own impending death. Me'ir never attempts to speak with the man, who for his part remains silent. He is like an ambiguous dark shadow upon whom the Israeli projects all his fears and despair. He serves as a mute and threatening background for Me'ir's desire to speak not with him but with residents of Amsterdam, who are Europeans: "after all, he is not as distant from them as those Asians and Africans . . . after all, he is an engineer and is learning history, Dutch history, or at least European history, and he read books, *Till Eulenspiegel*, and he admired the paintings of Rembrandt, Brueghel, and others." With no dialogue between them, the two remain unchanged, each in his place, one a muted Arab, the other an Israeli longing to be considered a European.[3]

Three-quarters of a century have passed, and this halting dialogue, which underneath the Arab's mask has exposed the possibility of being a new Jew, has been replaced by hostile silence and the breathless internal monologue of Shabtai's prose, in which the Arab can appear only as a phantom, an internal persecuting bad conscience (since Shabtai never confirms whether the man was an Arab or not). An inversion of sorts: the solid presence of the Arab, within which the new Jew could hide and take shape, has now itself become ethereal and internalized. My intention in this book is to describe and explain this transformation, not as a literary phenomenon but as a wholesale change in Israeli culture.

I chose to open with the stories of Shabtai and the First Aliya, not because I think they represent the development of Israeli literature, but because they each in their own way encapsulate a particular cultural structure, namely, the experience of encounter with what lies at the boundaries of Israeli culture. This encounter began under the sign of a myth of autochthony, a project of inventing a new Hebrew culture, almost out of whole cloth, and for this very reason it required the mask of the Arab. The invention of the Hebrew went hand in hand together with the invention of the Arab, and therefore the characteristic experience of this new culture was of this imaginary yet coherent space that contained the two within it and that contemporaries recognized as "the Orient." In this book, I try to trace the process of disintegration of this Orient and show how the contemporary experience of encounter was created out of its ruins. This experience is mostly a desperate attempt to affirm a separate Western identity. Desperate and futile, because the Arab keeps resurfacing as the phantom presence, or as Me'ir Ariel puts it, "sits at the end of the sentence," waiting for his turn, no doubt.

To describe and explain this transformation, I have decided to write a history of the cultural lens through which Israelis view their neighbors, or more precisely of the complex of knowledges and practices that mediate their encounter with the reality around them. Israelis have a generic name for this complex. They call it *mizrahanut* (literally, "orientalism") and typically use the term to refer to something larger than the academic study of the Middle East, Islam, or the Arab language and Arab literature. Typically, Israelis apply the term *mizrahan* (orientalist) not only to academics but also to all those government officials, army officers, journalists, and other experts who monitor the neighboring Arab countries, supervise the local Palestinian population, or participate in official and media debates about Arab, Islamic, and Middle Eastern affairs – in short, all those individuals who pronounce authoritative discourse about these matters and all those institutions in which such discourse is produced, packaged, and circulated.

Moreover, one of the main theses of this book is that it is impossible to disconnect the history of *mizrahanut* from the history of that social category that Israelis call *mizrahim*, namely, Jews who immigrated to Israel from Arab and Middle Eastern countries. As I show in the later chapters of this book, the sharp distinction between knowledge about Arabs and knowledge about the *mizrahim* – a distinction that is a defining characteristic of contemporary Israeli culture – was not self-evident before the establishment of the Israeli state in 1948, and these forms of knowledge and expertise were inseparably intertwined at that time. Therefore, I include within the rubric of *mizrahanut* all those who do research about the Jewish immigrants from Arab and Middle Eastern countries or who are in charge of absorbing and integrating them into Israeli society. This rather broad and diffuse sphere of expertise is the subject of this book.

Even such a broad definition, however, does not fully capture the social and cultural significance of the discourse of *mizrahanut,* which in an important sense is not the sole monopoly of the experts but is accessible as a sort of "inner orientalist" to almost all members of this culture. In this sense, *mizrahanut* is not merely a form of expertise but a core component of Israeli culture, of the way public discourse is conducted in Israel, of the way Israelis perceive the world around them, and of the manner in which they relate to themselves and define their own identity. In the same way that the linguistic codes of Israeli culture mandate speaking directly without beating around the bush (speaking *dugree*), they also include a certain orientalist function – an authoritative mode of speech that encompasses attitudes, opinions, tropes, and other discursive devices that can be used in ordinary conversation or in a political polemic and that position the speaker as someone who is observing from the outside (from the West), from a position of impartiality and superiority, what goes on in the Middle East or how Arabs behave.

The main argument of this book is that the role played by *mizrahanut* in Israeli society – both as a form of expertise and as a cultural-linguistic function that shapes the experience of encounter – has been profoundly transformed in the course of the last century, especially by processes caused by the establishment of the state. Just as from the First Aliya to Shabtai the figure of the Arab lost its capacity to mediate between old and new Jews, so too did Israeli *mizrahanut* turn separatist, and its knowledge now serves to confirm the cultural chasm between Israelis and their neighbors. The generation of prestate academic orientalists, for example, consisted of Central European Jews who were trained as philologists in German universities and construed their own role as building a bridge between Jews and Arabs to facilitate a "Jewish-Arab symbiosis." Even though they were experts in Islamic civilization, they also dedicated many of their studies to the Jews residing in Arab countries, especially Yemenite Jews, whom they regarded as "the most genuine Jews living among the most genuine Arabs."[4]

More importantly, as I show in chapter 2, in the years preceding the formation of the state of Israel, from 1926 to 1948, *mizrahanut* in the broader sense of a cultural-linguistic function applied itself to the "Orient" as a coherent and unified cognitive territory and as a meaningful metaphor signifying the renewal of the Jewish nation. Since Zionism exhorted Jews not only to return to Palestine in body but also to transform themselves, to shed the residues of the Diaspora and become pioneers, the "Orient" became the place where such transformation was possible as well as a rich source of tangible markers to signify the break between old and new Jewish identities.

The formation of the Israeli state in 1948, however, accelerated a process of divesting the metaphor of the "Orient" of the meaning it had in the past and of fragmenting its earlier coherence. The cognitive territory of the "Orient" was carved into different and separate jurisdictions, each claimed by a different group of experts: intelligence, government, *hasbara* (propaganda), and the absorption of immigrants. The Orient was disenchanted, while *mizrahanut* became separatist, no longer straddling the seams of the Jewish-Arab symbiosis but occupying a watchtower overlooking the hardening boundary between Israelis and Arabs. A younger generation of Israeli-born orientalists have applied themselves to this disenchanted and fragmented universe, no longer seeking there the secret of Jewish renewal but rather searching for "overt intelligence on the intentions, plans and deeds" of Arab leaders and regimes, which "often cannot be logically understood by an external observer."[5]

The Disenchantment of the Orient

Max Weber coined the term "disenchantment of the world" to denote the loss of meaning in modernity, or more specifically the loss of the ability to give the world a unified, organic, and coherent meaning. Weber argued that this loss was caused by the process of rationalization, which led not only to the severing of the bridges between this world and the next but to a more general process of differentiation and autonomization of the various spheres – religion, science, art, economy, politics, sexuality, and intellectual life – such that the coherent and meaningful world of our predecessors has fragmented into separate and competing jurisdictions.[6]

In coining the term "disenchantment of the Orient," I mean to refer to an analogous process of fragmentation in which the formerly coherent territory of the Orient was carved up into separate and competing jurisdictions (e.g., discourse on the Arab village is now distinct from Middle Eastern studies, which are themselves differentiated from the study of ancient Islamic civilization, which for its part has nothing to do with the sociology of *mizrahi* Jews in Israel). But unlike Weber, who argued that disenchantment was caused by a process of increasing rationalization, I argue the inverse: that disenchantment preceded rationalization and served as its condition of possibility.[7]

The first step in the transformation of the role that the orientalist function plays in Israeli culture was not recognition that the category of the "Orient" was imaginary and irrational but rather the arbitrary act of separation, of drawing external and internal boundaries, that took place as part of the state-building process during the 1948 war and its immediate aftermath: the expulsion of Palestinians from their villages and from the mixed cities; the decision to prohibit the return of the refugees and the war conducted against "infiltration"; the imposition of military government on the Palestinian population remaining within the confines of the new state; and the great migration of Jews from Middle Eastern countries and their forced settlement in the periphery. These acts not only separated Jews and Arabs but also provoked an intense conflict between different groups of experts, each presenting itself as capable of managing for the state the new external and internal boundaries and the new populations and problems. In the course of this struggle, the formerly coherent category of the "Orient" was carved up into different jurisdictions administered by different forms of expertise, and gradually the Orient was disenchanted and lost its capacity to endow the new Jewish existence with general and coherent meaning. Rationality, namely, the recognition by orientalists that the "Orient" was an artificial and essentialist category, as well as the new forms of rational knowledge – the discourse on the Arab village, Middle Eastern studies, the sociology of *mizrahi* Jews in Israel – only appeared much later, as a rather forced interpretation of the categories created by the state-building process.

To even formulate this project, to consider how and why *mizrahanut* has changed and with what consequences, is to break at once with two opposed yet symmetrical interpretations of orientalism. On the one hand, there is Edward Said's seminal analysis of orientalism as the way in which Europe sought to deal with the world around it, by essentializing the difference between "Orient" and "Occident." From this point of view, the orientalist function has no history and no development. Although there may have been some changes on the surface, on the "manifest" level, in what orientalists say, these changes never disturb orientalism at the "latent" level, where it has always and by definition functioned to position the West as separate from and superior to what lies outside it.[8] On the other hand, there is the testimony of orientalists themselves about what they do. They often depict themselves as educating an ignorant public about other cultures and peoples and thus, contrary to Said's view, as bridging the gap between them. The plausibility of this account is enhanced in the case of European Jewish orientalists, who were themselves branded as "oriental" by fellow Europeans and in reaction, so the argument goes, have espoused a much more sympathetic view of Arab and Islamic civilization than Said allows.[9] Yet, although their account may not ignore the historicity of orientalism, it obscures how orientalism functions on the discursive and institutional level. The history of orientalism is reduced to the story of a few individuals laboring at the margins to provide an accurate picture and combat prejudices with respect to Arab and Islamic civilization.

In one sense, my position can be seen as standing midway between those of Said and his critics: while Kremer and Lewis were right with respect to prestate Jewish orientalists, Said was right with respect to contemporary Israeli orientalists. But in another sense, what I am suggesting is altogether paradoxical from the point of view shared by Said and his critics: my argument implies that precisely because Jewish scholars in the prestate period were orientalist in Said's sense – that is, because they thought about the "Orient" in binary and essentialist terms – they construed their own role as bridging the gap between Jews and Arabs (i.e., they were nonseparatist). Contemporary Israeli orientalists, on the other hand, tend to disavow the old essentialist dogmas about the Orient,[10] but precisely for this reason they also tend to reinforce a separatist definition of Israeli identity. In short, as Israeli *mizrachanut* became less and less essentialist, it also became more separatist.

This is quite unthinkable from the point of view shared by Said and his critics, but it becomes thinkable if we understand the separatist effect of discourse not in terms of the prejudices and stereotypes it propagates but in terms of how it manages the boundary lines of identity. It becomes thinkable also when we sensitize ourselves to the paradoxes and hybridity of Zionism: this Jewish project of escaping internal colonialism via colonial settlement overseas also meant that in order to become "normal" (i.e., Western), the Jews had to go to the East and integrate themselves there; in order to constitute the binary division of East and West, they had to transgress it.[11]

Zionism and Its Boundary Signs

This argument derives from a conceptualization of orientalism that differs from the one developed by Said. From Said's point of view, orientalism is a Western discourse that invents an imaginary object – the "Orient" – and depicts it as radically different from the "Occident" (i.e., their difference is a difference of essences). In this sense, orientalism is not only a discourse about the orientals but also a way of defining the identity of the "West." As Said writes, "Orientalism is never far from . . . the idea of Europe, a collective notion identifying 'us' Europeans as against all 'those' non-Europeans."[12] Identity – whether European or Israeli – is created by drawing a strict boundary between East and West, thereby defining "us" and "them." This argument is by now a truism. Everybody knows that identity is defined against "the Other." Right?

Wrong. The problem with this approach, however simple and self-evident it may seem, is that it ignores the reality of the boundary itself. It basically requires us to think of the boundary as a nonentity, a "fine line" without any width to it, as in Euclidean geometry. If we conceive of the boundary as possessing a certain volume or width, if we analyze it as a real social entity, then what is inside the boundary is neither here nor there, neither them nor us; it is hybrid. Another way of saying this is that the very agents, social mechanisms, and symbolic materials that participate in the act of boundary making – the boundary signs themselves – of necessity also transgress the boundary just as they mark it.[13]

This point is well illustrated by the episode of the masked horseman with which I began. On the one hand, this figure is a boundary sign. One of its roles in the story is to mark the boundary between Arabs and Jews, since we are reassured at the triumphant end of the scene that the horseman was "really" a Jew (and the readers are also expected to learn in this way how to be a new Jew). On the other hand, however, if we freeze the frame and investigate more closely this figure in itself, just before it disappears, we realize that by the same token it also transgresses the boundary, since in itself it is neither Arab nor Jew but quite literally Janus-faced – a hybrid, an Arab-Jew.

Another illustration of this point is the wealth of terms that currently exist in the Hebrew language to signify the volume of the boundary, that social-spatial entity that at one and the same time separates and connects the two sides of the boundary: *Shetach Ha-Hefker* (no-man's-land), *Merhav Ha-Tefer* (seam zone), *Techum Ha-Sfar* (frontier area), *Ezor H-Gvul* (border zone), and many others. The first term, *Shetach Ha-Hefker,* is particularly apt and revealing. This was the name given, for example, to the no-man's-land separating Arab and Jewish Jerusalem before 1967. The Hebrew word *Hefker* is loaded with significance: it may mean a thing that is lost, without an owner, free for the taking, or it may refer to a deserted and empty zone, outside sovereign rule (or where sovereignty is disputed). Therefore, it also connotes an area outside morality, where no laws hold, where nothing is forbidden or protected – in short, a site of scandal (*Hefkerut*). In this sense, no-man's-land is a sort of antiborder, the opposite of the border (or of the law), which nonetheless always adjoins it and acts as its constant shadow. Moreover, linguistically *hefker* is also connected with another sort of transgression – losing one's religion, becoming a non-Jew (*Hitpakrut*), thus connoting a zone where identity dissolves, where the Jew merges into the Gentile.

The boundary, therefore, is not a fact established once and for all, but at any given moment it is an ongoing and rather precarious achievement. One can never stop marking it. At this point, I would like to return to the role of orientalist discourse and expertise. If the discourse of *mizrahanut* is separatist, this is not because once and for all it draws a boundary between East and West or between Arabs and Jews, since the very act of drawing the boundary also transgresses it and produces hybrids. Whether discourse and expertise are separatist depends on how they patrol, so to speak, the no-man's-land within the volume of the border; on the particular modes of control and supervision they exercise over the hybrids that exist therein; and on the forms of self-control and self-monitoring they exercise over the experts themselves. Separatism is a specific border regime that deals with the purification of hybrids (i.e., with the arbitrary relegation of them to this or that side of the boundary line).

The purification of the hybrids does not mean that they are eliminated. On the contrary, it is precisely what permits them to be manufactured on a large scale. This is Bruno Latour's argument concerning modernity. All premodern societies, explains Latour, manufactured hybrids, "monsters" that transgressed the carefully outlined boundaries of the cultural systems of classification and therefore were deemed to be a threat to the social order. For this reason, much of the ongoing cultural effort of these societies was directed at limiting the number of hybrids and controlling them, which is why the hybrids typically appear as carriers of impurity. An excellent example is furnished by the status of the pig in Judaism.

Modernity, on the other hand, multiplies the number of the hybrids exponentially, because at its disposal are forms of expertise that purify the impure hybrids and in this way reconstitute the cultural system of classification. The basic distinction of the modern classification system, according to Latour, is between nature and society, or between manipulable objects and right-bearing subjects. This distinction is a myth, but different groups of experts – doctors, psychologists, natural scientists, lawyers, and so on – have a vested interest in its persistence, and consequently their discourse obsessively endeavors to distinguish between "body" and "mind," between conscious and unconscious, between natural phenomena and human-made instruments.[14]

It is possible to apply this analysis, by way of analogy, to orientalist expertise, especially to the new forms of expertise that claimed jurisdiction over various departments of the Orient after 1948. This is where their significance lay. They produced rational accounts that legitimated the arbitrary fiat of purification, which explained why the hybrids "really" belong only to one side of the boundary, either Arab or Jewish, and which discounted their other features as nonessential, temporary, artificial, correctable, and so on. At the same time, however, the experts themselves, precisely because they endeavored to supervise the border zone, ran the constant risk of becoming themselves entangled in this no-man's-land, becoming identified with it, themselves perceived as hybrids who are not quite trustworthy. An important part, therefore, of the separatist border regime is the self-control and the self-monitoring that the experts exercise over themselves, the way their own discourse requires them to purify themselves because of their proximity to the hybrids.

At this point, the readers may justifiably wonder whether this rather complex and abstract theory has anything to do with history of Zionism and its relationship to the Palestinians. Isn't the story much simpler? Aren't the causes of the emergence of separatism much more straightforward? And wasn't the role of the experts in this regard altogether secondary and after the fact? It is fashionable today to compare Zionism with European colonialism and to point to their common origins. Zionism understood itself, so argue the critics, as a Western movement bringing the light of progress and civilization to the backward Orient. For this reason, it separated itself from its Arab surroundings, which it deemed inferior. In short, Zionism was a form of orientalism.[15]

Additionally, labor Zionism had economic reasons for separating from the Palestinians. In order for Jewish laborers to survive in the labor market, it was necessary to split the labor market (this was the notorious struggle over "Hebrew labor"), because the Palestinians laborers were much cheaper than the Jewish ones. The labor Zionist solution was to settle the land by means of purely Jewish agricultural cooperatives that relied solely on the labor of their members. In short, the economic exigencies that followed from the attempt to create a colonial settler society in the adverse conditions of Palestine led to the creation of a series of institutions – the General Federation of Labor, the kibbutzim, the Jewish National Fund – that gave Jewish society in Palestine its distinctive character and separated it economically and territorially from the local Palestinian population.[16]

This combination of separatist institutions and separatist identity, however, meant that the Zionist movement was on a collision course with the Palestinians, and it led directly and inevitably to their expulsion during the 1948 war. In comparison with this dynamic, rooted in the inescapable constraints of material existence and the ineluctable forces of identity, isn't the story about the hybrids, the experts, and the disenchantment of the Orient completely incidental and of marginal significance?

The aim of this book is to show that when the history of Zionism is considered from the point of view of the manufacture and purification of hybrids, it is possible to tell a different story about separatism. Separatism was not inevitable, a direct result of the essential nature of Zionism as a colonial-orientalist project, but a historical event overdetermined by multiple and sometimes contingent causes, of which some at least had to do with struggles among the experts and the relations between them and the state.

To substantiate this argument, chapter 2 deals with early Zionism and its experience of encounter with the Orient. This experience, I try to show, constituted something much more massive, complex, and meaningful than merely a sense of separateness and European superiority. To understand this point, we must recall that early Zionism was not only an organization mobilized to achieve political and economic ends but also a church seeking to disseminate a certain revealed truth and to instruct individuals on how to fashion their bodies and souls to attain salvation. To perform the magic of transforming old Jews into new Jews and to endow the new identity with a sense of authenticity and autochthony, early Zionism manufactured three different types of hybrids that at one and the same time marked and transgressed the boundary between Jews and Arabs in the prestate period:

1. The *mista'ravim*, that is, Jews who learned to imitate Palestinian customs and dialect to perfection.[17] Not only could they "pass" as Palestinians, but, as I will show, their imitation of the Palestinians functioned as a public sacrifice of their old selves for the sake of fashioning a new Zionist self. In this sense, the *mista'ravim* were similar to the early Christian martyrs and saints. They were virtuosi. The sacrifice of their old selves and the ascetic fashioning of a new self served as the basis for their claim to lead the flock of lesser souls by means of setting an example of virtuous conduct.

2. The Sephardim, that is, Jews who claimed to be descended from the exiles of Spain and who have lived for centuries under Ottoman rule – in Greece, Turkey, Syria, and importantly also in Palestine, especially Jerusalem. They were typically well integrated into urban Palestinian society. Intricate and dense networks connected their leadership with the Palestinian urban elite, thus providing confirmation for the idea that the goal of Zionism was to promote a harmonious synthesis between Orient and Occident.

3. The fellahin, that is, the Palestinian peasants, who were represented in Zionist iconography as "hidden Jews" (i.e., as the descendants of the ancient Hebrews or at least as their living image). This representation served to weave the Zionist narrative into the fabric of the settlers' everyday life in Palestine and transformed Palestine into *Eretz Israel* (the land of Israel).

These three hybrids joined together to create the experience of an open horizon of identity, a space of metamorphosis and the transmutation of identities. This was a coherent and meaningful experience of the Orient as a metaphor for the Zionist project of sacrificing the old identity and fashioning a new one.

I do not mean to claim that these were the sole forces shaping Zionist identity in the prestate period. The separatist institutions and acquired predispositions identified by other authors were no doubt dominant in prestate Jewish society, especially from 1936 onward. Consequently, all these hybrid figures were viewed with some suspicion, and numerous attempts to "purify" them were made. At the same time, however, as I argue in chapter 2, these hybrid figures and the practices associated with them were also central to key Zionist practices and rituals validating the new Jewish identity. In fact, they even played an important role in the functioning of the very separatist institutions that would seem opposed to them. As Latour argues, the production and mobilization of hybrids are intrinsically tied to their purification. They are not opposed to the purification of hybrids but feed it, and vice versa.

As I show in chapter 3, the key factor that explains the laxity of the prestate border regime and differentiates it from the current situation is the balance of power in the field of orientalist expertise: the two dominant groups of orientalist experts in the prestate period – the German-trained philologists and the amateur "Arabists" – not only did not seek to purify the hybrids but in fact modeled their own expertise on them: the philologists specialized in the "Jewish-Arab symbiosis," which they considered the Sephardim to embody most perfectly, while the Arabists claimed expertise in Arab affairs because, like the *mista'ravim*, they imitated the Bedouin and the fellahin and could "think like them." Thus, neither group of experts managed to disentangle themselves from the no-man's-land surrounding the boundary or to prevent their identification with the hybrids. On the contrary, their very authority depended on existing within the border zone, "between East and West," alongside the hybrids.

The 1948 war and the formation of the state of Israel certainly brought this state of affairs to its end and completely transformed the role that *mizrahanut* played in Israeli culture. In chapter 4, however, I show that it is impossible the attribute these changes to the war per se; rather, one must examine also the struggles between the experts that took place during and after the war. Even the most brutal and thoroughgoing attempt at separation, namely, the expulsion of Palestinians and the mass immigration of Jews from Arab countries to Israel in the aftermath of the war, did not completely separate Jews and Arabs, nor did it eliminate the ambiguity of the boundary between them. On the contrary, it led to the formation of three new hybrid figures:

1. "Infiltrators," whose movements blurred the boundary between what was inside the state and what was outside it.
2. "Israeli Arabs," whose status within the Jewish state remained ambiguous, between citizens and enemies.
3. *Mizrahi* Jews, the new immigrants, who were perceived as somewhere between Jews and Arabs.

This time, however, there was intense competition between different groups of experts, each seeking to present itself as better able to supervise and purify the hybrids. The difference between this period and the prestate period was not the fact of the war per se but more generally the project of giving Zionism the shape of a sovereign (Jewish) *state*. It was this project that produced the hybrids as a sort of a "byproduct" of the effort to draw external and internal boundaries, and it was this same project that changed the status of these hybrids and required their purification as well as the self-purification of the experts.

Like the boundary, the state is not a fact established once and for all but rather an ongoing and precarious practical achievement. Or as Timothy Mitchell put it, the state is an "effect" of a political practice that continuously blurs the boundaries between the state and society, or between the state and other states, and continuously redraws them. This effect has two components: first, the effect of sovereignty, the image of the state as a bounded unit with clearly defined jurisdiction, and second, the effect of agency, the image of the state as a cohesive and impersonal actor, strictly separated from the web of social relations and yet capable of effectively commanding it.[18] This image is in one respect a sham, because to be effective the state cannot avoid becoming entangled in the web of social relations. It cannot have recourse to the relationship of command alone. It must persuade, influence, bargain, mobilize, organize, and form linkages, networks, and coalitions; that is, it must act as if there were no boundaries between state and society, and in fact state elites benefit from "fuzzifying" these boundaries. But in another respect, the effect of the state is an important political reality, because without the boundary between the state and society, and certainly without a clear territorial boundary between the state and other states, the power of the state to issue commands would become illegitimate.

In the modern world, expertise has grown in parallel with the rise of the state, because it provides one crucial means of orchestrating the effect of the state: on the one hand, expertise establishes durable relations, which are not command relations, between state agencies, social actors, technology, and natural phenomena, thus producing and utilizing hybrids; on the other hand, it provides an ongoing account of its activities in which everything is separated carefully to its own proper realm – the natural, the scientific, the social, and the political – and the hybrids are purified.

The three hybrids mentioned above, therefore, were created as a result of the project to give Zionism the shape of a sovereign Jewish state, and as we shall see later, state elites benefited and continue to benefit from fuzzifying the external and internal boundaries. At the same time, however, it was also necessary to redraw these boundaries again and purify the hybrids in order to establish the legitimate authority of state agencies. This double movement of hybridization and purification was the basis for various alliances between state elites and groups of experts, who functioned in this manner as a sort of subsidiary arm of the state. As I show in chapter 4, this prompted an intense struggle between various groups of experts, each claiming to monitor the external and internal boundaries and to supervise the hybrids on behalf of state elites so as to assist in producing the effect of the state. In the course of this struggle, the previously coherent cognitive territory of the Orient, which earlier accommodated both experts and hybrids, both Jews and Arabs, was carved up into separate and competing jurisdictions, each controlled by a different group of experts. In particular, the expertise required to deal with Arabs outside the state ("intelligence") was differentiated from the expertise needed to deal with Arabs inside the state ("government"), and both were differentiated from the expertise needed to deal with the *mizrahi* Jews ("absorption of immigrants"). This process of differentiation is what I call the "disenchantment of the Orient."

I would like to accentuate the fateful importance, in particular, of the fact that the expertise required to absorb the *mizrahi* Jews was differentiated from other forms of expertise in Arab affairs "proper." It signaled a complete transformation in the role played by *mizrahanut* and the orientalist function in Israeli society: before the formation of the state, the orientalists in the Hebrew University took Judeo-Arab civilization as their main subject and dedicated many studies to the dialect, folklore, and religious traditions of the first communities of Middle Eastern Jews who immigrated to Palestine, especially the Yemenites and the Kurds. It was part and parcel of their expertise. After the formation of the state, however, succeeding generations of Israeli orientalists began to restrict themselves to the study of the Arab world in and of itself and abandoned the study of Jewish history to the field of Judaic studies. The communities of *mizrahi* Jews who immigrated to Israel were thus left outside the purview of *mizrahanut* and became an object of study for the social sciences. The social sciences, in their turn, tended to avoid the study of the Palestinians and only returned to it rather late, during the 1970s.[19]

From the point of view developed here, however, the social scientific discourse on *mizrahi* Jews and the orientalist discourses on Arabs outside and inside the state must be grasped together as a single "border regime," a device for the constant construction and purification of the *mizrahi* hybrid. One arm of this device undertakes to study Arabs, and Arabs alone, from a position of exteriority. This simple, staggering discursive fact reaffirms the boundary between Jews and Arabs and constructs *mizrahi* Jews as a hybrid in need of purification. The other arm accepts this construction as given and undertakes to "develop" and educate the *mizrahi* Jews – that is, to purify them. Nonetheless, it also continues to report a certain obstinate, irreducible difference that cannot be eliminated. The category of *mizrahi* Jews is thus the "hinge" between those two realms of discourse, making possible their separation and yet linking them inextricably. As I show in chapter 4, it is impossible to understand the emergence and significance of the category of *mizrahi* Jews without taking into account the project to separate Arabs and Jews. The attempt to draw such boundaries, especially through residential segregation, has produced as its inevitable byproduct a sort of "third space," a no-man's-land between the Jewish and Arab spaces, where the category of *mizrahi* Jews crystallized and acquired the meaning it currently has. From this perspective, the disenchantment of the Orient, the transformation of orientalist expertise, and the formation of the new category of *mizrahi* Jews appear as three sides of the same process, a process through which Israeli society produces and confirms itself as "Western."

The last part of the book deals with the forms of knowledge and expertise that developed over the years inside the jurisdictions of intelligence and government. These forms of expertise took upon themselves the task of purifying the hybrids and thus shaped how Israelis perceive the world around them. For example, as discussed in chapter 5, the discourse on the "Arab village" that developed within the framework of the military government imposed on the Palestinians from 1948 to 1966 purifies the Israeli Arab hybrid by separating what is "internal" to the village and hence "traditional" and "Arab" from what is "external" and hence due to the dynamic effect of the "modern" and "Western" Israeli society. In this way, modernization discourse – with its binary oppositions of modern versus traditional, West versus East – was inscribed upon the physical landscape of the state of Israel and has become part of the taken-for-granted spatial knowledge of all Israelis.

In a parallel development, as I show in chapter 6, a discourse of commentary about current events in the Middle East arose in the interface between military intelligence and academic Middle Eastern studies and has functioned to purify the refugee or infiltrator hybrid. It ignores and suppresses the complexity and ambiguity of the no-man's-land along the external boundaries and instead produces a dominant definition of Middle Eastern reality restricted to leaders and regimes whose intentions are well defined and whose responsibility is clearly formulated. The hybrids – the refugees and the infiltrators – are excluded from it.

The contiguity and proximity to the hybrids, as I have argued, pollutes the experts and therefore requires them to disentangle themselves from the no-man's-land inside the boundary and to purify themselves so they can appear as credible allies of state elites. For this reason, they have a vested interest in distancing themselves from the hybrids. The emergence of the discourse on the Arab village, for example, as I show in chapter 5, should be understood as part of a solution to the crisis of Arabist expertise, a solution that included the abolition of the military government and the withdrawal of its supervisory functions to behind the scenes. The reason for this crisis was that Arabist expertise became more and more identified with the no-man's-land inside the internal boundary and became polluted by the scandal and sensation that were linked to it and the rumors that grew around it. The expertise of intelligence officers and academic Middle Eastern studies specialists, on the other hand, was constructed from the very first as an extensive and hierarchical network that orchestrated the activities of various intelligence-gathering agencies (including those entangled in the border zone) while simultaneously permitting the researchers to remain distant from the hybrids. The result was a form of expertise that could afford to ignore the ambiguities of the border zone and thus was not polluted by proximity to the hybrids.

The final argument shared by chapters 5 and 6 is that the purification devices deployed by orientalist discourse no longer perform their role as well as they did in the past. Put differently, the dreaded "return" of the refugees has already taken place, at least at the level of the discursive mechanisms that were meant to supervise the hybrids. By now, after the Oslo Accords established the Palestinian Authority in the territories, and even more so with the eruption of the Al-Aksa Intifada, the discourse of intelligence experts is nothing but a desperate and futile attempt to impose its obsolete categories on a reality that no longer accords with them, a reality in which it is no longer possible to ignore the existence of the hybrids – both the residents of the territories, who are now all potentially refugees and infiltrators, and the Palestinian Authority itself, which is something between a state and a nonstate. The discourse on the Arab village was confronted with similar challenges even earlier. During the 1980s, it became clear that many so-called "villages" have grown to become more like towns and cities, while their residents were far more politically assertive and organized than was expected of peasants. Consequently, the discourse on the Arab village began to lose its relevance, and it has gradually been replaced by a debate conducted in categories taken directly from 1948. The specter of the internal enemy has returned to haunt public discourse, and with it have come renewed debates about the advantages and disadvantages of population exchange, transfer, autonomy, and assimilation.

Before embarking on this elaborate and difficult history, however, I offer, in chapter 1, a methodological excursus to clarify the subject of this book. I assume that many readers are already exasperated with my rather liberal and imprecise use of the terms "*mizrahanut*," "orientalism," "orientalists," "experts," "Arabists," "Middle Eastern specialists," and so on. What exactly do they mean? Who is an orientalist and who is not? Am I not fudging the issue by permitting myself to include all sorts of extra-academic actors and institutions within the scope of this study? The following chapter, therefore, is intended to serve as a methodological introduction to the rest of the book. There I take up the question of who is an orientalist and what is the scope of orientalism. I rule out definitions of orientalism based on its object (the "Orient") or on some clearly demarcated discipline and instead suggest we think of it as a set of practices that mediate historically changing forms of encounter within the boundary zone and as an open-ended field of struggle over the orientalist prototype – that is, over the definition of legitimate actors in the field, the rules of entry into it, and the hierarchy of worth within it.

CHAPTER 1

What Is Mizrahanut? *A Methodological Introduction*

IN THE INTRODUCTION, I said that *mizrahanut* is something larger than merely the academic study of the Middle East. I insisted that a working definition should include all those who, in various institutional locations, produce authoritative discourse on the Middle East, Arab culture, Islamic civilization, or even *mizrahi* Jews. I even suggested that such a history should address also something as fuzzy and ill defined as the orientalist function. By saying this, however, I probably have caused even more confusion and questioning: What is the subject of this book? What is *mizrahanut* (or orientalism)? Who are its practitioners (in Hebrew, *mizrahanim*)? Is it possible to give a straightforward and unequivocal answer to these questions? And if not, is it possible to write a history of *mizrahanut* at all?

There are two commonsensical ways of answering these questions, but neither will do in this case. The first is to define *mizrahanut* according to its topic, the slice of reality it studies, which is taken as given. In high school we were told, for example, that biology is the science of life or that chemistry studies the molecular structure of matter. Similarly, one could say that orientalism is the study of the "Orient." A different approach is to define *mizrahanut* according to the specific expertise wielded by its practitioners, who again are taken to form a given and well-defined group. Everybody knows that medicine, for example, does not have a single topic or object but that it is defined simply by what medical doctors do by virtue of their knowledge and jurisdiction. (What is the common denominator between, say, cosmetic surgery, the prescription of antihistamines, and sexual counseling apart from the fact that they are all under the jurisdiction of medical doctors?) Similarly, one could say that *mizrahanut* is the deployment of a particular kind of expertise, in particular, knowledge of the Arab language and

Islamic culture. In short, *mizrahanut* could be defined either by its object or by its subject. But even a superficial examination of these definitions shows that they are inadequate.

Suppose *mizrahanut* is the study of the Orient. What would be the geographical boundaries of this object? A very simple empirical test would be to collect all the articles published in a leading journal, such as the official publication of the Israeli Oriental Society, *Ha-Mizrach Ha-Hadash* (The New Orient), and to check to what geographical area they pertain. In the inaugural issue of *Ha-Mizrach Ha-Hadash*, the president of the society wrote that the new quarterly would deal with "events and developments in the countries of the Orient, especially the Middle East."[1] What did he mean by the "Middle East"? It could be a fairly well defined geographical area stretching from Turkey and Iran in the north and bounded by the Persian Gulf in the east, the Indian Ocean in the south, and the Suez Canal in the west. But my calculations show that only 60 percent of the 286 articles published in the period from 1949 to 1977 dealt with this area. However, as can be seen in Table 1.1, if one adds the articles dedicated to Egypt, a country commonly recognized as part of the Middle East even though it is in Africa, west of the Suez Canal, then 77 percent of the articles were dedicated to countries in the region. I might hypothesize, therefore, that the Middle East is not a geographical but a geopolitical unit and that its boundaries are determined by the intensity of relations between the countries included within it.

But in this case I would be hard pressed to explain why at least 10 percent of the articles were dedicated to countries further to the east – Pakistan, India, China, Japan, Burma, and so on – that are not commonly perceived as belonging to the Middle East geopolitical zone. I might hypothesize further that the topic treated by *mizrahanut* is not just the Middle East but the old, wide territorial expanse of the "Orient," as the president of the Israeli Oriental Society intimated. Even that would not do. Even if I ignore the fact that Egypt lies to the west of Israel and south of Europe, I would still be hard pressed to explain why approximately 8 percent of the articles were

TABLE 1.1. Geographical Focus of Articles in *Ha-Mizrah Ha-Hadash*, 1949–1977

Years	Near East and Egypt	North Africa	Far East	Sub-Saharan Africa	Other	Total
1949–1963	104 (73%)	3 (2%)	19 (14%)	7 (5%)	8 (6%)	141
1964–1977	115 (79%)	1 (1%)	10 (7%)	15 (10%)	4 (3%)	145
Total	219 (77%)	4 (1%)	29 (10%)	22 (8%)	12 (4%)	286

Source. Ilan Pappe, "Multi-Year Index," *Ha-Mizrah Ha-Hadash* 28, suppl. (1979): 4–31.

dedicated to countries of sub-Saharan Africa (Nigeria, Ghana, Ethiopia, etc.). I might hypothesize that the geographical boundaries of the Orient are not really defined by the boundaries of states but by the stretch of a certain civilization – the spread of the Islamic religion or of the Arabic language. This hypothesis, too, fails the test. While some of the articles dedicated to the countries of sub-Saharan Africa or the Far East focus indeed on Islamic elements in these societies, many others do not. Moreover, if this hypothesis were true, one would expect to see many more articles dedicated to the countries of North Africa (Libya, Algeria, Tunis, Morocco, etc.), whose inhabitants are predominantly Arab and Muslim, but only 1 percent concern these countries. To this evidence I must add the fact that many of the articles dedicated to countries of the geopolitical "Middle East" deal with non-Muslim and/or non-Arab populations, such as the Armenians, Assyrians, Copts, and Maronites.

This is admittedly a crude test. The reader may justly object that the contents of this one journal reflect not the boundaries of the object of orientalism but merely the vagaries of editorial decision-making, a fairly random process. The editors may have decided to provide their readers with articles on some less familiar topics or were simply inundated with submissions about Africa and the Far East. On this view, the object of *mizrahanut* remains easy to determine. It is composed of the geopolitical Middle East, which is the subject of 77 percent of the articles; the remaining articles are just "noise," wide blurry margins around a focused lens.

I tend to disagree. These margins are a little bit more patterned than one would expect if they were merely the result of a random process. As Table 1.1 shows, over the years there were some significant changes in the number of articles dedicated to the countries of the Far East and sub-Saharan Africa. Although from 1949 to 1963 14 percent of the articles were dedicated to Far Eastern countries and only 5 percent to sub-Saharan ones, these percentages were roughly reversed between 1964 and 1977, to 7 percent and 10 percent, respectively. The change is even more striking if we compare the first three years of the journal (1949–1952), when according to my calculations almost 20 percent of the articles were dedicated to India, China, and similar countries but only 2 percent to African countries, with the decade following the 1967 war, when the percentages were 6 percent and 13 percent, respectively.

Now, to anyone familiar with the history of Israeli foreign policy, these are not random fluctuations. In the first three years of the state's existence, its diplomats and experts followed closely the conflict and population transfer between India and Pakistan in order to derive evidence and arguments to bolster its position with respect to the Palestinian refugees; in the decade after the 1967 war, Israel was seeking ways to break out of the isolation imposed on it by the circle of "nonidentified" and Third World countries who supported the Arab states in the UN, and one of its strategies was to provide agricultural assistance to African countries, promising to help them develop and modernize. One starts to get the sense that the boundaries of the territorial area understood to be within the mandate of the journal are neither fixed nor random but change in quite determinable ways, in accordance with practices aimed not so much at reflecting a given reality but at shaping it and managing the encounter with it.

Or take another quality of the articles appearing in *Ha-Mizrah Ha-Hadash*. Even though a large proportion of them are dedicated to Arab communities residing inside the State of Israel, almost none deal with Jews – neither with Jews residing in Israel or Mandatory Palestine, nor with Jews residing in or recently emigrated from Arab countries, nor with the history of Middle Eastern Jewish communities. It is free of Jews.[2] If we go back a few years to prestate journals like *Mizrah u-Ma'arav* (Orient and Occident), which is discussed in the next chapter, we find the opposite picture. Practically all the articles were dedicated to Jewish issues and to Jewish communities of the Middle East, and only a handful dealt with developments in the Middle East.[3] Of course, the two journals are not comparable in a strict sense, but this is precisely the point: between 1922 and 1949, the orientalist function underwent a fundamental change and started to play a different role, and with this change came a revision in the ethnic boundaries of its object – boundaries that now marked a strict separation between Jews and Arabs.

This brief empirical test indicates that whoever attempts to define *mizrahanut* by its object – the "Orient" – inverts the real sequence: orientalist discourse defines and creates its own object, and not vice versa. As Said puts it, the "Orient" is not a place or a region but an idea, an imaginary entity, and from the geographical point of view, its boundaries are determined and changed quite arbitrarily.[4] Orientalism emerged, according to Said, in Europe in the period after the Crusades and before Napoleon's conquest of Egypt. It is not that Europe gradually discovered the Orient as over the centuries it probed further and further outward. On the contrary, Europe invented the idea of the "Orient" precisely when it was forced to be at its most insular, least capable of exploring what lay beyond it. The idea of the "Orient" served to aggregate together all that it did not know – all that it experienced as alien and threatening right at its door – and to master it, at least imaginarily.[5]

This argument implies another fruitful idea that one can find in Said: orientalist discourse defines and creates its own object, not from thin air, but in the context of a specific mode of *encounter* between Westerners and the world that surrounds them and through the mediation of specific *practices* that mobilize distant phenomena and transport them back to be represented on a Western stage. These practices shape the modality of knowledge through which the encounter is interpreted and experienced. For example, in the period discussed above, prior to Napoleon's conquest of Egypt, the mode through which Europe encountered the "Orient" is characterized by Said as a "textual attitude." This means, first, that in the absence of the colonial possession of foreign lands, the practices at Europe's disposal for mobilizing distant phenomena were mostly textual, specifically, the travel book and the dramatized polemic. Dante's *Inferno* is a good example: Dante masters Muhammad and represents him on the European stage by treating him as a "heretic," not only assigning him to a definite circle of hell but using him as an interlocutor within a dramatized polemic composed for European Christian audience.[6] But it also means that a textual attitude shapes the experience of the encounter and how it is interpreted. When Europeans traveled in the Orient, they planned their itinerary in accordance with what they read in books about the Orient, seeking to visit the places described in the scriptures, and they interpreted what they saw in this light as well. The correlate of the textual attitude was, thus, the "Orient" as an ancient, unchanging essence.

The terms "encounter" and "mediation" may be somewhat misleading here, to the extent that they connote the image of two distinct entities between which a messenger goes back and forth. Let me emphasize, therefore, that these practices and forms of expertise that mobilize the Orient must be grasped as networks that stretch across the boundary between the Orient and the Occident. In other words, the boundary is *internal* to these networks and is one of their effects. At one and same time, they ignore the boundary and go beyond it, only in order to turn back and erect it anew in their midst, in the form of a network property, an "obligatory point of passage."[7]

A good example is the status of ethnographic informants. To the extent that such informants are elucidating and describing local practices, they are already one step removed from the "native point of view." Indeed, typically they are individuals whose objective social position is somewhat removed from those upon whom they report, either because they are marginal or because they have already formed extralocal ties. This aspect of their existence is only reinforced by their connection with the ethnographer. In this sense, we are talking not about two distinct entities being mediated but about a whole set of graduated differences more and more removed from local context. We could say, therefore, that ethnographic expertise consists of a chain of connections reaching from the local context all the way to the air-conditioned office where field notes are reinterpreted in the form of a monograph and that the informant simply occupies one position in this chain. This reasoning can be formulated in one simple question: why isn't the ethnographer an "informant" as well? Asking this question immediately leads us to see the significance of the distinction between "ethnographer" and "informant" and the role it performs within this network of expertise. First, it serves to position the ethnographer at an obligatory point of passage (the point where "data" stops and "interpretation" begins); second, it purifies the hybridity of the informants and discounts all that is extralocal about them; and third, it purifies the hybridity of the ethnographers themselves, protecting them from becoming assimilated to their informants and infected by their hybridity.

These considerations are particularly relevant to what Said described as the second stage in the European encounter with the Orient, the colonial stage. The defining moment for Said, because he was specifically interested in the discourse about Arabs and Islam, was Napoleon's conquest of Egypt, but regardless of where one marks the rupture, the essential point is that when Europe began to penetrate and control the lands around it, the modality of knowledge and discourse consequently changed: Europeans could now observe the lives and bodies of the inhabitants of distant lands in close ethnographic and physiognomic detail; they mapped the precise topography of such lands; they ordered their colonial subjects to divulge the secrets of their language, civilization, and "mentality"; they ransacked their cities and temples and confiscated artifacts and treasures; and they transported everything back to the European centers, where maps, artifacts, bodies, and mentalities were further studied and analyzed.

In short, colonial practices and forms of expertise were networks that stretched all the way from the European centers to the distant colonies and constructed a new modality of knowledge – the gaze. While the object of the textual attitude was the "Orient" as an ancient, unchanging essence, mastery of which practically required ignorance of details, the gaze constructed objects of detailed and "anatomical" knowledge, such as the *Description de l'Égypte* commissioned by Napoleon, the comparative study of institutions in British anthropology, the anatomical-sexual analyses of scientific racism, and the detailed descriptions provided in development studies.[8] While the precolonial traveler journeyed in an Orient composed of prose, and what he saw there depended on a certain degree of blindness, the anthropologist and colonial agent were charged with seeing and describing everything, and the resulting total description was supposed to overcome and annul the mystery of the Orient.

This is why the end of colonialism must have spelled the transformation of orientalist discourse, that is, of the modality of knowledge shaping and interpreting the encounter between the West and its others. No longer available in the same way for the gaze, and yet no longer as impenetrable and inscrutable as in precolonial times, events in the Orient are now monitored from a distance – via electronic eavesdropping, the perusal of Arabic-language newspapers and official documents, and so on – and the results are accumulated, archived, and combined into surveys, chronologies,

reports, and assessments. In short, the political, economic, and military parameters of the encounter have changed, and with them also the networks
that mobilize and represent distant phenomena. Consequently, the object of
orientalist knowledge has changed as well. Here I must register again my
dissent from Said, who generally seems to equate orientalism with the textual attitude and with the essentialization and schematization of the Orient.
Orientalism is a "tradition," he says, implying that while some changes may
take place at the level of "manifest orientalism," at its core, at the level of
"latent orientalism," the attitudes, prejudices, and stereotypes have remained
the same.[9]

There is some truth to this assertion, as stereotypes about the Arabs and
Islam are clearly still prevalent in the Western media, for example,[10] but the
distinction between the "surface" of discourse and its "depths" is completely
unsatisfactory. It is a hermeneutics of suspicion, always ascribing the true
meaning of discourse to something hidden, something that is not completely
said and yet is "really" what is being said. Not only is the hypothesizing
of hidden meanings ultimately unverifiable, a self-confirming suspicion, it
in fact imitates the very orientalist procedure that Said himself powerfully
denounces. When orientalists search underneath the speech of modern Arab
leaders and intellectuals for signs of their "true" meaning, as determined
by the Orient, the tribe, Islam, or whatnot, they distinguish between the
manifest and the latent just as Said does.

Contra Said, I suggest that it is preferable to remain at the surface level
of what is being said and to seek to uncover not hidden meanings but what
made it possible to say the things that were said, "when and where they did –
they and no others."[11] At this level, the practices of eavesdropping, reading
documents, and monitoring events construct the object of orientalism not
as the Orient described by Said – an ancient, unchanging essence, a flexible
and all-encompassing metaphor of otherness – but as a continuous series of
events and developments catalogued by regions and states ("area studies").
Not only do these practices not construct the Orient as essence, they deconstruct it – they bring about the disenchantment of the Orient. Indeed,
the processes I describe in this book are not unique to Israel but characterize
the postcolonial mode of encounter in general. In a sense, it was this historical work of disenchantment that preceded Said's critique and served as its
precondition.[12]

The approach I take in this book, therefore, is to write the history of Israeli
mizrahanut as a history of the practices and forms of expertise that mediate the
encounter between Israelis and the world around them. Under this category
come all the practices that are concerned with drawing boundaries, with
patrolling the no-man's-land along the boundaries, with supervising and
purifying the hybrids, with controlling the passage across the boundaries,

and with mobilizing phenomena from "the other side" and bringing them closer for examination or contemplation. These practices shape, at each given period, a certain modality of knowledge and discourse that, in its turn, shapes how Israelis perceive, interpret, and react to this encounter.

This approach allows me to walk a fine line between the apologists for orientalism, who present orientalist discourse as reflecting, more or less accurately, a certain given reality (and who view the history of orientalism as merely a record of the mistakes and breakthroughs of more or less enlightened individuals), and its critics, who present orientalist discourse as a figment of the orientalists' imagination, essentially unchanged and without a history. To say that orientalist discourse is the product of an encounter is to emphasize that it is never merely a figment of the orientalists' imagination, because it is based on definite practices that mobilize phenomena and bring them closer for inspection, interpretation, and manipulation. And these practices have a history. They shift and change as they are interwoven with military, political, and economic institutions, as well as with the resistances mounted by those who are to be mobilized and represented. By the same token, however, to say that orientalist discourse is the product of an encounter is also to say that orientalist knowledge is never unmediated – never located outside discourse and outside the practices that shape how the encounter is structured, experienced, and interpreted.

Of course, I may have been on the wrong track all along. Things may not be so complicated. It may be true that the topic studied by *mizrahanut* is not quite stable and changes with geopolitical shifts, but what remains constant are the orientalists themselves and their specific expertise. They simply apply it to different cases as needs shift. Who, therefore, is an orientalist? The answer to this question is not self-evident. Even though Israelis do use the term *mizrahan* (literally "orientalist"), I note that Israeli universities never had departments for *mizrahanut*, and while in the past there were departments and institutes of *limudey ha-mizrah* (oriental studies), none exist any more, and in their stead were created departments for the "history of the Middle East," the "history of Islamic societies," or "Arab literature and language."

We can attempt another simple empirical test by scrutinizing *Ha-Mizrah Ha-Hadash*'s author index between 1949 and 1977. Are orientalists simply those academics employed in university departments specializing in the history of the Middle East, the history of Islamic societies, or Arab literature and language? Table 1.2 shows that such individuals wrote only 43 percent of the articles in *Ha-Mizrah Ha-Hadash*, while many other articles were written by social scientists (sociologists, political scientists, anthropologists, and geographers) and others. Is it possible that institutional location does not matter much and that individuals possessing orientalist expertise are distributed in various university departments?

TABLE I.2. Contributors to *Ha-Mizrah Ha-Hadash,* 1949–1977

Years	Academic Orientalists	Other Academics	Nonacademics with Degree	Nonacademics without Degree	Total
1949–1963	20 (32%)	6 (10%)	18 (29%)	18 (29%)	62
1964–1977	39 (53%)	22 (30%)	6 (8%)	7 (9%)	74
Total	59 (43%)	28 (21%)	24 (18%)	25 (18%)	136

Source. Ilan Pappe, "Multi-Year Author Index," *Ha-Mizrah Ha-Hadash* 28, suppl. (1979): 32–40.

We must reject this hypothesis, since, as Table 1.2 shows, university professors of all stripes constituted only 64 percent of the contributors to the journal. If we firmly believe in the existence of a well-defined orientalist expertise, we may press ahead and argue, nonetheless, that what matters is not whether one teaches at a university but whether one was taught by academic orientalists, possesses an academic credential, and is employed by those institutions requiring the practical application of such expertise – the Foreign Office, military intelligence, the office of adviser on Arab affairs, and newspapers and media organizations. After all, officials who are employed by the government Bureau of Statistics or the Central Bank and possess a university degree in economics are still considered to be economists; why should we shortchange the orientalists? As one Israeli journalist wrote, "The orientalists' community is a rather abstract concept, which begins with an intelligence officer decoding Arab broadcasts, and ends with a Professor of Egyptology and an expert on Islam."[13]

Even this hypothesis, however, fails miserably. Aggregating all nonacademics with a university degree, regardless of which credential they possess, shows that they add up to an additional 18 percent, bringing the total to 82 percent. We are still left with a residue of 18 percent of the contributors to the journal who never earned a university degree and were not academically employed.

Clearly, this too is a crude test. The reader may object that the editors of the journal may have decided to include contributions by individuals with different kinds of expertise, academic or not, for the benefit of the readership and that the decisions they made were random and do not reflect the "core" of orientalist expertise. But once again, when we inspect these seemingly random margins – and, in particular, when we pay attention to how the makeup of contributors changed over time – we see evidence to the contrary. Before 1963, more contributions were written by nonacademics than by academics, and a full 29 percent were written by individuals who were neither employed by universities nor possessed an academic credential (most of them were employed by the Foreign Office or by newspapers).

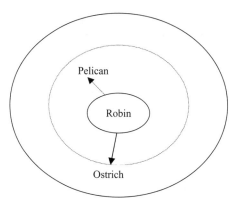

FIGURE I.I. Schematic Diagram of the Concept "Bird".

After 1963, however, academic orientalists alone accounted for a majority of contributions, and the percentage of nonacademic, noncredentialed authors dwindled to 9 percent.

This brief empirical test indicates that just as *mizrahanut* could not be defined by a certain topic proper to it, so it cannot be identified with a single type of expertise, since the credentials needed in order to write about oriental matters have clearly changed over the years. Does this mean that there is no way to characterize orientalists? I don't think so. The problem here is quite familiar to philosophers and cognitive psychologists. Most human concepts that serve to organize reality, they say, are constructed not according to strict logical rules of necessary and sufficient conditions but by means of "best examples" – prototypes – around which cases are organized by chains of different types and degrees of "family resemblance." For example, when asked to define "bird," people usually come up with a "prototypical" example, such as a robin. Rarely do they mention pelicans or ostriches, though in response to further probing they will agree that these are birds too. Robins are prototypes, while pelicans and ostriches are birds by virtue of different chains of family resemblance to robins. Figure I.I depicts the concept "bird" as charted by cognitive psychologists, with the degree of family resemblance measured by the distance from the center and the type indicated by the direction of the radial.[14]

I think that when Israelis use the term *mizrahan*, they similarly represent it by means of a prototype, a particularly good example standing for the whole class, and then by chains of cases linked to it by diminishing degrees of family resemblance. The prototype could be an academic orientalist researching contemporary Middle Eastern countries. In fact, such a prototype implicitly guided my investigations at first. But if pushed a little bit further, Israelis will readily add to this example professors of Islamic history and civilization (by virtue of similar academic qualifications and institutional proximity), intelligence officers and journalists (because they too interpret and comment on contemporary Middle Eastern events), and with diminishing levels of confidence also geographers and anthropologists (because they study the Palestinian citizens of Israel) and government officials (because they deal with the Palestinians).

There is an important difference, however, between a term taken from the social world, like *mizrahan,* and a term denoting a class in the natural world, like "bird": pelicans and ostriches are typically indifferent to the question of how similar they are to robins and which kind of bird is a better example of the class of birds. Not so with humans. The social world is rife with conflicts between different groups over the right to occupy the center of the circle, to present themselves as the prototype in relation to which all other groups must measure themselves and locate themselves, either in imitation or in opposition. The same holds for orientalists. It follows that the way Israelis use the term *mizrahan* reflects, unbeknownst to the conventional speaker of Hebrew, the history of struggles between different groups of experts over the right to position themselves at the heart of the orientalist enterprise, to present themselves as prototypical, or to improve their location with respect to an already dominant prototype.

These struggles are not a free-for-all or catch-as-catch-can. They take place according to certain rules inherited from the past and with respect to certain constraints. As *mizrahanut* involves the production and supply of cultural goods (commentaries, intelligence assessments, interpretations, advice, concepts, metaphors, points of view, dissertations, monographs, etc.), it operates under the constraint of consumer demand. As shown by Max Weber in his analysis of the development of religion, producers of cultural goods strive to attain a certain degree of independence from the consumers and to protect themselves from competition or critical evaluation of their services by imposing on the consumers a definition of what their needs and aspirations should be.

Magicians, for example, are dependent on the consumers in the sense that they provide services for pay, and they are contracted for the performance of a task specified in advance by the consumers. They must provide proof of the utility of their services, otherwise they will lose their reputation, and their consumers will turn to somebody else. Religion begins to differentiate itself from magic, according to Weber, when priests invent the idea of otherworldly salvation and thus seek to impose on the consumers a new definition of their needs and thus avoid having to show proof of the effectiveness of their services. They provide this good free of pay, but in return they demand that the consumers bring sacrifices, pray and confess, and obey the priestly group.

This solution, however, is not stable. It is truly a dilemma or a double constraint: too much dependence on the consumers exposes the group of producers to competition, critical appraisal, and devaluation, but too much independence may lead to isolation and loss of clientele. The strategies used by the suppliers of salvation to deal with this dilemma lead to another double constraint, this time regarding the nature of their knowledge. One way to create independence from the consumers is to "close" the scriptures – to pronounce them the word of God and hence immutable and to reduce the capacity of the consumers to interpret them (e.g., by not translating them from Latin to the vernacular, a strategy used by the Catholic Church for centuries). In this way, the priestly group attains a monopoly over the interpretation of the scriptures and limits access to its knowledge, which thereby becomes mysterious and esoteric (limiting access also requires the group to close the ranks through strict entry examinations and a long period of apprenticeship, thus instituting, in Weber's language, "closed social relations"). This is also what magicians do.

There is an inverse relationship, however, between how esoteric priestly knowledge is and the capacity of the priestly group to present their expertise as useful and relevant to the laity, the consumers of salvation. Consequently, as they close the scriptures and their ranks and monopolize interpretation, the priests leave themselves open to attacks by prophets, whose knowledge is based on the opposite principle of "revelation" (i.e., openness). Prophets cancel the need for entry examinations and apprenticeship (i.e., they institute "open social relations") as well as the need to consult interpretations of the scriptures at every step. They speak directly to the laity, revealing the word of God to them. The knowledge of elders too is open, as they provide advice and impart the wisdom of tradition to all who come to them. Any priesthood, if it is to exercise long-term domination over the laity, has to continuously balance the contradictory imperatives of monopoly over the interpretation of the scriptures and the need to engage in pastoral practice and instruct the laity. And this is a true dilemma, because pastoral practice of necessity means that priestly knowledge becomes more open so that even lay believers can become religious experts, but it also means that the pastor must go beyond the word of God, as given in the scriptures, or bend it to fit the everyday needs of the laity, thereby creating tensions and gaps through which prophecy may reappear.[15]

It is possible to describe this set of contradictions and constraints as a field of struggle between different suppliers of salvation over control of the consumers of salvation and over the capacity to define the prototype of the religious expert. This field – the field of religion, as shown in Figure 1.2 – is created by the intersection of the two dilemmas described above. Thus, the prophet is similar to the priest because both demand complete independence

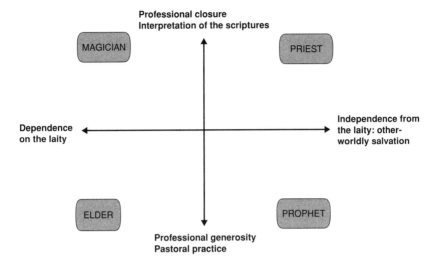

FIGURE I.2. The religious field as the prototype for other forms of expertise. *Source.* Adapted from Pierre Bourdieu, "Legitimation and Structured Interests in Weber's Sociology of Religion," in Max Weber, *Rationality and Modernity*, ed. Scott Lash and Sam Whimster (London: Allen and Unwin, 1987).

from the needs of the laity and both demand of the laity that they accept a new definition of their needs. But the prophet is also opposed to the priest in the "generosity" of his knowledge, in the fact that he reveals the word of God to all and demands the obedience of the laity solely on the basis of his charisma. Elders and the "wise" are similar to magicians because they supply advice in response to specific needs and requests raised by the consumers and usually accept some form of payment or gift. But they are also opposed to magicians and similar to prophets because their knowledge is open and they teach their listeners traditions, proverbs, maxims, and rules of thumb that can be applied in other contexts and times and passed on to others.

At this point, we no longer need to use nouns – "prophet," "priest," and so on – since it is clear that these terms do nothing but designate relatively unstable intersections of relations, relatively unstable positions within the religious field. Prophets threaten the priesthood because they challenge the esoteric quality of priestly knowledge, but if they actually manage to unseat the reigning priestly group, they are immediately exposed to pressures, first from their disciples to close ranks and codify the prophecy, then from the laity to translate the prophecy into instructions for everyday life. They thus begin to migrate this way or that, changing their position in the field as they seek, just like the priesthood before them, some sort of balance between the contradictory imperatives of the field. Field dynamics involve a constant migration toward the center and challenges from the margins offering new prototypes.[16]

Similarly, it is possible to write the history of *mizrahanut*, not as the history of a well-defined academic discipline or professional group, but as *a history of the field of struggle over the prototype of orientalist expertise and of the constraints and dilemmas within which this struggle takes place.* These constraints and dilemmas are not essentially different from those faced by the suppliers of salvation. The orientalist as well is under the double and intersecting pressures of balancing dependence on and independence from the consumers of orientalist knowledge, on the one hand, and balancing openness and closure of knowledge and social relations, on the other.

For example, the position of a professor of Middle Eastern studies in the field of orientalist expertise is analogous to that of the priest in the religious field. Membership in the professoriate is a form of social closure involving a long period of apprenticeship (undergraduate and graduate studies, along with some period of postgraduate training) and an arduous probationary period before tenure. Professors typically speak a variant of esoteric and learned discourse impenetrable to the laity. Membership in the academic community also entails a large degree of independence from the consumers of knowledge, represented by the well-known "academic freedom" to choose topics of research or to express opinions. As in the religious field, independence and closure grant academic orientalists a certain prestige and the capacity to define the taste needed to consume their products, but by the same token they disconnect them from the consumers and leave them open to the charge that their knowledge is impractical (i.e., that it does not respond to the needs of and problems faced by the consumers). This danger is even more acute (and herein lies the major difference between the field of orientalist expertise and the religious field) because the consumers of orientalist knowledge are typically politicians, military decision-makers, and state officials – in short, people who possess political power and administrative authority. It is typically difficult to persuade these individuals to listen to the advice of experts, and it is even more difficult, in fact, nearly impossible, to impose on them a new definition of their needs. Strict adherence to independence and closure, therefore, leads to the notorious "ivory tower" – to isolation and lack of influence.

As we shall see in Chapter 3, an opposite position in the prestate field of orientalist expertise was occupied by nonacademic experts, typically identified as "Arabists." They were Jews who had mastered the local Palestinian dialect and customs to the point that they could behave and speak like Palestinians, had Palestinian friends, and claimed that they knew how to think like them. Their position in the field of orientalist expertise was analogous to that of elders in the religious field. To become an Arabist, one did not need credentials or to undergo elaborate initiation rites, one only needed to immerse oneself in the local community (i.e., Arabism was a form of open social relations). Arabist knowledge was open as well, because the Arabists' role was to impart advice to decision makers and teach them what the Arabists knew about Arab society. Like elders, Arabists were also dependent on the consumers of their advice – the politicians and paramilitary leaders – because they served as junior officials under them, within the administrative hierarchy of Jewish proto-state institutions. As in the religious field, openness and dependence meant that the consumers actually listened to the Arabists and sought their advice; they were thus influential, but they were also incapable of controlling the dissemination and attribution of their knowledge. Their superiors routinely appropriated the insights provided by the Arabists and presented them as products of their own thinking. Strict adherence to openness and dependence, therefore, led to the loss of prestige.

Moreover, another difference between the field of orientalist expertise and the religious field is that those vying to impose their expertise as prototypical must also be careful to purify themselves from association with the hybrids without at the same time completely losing touch with them and becoming unable to supervise them. Just like the relation between the ethnographer and the informant, the distance between the Arabists and their informers had to be carefully managed and negotiated. Over time, as we shall see in Chapter 5, since the Arabists were entrusted with the task of close supervision and monitoring of the Palestinians in the framework of the military government, they became increasingly polluted by their proximity to the hybrids and began to be viewed with equal suspicion. Hence, they needed to withdraw further from the hybrids and protect themselves through academic mechanisms of closure and distancing.

It is clear, therefore, why it is so difficult to define who is an orientalist and why the articles in *Ha-Mizrah Ha-Hadash* were written by such a diverse group of contributors, boasting different types of expertise and different credentials. A field of cultural production such as orientalism, which is under strong cross-cutting pressures because of its input-output relations with the state, the army, and the political sphere, is particularly unstable. No position within it is stable, and no prototype enjoys longevity. The balance attained between the different constraints and imperatives is precarious, short-lived, and constantly open to challenges from different directions. The history of the field of orientalist expertise, as narrated in this book, is a history of constant and intense struggles, of desperate rearguard battles, of daring maneuvers to outflank the enemy, of coups and countercoups.

To summarize, the topic of this book, *mizrahanut*, is not a clearly defined object or subject – a given slice of reality or an easily identifiable group of experts – but a relatively open field of struggle between different groups of experts, each seeking to impose itself as the prototype of orientalist expertise. To do so, these experts need to weave extensive networks that at one and the same time mobilize distant phenomena and bring them closer, yet also draw a boundary right in their very midst. Put differently, they need to present themselves as capable of managing the hybrids at the same time as they neutralize their own hybridity, the inevitable contamination that is their inevitable "occupational hazard." In this way, they shape the encounter between Israelis and the others who surround them, or are in their very midst.

The Jew underneath the Arab's Mask: The Experience of the Orient in the Prestate Period

> Out of the abyss of forgetfulness there rises, like a phoenix out
> of the ashes, the balcony . . . upon which sat my great father and
> flung his hand towards the [Palestinian] villages of Chiriya and
> Sakiya, like Napoleon surveying the battlefield, and in a voice
> which was altogether on the right side of creation told me, and I
> was a child then: *dort ist Arabien* [yonder lies the Land of Arabia].
> —Yoel Hoffman
> *Ha-Shunra ve-Ha-Shmeterling*
> (The Cat and the Butterfly)

THE FIRST "HEBREW CITY," Tel-Aviv, was established because its founders
sought to escape their cramped residences in Arab Jaffa, to escape the smoke,
the noise, the dirty streets, and the foul language, and to design a European
"Garden City" with wide boulevards, modern installations, proper distance
between the houses, private gardens, and large rooms. From its very inception
in 1906, Tel-Aviv, the "city that sprung from the sands," embodied almost in
a pure form the Zionist utopia of inventing a new culture and a new identity
from whole cloth. Opposed both to the Jewish shtetls of eastern Europe and
to the Arab towns and villages around it, it perfectly encoded the double
Zionist rejection of the Diaspora and the native culture – forgetfulness and
separation. And yet, as Yoel Hoffman reminds us, it was also a city under the
sign of the Orient, a city whose inhabitants identified themselves in relation
to an Orient that lay just beyond its boundaries, menacing and corrupting for
some, enticing and reinvigorating for others, but always potent and solid, a
coherent presence, capable of engulfing one the moment one set foot outside
the city. Moreover, the Orient not only surrounded Tel-Aviv but was also
present within it, as a sort of a palette, a compendium of colors and forms,
serving to "fill up the gap between biblical times and the modern age."[1]

In this chapter I show that the experience of the encounter with the
Orient during the prestate period, especially in the very early days of Zionist

settlement in Palestine, roughly till 1936, constituted indeed something much more massive, complex, and meaningful than rejection and separation. It was the experience of an open horizon of identity, of a liminal space of metamorphosis and the transmutation of identities, of a no-man's-land populated by hybrids. But in order to do so, I need first of all to deal with two prevalent arguments about early Zionism that tend to minimize the complexity of the prestate experience of the Orient and reduce it to the negative gesture of separation.

Zionism as Orientalism

The first argument is that Zionism was a form of orientalism in Said's sense, that is, a discourse of European superiority and denigration of the Orient. Indeed, the writings and speeches of early Zionist leaders, as well as of the first Jewish Settlers in Palestine, are replete with orientalist expressions of superiority and scorn toward the local inhabitants of Palestine and Arabs more generally, along with repeated assertions of their own European identity. This sort of discourse was prevalent and explicit in the prestate period. In the eyes of the first Zionist settlers, the *biluyim* arriving in 1882, the local inhabitants were "savages," "primitives," and "backward." They were part of the "Asian throng," "people of the Orient," "sons of Arabia," while the settlers were "Europeans."[2]

Zionist leaders, like Hertzel and Nordau, tried to sell Zionism to the European powers as a European bulwark against Asia and as a way of bringing European civilization to the Orient. Mordechai Hillel Ha-Cohen, one of the founders of Tel-Aviv, thought that Ashkenazi Jews were "the most civilized group in Palestine," the Arab fellahin and Bedouin were still "half-naked savages," and Sephardi Jews were similar to the Arabs. They were "Levantine," and it was better to keep one's distance from them. Teachers and educators in the early Yishuv praised the "mental energy" of Russian, Polish, and Austro-Hungarian Jews and derided, by comparison, the "Oriental lethargy" of Yemenite Jews. Jabotinski, another Zionist leader, declared that "we are immigrating to Palestine in order to erase within us the remnants of the Oriental soul. We can do a favor to the Arabs in Palestine by helping them to rescue themselves from the Orient." Haim Weitzman, president of the Zionist Federation and later the first president of the State of Israel, repeatedly demanded from his British interlocutors not to refer to the Jews in Palestine as "natives," despite the obvious fact that this designation could bolster their claim to the land. Ben-Gurion, debating with Jewish intellectuals who advocated a binational state of Jews and Arabs in Palestine, warned that "no exemplary Jewish society would develop under the rule of the Arab Orient – just a new Yemenite Diaspora, perhaps the poorest and most destitute Diaspora."[3]

How to understand these expressions? No doubt they betray a deep-seated need among early Zionists to distinguish themselves from Arabs and Middle Eastern Jews and feel superior to them. It is also quite likely, as some authors have suggested, that this need to orientalize others was a reaction to the fact that European Jews were themselves stigmatized as "oriental" by European Christians. Having internalized the stigma, and needing to prove themselves "Western" and "modern," they turned around and orientalized others who were weaker. This pathos of distinction has consequently exacerbated relations between Jews and Palestinians at the same time that it led to discrimination against Middle Eastern Jews.[4]

The chief problem with this argument is simply that it is partial. As Khazzoom notes, the psychosocial consequences of the internalized stigma of being oriental are indeterminate. For some individuals, it may have prompted a desperate bid to be considered Western by orientalizing others; others might have chosen, on the contrary, to embrace the stigma and affirm the kinship of the Jews with the nations of the Orient. For most, it probably meant an ambivalent attitude that incorporated attraction and repulsion, fascination and disdain.[5] Indeed, as we shall see, alongside expressions of rejection and disgust with the Orient, early Zionist texts were also filled with expressions of attraction toward and fascination with it. Some of the very people just mentioned could sometimes write in completely different terms, with the opposite valuation. They were fascinated with the image of the Bedouin as noble warriors and sought to emulate them; or they were enamored of the diversity and tolerance of the Oriental city; or they contemplated the life of the fellahin as a window onto biblical times.

In short, the desperate bid to be considered Western by orientalizing others was only one side of a much more complex reaction. There were some European Jews, especially German Jews, who opted for affirming the stigma, affirming the oriental identity of Jews, and seeing in it a source of distinction. The Jews were entrusted, in their eyes, with a unique mission of cultural mediation of world-historical significance. Being oriental by origins but living in the West, being European-born but migrating to the Orient, they would mediate between Orient and Occident and reconcile their differences. This sort of reaction played an especially important role in German Reform Judaism and the German Zionist movement, the largest and most influential branch of Zionism before its decimation by the Nazis. Late nineteenth-century German Jewish synagogues, for example, were designed in a distinctly "Moorish" style taken from the canons of nineteenth-century romantic orientalism, and a leading intellectual journal was named *Ost und West*. Further, this sort of reaction was important in the creation of the

German Jewish brand of orientalist scholarship, intimately connected with reform Judaism and Zionism.[6]

How to understand, therefore, the more general discursive fact of the coexistence, side by side, of disgust and fascination, attraction and rejection? My critics no doubt will be justified in pointing out that the more positive expressions were also orientalist in Said's sense: stereotypical, essentialist, condescending, related to a fictionalized and romanticized Orient, not to its "concrete cultural reality," nor to the real aspirations of its inhabitants.[7] All this may be true, but it is beside the point. While romantic orientalism no longer satisfies our contemporary taste for an authentic dialogue among equals, to pronounce it as false, and hence separatist, from our vantage point in the present is to practice the worst sort of anachronistic historical scholarship. We should be well warned that today's truisms are tomorrow's prejudices. We need to evaluate these gestures of orientalization and self-orientalization within their own context, without appealing to a knowledge of "concrete cultural reality" or "real aspirations," a knowledge that can be nothing but the false wisdom of hindsight. The crucial point about these no doubt stereotypical images of the Bedouin, the fellahin, and the city dwellers – a point that is discussed later in this chapter – is not that they occluded "reality" (since reality is never available except in a foggy and distorted mirror) but that they expressed the idea that modern Zionist identity, rather than shaped by the exclusion of the Orient, should be shaped through an imaginary (and no doubt paternalist) relation of affinity and kinship with it.

How to think, therefore, of the discursive coexistence of these contrary valuations? As against the attempt to minimize the significance of one set of valuations, to try to read "beneath" what was said a more fundamental attitude that annuls it, I would like to register and describe this discursive fact in all its complexity and superficiality. *The experience of the early Zionist encounter with the Orient was multifaceted and could easily encompass all these opposite valuations, all these contradictions and oppositions, because, as we shall see, it was primarily an experience of an open horizon of identity, of metamorphosis and the transmutation of identities.* Consequently, prestate *mizrahanut* and its various discourses played a decidedly nonseparatist role – not because they always affirmed a relation of affinity and kinship with the Orient and with its inhabitants (not by a long stretch!) but because they provided the Zionist project of personal and national transformation with the liminal place where identities were destabilized, suspended, and reinvented.

Zionism as Colonialism

The second argument compares Zionism with colonialism rather than orientalism. In this narrative, Zionism was akin to other European projects of establishing a colonial settler society (South Africa, Algeria, etc.); that is, it involved the conquering and exploiting of a colony and also the immigration of large numbers of Europeans, who came to stay typically as farmers and landlords. One does not need to embrace the more controversial claim that Zionism *is* colonialism to appreciate the analytical leverage gained by such comparison. It highlights the material – economic and territorial – exigencies that all settlement endeavors must face and that constrain the range of options open to participants. It highlights as well the available models from which they might draw inspiration.

Gershon Shafir and Baruch Kimmerling, among others, have used this comparative framework to develop an account of the origins of the Israeli-Palestinian conflict. All settlement, they explain, entails a struggle over land and labor. What distinguished early twentieth-century Jewish settlement in Palestine are the particularly adverse conditions under which this struggle was conducted. The Jewish settlers lacked political-military control over the colony, they could not acquire land freely, and the wages they deemed necessary for survival were much higher than those needed by the native Palestinian workers. Shafir and Kimmerling show that after a short but intense struggle within the Zionist movement and under the inspiration of ideas based on German colonization in eastern Europe, the settlers opted for a "separatist method of pure settlement."

The two hallmarks of this method were the splitting of the labor market – so that Jewish labor would not need to compete with the much cheaper Palestinian labor – and the conquering of swaths of land for purely Jewish settlement by means of agricultural cooperatives. The result was separatism. A series of institutions were built – the General Federation of Labor, the Kibbutzim, the Jewish National Fund, and so on – that gave prestate Jewish society its distinctive character and organized it on the basis of thorough economic and territorial separation from the local Palestinian population. From this perspective, it is immaterial whether the settlers were attracted to the Orient or repulsed by it, admired or despised it. The economic imperatives were decisive and led to the formation of a separatist economic and political structure. Separatism, in its turn, meant that the Zionist movement was on a collision course with the Palestinians, since Jews sought to open the land market and bifurcate the labor market whereas Palestinians sought to achieve the opposite. Moreover, separatism shaped the experiences and predispositions of the younger generation, who grew up with a sense of being separate and superior. The result was war, expulsions, and de facto division of the country.[8]

The analysis developed by Shafir and Kimmerling is a valuable corrective to earlier Zionist historiography, which tended to be apologetic and explained the same developments in terms of the lofty ideals motivating Zionist settlers. Nonetheless, there are also two problems with it. First, it too is a partial account. The focus on the labor movement means that other actors and alternative centers of power are ignored. The critics share with the official Zionist historiography an emphasis on the organizational power of the labor movement and on the process of building the institutions of the state-in-the-making, an emphasis that involves a certain measure of anachronism, of projecting backward as explanation the later hegemony of the labor movement.[9] Jewish society under Ottoman and British rule, however, not only was ruled by bureaucratic institutions staffed with expert officials, it was also a society administered by *notables*. As consequence, Jewish society was not altogether different or separate from Palestinian society.

The administrative structure of the Ottoman Empire relied to a great extent on administration by notables, and though bureaucratic reforms in the late Ottoman period reduced the power of the notables, they did not eliminate it altogether. The British Mandate government, in its turn, employed a rather small number of professional officials, as it was wont to do in the colonies, and found it expedient, therefore, to use the notables as intermediaries in its dealings with the population. In each village, the British administration appointed one of the notables as a *mukhtar* (village leader) and conducted all its official business through this person; it treated the urban leadership similarly, as high level *mukhtars* directly answerable to the county or district governor. A relation of patronage with a degree of give-and-take was forged between the governors and the notables. The governor supplied the notables with resources – with jobs and favors they distributed to their own clients – and they repaid with information, with political backing, and, most importantly, with their capacity to mobilize social networks to get things done. Typically, therefore, the local and municipal leadership of notables was more politically moderate than the "national" leadership, and this was true for both Jews and Palestinians.[10]

The Jewish notables included large citrus growers, merchants, industrialists, members of the association of farmers, rabbis, leaders of the Sephardi community in Jerusalem, mayors and *mukhtars*, judges, intellectuals, and professors. Many of them were elected to the representative body of the Jewish community in Palestine and were members of its permanent committee (Ha-Va'ad Ha-Leumi). More importantly, many of the Jewish notables had extensive ties of commerce and friendship with Palestinian notables, especially those among the educated and Europeanized elite.

The significance of the notables should not be underestimated. In hindsight, it is easy to dismiss them as weak and ineffectual, since they were marginalized by the labor movement. In fact, in the parlance of the labor movement, the term "notables" was a slur and was meant to indicate that its competitors were "bourgeois" and "reactionary."[11] Yet, their existence indicates that the story of territorial and economic separatism is incomplete, because on the administrative and social levels a different mode of encounter existed, characterized by networking and mediation among notables.

Furthermore, it is important to remember that the notables, especially the so-called civic circles and the Sephardi elite (about which more later in this chapter), competed against the labor movement for leadership of the Jewish group in Palestine. The struggle between the notables and the labor movement continued throughout the prestate period and even to some extent after the formation of the state. The hegemony of the labor movement was far from perfect. Probably a majority of Palestinian Jews were not members of its organizations, but almost all were under the administration of notables in the framework of municipal government.

On the other hand, and to complicate the picture, one must add that the interethnic networks of the notables were not simply an external alternative to separatism; they were also integral to its functioning. The most obvious example is the purchase of land. In order to pursue what Shafir called a "separatist method of pure settlement" in a situation where the Palestinian national leadership was exhorting Palestinians not to sell land to Jews, the Zionist leadership had to rely on the notables' social ties with Palestinian notables and on their ability to collect information, contract with their acquaintances, and bribe, persuade, and cajole in the native tongue when necessary. In chapter 4, we shall see that even the ultimate gesture of separation – expulsion – needed the mediation of the notables. This is but another illustration of the thesis offered in the introduction: a boundary, even the strictest boundary, of separation cannot exist except by means of something that transgresses it. Auxiliary but essential, the mode of encounter represented by the notables must have given rise to a different experience of the Orient.

The second problem with the analysis developed by Shafir and Kimmerling has to do with how it represents labor Zionism itself. The argument that the origins of separatism lay in the economic constraints of settlement depends on depicting labor Zionism as an organization that was mobilized to achieve political and economic ends and that demanded obedience from its members. Labor Zionism, however, was also something else: it was a church, seeking to disseminate a certain revealed truth – and seeking to do this not by means of commands but through pastoral guidance on how individuals should fashion their bodies and souls in order to attain salvation. While it attempted to impose on Jewish society political domination of the more conventional sort, it also sought to exert a pastoral power.[12] Individuals were required not only to obey but also to sacrifice their old identity, to mend their souls, and to represent this internal change by shaping their bodies, acquiring new habits, and providing testimonials.

In return, the Zionist pastors, themselves virtuosi of sacrifice and asceticism, would certify that they were saved, that they had transformed themselves and become "pioneers." It was a movement of ethical improvement no less than it was a workers' organization. Put differently, many of these so-called workers came to Palestine not so much to work for their livelihood as to work on themselves. When they campaigned for "Hebrew labor" and the splitting of the labor market, they were both struggling against cheaper Palestinian labor and seeking to purge themselves of the vices of "dependency" and "parasitism."

It was this pastoral power and the inevitable opposition that it provoked that gave the politics of prestate Jewish society their flavor as "identity politics" characterized by a public and intensive preoccupation with the self, a constant struggle between different groups of pastors, and the massive production and dissemination of icons meant to symbolize the transformation of identity and weave it into the fabric of everyday life. This is why the hybrids and the practices of imitation, mediation, and iconographic representation that produced them (described later) were not marginal but central to the project of labor Zionism, since they served to turn individuals into Zionist subjects. As we shall see, together they created the experience of the Orient as an open horizon of identity, a liminal space populated by hybrids, where the immigrants and settlers could shed their old identities and acquire the qualities of the new Zionist man. This space was the correlate of a form of power that sought to dissolve the old identities and endow the new ones with authenticity.

Before I describe the hybrid practices that constructed this space, I would like to emphasize that the alternative account I offer here is not meant to replace the two theses of Zionism as orientalism and Zionism as colonialism but to supplement them. In fact, I believe that when the two theses are combined, they provide a formidable explanation for the emergence of a strong separatist current in prestate Jewish society. The economic constraints of settlement, in a sense, explain why the initial ambivalence toward the Orient could turn into rejection and separation.

Moreover, the combined theory pinpoints the specific sector of Jewish society that would be most likely to hold a separatist worldview and to work for economic and then political separation, namely, the sector consisting of purely Jewish agricultural cooperatives, whether *kibbutzim* or *moshavim*.[13] Planted amidst Arab villages but declining to employ Palestinians as hired labor and gradually minimizing commercial contacts with them (although such contacts could never be completely eliminated before 1948), these cooperatives were often depicted by their founders as islands of Western progress in the primitive and barren Orient. Thus Moshe Dayan's father, who was a founder of Nahalal, the first *moshav*, would take his son with him on a trip to the adjoining Palestinian village and point out the unpaved roads, the lack of trees and flowers, the laziness of the inhabitants, the lack of water pipes, the ignorance about the use of fertilizers, and the low productivity, and he would contrast these with the achievements of their own "model Hebrew village."[14] This was an attitude held by many within this sector.

When I say that my account supplements these theses rather than contradicts them, I mean two things: first, and most obviously, that there were many people in other sectors of prestate Jewish society that did not necessarily share such a strong sense of being apart from and elevated above the Orient, especially because they were in close contact with local inhabitants. Among these were the Jewish notables, who appear prominently in my story. It is well known that some of the most sympathetic, though paternalist, pages written about the lives of Palestinian peasants were penned by those who employed them, such as the citrus grower Moshe Smilanski.[15]

Additionally, my account supplements these theses by problematizing the boundary, as I suggested in the introduction. The cultural significance of the separatist sector was not given in advance because precisely in order to separate Jews from Arabs it also needed to transgress the boundaries between them. Planted amidst Palestinian villages, the Jewish agricultural cooperatives produced social types who managed the cooperatives' relations with their neighbors – Jewish *mukhtars*, guards, and local notables – by imitating their customs (I will say more about this social type and its significance in the next section). No less importantly, and for the same reasons, the formative experiences of the second generation, who grew up within this sector, were not solely shaped by a strict separation between Jews and Arabs but in some respects seem to reflect this generation's inhabiting of a fuzzy boundary zone between the two.

As his biographer notes, the young Moshe Dayan, for example, did not imbibe the lesson that his father sought to impart to him. On the contrary, he was deeply impressed by the Palestinian peasants, by their steadfastness and their rootedness in the land, which stood in such stark contrast to the rootlessness of his own father, who after a few years hired a farmworker and went to Europe as a Zionist emissary.[16] Dayan's sentiments were shared by many of his generation. They who were brought up in purely Jewish settlements as the first generation born in the land sought to distinguish themselves from their parents' generation and to accentuate their autochthonous distinction by inhabiting a sphere that was solely theirs and to which their parents did not have access. In this sphere they met with neighboring Palestinian kids and learned some of their language and customs; in this sphere they played together but also competed and fought.[17] Their identity and selfhood were tied to this agonistic in-between sphere no less than they were tied to the purely separatist space wherein they were born.

It is probably of no great importance, but there is a story written by the young Moshe Dayan when he was eleven that captures very well this sense of an ambivalent in-between sphere composed of both enmity and friendship.

In the story, he rides into the desert accompanied by two Bedouins. He does not know whether they are his friends or enemies and so keeps his guard up. He dresses like them and shares their food, and gradually they become friends. They are attacked by robbers (of unknown extraction), and the fight takes place during a desert storm in which it is not possible to tell who is fighting whom, nor whether his new friends have joined his attackers. At the end of the story, however, we learn that his new friends saved his life.[18] The confusion between friend and foe stands unmistakably for the confusion between Jew and Arab, and the desert storm provides a potent metaphor for the ambivalent in-between sphere that the young generation claimed for itself.

I will have more to say about the life experiences of this generation in the next chapter, but let me note that they are crucial to the story of separatism, because out of this generation came the military commanders – Moshe Dayan, Yigal Alon, and Yitzhak Rabin – who orchestrated the expulsion of the Palestinians in 1948. If their life experiences were completely shaped within a purely Jewish sector, it would be easy to understand the expulsions as emerging directly out of the social and economic structures shaped by orientalism and colonialism. If, as I have argued here, their life experiences were shaped within a more ambivalent and agonistic boundary zone, then it is possible to make sense of the expulsions, not as the outcome of a determinist causal chain, but as an attempt by this generational group to resolve the ambivalence inherent in its own identity and sense of selfhood – as a gesture of self-purification tied, as we shall see in the next chapter, to its failed claim to appear as experts on Arab affairs.

The Desert, the Bazaar, and the Village

A text written by Ben-Gurion in 1917, while he was in the United States, divides the inhabitants of Palestine into three groups. The first were the Bedouin, who roam the desert and live in tents. He considered them to be "pure Arabs":

By origin and race they are all one unit without any foreign elements mixed into them. For thousands of years they have been roaming the deserts of Syria and Arabia, in the lowlands of the Negev and in the land of Judea, and have hardly changed their traditions, their customs, their garb, their occupation, their manner of speaking and the conduct of their households since the days of Abraham our forefather and up till now.[19]

It is interesting to note that the orientalist Shlomo Dov Goitein, whom nobody could suspect of sharing Ben-Gurion's convictions, and who later decided to emigrate from the state that Ben-Gurion built, used almost the same expression to describe the Bedouin – "real Arabs, i.e. camel-breeders." The Bedouins were, therefore, an absolute otherness, inhabitants of the very same

"Land of Arabia" upon which Yoel Hoffman's father gazed. An immutable Orient, outside history, essentially and radically opposed to Europe.[20]

The Jewish immigrants met this otherness with an attitude that mixed both fear and admiration. The Bedouin were clearly their model of the "noble savage," and when referring to them, they typically spoke of a sort of "ancient majesty." More importantly, around the Bedouin there developed an exclusive and masculine subculture of virtuosi, the *mista'ravim*, who imitated what they perceived to be the Bedouin way of life. Visitors to the Jewish colonies at the turn of the century reported that

many of the youth of the colonies . . . have learned the customs of the neighbors. When they join the company of Bedouin, *Abayas* on their shoulders, *Kafias* on their heads, guns slung on their back, riding a galloping horse, it is impossible to recognize them as the children of Israel, also because they speak Arabic as fluently as a real Arab. They also know how to deal with the Bedouin in accordance with all their customs and etiquette.[21]

A little bit later, among the immigrant laborers who came during the first and second decades of the twentieth century, the members of the guards association Ha-Shomer were famous for similar virtuoso imitation of the Bedouin (Fig. 2.1). Among them, there was an even smaller and more radical group known as Ha-Ro'eh (the Shepherd), who actually took upon

שומרים ראשונים

אברהם שפירא   סנדר חדד

FIGURE 2.1. Abraham Shapiro and Sander Haddad, Jewish guards, ca. 1900. *Source.* Ben-Tzion Dinur, *Sefer Tòldot H-Haganah* (History of Self-Defense) (Tel-Aviv: Maarachot, 1954).

themselves to work for a year tending the flocks of Bedouin chieftains and to live among the Bedouin shepherds exactly as they do, out in the fields. They were "attracted to the free life of the Bedouin. They yearned for this life, which became for them a symbol for all that is lofty and grand in life."[22]

My point here is not that the figure of the Bedouin was romanticized and admired by the Jewish settlers – there is much evidence to the contrary as well – but that the Bedouin was imagined as a radical and immutable other and that this image was, to a great extent, manufactured by the practice of imitation. This practice was central to Zionist self-fashioning.

As the Zionist settlers arrived in Palestine, which they called *Eretz Israel*, they sometimes seemed to have expected that the very journey, the very return to the cradle of the nation, would permit them to overcome the distortions of national character caused by exile. They attributed almost magical qualities of purification and liberation to the land upon which they settled. Thus, Ben-Gurion reported to his father in astonishment that the Palestinian servant in the Jewish agricultural school of Ben-Shemen spoke a fluent and vivid Hebrew, better than the teachers who taught him the language back in Plonsk. He surmised that "this is the effect of the land of Israel, where no external and alien elements obstruct the free development . . . of our nation's spirit." But very quickly he discovered his mistake. To one of his brothers, who wished to immigrate to Palestine and start a lottery, he wrote back in anger,

Do you think that it is enough to change places and to go to the land of Israel, without leaving behind all the dirt and refuse which have attached itself to our lives in exile, all this etherealness, abnormality and this ugly, unnatural life in which we are mired in the ghetto – and be saved? This is a mistake. The land of Israel is not only a geographical concept. The land of Israel should be also the improvement and purification of life, a transformation of values in the highest sense of the word – for if we bring the life of the ghetto to our land – what have we done?[23]

In short, the new immigrants were required to fashion themselves anew, to work on themselves so as to leave behind the spirit of the Diaspora and acquire new habits and a new character.

In this situation, imitation of the native Palestinian culture and customs served to symbolize the desired internal change, to symbolize that one has broken with the old self. Anything in this culture and way of life that could be construed as the inverse of the Jewish way of life in the Diaspora was particularly useful for this purpose. Ben-Gurion, for example, would pepper his letters to his family with Arab words, especially when he wanted to express dissatisfaction and impatience with their "old Jewish" fears and indecisiveness. Apart from burrowing words, the settlers imitated Palestinian dress and food, and they rode horses and carried weapons in the same fashion as the

Palestinians. All of this was fairly superficial imitation, a sort of a thin layer of stereotypically "Oriental" signs spread on the surface of settler culture, much like in other colonial societies.[24]

It is possible, however, to understand this superficiality differently. The imitation of Palestinian culture and customs was a practice that created hybrids – *mista'ravim* – as it sought to assure the Zionist self of its authenticity. The claim that the imitation was superficial, therefore, was in this sense a purification device. It permitted the great majority of Jewish settlers, as it still permits Israelis today, to purify the *mista'rev* hybrid and present the transgression of boundaries as mere artifice, a charade. It could be easily suspended. The mask could be taken off to prove that one was "really" a Jew. In a sense, this claim was also a social demand directed at the imitators, reminding them not to delude themselves that they have really become different and not to be taken in by their own art. In this way, the transgressed boundary could be reconstituted and redrawn, and yet it would still be possible to imitate – to multiply the hybrids without admitting their existence.

At the same time, it is important to recall that among the settlers there were always a few individuals who were not satisfied with superficial imitation and who became virtuosi of imitation. Even though they were relatively few, as hybrid figures they played an important role in marking and transgressing the boundaries of the new Zionist identity, and they typically enjoyed a special status and prestige among the settlers. These virtuosi transformed imitation into a "technology of the self" that was meant to deal with the psychological and ethical problems caused by Zionism.[25]

The problem for the immigrants was how to convince themselves and others that they had indeed attained the Zionist goal of self-improvement and purification from the effects of the Diaspora and had indeed become "new Jews." The official Zionist answer – manual labor, particularly in agriculture – was actually ambivalent and left a doubt that gnawed at the heart of the settlers. The reason was simply that the first Zionist pioneers never managed to earn enough to cover their costs and were always dependent on external support from wealthy European Jews, from the organizations of the World Zionist Federation, or even from their own families. Ben-Gurion, for example, subsisted on money sent by his father, and his letters are full of complaints that the money was late to arrive. Unlike Shafir, I am less sure that this was a problem of material survival for the fledgling Zionist settlement effort. But what is clear is that it constituted an ethical problem of the utmost urgency. The settlers, especially the socialists who arrived in the first two decades of the twentieth century, were trained to recognize in this money the old stigma of dependency. They referred to financial support using words that indicated their disdain: *apotropsut* (guardianship), meaning that such support came at the price of turning the receivers into minors, under the paternal authority of the giver, and *tapilut* (parasitism), meaning that the receivers reverted to the Jewish condition in the Diaspora, working in unproductive occupations or, worse still, subsisting on charity.[26]

Any financial support prompted the suspicion that the Diaspora had crept back into their hearts and was erecting itself anew in Palestine. This continuing sense of failure and doubt, masterfully captured by the writer Hayyim Yosef Brenner, turned at least a few of the settlers into virtuosi of imitation. The goal was to eradicate in themselves all signs of dependency. And if they wanted indeed to convince themselves that they had turned into exemplars of the "new Zionist Man," their imitation could not be superficial; it must entail a complete sacrifice of their former selves. The members of Ha-Ro'eh, for example, undertook to spend a whole year among the Bedouin, without any contact with their friends or other Jews. This absolute isolation, this asceticism, this living outside in nature was meant not only to turn them into accomplished shepherds but to fashion them into a new human type: hardened, resourceful, capable of taking care of themselves, and without need of anybody's help or support.[27]

This absolute sacrifice of their former identity gave them the status of virtuosi among the settlers, that is, the status of those who have mastered a certain moral ideal to perfection – perhaps too perfectly. They were an object of admiration but also of criticism. Their critics used a certain codeword, *gandranut* (dandyism), to express their disapproval. When applied to the members of Ha-Shomer, it clearly referred to the fact that, in the manner of Bedouin horsemen, they wore fine clothes and invested a lot of money in showy rifles and horses. But the criticism was voiced also against the members of Ha-Ro'eh, who wore the simplest of garments, and precisely because they preferred to walk barefoot![28] This shows that this codeword had another, more important meaning: sense of superiority or arrogance. The critics admitted that the *mista'ravim* had indeed presented the rest of the settlers with an exemplary model of the new Zionist identity, but they blamed them for doing so only to enjoy personal prestige and not for the sake of a higher cause. Finally, the accusation of *gandranut* was a purification device. On the one hand, if the virtuosi of imitation were merely dandies, then this meant that their imitation was superficial and they were truly only Jews. On the other hand, if even the barefooted shepherds could be accused of *gandranut*, it must have been because their concern with external appearances betrayed a tendency to cross over to the other side and to identify with the Arabs they imitated. After all, wasn't the opposition between West and East also an opposition between inwardness and exteriority, depth and surface?

This accusation seems, therefore, to betray a characteristic anxiety: might not the virtuosi "go native"? Spending too much time on the other side, they might get so invested in the role they were playing that they could no longer distinguish it from reality. By imitating the Arabs, did they not run the risk of *hitpakrut*, becoming one of them and losing their Jewish identity? Their critics reminded them that "the ideal of becoming a Hebrew guard [*shomer*] does not require at all imitating the Arab's dress, language and manners. It is possible to see much beauty and utility in a Hebrew hero, but when the Hebrew element is spoiled, beauty and utility will be spoiled too."[29]

In short, the hybrid virtuosi of imitation were accused of transgressing the boundary, and the accusation itself served to redraw the boundary, without of course annulling the need for transgressing it yet again. The boundary was imagined as extremely easy to cross in one direction, much less so in the other; the Orient was penetrable and superficial, yet also a deep labyrinth, a "Heart of Darkness" where one could be lost for ever. These fears, which are very typical of colonial societies, provide evidence for the need to manage the boundary zone, to purify the hybrids and separate in them what is "Arab" and what is "Jewish."

Despite the attempts at purification, the virtuosi of imitation still enjoy an iconic status in the Zionist narrative. They were never completely purified. Why? First, because the self-fashioning of the virtuosi was a form of exemplary leadership. It was an important tactic utilized by the pastoral form of power that ruled prestate Jewish society. The virtuosi were at once the prototype of the new Zionist identity and of what lay beyond it, the experience of the Orient as a radical and immutable otherness. Second, as I argue in the next chapter, because the hybrid practice of imitation was an important source of legitimacy and credibility for orientalist expertise in the prestate period. For this reason, orientalist discourse could not purify the hybrids, since its very authority depended on proximity to Arabs, mixing with them and imitating them.

The second group that Ben-Gurion identified was the urbanites. They were the exact opposite of the Bedouin, not only because their lifestyle was completely different but also because "by their years, most of the urbanites are relatively new and young," and even more importantly because they had no essence: "This group is many-colored and diverse, a chaotic mixture of races, nations, languages and religions that is very difficult to find anywhere else . . . a great confusion of languages . . . all sorts of racial and national types from the children of Shem, Cham and Yephet live together in one place . . . all the religions . . . and all the sects . . . are represented here."[30] The radical, eternal, and pure otherness of the Orient, represented by the Bedouin, dissolved in the city into a mishmash, the absence of essence, a fleeting and weightless nullity, which, by the same token, was also outside history. The same image was also repeated by one of the founders of paramilitary intelligence: "It is in the nature of Arab society that nothing is fixed, everything is fluid and changing."[31]

This image is no doubt that of the oriental bazaar, an image of a busy chaos where nothing is stable and everything could be bought and sold, a carnival in which identities dissolve into one another or are inverted in a sort of sensual and frivolous transgression. We find this image again in Goitein when he complains (indirectly) about the love of boys practiced by men in oriental cities and attributes it to the inheritance of a Greek-Persian urban culture that the Arabs acquired after they lost the purity of their own tradition.[32]

It is easy to mock Goitein's puritanical censure or Ben-Gurion's modernist desire for order and clarity. The novelist Amos Oz, for example, has attributed the separatism of the settlers to a clash between the repressed and puritanical sexuality they brought from Europe and the colorful and sensual promiscuity of the oriental cities. He tells of his grandmother, who after arriving in Palestine

took one shocked look at the sweaty markets, at the colorful stands, at the busy alleys that were full of the voices of vendors, and the braying of donkeys, and the bleating of goats, and the screams of chickens hanging with their legs tied, and the blood-dripping throats of slaughtered fowl. She saw the bare shoulders and arms of oriental men, and the scandalous noisy colors of fruits and vegetables . . . and immediately she rendered a final verdict: the Levant is full of microbes.

He speculates that it was not the dirt but "the throbbing sensuality of the Levant . . . the sights, colors and odors of the Orient" that evoked "in my grandmother's heart, and possibly also in the hearts of other immigrants and refugees" such fears that they "endeavored to build a ghetto for themselves, to barricade themselves from the threats and sensual temptations [of the Orient]."[33]

But this is a spurious argument, since the mocking gesture itself is part of the very same discourse, the same image of the Orient as carnival. The only difference is that it affirms this image rather than censure it. Yet this affirmation is not new, it was present already in the prestate period, for example, in Goitein's celebration of the freedom and tolerance of Mediterranean society: the freedom to disappear among the crowd, to change personas and identities; the tolerance that permitted different ethnicities and denominations to coexist without any of them standing out or being persecuted; the very sort of tolerance that Jews have sought, with little success, in European cities.[34]

The other side of the image of constant change and the absence of essence, of carnival and the transmutation of identities, was the ideal of a productive synthesis or symbiosis between the different groups and races and between the Orient and the Occident. This ideal of synthesis was the distinctive ethos of the notables. Just as the image of the Orient as absolute otherness was manufactured by the practice of imitation, so the image of the Orient as carnival and synthesis was manufactured by the practices of association, networking across ethnic lines, and mediation among notables.

In the imagination of contemporaries, the hybrid figure of the Sephardi Jew was the concrete embodiment of this ideal of synthesis.[35] There was a whole set of hopes and interests invested in the invented memory of Sepharad (Spain) as a zone of cultural encounter and mixing. Take, for example, the bimonthly *Mizrah u-Ma'arav* (Orient and Occident), started in Jerusalem in 1919 by Avraham Elmaliah, a Sephardi intellectual, educator, and notable. Many other Sephardi intellectuals and notables wrote for it, and so did many prominent Ashkenazi intellectuals. By *Sepharad* they specifically meant "the golden age of Sepharad," the time when Jews lived under Islamic rule in Spain, and they interpreted this period as a moment when Jews managed to perfectly balance East and West, to synthesize the "emotional poetry" of the first with the "calculating reason" of the second in "superior harmony."

The contributors to *Mizrah u-Ma'arav* thus constructed the Sephardim as hybrid, but unlike the *mista'ravim*, their hybridity was understood as a "harmonious synthesis," not artifice or self-fashioning. Nonetheless, just as the *mista'ravim* garnered admiration and respect, so were the contributors to *Mizrah u-Ma'arav* attempting to present the Sephardi synthesis as a model worthy of emulation by Ashkenazi Jews. They argued that the goal of Zionism was "to connect what is worthy in the East with what is excellent in the West, to serve as a bridge and a tie between Europe and Asia.... This ambition for a synthesis between East and West is our legacy from the period of *Sepharad*." From this point of view, Zionism must be a return to the ideal of *Sepharad*, and "*Sephardi* Jews especially must turn it into a fertile inheritance."[36] Their bodies as well expressed a more complete synthesis of human qualities. They were possessed of "this health of the body and the spirit, this internal calm and confidence, this straight and piercing gaze, so lacking in the hasty, capricious and boastful sons of Russia and Galicia."[37]

The construction of the Sephardim as hybrid was not just a romantic attribution by European-born intellectuals; it was also a form of self-understanding and self-presentation by the Sephardi notables. They attempted to use their mediating position, between the Orient and the Occident, to claim leadership of the Jewish community in Palestine. From their point of view, the Jews did not need to imitate the Arabs, because the Jews themselves were "oriental," an integral part of the Levantine urban mosaic. Some spoke about the unity of the Semitic race: "Here the Jews will meet a people similar to them in race, and with a culture similar to their culture ... out of this encounter new values will emerge, which would be a blessing for both races together ... a great Semitic culture."[38] They cautioned, however, that since the Jews have spent millennia in Europe, they must work to recover their forgotten roots and learn how to integrate once again in the Orient:

The Jews are of oriental origins, despite their long exile in occidental lands. The land of Israel is in the Orient and our first duty in returning to it is to acquire again the good oriental qualities, but also to maintain the good qualities we have acquired in the Occident. The Arabs, like the Jews, are Semites and therefore they are cousins. Our languages derive from the same origin and so do our beliefs and much of our nature is similar.[39]

Obviously, the Sephardi notables offered themselves as leaders and guides of such a process of integration. They would teach the Jews about Arab culture and language, and vice versa – they would explain the ideas of Zionism to the Arabs, and in this way they would mediate between the two groups. When accusations were made that they would be dragging the Jews down to the level of an inferior culture, they responded with the ideal of synthesis. The goal of Zionism was not for Jews to cease to be European, but neither was it for them to remain a "foreign implant" in the Orient. Zionism had a higher goal, a world-historical mission to mediate between the two rival civilizations, Orient and Occident, and synthesize them into a higher and more complete form. Only the Jews could perform this task, because only they had existed in the past in a "Jewish-Arab symbiosis" as well as deep within the folds of Western civilization. In a sense, the Orient of the notables included the Occident within it, because unlike the Occident it was an open space permitting productive syntheses between different cultures.[40] To achieve this synthesis, they translated classical Arab literary works into Hebrew and taught colloquial Arabic to Jewish high school students. Together with Ashkenazi intellectuals such as Bia'lik and Tortchiner, the Sephardi notables and intellectuals argued that the purpose of learning Arabic was not only to allow Jews to understand their Palestinian neighbors and be able to converse with them but more importantly to deepen their understanding of the Hebrew language itself. For those who would like to invent new Hebrew words and improve the everyday Hebrew spoken by the settlers, colloquial and literary Arabic would provide a rich and relevant source of inspiration.[41]

My point here is not that the notion of Semitic racial unity was idealized and romanticized by the notables. This idea was by no means unanimously accepted. Max Nordau, for one, called it "an idiotic expression of false science," and Goitein too considered it an anti-Semitic invention of the nineteenth century.[42] My point is that the Orient was imagined as a space of heterogeneity and hybridity characterized by constant flux, absence of essence, synthesis, and an open horizon of identity, regardless of how one might value these qualities. Such an image was tied to the hybrid figure of the Sephardi Jew and to the practice of mediation among notables. It expressed not simply their greater affinity to the Arabs, their wish to promote peace and understanding among Jews and Arabs, but also their claim to provide an alternative political and cultural leadership for the Jewish community in Palestine. They competed against the labor movement in the political field and promoted the practice of mediation among notables as an alternative to its strategy of economic and territorial separatism. At the same time, they were also competing against the group of Hebrew writers and intellectuals who had immigrated from the cultural centers of Odessa and Warsaw (the most famous were Haim Nahman Bialik, S. Ben-Zion, Asher Berash, Yosef Klausner, Ya'akov Rabinovich, and Shaul Tchernichovski), who dominated the cultural field by virtue of their coalition with labor, and whose discourse focused on the formation of an insular Hebrew identity. The Sephardi notables typically found themselves excluded from this coalition, and the resources composing their cultural capital – social network ties across ethnic boundaries and knowledge of the Arab language – were devalued within this new discourse. Against this coalition, therefore, the notables mobilized the image of the Orient as an open space where Jews could and should blend, and they asserted their superior credentials for cultural leadership because, unlike the Hebrew writers, they were born in Palestine or at least well integrated with its people:

Now the time is ripe for the young land of Israel, and especially for her maturing children, to come out with their aspirations and demands. . . . We too want to live our happy lives, free from all external worries and from the influences of the Diaspora, which even here, in the land of our fathers, still haunts us. Now, at last, there's a new spirit in us; after all, it is with our brothers, kindred of the same race, that we have lived most of our days, and thus the splendor of the Hebrew-Arab Orient had spread in our veins. . . . Orientals we wish to remain wherever we are and whatever we do – Orientals, with all that is good in that beloved expression, and despite of its less appealing sides. Orientals as our fathers were, and as surely will our sons be tomorrow . . . and Occidental as well; this means that we will always march forward . . . till the day will come and the Orient once again will give to the Occident much more than it gave in the days of Judea and Arabia – maybe even perfection itself.[43]

It is significant that even those who rejected the ethos of the notables employed the same image of the Orient, though with a different valence. Against the vision of Semitic unity or urban hybridity, they countered with fears of racial miscegenation. For them, the urban mixture of races was not a lighthearted mishmash but a dangerous dilution of racial purity. They perceived synthesis – the very same quality celebrated by the notables – as a power that the Orient possessed to absorb all newcomers from the Occident and corrupt them so they disappeared within it without a trace, "just as the desert sands crawl back and cover all the places, which were once desert, and then settled, and then once again abandoned under its dominion."[44]

There were all sorts of fears and suspicions directed at the Sephardi hybrid, and all sorts of devices meant to purify him, to separate within him what belonged to the new Hebrew and what to the old oriental. One argument frequently heard was that the Sephardi blending of East and West was not a harmonious synthesis of the best qualities of the two civilizations but, on the contrary, a synthesis of their worst ones. It was a superficial synthesis, producing a Levantine creature of external brilliance but rather hollow on the inside. Typically, French education was held to be at fault. Seemingly hybrid, the Sephardi actually had crossed over to the oriental side, displaying the oriental quality of fascination with the exterior and with appearances. Dandyism all over again!

Another device was the theme of degeneration. The Sephardi blending of East and West did not produce a harmonious synthesis of body and mind but, on the contrary, resulted in a dangerous infection that led to degeneration and decline. This is how a young Sephardi intellectual expressed it: "Here in Turkey the Jew sits peacefully and serenely next to his Turkish neighbor, legs folded underneath him, and both are smoking their hookahs with pleasure and oriental sloth, calmly and quietly rolling their prayer beads in their fingers, praising Allah for all the goodness he provides to the creatures of his world."[45] The "oriental" way of sitting, the hookah and the prayer beads, all these symbols of "oriental sloth," are used to prove that Sephardi Jewry had declined, degenerated, and gone over completely to the oriental side. Sephardi Jewry could not be counted upon to assist in the national revival, unless it is itself awakened, shaken to its feet, so to speak, and separated from its oriental neighbors, the Arabs and the Turks.

This equivocation, however, between celebration of hybridity and attempts at purification remained unresolved, and it proved impossible to separate within the Sephardi hybrid what belonged to the new Hebrew and what to the old oriental. The "golden age of *Sepharad*" remains an important part of the Zionist narrative to this day. The Sephardi form of pronunciation overcame the Ashkenazi one and was adopted as the official manner of speaking Hebrew. It became an audible symbol of the rejuvenation of the Hebrew language and an integral part of the somatic equipment of the new Jew, the *sabre*. Certainly this was due to the fact that the notables still held an important position in Jewish society and commanded public attention. Moreover, they were crucial to the Zionist case because their community had lived in Palestine for hundreds of years, thus proving the continuity of the Jewish connection to Palestine. In this capacity they testified before the various committees of inquiry that came to Palestine periodically to try to sort out the competing claims of Jews and Palestinians. The appearance of one of these "Palestinian Jews," as they presented themselves, before such a committee, the proud assertion of hybridity, allowed the Jewish side to resist the definition of the situation as a struggle between natives and newcomers.

But as we shall see in the next chapter, there was also another reason: orientalist discourse did not seek to purify the Sephardi hybrid. On the contrary, the German-educated philologists at the Institute for Oriental Studies in the Hebrew University were the allies (and sometimes personal friends) of the Sephardi notables. They identified with the ideal of *Sepharad*, they studied the period of Sepharad as the most glorious moment of the "Jewish-Arab symbiosis," and they dreamt about recreating it in Palestine. Put differently, orientalist discourse in the prestate period was enunciated from a position very similar to that of the Sephardi Jew. Orientalist expertise was legitimated by a similar appeal to the principle of synthesis. Consequently, orientalist discourse could not purify the Sephardi hybrid. On the contrary, it participated in manufacturing it.[46]

We see, therefore, that the early Zionist experience of the Orient was composed of opposites: at once an essence and its absence, immutability and constant flux, ancient majesty and a fleeting, frivolous nullity, clear identity and total chaos. To this complex experience we must add another layer, represented by Ben-Gurion's third and final group, the most important from his point of view – the fellahin. Ostensibly, they were similar to the urbanites in that they too were "many-hued and different from one another in their religion and race . . . here too chaos and confusion reign . . . no less than eight different races." Moreover, they too were the inverse of the Bedouin: "If we try to trace the origins of the fellahin . . . we see that there is almost no connection between them and the real Arabs, members of the Arab race." Yet, they differed from the urbanites because Ben-Gurion thought that it was possible to trace their origins. He thought it was possible to show that "most of the fellahin . . . were the descendents of the very same farmers the Arabs found when they conquered Palestine in the Seventh Century." His conclusion was that they really were "the ancient Jewish farmers who remained in their land despite all the persecutions." Although they converted to Islam under the pressure of the Arab conquerors, this religious veneer was rather superficial, and underneath it, particularly in peasant folklore and place names, one could glimpse the very same traditions handed down from the days of the Bible.[47]

Unlike both the Bedouin and the urbanites, therefore, the fellahin were not outside history. Their origins could be traced, and it was possible to tell their history and all that befell them from biblical times and until now. Or more precisely, more than the fellahin being inside history, they were the mediators making possible the Zionist "return to history." This was no longer the immutable Orient, an absolute otherness to be imitated; nor was it the changing and essenceless Orient, making possible mediation and synthesis. Rather, it was the experience of an Orient in which the new Jews saw themselves reflected, a mirror image of their ancient selves because it harked back to biblical times. The image of the fellahin as "hidden Jews" served to connect the modern Jewish settlement of Palestine with their biblical roots in the land of Canaan, less because this curious genealogy validated the Jewish "right" to the land than because the fellahin became the mirror through which the everyday lives of the settlers were endowed with the stamp of authenticity and autochthony – they were not colonizers because they were "living with the Bible," as claimed by one famous settler, soldier, and self-styled archeologist and orientalist.[48]

The fellahin were not typically an object of admiration or imitation and were not included in the social networks of the notables, unless as subordinates. But around them was woven a whole web of observation and contemplation, ethnographic description and biblical lore. There is no doubt that one of the motives behind the identification of the fellahin as descendents of the ancient Hebrews was the desire to fit the local inhabitants of Palestine within the Zionist project and thus to "solve" the problem they posed. In fact, this identification was always accompanied by speculations about the future assimilation of the fellahin into Jewish society and even ideas about establishing a "mission" among them charged with converting them to Judaism. On this level, the genealogy and ethnography of the fellahin perhaps constituted a cul-de-sac, and the role they played in the life of the Jewish community in Palestine was short-lived. (Although not as short-lived as may seem; we shall see how the idea of a mission in the Arab village and of assimilating the peasants was raised anew in 1948.)

On the symbolic level, however, the figure of the fellahin played a much more significant role as an ideological mirror placed in front of the Jewish immigrants, endowing their presence on the land with a sense of authenticity, yet demanding of them that they fashion themselves as farmers and agricultural workers.[49] Even without tracing a direct genealogical link between the fellahin and the Jews, the literature about the fellahin sought to endow the new Hebrew identity with a sense of continuity:

The general reason for my trying to acquaint other [Jews] with the life of our neighbors ... is because this life, and especially fellahin life, could serve as a living interpretation of our living book, the Bible. ... We Jews have an urgent need to become familiar with the life of the Arabs in our land, especially the life of the fellahin, before they also will become Europeanized, so that through them we will become acquainted with our own ancient and typical self.[50]

My point, again, is not that the fellahin were romanticized and idealized but that the literature about them presents us with a third Arab-Jewish hybrid and with another modality of experience of the Orient, this time as a mirror in which the Jewish immigrants could see themselves reflected and convince themselves that they had a right to the land. No less importantly, this mirror image also allowed them to convince themselves that their rebellion against the Jewish culture of the Diaspora did not alienate them from their identity but actually brought them closer to its true essence.

This point is confirmed by the fact that this same mirror image was applied not only to the fellahin but also to oriental Jews, especially the Yemenites, whom Goitien called "the most genuine Jews living amongst the most genuine Arabs" and whose customs and language he used to clarify points about Jewish life as depicted in the Bible and the Talmud. This idea was prevalent. The linguist Eliezer Ben-Yehouda, who produced the first modern Hebrew dictionary and is celebrated as the "reviver of the Hebrew language," was fascinated by Yemenite Jews and claimed that in them one could discern the social character of the people of Israel in the times of the *mishna*. But the most important contribution to the shaping of this image was made by the visual arts – painting, sculpture, and handicrafts. For example, the paintings of Nahum Gutman, who believed that "the biblical type is most accurately represented by Arab figures," or the combined works of the artists of the Betzalel academy in Jerusalem, who typically hired Yemenite Jews to serve as models for Biblical figures. In their works, for example in the illustrated *Song of Songs* produced by Ze'ev Raban, the Betzalel artists created a romantic image of the Orient as the site where biblical stories took place, and they populated it with "Arab" and "oriental" figures taken from the imagery of nineteenth-century romantic orientalism (Fig. 2.2). Additionally,

FIGURE 2.2. Ze'ev Raban, "I implore you, O daughters of Jerusalem." *Source.* Ze'ev Raban, *The Illustrated Song of Songs* (Jerusalem: Shulamit, 1923).

the workshops of Betzalel employed Yemenite artisans and goldsmiths, partly because they were cheap and were perceived as docile and hardworking, but partly also because they lent authenticity to the artifacts that were sold to Jewish communities around the world.[51]

I have used the terms "mirror image" and "reflection" to highlight the iconographic dimension of the practice that created this experience of the Orient – "iconographic" in the double sense of visual representation and of the production of icons used for daily, domestic worship. The fact that this iconographic practice played an important role in the Zionist project provides further support for Yehouda Shenhav's argument that Zionism – which presented itself as secular nationalism – relied on continuous mobilization of religious practices.[52] Even though Judaism is usually perceived as being opposed to icon worship, there was a distinct iconographic dimension to European Jewish worship in the nineteenth century. The role of icons was to serve as a visual device for contemplation, a tangible symbol that made it possible for the believers to concentrate their thoughts on a certain religious meaning.

Examples included the *mizrahim*, painted plaques that were hung from the walls of many European Jewish homes to indicate the eastward direction toward which the family should turn in prayer. These plaques, which typically depicted places or landscapes in Palestine, served also as visual reminders of the holy country from which the Jews were exiled, a means of performing the divine instruction never to forget it and always to have it at the center of one's thoughts. By contemplating them, the believers could, in the language of the divine instruction, "direct their hearts," that is, forget their daily worries and earthly concerns in order to concentrate on that which was lost and in this way complete in their hearts what history took apart and relegated to oblivion. As their name indicates – *mizrahim* is derived from the Hebrew word for "East" – these plaques represented an iconographic practice that did not distinguish sharply between the concepts of "Eretz Israel" and the "Orient" and treated the two as interchangeable. The plaques were typically painted by artists residing in Palestine who used the landscapes, places, and figures around them to represent biblical events, sites, and personages and who then sold them to European Jews. For example, a *mizrah* plaque painted in Jerusalem in the early twentieth century by Moshe ben Yitzhak Mizrahi depicts the mosque at the Dome of the Rock in order to symbolize the Temple Mount (Fig. 2.3).[53]

Only a short distance separates these plaques from illustrated books, such as *Treasures of the Bible*, published in Berlin in 1925, which contains illustrations, reproductions, and photographs of archeological findings and ancient artifacts (Fig. 2.4). The purpose of this book, as its editor wrote, was to "shed a new light on almost all the images of life that are revealed by the Bible. . . . A

FIGURE 2.3. Moshe ben Yitzhak Mizrahi, *Mizrah* plaque, ca. 1920. Oil paint on glass. *Source.* Israel Museum, Jerusalem.

living understanding of a book as saturated with stirring reality as the Bible is impossible if the written words are not accompanied by actual pictures that draw the [readers] closer to concrete observation." This secularized rendition of the religious commandment to remember and imagine the Holy Land enjoyed immense success, and not only among German Jews. We know that many in the Jewish community in Palestine possessed this book and that artists like Boris Shatz and Yitzhak Danziger (whose sculpture *Nimrod*, modeled on "Assyrian" motifs, became a Zionist icon) used it for inspiration.[54] Again, there is no doubt that these books drew, to a great extent, on the imagery bequeathed by nineteenth-century romantic orientalism, but their intended role – "living understanding," "concrete observation" – was similar to the role of the *mizrahim* plaques; they were to be used as visual devices for contemplation, aiding memory to overcome what history had destroyed and buried.

Moshe Dayan's *Living with Bible*, a book that was authored by one of Israel's best-known soldiers and statesmen and enjoyed immense popularity among both Israelis and Jews all over the world, can be viewed as a direct continuation of *Treasures of the Bible*, since it had a similar status as an icon

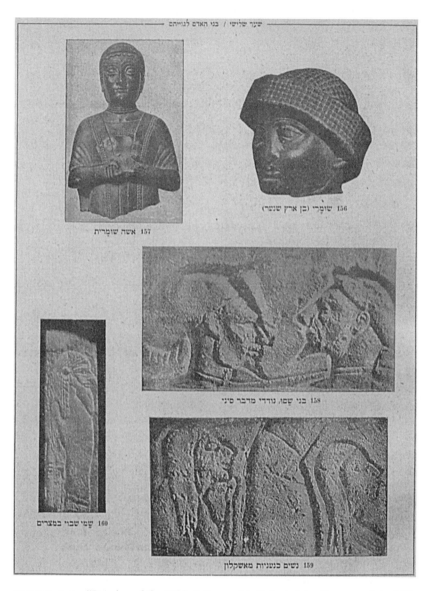

FIGURE 2.4. "Peoples of the Bible." *Source.* M. Solovitshik, *Treasures of the Bible* (Berlin: Dvir, 1925).

and a device for contemplation. The need for these visual devices was not unique to European Jews, dwelling far away from the Promised Land, but was voiced also by the Jewish settlers in Palestine itself. We find the young Ben-Gurion, shortly after he arrived there, yearning after such a device. His letters to his father are full of romantic descriptions of the scenery, and he strains to find in it any visible traces of the ancient Hebrews or at least some special majesty.[55] His expressed need for a visual device gives us a sense of how important to the new settlers was the iconographic practice of depicting the fellahin or the Yemenites: it converted Palestine into Eretz Israel. From the Palestinian raw materials, it actually shaped this "magical" Eretz Israel, a place where one could directly observe biblical reality, and it wove these materials into the fabric of everyday life in the form of artifacts and images surrounding the settlers and adorning their homes. Boris Schatz, for example, envisioned a situation in which every Jewish home would include "a Jewish corner, or better, a special room set aside for Jewish artifacts," especially those manufactured by Betzalel's workshops (Schatz was Betzalel's founder and first director). This room was meant to serve as a device for contemplation and recollection: "In this room one could sense the great spirit of our free forefathers; the intense spiritualism, the exalted idealism of our prophets; the boundless courage of our warrior forefathers who defended our land."[56] In a sense, the hybrids were all around the settlers. However many times they were purified, however many authors wrote with derision about the "primitive" fellahin, comparing them with savages[57] and thus separating again within the hybrid what was "Arab" and "backward" from what was "Jewish" and "developed," the purification devices could not catch up with the production of these hybrid icons, which were an intrinsic part of visual culture.

The literature on the fellahin undertook to provide a similarly tangible representation, and hence there was a distinct iconographic dimension to its descriptions. Take, for example, the opening passage of Stavski's *The Arab Village*:

The village gazes far from on high, spreading the odors of habitation and population, voices and commotion, which fill with rejoice the hearts of any traveler, foreigner and *ger* [a biblical word for a non-Jew who resides among the Jews and undertakes to follow their faith], who happens to pass by, promising lodgings ... for the night's rest. . . . When the traveler draws near to the boundary of the village, a refreshing smell of water comes to his nostrils – the water of a well, a pool, a tub. . . . The well is the heart of the village and the first condition of its existence. . . . Without a well there is no peace and no comfort, no life and no fertility.[58]

This introduction is meant to give the reader a sense of observing the village from without, slowly drawing nearer to it so it is possible to see, hear, and even smell it. The rhythm of the book's first chapter is dictated by this movement, which begins with observation from outside and then penetrates the village through its gate, moves to the communal barn and then along the winding streets to the traditional guesthouse, progresses to the home itself, the wall protecting it, the courtyard and all the different fixtures in it, then enters by the door into the home's interior, and finally touches upon "marital relations." There is no doubt that this mode of description was meant to assist the readers in imagining a "living picture," and even if this was not strictly a visual device for contemplation, there is no doubt either about the purpose behind this technique of writing: it allows Stavski to draw the reader slowly into the world of the Bible, into an Orient in which biblical times and our own times are one and the same. This is shown by the reference to the *ger* (the biblical term for a convert to Judaism) as well as by the fact that Stavski later purports to have witnessed the story of Jacob and Rachel unfolding once again at the village's well. The book is replete with biblical and Talmudic references, which are meant to shed light on the customs of the fellahin and to be rendered living and relevant once again through observation of the village.[59]

These were the parameters of the experience of the Orient in the prestate period: an absolute otherness constructed by the practice of imitation; a carnival orchestrated by the art of mediation between notables; and a mirror image woven into the fabric of everyday life by an iconographic practice. The first and the second images were opposed to one another as essence and its absence, immutability and changeability, and both were opposed to the third image as painting and narrative, representation and development. Nonetheless, all three images joined together to compose a coherent and meaningful experience of the Orient as a metaphor for metamorphosis and the transmutation of identities. It was less important whether such metamorphosis was understood as imitation, assimilation, synthesis, symbiosis, or mirror identification, also less important whether it was affirmed as rejuvenation or negated as degeneration.

There is no doubt that as the years passed, especially after 1936, when the conflict with the Palestinians intensified and the separatist institutions of labor Zionism gained dominance, the emphasis on the negative valuation of metamorphosis, on the dangers inherent in the Orient and the need to separate from it, grew as well. In the next chapter, I trace the history of new practices that from 1936 onwards began to change the mode of encounter with the Orient and that after 1948 clashed in a jurisdictional struggle that led to the disenchantment of the Orient. And yet the experience of the Orient described in this chapter was still valid up until 1948, because, as explained earlier, it was closely tied to the alternative politics of the notables and was the correlate of the pastoral power exercised by the church of labor

Zionism. It was this pastoral power that gave rise to the distinctive identity politics that characterized the Jewish community in Palestine and that only the formation of the state began to subdue. From it followed also the role of the Orient as the site of identity metamorphosis, a liminal space populated by hybrids.

CHAPTER 3

The Field of Orientalist Expertise before 1948

IN THE PERIOD BEFORE 1948, there were two key contenders in the struggle to impose the prototype of orientalist expertise. The production of orientalist knowledge was, to a large extent, divided between them, and the struggle was undecided. On the one hand were professors of oriental studies who taught at the Hebrew University and had been trained in German universities; on the other hand were Arabists who spoke the local Palestinian dialect and served as advisers to the political leadership.

As shown in Figure 3.1, these were not the only groups claiming some form of orientalist expertise, but they represented two radically different principles of expertise, and to a large extent the opposition between them was the main dynamic determining the shape of the field and the range of options open to other groups of experts. These principles, and herein lies the importance of the argument of the first part of this chapter, were analogous, one to the Sephardi hybrid and the other to the *mista'rev* hybrid, and for this reason orientalist discourse could not purify these hybrids. Nonetheless, as I show in the second part of this chapter, from 1936 onward the competition between different groups of experts, along with the relations between them and the political and military leadership, led to the formation of new claims for expertise and new practices of intelligence, government, *hasbara* (literally "explaining"), and the absorption of immigrants that after the establishment of the state in 1948 divided between them the cognitive territory of the orient and purified the hybrids.

The Institute of Oriental Studies was created at the Hebrew University in 1926, a year after the university itself was established. From its inception, it was staffed by professors who were brought from Germany by the university's chancellor, Yehouda Leib Magnes, to make up the institute's faculty and who were trained as philologists in German institutions. In German universities,

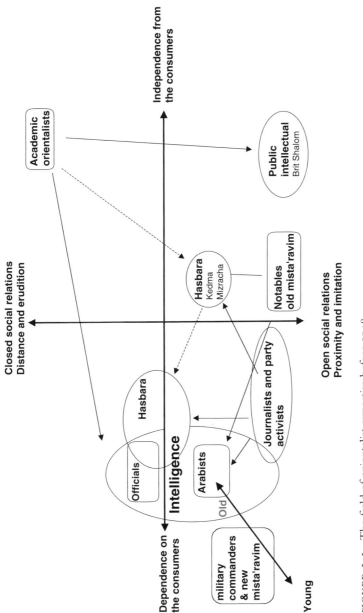

FIGURE 3.1. The field of orientalist expertise before 1948.

Islamic studies and Judaic studies were taught together, as a single unified branch of knowledge, and the German-trained professors were well educated in both. Moreover, many of them came from religious families and thus were deeply committed to the study of Judaism, especially the interaction between Jewish and Islamic civilizations. Thus, their expertise was analogous to the Spehardi hybrid, and they socialized with Sephardi intellectuals, teachers, and translators.[1]

Their claim to be recognized as experts on Arab affairs was based on a principle of distance and academic closure, though expressed in three different ways: First, it was based on distance in time, because they studied medieval Islamic history and considered the study of the contemporary Orient, in the absence of established archives, to be unscientific.

Second, it was based on distance from the Orient and Arabs themselves, because they considered someone to be an expert only if he possessed a credential from a respectable European university. Firsthand knowledge of the "natives," on the other hand, did not count for much in their eyes. They themselves were all but one born in Europe, and the only native-born professor – Yosef Yoel Rivlin – completed his Ph.D. in Frankfurt under the first director of the institute, Professor Yosef Horowitz. Even when it came to Arabic instruction in elementary schools, Goitein considered the Sephardi and Palestinian teachers to be inferior to Ashkenazi teachers because they lacked European or Hebrew (i.e., Ashkenazi) education.[2] In this way, the professors exercised near-perfect control over the supply of their own expertise. The rules of entry into their portion of the field were strict and fixed and required a long period of preparation and a serious investment in academic studies.

Third, it was based on distance and independence from the consumers of orientalist knowledge. The professors fought mightily against demands that research and teaching in the institute should be more attuned to practical needs, especially the political needs of the Jewish community in Palestine. Thus, the central quality of the prototype of orientalist expertise that they represented was distance, which they interpreted as guaranteeing autonomy, independence, objectivity, and scientificality. In short, they combined academic closure with a radical autonomy from the consumers of knowledge,[3] and for this reason I place them at the top right of Figure 3.1.

Nonetheless, adherence to this principle of distance was not necessarily the final position of the professors. It was more like a gambit in a complex dynamic caused by the struggles in the field of orientalist expertise as well as by the relations between this field and the political sphere. The fact that they protected themselves by distance and academic closure did not mean that the professors undertook to avoid all political involvement but simply that in taking political stances they were limited (and enabled) by the constraints associated with their position in the field of orientalist expertise.

Several strategies were open to them: One was to try to convert their academic standing, validated by distance, erudition, and academic closure, by moving toward the bottom right corner of Figure 3.1 (i.e., in the same position as the prophet in Figure 1.2), that is, by becoming public intellectuals, who seek to shape the public agenda and subordinate it to moral considerations. The second possible strategy was more moderate; it involved a movement not only on the vertical axis but also along the horizontal axis in the direction of greater dependence on the consumers and greater dialogue with them while maintaining a semi-independent status in the public sphere. The third strategy was to renounce altogether their claim of independence and become employees of the institutions of the "state-in-the-making." The first strategy was displayed in the orientalists' activities in Brit-Shalom (Covenant of Peace). The second materialized through their connections with the notables in the context of Brit-Shalom's successor – Kedma Mizracha (Eastward) – and the practice of *hasbara* (explaining). Finally, the turn to the third strategy was typical of their students and was caused by the slow pace of promotion in the institute.

Brit Shalom and the Institute for Oriental Studies were created almost exactly at the same time by the same individuals and with similar goals in mind. Brit Shalom was established in 1925 after a lecture on "The Position of the Arab-Islamic World with Regards to Zionism" delivered by Professor Yosef Horowitz at a conference marking the inauguration of the new university. A year later, the Institute for Oriental Studies was created, with Horowitz as its first director. Almost all the professors of the new institute were members of or sympathizers with Brit Shalom.[4]

It was a natural union, because the members of Brit Shalom were strongly influenced by the charismatic philosopher Martin Buber, who taught that the task of Zionism should be to bridge the divide between the rising East and the declining West. This was, as we have seen, an idea espoused by many German Jewish intellectuals. They had reacted to the anti-Semitic stigmatization of Jews as "oriental" in a manner that expressed a great deal of self-confidence and a sense of being well integrated into German society and culture. From this point of view, academic orientalism was a form of Zionism, a form of mediation between East and West. For this reason, the professors emphasized in their research the deep historical, linguistic, and cultural affinities between Jews and Arabs: They studied not only the Jewish-Arab literature and poetry composed during the "golden age of *Sepharad*" but also the Hebrew-Arab dialect of Yemenite Jews, the mutual influences between Jewish and Islamic philosophies, the modification of Jewish legal thought and prayer practices due to the impact of Islam, and the similarities between the folklore and folk arts of the two peoples. In short, they attempted to demonstrate the scope of the "Jewish-Arab symbiosis" in the past in order to promote its possibility in the present.[5] They were the distinct carriers of the image of the Orient as synthesis as well as the place where the Jews originated and from which they derived their essence.

In the first three years of its existence, Brit Shalom concentrated its efforts mostly on *hasbara* – on "explaining the values and culture of the two peoples in speeches and in writings to Hebrews and Arabs and developing friendly relations between them . . . influencing public opinion in the spirit of agreement and peace." In 1926, for example, it started a program of evening classes in Arabic for the Jewish public.[6] But after the events of 1929, particularly after the murderous attack on the Jewish community in Hebron, Brit Shalom began to appear in the public sphere as a group of public intellectuals claiming to provide moral leadership for the Jewish community. They wanted Jews to understand Palestinian grievances and, despite the attacks, to reach out to them with a program of peaceful coexistence, even if that meant accepting limits on land purchases and immigration quotas. But their attempt to convert their academic standing into moral authority failed miserably. They came under sharp attacks from the leadership of the labor movement as well as from the cultural leadership, the Hebrew writers, and they were ridiculed as "naïve," as lacking any practical knowledge or firsthand acquaintance with Arabs. That is, their critics singled out precisely the very distance and academic closure that provided the professors with their prestige to begin with. Disappointed, they retreated back into the ivory tower of academic closure and nursed their wounds.[7]

Between prophetic ire and academic distance there was another possible strategy, *hasbara*. The meaning of this term has changed over the years. When Israelis speak about *hasbara* today, they usually mean a polemical discourse representing Israel's position on the world stage, though sometimes they also use the term to refer to internal educational campaigns, such against smoking or to promote AIDS awareness. In the prestate period, however, the term *hasbara* was principally used to denote educational efforts among the Jewish public (and only secondarily and by extension among Arabs, explaining to them the purpose and peaceful nature of Zionism). After the collapse of Brit Shalom, the academic orientalists did not dare venture any more into the public sphere and were content to research the Jewish-Arab symbiosis of the past. With the eruption of the Palestinian rebellion in 1936, however, some former members of Brit Shalom joined together with a group of notables – leaders of the Sephardi community, citrus growers and farmers, mayors of mixed cities and *mukhtars* of settlements, and leaders of the "civic" (i.e., bourgeois) German Jewish circles – to form a new association, Kedma Mizracha. Its purpose was defined as "encouraging familiarity with the

Orient, creation of economic and social ties with the nations of the Orient, and correct *hasbara* about the work of the Jewish people in this land."[8]

The term *hasbara* captured well the position that the members of Kedma Mizracha sought to carve for themselves. First, unlike Brit Shalom, they did not present themselves as self-appointed moral leaders. They justified their intervention in terms of dependence on the consumers of their knowledge. There existed, they said, public demand for their merchandise: "The public demands *hasbara*, and *hasbara* is extremely necessary."[9]

Second, they took pains to avoid direct confrontation with the political leadership and presented themselves as its allies. At the same time, however, their actions entailed an implicit criticism of the leadership. This was exactly the ambiguity of the term *hasbara*, for if it meant "propaganda among the Arabs," it denoted the service they would perform for the leadership, but if it meant "explaining to Jews the Arab question," then it meant that this question was not well understood by many of the Jews, perhaps even many of the leaders, who were born in the Diaspora. This term – *hasbara* – expressed a careful strategy that sought to convert orientalist expertise into political influence and that relied on the fact that the notables could present themselves at one and the same time as experts possessing orientalist knowledge, and as representatives of sectors of the Jewish public, i.e. the consumers of orientalist knowledge. Precisely for this reason, when the members of Kedma Mizracha met with Ben-Gurion, then chairman of the Jewish Agency, the latter pressed them to define exactly what was their goal: Was the association "for research about the Arabs or for actions"? Did they want to explain Zionism to the Arabs or explain to Jews the value of cooperating with the Arabs?[10]

Third, the members of Kedma Mizracha highlighted the fact that they had business and friendship ties with Palestinian notables and presented these ties as useful in persuading Palestinians to take a more favorable stance toward Zionism. Despite Ben-Gurion's skepticism, Kedma Mizracha enjoyed some success, even in the labor movement. Some of the leading experts on Arab affairs in the labor movement were among its founding members, and many of the rank and file attended its lectures and debates. This meant, however, that the term *hasbara* also expressed the fact that Kedma Mizracha was composed of a large number of groups and personalities with different interests and worldviews. *Hasbara* was a sort of compromise between them, a lowest common denominator. In the end, the forces of attraction and repulsion emanating from the political leadership acted to fragment this fragile unity and to sever the weak ties among its different groups. Some were left out in the cold, while others were pulled closer to the leadership. Moshe Sharet, who was the director of the political department of the Jewish agency and considered himself also an expert on Arab affairs, acted vigorously to co-opt

Kedma Mizracha and turn it into an organ of the Jewish Agency, entrusted with promoting better relations between Jews and Arabs on a local basis.[11]

Indeed, the second important group claiming orientalist expertise, the Arabists, emerged to a large extent out of this attempt to co-opt the notables. The notables typically lacked academic orientalist education, but they spoke colloquial Arabic in the local Palestinian dialect and, as merchants, citrus growers, guards, and *mukhtars* of Hebrew settlements, were in daily contacts with Palestinian notables and peasants. This is why I place them at the bottom of Figure 3.1: their claim to be recognized as experts on Arab affairs was not based on some sort of esoteric knowledge or academic closure but on open social relations and a principle diametrically opposed to that of the professors – proximity.

The Arabists were in direct contacts with Palestinians, who were their neighbors and contemporaries, and in this way they acquired knowledge of local customs, dialects, relations, and events taking place in the here and now. This sort of knowledge involved to a great extent an element of imitation. Like the *mista'ravim*, the Arabists also learned to behave and speak as Palestinians did, and by virtue of this imitation they claimed that they could understand how Palestinians thought and could predict their behavior. In this sense, Arabist expertise was analogous to the *mista'rev* hybrid, and indeed some of the guards who in the past imitated the Bedouins and now were *mukhtars* of Jewish communities joined the paramilitary intelligence services of the Jewish side and became Arabists. Put differently, unlike the professors, the Arabists did not have much control over the supply of their own expertise. Anybody who learned the local Palestinian dialect from their neighbors and became adept at imitating them could be considered an Arabist. Unlike the professors, Arabist expertise was generous and open, not only because there were no fixed and strict criteria of entry into their ranks but also because it was in the very nature of Arabist discourse that it sought to enlighten its audience and equip them with an understanding of "Arab mentality" (i.e., to turn its audience into semi-Arabists themselves). By contrast, it is in the very nature of professorial discourse that it is esoteric and that it presents itself as inaccessible to laymen.

The expertise of the Arabists, even before they began working for the Jewish intelligence services, and especially in their role as notables, was not academic but directed at a practical purpose, namely, mediating between Jews and Arabs, maintaining "neighborly relations" between them, and making sure that no conflicts developed because Jews misunderstood the "Arab mentality." As we saw earlier, the political and cultural leadership was gradually marginalizing the notables. One strategy the notables employed to regain influence was *hasbara*, that is, offering themselves as guides to the intricacies of dealing with Arabs and the Orient without challenging the political leadership but also without serving it directly. Another possibility was to offer themselves as advisers, paid or unpaid, to the political leadership, that is, to move along the horizontal axis toward a position of greater dependence on the consumers of orientalist knowledge, which by the same token meant also a greater capacity to influence the political leadership.

This was the position of the Arabists. On the one hand, the Arabists were required to provide "information," which meant that their knowledge was directly subordinated to the needs of decision-makers. On the other hand, the expertise of Arabists was not really in "intelligence," as we understand the term today, but was directly continuous with the role of the notables as mediators between Jews and Arabs (as such, their knowledge was open and accessible to all). For example, the Arab intelligence branch of the Haganah (the main Jewish paramilitary organization), which formed in response to the 1936 Arab rebellion, was based in large part on the private network of Ezra Danin, a citrus grower and a Jewish notable, who created it in earlier years in order to protect his citrus groves – to collect information about gangs and thieves, to cultivate contacts in the villages so he could pursue the thieves and get his property back, and to do all this without harming neighborly relations.[12]

The Arabist as a social type, therefore, was based on a principle akin to the hybrid practices of the *mista'ravim* and by no means could purify them. The knowledge and expertise of the notables, when applied to intelligence work, did not develop into a method for evaluating and assessing information but became an art of recruiting and employing informers, directly continuous with the art of mediation between notables. The first Arabists saw themselves, not as intelligence operatives in the strict sense, but as mediators and advisers operating in a defined geographical area, a sort of county that they represented vis-à-vis the central authorities (in this case the Haganah central command and the Jewish Agency). Even as they collected information and passed it on, they understood their work as subordinate to the larger task of preventing conflicts between Jewish and Palestinian settlements, conflicts that they attributed in part to lack of understanding of the "Arab mentality." Yet the emphasis on neighborly relations was also a necessary tool for operating informers, since the latter (many of whom were notables of adjacent Palestinian communities) typically supplied information on the condition that it be used to avert conflicts between Jews and Palestinians (i.e., to maintain good relations) and not be used to harm general Palestinian interests.

Thus, employing informers was an art, both in the sense that it was practical, embodied knowledge that typically was learned on the job in a process of apprenticeship and in the sense that it was a blend of skilled mediation, negotiation, and haggling within which it was difficult to make a strong distinction between the task of collecting intelligence and the task of maintaining neighborly relations. The Arabists' self-understanding also caused them to view their reports not merely as "information" but as part of a dialogue with the political center, toward which they directed complaints and warnings, just as the notables did with the Ottoman and British authorities. For example, they frequently complained that the center did not "react" to their reports and that they saw no action as a result of what they reported.[13]

Many of the Arabists acted indeed as notables in the technical, Weberian sense of the term: many were unpaid or were employed on a temporary basis (at the beginning, Ezra Danin even used his own funds to pay informers), and they submitted reports as a sort of side job. Over time, however, some of them became employed as intelligence operatives on a regular basis, and some – Ezra Danin and Josh Palmon – were appointed as advisers to the political leadership. The position of adviser was characterized by a high degree of dependence on the consumers of orientalist knowledge and by open social relations: not only did the Arabists no longer enjoyed the relative freedom of the notables to define the purpose of their expertise, but as advisers they lost control over the attribution and dissemination of their discourse. Indeed, it was easy for the consumers to appropriate it: "I found out, that every time I tried to explain to him the situation based on the information I had, and to formulate my own assessment, Eliahu Golomb [commander of the Haganah operations branch] always pretended to know more and better than me and my colleagues."[14]

The Arabists also did not enjoy a monopoly over intelligence work and had to share it with another group of advisers and officials. In order to characterize this group, it is necessary to return to the Institute of Oriental Studies at the Hebrew University and to the third strategy available to the academic orientalists. As the reader may recall, the professors vehemently rejected the suggestion that research and teaching at the institute should cater to practical needs. Especially after the fall of Brit Shalom, they retreated to the academic ivory tower and to a position of radical independence from the consumers. Their sense of being under attack increased in 1934, when an external review committee criticized the institute for restricting itself to the study of Islamic culture in the distant past and not teaching topics related to the modern Middle East, colloquial Arabic, and so on. There is no doubt that this attack was partly in reaction to the role the orientalists played in Brit Shalom. The committee's report was quite scathing on this count:

The Jewish land of Israel is surrounded on all sides by the Muslim world, a thorough acquaintance with which is of the utmost importance to the economic and political development of the country. For this purpose, neither the study of pre-Islamic poetry nor research on ancient Arab historians are decisive, but research on the living Muslim world, its geography, dialectology and commerce are much more important to the

Jews in the land of Israel than Islamic art and archeology.... Whatever one may think about the means to promote a better understanding between Jews and Arabs, which is so crucial for the building of the land of Israel, it is patently clear now that no Arab will change his political views on the Jewish question because the Hebrew University prepared a concordance of ancient Arab poetry.[15]

Such blatant dismissal of their aspirations must have been difficult to swallow, and the professors showed their disdain for the report by doing hardly anything to accommodate its recommendations. Two new faculty members were added, one from the Economic Research Institute of the Jewish Agency to teach economics and sociology of the Middle East and another, a Syrian Jew, to teach modern Arab literature, Arabic composition, and translation. But both remained junior members of the institute (the second remained a doctoral candidate for many years), and the senior staff did not change their teaching or research one iota.

The criticism did not go totally unheeded among their students, however. The professors warned them indeed that "there is education for an orientalist ... and there is education for one, who would like to act in the Orient" and the two are not the same,[16] but the students were attracted to action and practical work partly because their academic mobility was blocked by their professors. My calculations show that the average time from M.A. to Ph.D. in the Institute of Oriental Studies was nine years and that five more years were needed on average to attain the position of a nontenured lecturer, if it was achieved at all.[17] The significance of these numbers must be appreciated in the historical context. This was a time when many of their peers were taking influential positions in the institutions of the state-in-the-making. It was a period of accelerated mobility, and the longer they waited, the greater the pressure they experienced to bypass the barriers created by their professors.

This is why they chose the third strategy, and instead of following their teachers, they crossed the boundary between academia and officialdom and took positions in the intelligence services of the Jewish community. Some joined the Arab intelligence branch of the Haganah, and others were employed by the Arab division of the political department of the Jewish Agency. As officials, their status was similar to that of the Arabists. They were required to supply information and cater to the demands of the consumers – the commanders of the Haganah and the top political echelon at the Jewish Agency – to whom they were subordinate. On the other hand, they were different from the Arabists because their academic training led them to develop a different method of intelligence work, one that was based to a much larger extent on being able to read literary Arabic. They read Arab newspapers and summarized their contents on a regular basis, they used the summaries to create intelligence archives and chronologies, and they prepared concordances and keys to facilitate access to the information stored in the archives. This method typically required some academic credentials – that is, some degree of closed social relations. For this reason I placed them near the top left corner of Figure 3.1. Like the Arabists, they were dependent on the consumers; like their teachers, they possessed a certain degree of control over the supply of their own expertise.[18]

Finally, there were two additional groups of experts on Arab affairs that must be mentioned. They are less important for understanding the two main oppositions structuring the field but are still crucial for capturing the full range of dynamic contradictions and secondary oppositions operating in it. The first of these groups was composed of journalists and political activists in the labor movement. Members of this group were sometimes employed as advisers alongside the Arabists, but most of their activities were typical of *hasbara* – editing a newspaper in the Arab language for the General Federation of Labor (Histadrut), organizing Palestinian workers, and so on. Their expertise was heterogeneous: Some had studied orientalism in European universities, some were autodidacts, but most seemed to have shared with the notables the principle of proximity to Arabs, knowledge of colloquial Arabic, and friendship and close relations with Arabs, typically on the basis of experience accumulated through mediation between Arab and Jewish settlements. A few others were Jews of Middle Eastern extraction. Such heterogeneity meant that their capacity to control the supply of their own expertise was rather limited. Their degree of dependence on the political leadership, on the other hand, was rather high, and they were loyal to it. They were an integral part of the intelligentsia, out of which the leadership itself developed. Thus, even if they sometimes disagreed with the policies of the political leadership, they typically saw themselves as serving the party and, by the same token, the leadership. For this reason I placed them at the bottom of the lower left quadrant of Figure 3.1.[19]

The second group is more interesting for its role in later developments, especially after 1936. It was composed of young, lower-echelon military commanders of the Haganah, and after 1941 of its shock troops – Ha-Palmah. This was a generational group, composed of youths who were born in Palestine, typically first-generation *sabres* whose parents came from Europe. Thus, their position in the field expressed a secondary generational opposition between the middle-aged and the young, the European born and the native born. The three most famous representatives of this group were Moshe Dayan, Yigal Alon, and Yitzhak Rabin. Dayan and Rabin, for their part, grew up within the purely Jewish separatist sector, Dayan in a *moshav* and Rabin in Tel-Aviv. Yet both report as one of the crucial experiences of their early years the encounter and interaction with Palestinian youths, the two groups cohabiting this partly agonistic, partly amicable in-between sphere that I described in the previous chapter, straddling the boundary between Jewish and Arab spaces.[20] Alon, on the other hand, grew up in a mixed Arab-Jewish environment. In his village, most Jewish farmers employed a Palestinian worker, whose family lived with the farmer's family. This was also true of Alon's household. Rumor has it that as a baby he was breastfed by the worker's wife. His father had many Palestinian acquaintances, and Alon, whose mother passed away when he was a young child, used to spend summers with the family of one of these acquaintances. Relations with neighboring Palestinians, however, were not always amicable, and as teenager Alon had his fair share of skirmishes with them over grazing rights, theft, and so on.[21]

Because this generational group grew up in the vicinity of Palestinians or among them, and because the experience of the agonistic in-between sphere crucially shaped their generational identity, the practices of imitation were important insignias of membership in this group. They all had observed the fellahin and the Bedouin and imitated their customs as an element of their own project of self-fashioning, partly inspired by the image of these as a mirror on biblical times and partly as a way of establishing their own difference from the adult world. Only a few of them became truly proficient in such imitation – Dayan and Alon did, Rabin did not – but such proficiency was typically recognized among this group as a mark of distinction and a source of prestige. In this sense, they competed with the Arabists, from whom they were typically separated in age, for the position of experts and advisers on Arab affairs. For these reasons, I placed them in roughly the same position as the Arabists in Figure 3.1, but removed from them along a secondary, generational axis. As we shall see later in this chapter, there was no love lost between these two groups. The youths were no match for the Arabists in knowledge of Palestinian society, but they had on their side their fighting spirit, their experiences in the agonistic in-between sphere, and gradually also military training, which they acquired either in the Haganah or from the British. The slide of this group toward a distinctive activist and militaristic ethos – seeking to solve the political problem of relations with the Palestinians through force of arms, as described so well by Uri Ben-Eliezer[22] – is partially explained, therefore, also by their clash with the Arabists, who were typically recommending more moderate and local means.

Intelligence Expertise in Infancy: The Competition between Arabists and Students in the Paramilitary Intelligence Services, 1936–1947

What is the utility of the scheme presented in Figure 3.1? Its main purpose is to suggest a certain causal argument: the actions of experts should be understood in the context of the struggle that occurred over the legitimate prototype of orientalist expertise. Each group of experts was interested in presenting its own unique qualities as a model others must emulate, as the necessary equipment for functioning as an expert on Arab affairs. Moreover, as I argue in Chapter 1, this struggle took place under a distinctive set of constraints, especially those associated with the relations between the experts and the consumers of their knowledge. On the one hand, it was possible to mobilize the consumers as allies and in this way to obtain superiority over other experts; on the other hand, especially when the consumers were a powerful group, such as the political and military leadership, the consumers could eliminate altogether the independence of the experts and prevent their contribution from being recognized.

This argument implies another: the distinctions favored by the contemporary critics of orientalism – between those who were more or less "essentialist" or between those more or less loyal to the prospect of Jewish-Arab coexistence – are much less relevant for explaining the actions of the experts.[23] The image of the Orient presented in the previous chapter was common to everybody in this period, Arabists as well as academic orientalists, right-wingers as well as leftists. They were all orientalists in Said's sense – essentialist, condescending, prejudiced – at least from our vantage point today. Nonetheless, the struggle in the field of orientalist expertise, fought out under the pressures emanating from the political field, especially after 1936, began to create something new – new claims for expertise in managing and mediating the encounter between the Jewish community and the Arabs. There emerged incipient practices of intelligence, government, hasbara, and the absorption of immigrants, which eventually divided between them the cognitive space of the Orient.

The migration of Arabists and students into the intelligence services of the Jewish community, especially after 1940, led to a clash between these two groups and a struggle over the prototype of orientalist expertise. From the students' point of view, the methods of the Arabists were "primitive," and they thought little of these "mustached men of the field" who could not even spell correctly in Arabic. The Arabists, for their part, did not think much of the students, "who did not understand colloquial Arabic and have never before worked with Arabs," and considered them to be the "antitype" of how an intelligence officer should look and behave. Typically, the Arabists had the upper hand in these struggles, and they tended to dominate the branches of practical orientalist work. Nonetheless, gradually during the 1940s a division of labor began to emerge between the two groups, and a certain balance of forces was established.

The Arabists dominated the Arab intelligence branch of the Haganah – a semiautonomous apparatus that developed out of the networks of Ezra

Danin (the citrus farmer) – while the students worked together in the Arab division of the political department of the Jewish Agency, under the direction of Eliahu Sasson, a man who in many respects combined the academic expertise of the students with intimate knowledge of the contemporary Arab world (he was a native of Damascus). This division of labor not only was between different administrative bodies but was also understood by both sides as reflecting the opposition between two prototypes of orientalist expertise: between "political intelligence" and "security intelligence," between a focus on the urban elites and a focus on Palestinian villagers and more generally the lower rungs of Palestinian society, and between two different ways of rendering the utility provided by intelligence work – as a method for formulating assessments, on the one hand, and as a guide for practical action, on the other.

The struggle was provoked by the young students' attempt to impose the philological modus operandi that they acquired in the course of their studies at the Hebrew University on intelligence work and on the Arabists. They argued that intelligence work was similar to philology as well as to archeology: "In both cases . . . the researcher has to acquire an image of a distant reality, by piecing together patiently and slowly bits of information and hints, classifying and sifting them, and trying to bring them into an orderly system." The working assumption of philology, after all, is that one studies a distant reality that is impossible to know firsthand. This assumption guided all the reforms of intelligence work that the students suggested, but it was the exact inverse of the ethos of the Arabists, who collected their information through face-to-face contacts with their informers on the basis of proximity and even imitation.[24]

Another assumption embedded in the philological training of the doctoral students was that it is primarily through texts and language that one gains access to such distant realities and comes to know them. This is, after all, what philologists do. They compare texts and trace the meaning and origins of words in order to learn about the people who used them. The students suggested that open sources, such as the Arab press, could in fact provide valuable information, and they began acquiring the daily Arab newspapers and combing them for information. They claimed that the information gotten in this way was more reliable and systematic than the reports of informers. They considered the reliance on informers to be "primitive." The Arabists, on the other hand, argued that "written facts do not represent the Arab truth, which is undergoing a process of constant change." They warned that "information which does not deal with concrete affairs is insufficient and even dangerous, if it is not accompanied by an understanding and feel for the context which nourishes the reactions and behaviors of the society one is attempting to study."[25]

The modus operandi of philologists requires archives where texts are accumulated and compared to one another in order to determine when were
they written and by whom and to identify perjuries and selective omissions.
The students indeed took it upon themselves to create intelligence archives
and to supply these with the necessary concordances and indexes. They
claimed that in this way they could cross-check the information submitted
by the Arabists and determine its reliability. One student became secretary
of the Arab intelligence branch of the Haganah and reorganized its files into
a systematic archive and a name index. He toiled to make sure that all field
reports were filed, cross-checked, and sifted so that it would be possible to
access the necessary information quickly, verify its reliability, or determine
which information was missing (in the latter case, field officers could then
be instructed to get the missing information). In 1945, after his relations
with the Arabists soured, he moved to the Arab division of the political department of the Jewish Agency and brought with him "his" archive, which
mostly covered Palestinian society. Three other students were employed in
the archive, and together they prepared summaries of the Arab press as well
as a thesaurus of basic terms used in the daily Palestinian press. At the same
time, another student was entrusted to create a parallel archive at the Jewish
Agency containing information about neighboring Arab countries. The
Arabists were not impressed. They were "antiarchive," as one of them later
put it. Life, especially life in Arab society, was too dynamic to be studied by
collecting information about the past: "While in our meetings we had real,
living people discussing and debating, his archive was something completely
different . . . something scientific, something written."[26]

Finally, the philological modus operandi presumed the existence of a
certain hierarchy in the process of knowledge production. At the bottom
of the ladder were *apprentices*, students whose task was to collect the raw
materials for the archive and the concordances and in the process to acquire
the skills necessary to read ancient texts. Directly above them, the next
rung in the hierarchy was occupied by a figure with an easily recognizable
and characteristic social and intellectual makeup, who might be called the
pedant: a professor who organized the work of the apprentices and made sure
that the texts were accurately dated, referenced, and indexed. The pedant
embodied, in his personality and style of work, the values of rigor, precision,
objectivity, modesty (in the sense of avoiding speculative interpretation), and
reliability. He usually wrote long surveys based directly on the archive. At
the apex of the philological hierarchy was the *speculative interpreter*, famous
for his insight, empathy, and synthetic powers. He no longer dealt with the
archive directly but on the basis of his known erudition wrote monographs
penetrating into the collective psyche of a people through the exegesis of a
few words. If the pedant created the objective infrastructure, the role of the

speculative interpreter was to use it to reconstruct the subject behind the original language. From the very first day they set foot in the Institute of Oriental Studies, the students were employed in a huge project of producing a complete concordance of ancient Arab poetry, a Herculean task that even today, after more than seventy years, has not been completed. This project was chosen for the institute by its first director, Horowitz, himself a pedant type, in order to prove the scientific quality of the new institute.[27]

No wonder, then, that the students, when they turned to intelligence work, attempted to recreate this hierarchy. For reasons I will discuss – reasons having to do with their status as officials and their relations with the political leadership – the position of the interpreter was not accessible to them. This position was created only much latter, in the research branch of military intelligence, as I describe in Chapter 6. Early on, however, the students first endeavored to turn themselves into pedants of a sort and then to turn the Arabists into their apprentices. They tried to instruct the Arabists about the proper rules for the transliteration of Arab names; they prepared questionnaires for the Arabists to follow in composing their reports; they demanded that the Arabists properly check the information they got from their informers and not report rumors as if they were facts; and they begged the Arabists not to mix their own assessments and speculations with the facts being reported. Most importantly, they lobbied to create a strict division of labor between "field officers," whose role, as apprentices of a sort, would be to "collect and report the information in a dry and precise way" and "convey only the naked information," and a "central office," where the students, in their new role as pedants, would "classify and sift the material, draw the conclusions, and write the summary." The students argued that such a central office, armed with archives and indexes, would be able not only to cross-check and verify reports but also "to find connections between them that the informer could not imagine, and combine the different details into a complete picture." The Arabists, however, did not accept the role of apprentices. They continued to send "juicy letters" that impressed the leadership much more than the dry reports of the students, and they continued to add their own opinions and assessments to the information.[28]

The Arabists won this struggle, and when the students left the Arab intelligence branch of the Haganah, and moved to the Jewish Agency, their philological expertise became identified with a specific domain of "political intelligence." At the same time, Arabist expertise began to change too, partly because of the competition with the students, and it gradually crystallized into what the Arabists called "security intelligence." The distinction between these two domains had to do, first, with the object of intelligence work, the target that each side focused on and considered key for understanding events. By "political intelligence," the students meant collecting information on the actions, moves, attitudes, and internal relations among the urban, educated elite of Palestine and neighboring countries, usually through monitoring the Arab press. Even when they too operated informers, these were typically educated individuals who knew literary Arabic and who were members of the Arab political establishment. The Arabists, on the other hand, defined their task as "infiltrating the circles of the masses and listening to the echoes of the conspiracies and schemes that are plotted from above, and not the upper circles of the leadership and the aristocracy – the workshop where these schemes and conspiracies are hatched." By "infiltrating the circles of the masses" they meant using informers, particularly in the villages and strictly within Palestine, to get information on gangs, planned attacks, ambushes, thieves, and so on. The distinction between elite and mass, city and village, reflected the opposition between open and closed social relations. The students disparaged the information supplied by the Arabists as consisting of disconnected reports on the security situation that were of limited value by themselves and did not reflect an "understanding of the political background." The Arabists, on the other hand, doubted the assessments of the students and considered them to be the product of salon conversations between intellectuals who were not field operatives and thus give too much weight to the ideas of Arab intellectuals and the maneuverings among the Arab leadership.[29]

But the distinction between political and security intelligence had to do not only with the object of intelligence work but also with how its goal was perceived. Each group of experts rendered this goal differently in accordance with their training and in order to establish the usefulness of their services. Political intelligence was the translation of philological expertise into intelligence work. The information was accumulated in archives and used by the students, acting as both apprentices and pedants, to write daily and weekly surveys disseminated to the political and military decision-makers. However, just as the crowning achievement of philological expertise was not the erudite survey but the speculative interpretation capable of reconstructing the subject (collective or individual) whose spirit animates the text, the crowning achievement of intelligence work, in the students' view, was not the intelligence survey, not even the piecing together of bits of information into a complete picture, but rather the "assessment," the drawing of conclusions about the *intentions* implied by the information – the hidden plans or the fundamental ideas orchestrating all the different events reported. It is easy to see that the students were trying to arrogate to themselves the role of "interpreters," which they had internalized as the apex of the philological hierarchy. Unfortunately for them, this status was not accessible to them. Only Eliahu Sasson, director of the Arab division of the Jewish Agency, had direct access to the political leadership and could convey his assessments to them. The students were junior officials under his authority, and their surveys were appropriated by him or by other senior officials. Like the Arabists, the students acquired a certain measure of influence on the decision makers, but at the price of surrendering control over the attribution and dissemination of their discourse.[30]

Moreover, the political leadership had grave doubts about the claim to interpret "intentions." Here is what Moshe Sharet, director of the political department of the Jewish Agency and later the first minister of foreign affairs of the State of Israel, had to say about it: "The guys in the Arab division are working with exemplary efficiency, and bring us accurate and speedy news about what is taking place in the opposing camp. We do not have the capacity, of course, to penetrate the realm of hidden thoughts and secretive intentions, but decisions and movements are brought to our attention immediately." Clearly, the political leadership sought to protect its privilege in this way and to bar the experts from gaining a foothold within the domain of political decision-making. But they seemed to be genuinely perplexed by the naïveté of the experts. In another context, Sharet's words were more explicit and criticized the naïve hubris animating the claim to interpret intentions:

Is there in the [British] Ministry of the Colonies some kind of box, and inside it a piece of parchment, and on it is written all that Britain would want in Palestine? Does the Minister of the Colonies himself know what Britain might want in a few years in Palestine . . . ? Absolutely not. For [the British], in the given situation there are certain things that are fixed, and many others that are not fixed.[31]

We should remember Sharet's words because, as we shall see in Chapter 6, today the interpretation of intentions plays a crucial role in shaping how Israelis perceive the reality around them. Indeed, its current importance indicates that the economy of relations between the experts and the political leadership is now markedly different.

The Beginnings of Hasbara: The Polemics on Arab Nationalism

Since the leadership did not accept the students' claim to interpret intentions, the students often labored under a different rendering of the utility of their expertise. Through this rendering they sought to protect their claim to interpret the data but without mounting any challenge to the political leadership. Even if they could not really fathom Arab intentions, they argued, there was utility in such interpretation, even the interpretation of intentions, for the purpose of *hasbara*. Because the students were now officials employed by the political department of the Jewish Agency, the nascent "foreign office" of the state-in-the-making, *hasbara* ceased to consist in the education and enlightenment of Jews about Arab culture and politics and instead became restricted to propaganda meant to confront Arab claims in the international arena. The surveys of the students were passed to the leaders of the Jewish Agency in order to "equip them with *Hasbara* material and with arguments that they could use in their propaganda and diplomatic activity in the west."[32]

As the crucial decision about the end of the British Mandate drew near, consumer demand became stronger and overcame the students' attempt to create a certain measure of autonomy. As the pressure on them intensified, they were required to provide materials directly addressing immediate political and propaganda needs and to drop all pretense of formulating independent assessments.

In the summer of 1947, the political department of the Jewish Agency authorized the creation of a research division headed by one of the students, something the students had demanded for a long time. This division, however, was meant not to function as a relatively autonomous center of intelligence assessment (e.g., a center like the current research branch of military intelligence) but to "provide answers to questions submitted by officials of the political department in the country and its representatives abroad, and to publish summaries and surveys in selected topics of special interest to Zionist policy." Given such a mandate, it was in fact difficult to distinguish between the needs of intelligence and *hasbara* in what the students were requested to do. Even a detailed survey of Arab armies prepared by one of the students in 1946 was commissioned by the political department not so much to prepare for a confrontation with the Arab states as to provide the representatives of the Jewish Agency appearing before the Anglo-American commission of inquiry "with arguments that will disprove the claims that [if given independence] the Jewish community will need the protection of American and British troops, and will convince the commission that there is no reason to be worried about an attempt by the Arab states to thwart an Anglo-American solution of the problem of Palestine, and that the western defense strategy will benefit much more from a Jewish state with a regular army than from the Arab armies."[33] Accordingly, the survey underestimated the strength of the Arab armies.

Thus, the students labored under two competing interpretations of the significance of their expertise – assessment or *hasbara*. As the moment of fateful decision about the future of Palestine drew near, the political leadership tended to ignore their claim to assess the information – that is, to draw conclusions about political and military intentions – and to limit their role to *hasbara*. Hence, only in the next chapter, which deals with the years after the war and with the rise of the research branch of military intelligence, will I have occasion to return to the students' claim to formulate intelligence assessments. For the time being, however, I note that the limiting of the students to *hasbara* meant that in terms of their position in the field of orientalist expertise they drew nearer to the journalists and the political activists, especially the educated among them, and together they shared a polemical discourse about Arab nationalism.

It is fashionable today to argue that Zionism denied the existence of the Palestinians or their being a nation. According to this view, "A land without a people to a people without a land" was the formula before the bitter clash with the inhabitants of Palestine, followed afterwards by the obstinate refrain "There is no Palestinian nation." The Zionists supposedly engaged in "a complete denial of the existence of the Palestinians as a nation or as a public imbued with national sentiments" because of an orientalist tendency to underestimate the natives and think it would be easy to buy them off or because of a psychological need to believe that it would be possible to realize Zionism without resorting to the use of force.[34]

In fact, the inverse is true. The Zionist movement never stopped debating Palestinian nationalism, arguing with it and about it, judging it, affirming or negating its existence, pointing to its virtues or vices, and seeking after signs that would confirm its existence or predict its demise. The accusation of "denial" is simplistic and disregards the historical phenomenon of a polemical discourse revolving around the central axis provided by Arab or Palestinian nationalism, a sort of "point of diffraction," a locus of dissension that makes possible a complex game in which "denial" is but one strategy among many.[35]

Already in 1930, Ben-Gurion gave this warning to the members of the acting committee of the General Federation of Labor:

There are some members who deny the existence of a national movement among the Arabs. They see the internal divisions among the Arabs.... It is true that the Arab national movement lacks a positive content...but we will be mistaken if we measure the Arabs and their movement according to our own standards. Each nation gets the national movement it deserves. The clear identifying sign of a political movement is that it knows how to organize the masses around itself. According to this consideration, there is no doubt that what we have before us is a political movement, and we should not underestimate it.[36]

Sharet, too, did not mince his words:

There was a time when we said: there is no Arab movement; there are Effendis who protect their own personal interests and nothing else. Already in the congress at Carlsbad I spoke against this view. I said that the Arabs have a natural national instinct that leads them to resist us.... There is not one Arab in the land of Israel who is not offended by the entry of Jews to this land; there is no Arab who does not see himself as part of the Arab race, which ruled this land for hundreds of years. And he does not have to consider himself as part of the Arab nation that has states and countries in Iraq and Hejjaz and Yemen. For him the land of Israel is an independent unit that once had an Arab character, but is now changing; . . . and his reaction to that cannot be but resistance. . . . None of this is artificial; there is something in their hearts that turns this movement into a mass movement.[37]

It is true, of course, that many of the participants in this debate undertook to deconstruct the Palestinian national claim: "Do the Arabs of the land of Israel constitute one nation or different ethnicities that do not compose a single national unit? . . . We are interested in knowing the true situation in an objective manner, and therefore we have to find out from which aspect do the Arabs constitute one body, and from which aspect do they appear as separate bodies?" The answer of some was that "a long chain of differences sets apart the Christian group and turns it into a separate sect. . . . The common cause uniting Muslims and Christians is only a thin layer of ashes covering over the hot embers, underneath it all the differences are still burning."[38]

But the goal of this deconstruction of the nation as an objective entity was not necessarily to deny its existence or its authenticity but to argue against the Arab national movement and show that it ignored the rights of minorities in the Middle East – Christians, Druze, Assyrians, Copts, Kurds, Armenians, and of course Jews – and was "reactionary," "imperialist," and "fascist."[39]

Put differently, the point of diffraction of the debate about and with Arab nationalism was the question of *right* – Who has the right to the land? Is this right divisible? – while the denial of the existence of an Arab or Palestinian nation was only one strategy in this debate and not necessarily a very important one. The strategies of the participants in the debate about Arab nationalism, the answers they gave to the question of right, were intrinsically tied to the position they occupied in the internal Zionist polemics. The two national movements were entangled with one another and mutually dependent on one another – what was said about one from without could immediately be diverted for internal purposes. There is no doubt, for example, that the analysis of the Arab national movement as fascist and reactionary was meant to be also an attack on the Zionist Revisionist movement of Ze'ev Jabotinsky and a means of highlighting the difference between labor Zionism and its internal opponents. Unlike the revisionists, labor Zionism was socialist and progressive. It struggled against the forces of reaction on the Jewish as well as the Arab side.

The main difference, therefore, in what could be said about Palestinian nationalism in the prestate period and what is said about it now does not derive from the fact that Israelis today are more enlightened and are willing to admit the existence of the Palestinians as a nation. Instead, as we shall see in Chapter 6, it derives from the fact that, especially after 1967, in both *hasbara* and the military government in the occupied territories new discursive positions were institutionalized from which it became possible for

an Israeli expert to represent the will of the Palestinians to the Israeli public. The result was the appearance of a new form of expertise that could
lay claim to knowledge about what Palestinians really wanted, what their
true intentions and ambitions were, and that would purport to speak in
their name and represent them to the Israeli public. In other words, what
changed between the prestate and the contemporary period was the discursive point of diffraction – from the question of right and national character to the question of identity and the fundamental will of a collective
subject.

Operation *"Arab Village"* and the Development of the Practice of Government

Although the interpretation of their work as *hasbara* limited the competition between the students and the Arabists and to a certain degree even
forced the former to recognize the superiority of the hands-on knowledge
of their competitors,[40] their attempt to claim the authority to assess intelligence nonetheless did threaten the Arabists and led them too to reformulate
how they understood the utility of their expertise. Put differently, when
the students doubted the value of the information supplied by the Arabists,
"without an understanding of the political background," they pushed the latter to formulate a new justification for their expertise. And this justification,
to differentiate themselves from the "theoretical" expertise of the students,
had to be that their expertise was "practical."

From this point onward, Arabist expertise in operating informers began
to crystallize into a practical technique of brewing and exploiting internal
conflicts and divisions in the Arab village as well as directing retaliatory
attacks against it. In a sense, Arabist expertise was never in "intelligence." It
was only interpreted as such for a short interval between its origins in the
art of mediation among notables and its future as a technique of government
over the villages. This trend was already in evidence during the first six
months of operation of the Arab intelligence branch of the Haganah. Danin's
instructions to the field officers included the following:

[a] One should . . . get the information from several informers, preferably ones who
are enemies of one another, and not just from one informer; [b] One should thoroughly learn the game of forces that motivate the environment, in order to understand the visible results; . . . [f] The technique of the government and the police in
the vicinity, whom do they draw to them, and whom do they push away, the reasons and the consequences. . . . One should look for individuals who are bitter, have
been cheated or insulted, who have been treated badly. . . . It is necessary to make
the informer economically dependent [on us] . . . by arranging a job for him.

A little bit later, during the first course for intelligence officers of the Haganah, Danin brought

one of our Arab friends, who, in an exciting lecture, explained to the cadets how intrigues [*fasaad*] are brewed in an Arab village, stage by stage, so as to provoke internal quarrels and suspicions, which will weaken and neutralize the inhabitants during a period of Jewish-Arab tensions. Many of the cadets were appalled to hear this, and they considered the Arab lecturer, the master of intrigues, to be a despicable and vile creature, lacking all moral inhibitions. I had to explain to them the basic facts of life in the Arab sector, and especially in the villages. "My dear children," I said, "this is a living reality. It is a way of life that has existed for generations. These are the customs of the Ishmaelites, whose villages are sometimes mortal enemies for 500 years."[41]

This does not mean that the Arabists became governors in 1945. The old justification of their expertise as promoting "neighborly relations" remained, interwoven with the art of mediation among notables and the operation of informers. In 1944, for example, Danin organized a course in colloquial and literary Arabic and in cultivating ties with Arab neighbors for the *mukhtars* of Jewish settlements – "both for the purpose of neighborly relations and for intelligence purposes." In the same year, the budget of the Arab division of the political department of the Jewish Agency still included sums earmarked for cultivating neighborly relations with Arab villages and for financing local gift exchanges for the purpose of reconciliation (*sulha*). In fact, at this stage there was no clear differentiation between the monies used for intelligence and the monies used for cultivating neighborly relations. The funds allocated to field officers by the Arab intelligence service were used, quite interchangeably, to pay informers as well as to organize reconciliation parties, gift exchanges, and so on.

Even the role that the Arabists played in directing retaliatory attacks could not be described without reference both to the goal of cultivating neighborly relations and also to the art of governing the villages. "Retaliation" was a complex concept that included the notions of revenge, punishment, and deterrence: it was possible to justify violent action against Arabs by citing purely military considerations (deterrence), judgments about justice (punishment), or knowledge of Arab culture and neighborly relations with Arabs (revenge). Typically a mixture of all three was involved. The Arabists participated in perfecting the logic of retaliation by educating the military decision-makers about the traditional rules of Arab revenge but also by finding out who were the perpetrators and whence they came and by mediating between Arab and Jewish settlements and explaining to both the cultural logic of the other side's violence. They did all this believing that they would thus minimize the amount of friction between Jews and Arabs and prevent misunderstandings (i.e., the old role of mediation). But as they became involved in the calculus of justice, punishment, and deterrence, they also began to develop a sort of governmental relationship with the villages. Especially during the 1948 war, as we shall see in the next chapter, when they functioned as advisers to brigade commanders, they began to represent the considerations of good government – justice, divide and conquer, distinguishing between "good Arabs" and "bad Arabs" – vis-à-vis the military logic of pure deterrence.[42]

The distinctive character of Arabist expertise was further crystallized in the course of "operation Arab village," conducted by the Arab intelligence branch of the Haganah in 1945–1947. During the operation, between 600 to 1,000 villages were surveyed by scouts and informers as well as by aerial reconnaissance, and the reports were collected in the "Green archive." An examination of these files reveals the various interests and forms of expertise that were invested in obtaining knowledge about the villages in this period. First, some of the items of information in the village files answered the needs of combat intelligence: the number of the men in the village, the number of weapons, the topography, and so on. Another set of items had to do with the needs of *hasbara*, with which was blended also the old iconographic practice that sought to find in the villages traces of the ancient Jews: the year in which the village was established and the place of origination of its inhabitants (in order to prove that many of the Palestinians were relatively recent immigrants), the ancient ruins found in or near the village ("to show its ancient origins"), the meaning and origin of the village's name (some of the files used Ben-Gurion and Ben-Tzvi's book as reference), and so on. Another important interest was buying land from the villagers and settling it. This is why the files also included information about land ownership in the village, how the plots were cultivated, and so on.

But the bulk of information in the files reflected the needs and point of view of the emerging Arabist expertise. Information was collected, first of all, about the leading families in the village, the kinship ties among them, the blood feuds and conflicts between them. The Arabists could use this information to interpret the events in the village, but more importantly they could use it to act against the village and weaken it when needed. After 1948, these files were picked up by the military government in charge of the Palestinian citizens of the new state and were used to devise a system of control over the villages. Information about the major personalities and officeholders in the village – the mayor, the *mukhtar*, teachers, midwives, guards, policemen – served a similar purpose. Another set of items were to be used by the Arabists to aid in retaliation, whether as a form of "just punishment" (who of the villagers participated in the Arab rebellion, who were gang members, who were the "chief instigators," who were their family members) or as a means of deterrence (the location of targets, such as the well, the barn, and the bakery, that could be destroyed in order to make clear to the villagers the price of acting against the Jews).[43]

The "One Million Plan" and the Development of a Discourse about the Absorption of the Jews from Arab Countries

During these same years, between 1936 and 1947, there developed another practice of great significance. In the Introduction, I emphasized that a crucial condition for the change in the social role of *mizrahanut* was the invention of the category of *mizrahi* Jews and the fact that the expertise mandated to speak about them was differentiated from the expertise mandated to speak about the Arabs. In Chapter 2, however, I sought to demonstrate that such a differentiation was not yet possible in the period preceding the formation of the state, particularly because of the crucial role that Sephardi Jews played in this period, as Arab-Jewish hybrids of a sort who at one and the same time marked and transgressed the boundary of Zionist identity and around whom was woven a whole discourse about the common roots of Jews and Arabs and the possibility of a harmonious synthesis between East and West.

This state of affairs had already begun to change, however, before 1948. Jews residing in Arab countries were increasingly marked as candidates for mass immigration and thus became the focus of discourse about the absorption of immigrants. Correspondingly, the right to represent them and speak in their name began to be removed from the hands of the Sephardi leadership. In 1942, when they grasped the extent of the destruction of European Jewry, the Zionist leadership began to search for substitute pools of immigrants. Ben-Gurion formulated an ambitious plan to bring one million Jews to Palestine after the war, and he zeroed in on the Jews from Middle Eastern and North African countries as the most promising candidates for immigration. His considerations were purely quantitative.

The principal significance of this plan lies in the fact, noted by Yehouda Shenhav, that this was the first time in Zionist history that Jews from Middle Eastern and North African countries were all packaged together in one category as the target of an immigration plan. There were earlier plans to bring specific groups, such as the Yemenites, but the "one million plan" was, as Shenhav says, "the zero point," the moment when the category of *mizrahi* Jews in the current sense of this term, as an ethnic group distinct from European-born Jews, was invented. I will return to this point in the next chapter.[44]

According to Ben-Gurion's plan, there were to be separate absorption camps for "Jews of Islamic countries" and "European Jews." European immigrants were to sojourn in their camps, located in the north and next to the

Gaza strip, for a period of only three months. These were camps for people in transit. The immigrants from Islamic countries (all immigrants from North Africa, the Middle East, and Aden), on the other hand, were to be housed in larger camps, where they would stay for a period of one to two years. These camps were to be located in the south of the country so they could serve as "seeds for permanent settlements for the immigrants from the Orient, who were earmarked for agricultural work in the south ... because they were more used to work in these climate conditions." The one million plan was thus a complete innovation, because before its formulation, and really up till 1948, the few immigrants who arrived from Middle Eastern and North African countries were cared for by the communities of their compatriots already settled in Palestine. If there was a universal claim to represent all of them together, it was made only by the Sephardi leadership, who measured them by their degree of proximity to the Sephardi prototype. From the mid-nineteenth century onward, however, the Sephardi claim coexisted uneasily with the fact that typically each group of immigrants – North African Jewry, Syrian Jewry, Persian Jewry, and so on – was represented by its own notables and associations, which handled the affairs of their communities and their own immigrants autonomously and were only loosely affiliated with the Sephardi organizations. Ben-Gurion's plan for massive immigration, were it to be realized, would have expropriated the "absorption of immigrants," as it was now called, from the hands of the communities, the notables, and specifically the Sephardi leadership. It was part of his declared campaign to "start thinking in new concepts ... concepts of a state."[45]

Significantly, this new category of immigrants was constructed from the very beginning as an Arab-Jewish hybrid. Expounding on Ben-Gurion's plan, the chief of the immigration department of the Jewish Agency noted that this new pool of immigrants presented special difficulties. "Despite being geographically quite close to us, they are alien and distant, and this lack of familiarity is mutual." He especially noted a "cultural rift" due to the Arab nature of these Jews: "A further obstacle is the Arab reality, which makes it difficult for our cultural concepts to penetrate." As Shenhav shows, the Zionist emissaries who were sent to Middle Eastern countries in the wake of the plan and met there with local Jews to assess their potential for immigration and absorption expressed similar sentiments, and they too thought of their interlocutors as hybrid Arab-Jews.

Shenhav's argument, however, is not that the emissaries discovered the hybridity of Middle Eastern Jews – discovered that somehow the latter were "really" Arab-Jews in their essence – but rather that the emissaries constructed this hybridity as a mirror-reflection of the split nature of their own consciousness: On the one hand, they met their interlocutors in their capacity as Zionist emissaries sent to liberate them (i.e., they met as Jews); on the other hand, they met them as colonial agents separate from the native population, since they arrived as members of a construction team contracted by the British government, and they employed the locals in the same way the British did (i.e., they met as Europeans).[46] It is completely immaterial for my task in this book, and indeed impossible to determine, whether the Jews of Iraq or Iran were "really" Arab-Jews or not. What is crucial, however, is that they were constructed as such, and this construction had far-reaching cultural significance. Unlike the Sephardi Jews, for whom hybridity was to a large extent a self-designation within the framework of a project to mediate and act as a bridge between Jews and Arabs, the new immigrants were constructed as hybrid by others in relation to a project of separating from the Arabs. From the moment that the Zionist leadership began to "think in concepts of a state" and formulate concrete plans that gave the Zionist project the form of a state with sharply delineated internal and external boundaries between Arabs and Jews, it began to create the no-man's-land within which the category of *mizrahi* Jews was to crystallize.

A final point I would like to make is that Ben-Gurion's plan, if realized, not only would have removed the absorption of immigrants from the communities and from the Sephardi leadership but would have brought a newcomer into the field of orientalist expertise. To formulate his plan, Ben-Gurion sought the advice of statisticians about the numbers of Jews in various countries; of economists about the creation of jobs and the financing of settlement and construction; and of health specialists about hygiene, inoculation, selection of able-bodied immigrants, and so on. He was completely uninterested in orientalists as experts on the immigrants' countries of origin and culture or in their advice on how the immigrants should be treated. It seems that he ignored these issues because his paramount interest was in facilitating rapid absorption of the immigrants and in assimilating them as quickly as possible into the existing society.

This approach created an opening for specialists in the "absorption of immigration" who could provide a justification for treating the immigrants from Middle Eastern and North African countries as a single category (despite the obvious differences between them) and as distinct from European Jews but capable of being integrated and assimilated rather quickly (i.e., as different but fixable). Precisely such specialists – sociologists, psychologists, and social workers – were then beginning to conduct research on "oriental" Jews, as they named them, typically under the auspices of the Institute for Economic Research of the Jewish Agency, its department of youth immigration, or the social department of the National Board (Ha-Va'ad Ha-Leumi). They did not claim to possess specialized knowledge about Middle Eastern societies and their Jewish communities, though they undertook to learn the necessary "background" from secondary sources. Instead, they claimed to possess a universal form of expertise in the diagnosis and treatment of "social problems" – deviance, poverty, maladjustment, and so on. They typically suggested that such problems stemmed from the failure of immigrants from "backward" cultures to adapt to the "modern" society built by European immigrants.[47]

The New Mista'ravim

Finally, in the same years during which the practices of intelligence, government, *hasbara*, and the absorption of immigrants began to be elaborated, a parallel change took place that in many respects serves as the best proof for my argument about the interconnections between the emergence of the category of *mizrahi* Jews, the transformation in the social role of *mizrahanut*, and the disenchantment of the Orient. This was the change that took place from 1942 onward in the social significance of the practice of imitation. In 1942, as the possibility of a German invasion became palpable, the British authorized the creation of a new unit for special operations and collecting information whose members were to disguise themselves as Arabs. The idea was that they would stay behind as undercover agents in case of a German occupation of Palestine. When the Germans were defeated by Montgomery, and the British lost interest in the unit, it was incorporated into the Palmach – the shock troops of the Haganah. It was named Ha-Shachar (The Dawn), because its original name, Ha-Shchorim (The Blacks), was too politically incorrect even for this period. The most important point about Ha-Shachar is that, though all of its commanders were Jews of European origin, all of the rank and file, the actual *mista'ravim* (as they were indeed called), were Jews who had immigrated from Arab countries – Yemen, Syria, Iraq, Egypt, and so on. Originally, this was something that the British insisted upon. Over time, however, this feature became institutionalized as part of the official doctrine of the Haganah and of the IDF after it: "A candidate to become a *mista'rev* first and foremost must be of a *Mizrahi* Jewish ethnicity, originally born in one of the neighboring Arab states or in North Africa, his mother tongue must be Arabic, and he must have been in regular contacts with his Arab neighbors in his country of origin, living among them or in proximity to them."[48]

Put differently, the principle according to which the new *mista'ravim* were to be selected was the same as the principle at the core of the one million plan. Indeed, the two were contemporaneous. Recall Shenhav's argument that the one million plan led to the invention of the category of *mizrahi* Jews and gave the term the meaning it has today because the plan treated all Jews who originated in these countries as belonging to a single category of candidates for immigration. At the same time, however, the emergence of the new *mista'ravim* added another layer of meaning to the newly minted and still crystallizing *mizrahi* category, that is, as implying a quasi-racial division between those who had an "oriental appearance" and those who did not.

What was the significance of this new layer of meaning? One way to get at it is to compare the old and new *mista'ravim*. Unlike the new *mista'ravim*, the old virtuosi of imitation never sought to disguise their real identity. Imitation was not deception. On the contrary, the role they played demanded that they appear publicly as hybrids, as Jewish notables and *mukhtars* who also wielded some influence in Palestinian society and were on friendly terms with Palestinian notables. The practice of imitation was not meant to create a perfect replica of the Arab original but consciously left a certain gap between the original and the imitator, and exactly this gap permitted the transmutation of identities and the self-fashioning of the new Jew. No less importantly, the practice of imitation and the status of hybrids – as with the Arabists or the notables – were perceived as a crucial fount of knowledge and expertise in Arab affairs.

The new immigrants who were recruited to Ha-Shachar, on the other hand, were selected primarily on the basis of their personal appearance, which was crucial for successful deception and undercover operation. In terms of personal appearance, they had to be perfect replicas of the Arab original, but they had to be educated about everything else because they did not speak the Palestinian dialect and were unfamiliar with Palestinian society and its customs. Typically, even their familiarity with Arab society in their countries of origin was rather superficial, as they were selected from among those who had "already received Zionist education" and had immigrated to Palestine at a rather young age. As one of them said many years later: "We sat around the campfire and sang songs [in Arabic], but if you went to a Palestinian village and began to sing they would consider you insane. This was good enough maybe to impress the European Jews, but it was not good enough for the Arabs."[49]

Instead of possessing a well-recognized public status in Palestinian society, they had to infiltrate it undercover, and at least during their first assignments they tended to keep silent and look around them. Instead of giving shape, in their bodies and conduct, to the possibility of being a new Jew by virtue of imitating the Arabs, it was almost as if precisely the demand to be an exact external replica of the original meant that their version of imitation left the two categories intact, undisturbed. The purification device was built into the new practice of imitation in advance, as a distinction between inside and outside, between an external "oriental appearance" and an internal Jewish-Zionist essence. Indeed, unlike the Sephardi hybrid or the Arabists, they were not familiar with the whole universe of common Jewish-Arab life and coexistence in Palestine and were astounded to discover it during undercover missions in Tiberias, for example:

Jews and Arabs sitting one next to the other around restaurant tables...speaking Arabic interspersed with Hebrew words. . . . Young Jewish men and women strolling along the beach amongst Arab fishermen. We were particularly impressed by the fact that Jews and Arabs live together in the same neighborhood, even in the same building. . . . In the public bathhouse, there were two Arabs sitting with the Jews and talking about everyday affairs. Their conversation was very friendly and intimate.[50]

For this reason, probably, there was mutual mistrust between them and the Arabists. The leading Arabists refused to use the new *mista'ravim* to collect intelligence and claimed that they were not professionally trained. The commander of Ha-Shachar, for his part, expressed suspicion toward the Arabists' use of paid informers and argued the latter's motives could not be trusted. In this way, Ha-Shachar corresponded to the interests and worldview of the young military commanders. As I noted earlier, the latter competed with the Arabists for the position of experts on Arab affairs but were unable to unseat them. The political leadership was suspicious of the young commanders, who typically belonged to a competing political faction and whom it perceived to be potential challengers in the future. The Arabists, on the other hand, were much safer allies, and their subordination to the leadership's authority was not in doubt. This is one of the reasons why the young military commanders began to adopt a distinctive militaristic and activist worldview, which during this period, the early 1940s, still contrasted sharply with the position of the political leadership and the Arabists. Hence the new *mista'ravim* were useful to them as a means of bypassing the Arabists and developing their own network of expertise in Arab affairs. The new *mista'ravim*, after all, were Jews and not paid Palestinian informers, and thus operating them did not require immersing oneself in the networks of common Jewish-Palestinian life, where the notables and the Arabists possessed a distinct advantage.

At the same time, however, the new *mista'ravim* were useful to the young military commanders because their practices of imitation were adopted by the paramilitary units and became part of their distinctive lore and ethos. In this way, as I noted earlier, the younger generation of mostly native-born *sabres* sought to mark the difference and distance separating them from their parents' generation and thereby also from the political leadership and by way of opposition to characterize the latter as still marked by the Diaspora, unable to provide the proper model of the new Jewish man. Imitation, therefore, played the same role as the militaristic-activist ethos and was blended with it as part of the new generation's challenge to its elders. Additionally, by imitating the Palestinians, the young commanders and their troops acquired confidence in the authenticity of their existence in Palestine. The bitter irony is, of course, that they gained this confidence only a few years before they purged Palestine of the Palestinians themselves. Just before he became commander of all of the shock troops, Alon took part in organizing and commanding the unit of *mista'ravim,* because, as he put it, he wanted "to make sure that their historical mission, as Jews imitating Arabs, will be preserved." Even before they undertook any operations, the members of Ha-Shachar became well known for the colorful parties they threw, singing in Arabic and dancing Arab dances. "Very soon there was not a single soldier of the *Palmach* who did not intersperse a few Arab words into his conversation." Many Arab words thus became part of the unique slang of the paramilitary units and after them the IDF – the Hebrew of the *sabre* is a Hebrew-Arab hybrid. Occasionally, the top political leaders of the Jewish Agency were invited to these parties. In their honor, the *mista'ravim* built a quasi-Bedouin tent and sat on its carpeted floor dressed as Bedouin. "The honorable guests were greeted in a traditional Arab greeting, in handshakes and by putting one's hand on one's forehead and heart . . . the Islamic midday prayer was conducted in accordance with the strictest costumes, with bows and shouts of 'God is great.' . . . The meal ended with song, dance and drinking black coffee."[51]

Even more significantly, the new *mista'ravim* were useful for the military commanders because they were perceived as a *tabula rasa,* as completely ignorant, thus needing to be taught everything. Instead of knowledge and expert authority flowing from the status of hybrids and from the practice of imitation, as in the past, they were completely detached from one another. Not only were the new *mista'ravim* invariably subordinate to European-born commanders, but they were also under the tutelage of a special teacher appointed to guide and educate them. He was an Iraqi Jew, indeed, but academically trained. He was educated as a teacher of Arabic, and he also audited courses at the Institute for Oriental Studies at the Hebrew University. He was employed by the culture department of the General Federation Labor to teach Arabic to Jewish activists. From there he was brought to Ha-Shachar and immediately took it upon himself to educate the new immigrants in everything they would have to know in order to pass as members of Arab society:

Language – improving reading and writing, proverbs and fables, classical poetry, reading a newspaper, listening to the radio, writing letters, typing on a typewriter . . . ; Basics of religion – Qura'n, Hadith (proverbs and stories about the prophet), the Islamic calendar, the sects in Islam, rules of purity and impurity in sexual matters, dress, food and drink, rules of inheritance, marriage and divorce, the status of women; Society – the social structure of the Arabs in *Eretz Israel,* families, personalities and leaders, parties and organizations, the press, public institutions, economy; History and geography – Islamic history from pre-Islamic times (*Jahilya*) to the present, history of *Eretz Israel* from the period of Arab conquest, the Arab national movement in general and especially in Palestine, arithmetic and geometry in Arabic; Customs and folklore – clothes and modesty, the Arab house in the city and the village, the market, the street and the coffee house, manners, swears and curses, holidays, superstitions, the custom of blood revenge, etc.

To improve his knowledge, he even spent some time studying with a Muslim sheik in the old city of Jerusalem.[52]

We see, therefore, what was the layer of meaning added by Ha-Shachar to the newly crystallizing *mizrahi* category. It had to do with the social construction of ignorance, with a redivision of roles that concentrated all knowledge and expert authority in the position of the teacher, whose task was to accumulate and inculcate scholastic knowledge, while it dismissed and devalued embodied knowledge, the practical knowledge acquired and put to use in and through doing, construing it to be merely a matter of "appearance."[53]

On the eve of the 1948 war, the balance of power in the field of orientalist expertise was rather fragile. A certain division of labor emerged, indeed, between Arabists, student-officials, notables, *mista'ravim*, military commanders, professors, journalists, and political activists, and this division of labor was institutionalized as a set of organizational distinctions between political intelligence, security intelligence, *hasbara*, special operations, and the absorption of immigrants. None of these groups was satisfied with its position, however, and each interfered in the jurisdictions of other groups. Yet certain areas of crucial importance – especially intelligence about the armies of the neighboring Arab states – were not covered and remained as interstitial domains over which none of the groups of experts claimed jurisdiction. Moreover, there were newcomers to the field, sociologists and psychologists, whose claim of universal jurisdiction over "social problems" was likely to undermine the position of the notables as well as the academic orientalists. Similarly, the militarist practices of the military commanders and their use of the new *mista'ravim* challenged the expertise of the Arabists and the notables and threatened to make them irrelevant. The war and the huge demographic changes that followed in its wake easily threw this fragile state of affairs off balance and initiated a short period of intense struggle over the right and authority to manage the new reality.

CHAPTER 4

The Struggle over Jurisdiction, 1948–1953

FROM 1948 TO 1953, between 600,000 and 760,000 Palestinians were expelled from the areas that became the State of Israel and were not allowed to return. Their place was taken by 687,024 new Jewish immigrants, who arrived within the first three years (and more were to come later); at least half of these came from Middle Eastern and North African countries. The immigrants were settled, for the most part, on the lands taken from the Palestinians. Nonetheless, within the territory of the State of Israel there remained about 100,000 to 150,000 Palestinians who were put under military government.[1] Mandatory Palestine was hastily destroyed, and new lines of separation were demarcated on its ruins. Expulsion, prohibition of return, and immigration determined the external boundaries between Jews and Arabs, while the military government drew the outline of the internal boundary that separated them as well.

The focus of this chapter is not on this geopolitical and demographic transformation per se but on the intensified struggle among experts it provoked as each group of experts sought to present itself as capable of dealing with the new situation. The reader, however, may justly wonder why I accord such significance to the struggles among experts. Isn't the plain devastating fact of the expulsions evidence enough that the war completely and irrevocably separated Jews and Arabs and erected a wall of enmity between them? Sovereign borders were drawn between the new state and the Arab states around it. It was emptied, as much as possible, of Palestinians. Whether forced or done of their own accord, many Jews left their homes in Arab countries and immigrated to Israel. Whatever small remnant of Palestinians were left behind were segregated from the rest of the population. Most of the mixed Arab-Jewish cities became purely Jewish, and the captive Palestinian minority was concentrated in the villages, far away from the centers of Jewish population, under a military government that restricted their movements. This was indeed the garrison Jewish state, "clean of Arabs and as a lone island in the Arab sea surrounding it."[2] Moreover, it seems pretty clear that this transformation was merely the culmination of a historical process of separation that had begun earlier and that the expulsions probably brought to fruition, whether by conscious design or not.

Simple and self-evident as this story may seem, I think it is also partial. As a result of the war and expulsions, boundaries were drawn indeed to separate Jews and Arabs, but they were very fuzzy and quickly ballooned into frontier zones and no-man's-lands where three new hybrid figures appeared: the "infiltrator," the "Israeli Arab," and the "*mizrahi* Jew." The armistice lines that separated the new state from its neighbors were not clearly demarcated on the ground and even on the maps were drawn "with a thick pencil." Consequently, they became a no-man's-land that was hotly contested. Moreover, through these contested border zones, Palestinian refugees were trying to return to their homes and fields within the state. The Palestinian "infiltrators" (as they were called then) appeared as hybrids who on one side of the border were refugees and enemies but on the other side were "present absentees" and therefore residents of the new state. Inside the state as well, Palestinians were neither completely separated nor completely integrated. "Israeli Arabs" had an ambiguous status, hybrids of a sort between citizens and internal enemies. Consequently, the internal boundary between Jews and Arabs was not yet an established fact. Finally, as we shall see, there were deep suspicions and misgivings with respect to the new immigrants from Middle Eastern and North African countries. Were they Jews or Arabs? Could they be trusted to maintain the fragile new boundaries between the two? *Mizrahi* Jews made up a third group of hybrids that appeared in this period.[3]

These arguments derive from the approach I outlined in the introduction: the boundary is not a fact established once and for all, even by such an abrupt, violent, and complete transformation as the war. It is an ongoing and precarious accomplishment of practices that, at the same time as they mark it, also continue to transgress it and require that it be drawn anew – the proverbial "thick pencil" of the armistice committee. As we shall see below, even the supreme act of separation – the expelling of the Palestinians – was accomplished through the mediation of notables, who were thus positioned neither on this nor that side of the boundary but within its volume. For this reason, the attempt to draw internal and external boundaries inevitably led to the appearance of new hybrids, who marked and transgressed these borders at one and the same time. Moreover, there was a sort of dependency or a vacancy chain between these hybrids. As I show in this chapter, the attempt to purify one of them inevitably led to the formation of another. For example, the attempt to purify and control the infiltrators required creating a strong distinction between the refugees outside the state and the Palestinians who remained inside it. How arbitrary was this distinction is evidenced by terms like "internal refugees" and "present absentees" that were used to describe at least some of the Palestinians who remained behind. The result was the formation of the hybrid and ambiguous category of "Israeli Arabs." By the same token, the attempt to purify the Israeli Arab hybrid and create rigid internal boundaries between Jews and Arabs led, especially in the mixed Jewish-Arab cities, to the formation of a "third space" between them where the *mizrahi* category further crystallized. As in the famous nursery rhyme about the hole in the bucket, any attempt to plug up the holes and prevent the state from flowing beyond its boundaries merely created new holes.

I would not like, however, to create the impression that the hybrids were simply "obstacles" that stood in the way of the project to establish a sovereign Jewish state. On the contrary, these three hybrids were produced as a necessary byproduct of the technology of state building and played a productive role with respect to it. This argument also stems from the approach I outlined in the introduction: the state is an ongoing practical accomplishment as well, the effect of a political practice that continuously "fuzzifies" the boundaries between the state and society, or between the state and other states, and continuously redraws them.[4] The hybrids serve as a particularly dense and fruitful "point of transfer" for this process in which the state continuously flows beyond its boundaries and continuously erects them anew.

These general theoretical considerations are even more pertinent when dealing with the first few years of the State of Israel. As others have noted, and as shall be seen below, the technology of state building consciously relied on fuzzifying the boundaries and creating areas of strategic and creative ambiguity. A favorite strategy was to delegate, in effect, legal authority and administrative jurisdiction to pre- and proto-state agencies without formally constituting them as state apparatuses. Such agencies included the General Federation of Labor (the Histadrut), the Jewish Agency, and the Jewish National Fund (JNF). From the point of view of state elites, this form of delegation had many benefits: It enabled the mobilization of individuals through the organizational and pastoral structures created in the prestate period; it served to protect the state budget from increasing demands; it afforded a means of bypassing legal or political hurdles; it increased the power of the dominant party, Mapai; and, most importantly, it was a flexible mechanism for monopolizing state resources in Jewish hands – through institutions like the Jewish Agency and the JNF – and thus monitoring the internal boundary between Jews and Arabs.[5] The ambiguity of the limits of the state thus matched the ambiguity of the hybrids and permitted exploitation of them to the full. As we shall see later in this chapter, this was also true for the external boundaries of the state. They too were fuzzified, and with similarly useful results from the point of view of state elites.

But to the degree that the hybrids were produced as an integral part of the technology of state building, it was necessary, in a sort of parallel movement, to purify them, to redraw the blurred internal and external boundaries, so as to produce the appearance, the effect, of the state as a sovereign agency in clearly demarcated territory, clearly demarcated also from the society over which it exercised the power of command. This is why I deal with the struggles among the experts. As I explain in the introduction, the experts played an important role in producing the effect of the state because their discourse separated what "really" belonged to this side of the boundary and what to the other. For this reason, there were all sorts of alliances and coalitions created in this period between various groups of experts and various factions within the state elite. To a certain extent, these were exchanges based on mutuality of interests, a sort of a bargain in which the experts assisted the elites in creating the effect of the state and received in return jurisdiction over management of the hybrids.

I do not wish to create the impression, however, that this was a premeditated conspiracy that the two sides entered into in order to realize clearly defined goals and interests. This for two reasons. First, the two sides found each other almost in a blind fashion, on the basis of the structural homology between the political struggle and the struggle among the experts. It is customary to depict the struggles and debates that this chapter deals with – over the expulsions of the Palestinians, how to deal with infiltration, the retaliatory attacks, the military government, and the absorption of immigrants – as political struggles between hawks and doves, left and right, secular and religious. I would suggest, however, that they could be viewed from a different (sociological) perspective as struggles between different groups of experts over professional interests. Each of these groups of experts claimed that it should be granted jurisdiction over dealing with problems like infiltration or the absorption of immigration, or at the very least that it should be consulted on these matters by the relevant agencies, because its knowledge was relevant to these problems.

The war and the establishment of the state indeed destabilized the precarious equilibrium of the field of orientalist expertise. Groups of experts that had previously been in a relatively subordinate position perceived here an opportunity to improve their situation. Others perceived a threat and felt a need to protect their position. In short, the experts acted not on the basis of a clearly articulated political conviction but on the basis of their position within the field of orientalist expertise, relative to other experts, and they were motivated by a sense that a new range of opportunities had become available. If an alignment of interests began to form between them and a faction of the state elite, then this happened because of structural reasons, because of the homology between the political and the professional struggles, in the sense that "my enemy's enemy is my friend."

The second reason the notion of conscious conspiracy is inadequate for describing what took place is that once such a temporary alliance was formed, its stability and longevity depended on the process by which the two sides gradually taught each other to speak the same language – the language by means of which the hybrids would be purified and the boundaries of the state would be reconstituted. Gradually they would come to share a common universe of discourse, a common definition of reality, and it was precisely this common language that would translate the interests of the two sides and establish an alignment between them. In other words, the alliance between the two sides was not caused by their interests but precisely the opposite: the existence of an alliance between them is what allowed the two sides to interpret and understand their interests as satisfied by it.[6]

In this chapter, I focus on four sets of struggles that took place in the period from 1948 to 1953. First, during the 1948 war, the experts tried to wrest some control over the expulsions from military commanders. This was not, as many have thought, a struggle between hawks and doves over *whether* Palestinians should be expelled but rather a struggle over defining the expertise and authority necessary to decide *who* among them must leave and *who* may stay. In a sense, it was an early trial of strength between the protagonists – Arabists, notables, the students (who by this point had become Foreign Ministry officials), military commanders, intelligence officers, and academic orientalists – who carried their conflicting claims into three sorts of subsequent struggles. One such struggle was over the management of the border zone between Israel and its neighbors and the control of the infiltrator hybrid. The second multifaceted struggle was over the proper treatment of the Palestinians who remained under Israel's rule (i.e., the Israeli-Arab hybrids). Finally, the third struggle was over the expertise necessary to best absorb the immigrants from Middle Eastern and North African countries (i.e., the *mizrahi* hybrids).

The Struggle over the Expulsions

Why were the Palestinians expelled? I am not an expert on the history of 1948 war, but I think there is something misleading about Benny Morris's claim that the first expulsions were unplanned local events and that only after the event did the Zionist leadership understand what was taking place and choose to affirm it. In Morris's language, the war was a "transformative event" that changed what the leadership perceived as possible or desirable.[7]

The problem with this argument is that it seems to echo, without much critical reflection, the justifications provided by some of the key actors themselves for their actions. The image of the war as a transformative event was Ben-Gurion's. As early as 1942, in a discussion about Jewish immigration, he spoke about the possibilities opened up by the world war, "one of the most dynamic periods in human history." He said that it required one "to think in new concepts and not to be tied to obsolete concepts. . . . There will be a new order in the world. Tens of millions of people will be dislocated. All the concepts about people's movement have changed as result of the war."[8] In the course of the 1948 war, he made continuous use of this image to justify violent acts, and there is no doubt that he thought in these terms – the concepts "ours" and "not ours," he said, "are concepts that belong only to a state of peace, and in a period of war they completely lose their meaning."[9] This image accords war an independent, almost transhuman agency. Wars, however, are fought by people, and some people are better placed than others to shape the rules about what is and what is not permitted in their course. Benni Morris has done more than anybody else to change Israeli public discourse with regards to the expulsions, but in this respect there is in his account a vagueness that uncannily resembles the vagueness with which Ben-Gurion enshrouded the war.

Should we accept, therefore, Nur Masalha's argument that a Zionist master plan for the expulsions, the notorious "Plan D" (*Tochnit Dalet*), was drawn already before the war?[10] I do not think so. As Benni Morris has already pointed out, no "smoking gun" has ever been found, no detailed master plan or explicit government decision instructing the forces to generally clear the country of Palestinians. More importantly – since Morris's refrain relies too much on legal formalism – such an argument severely underestimates the divisions within the Jewish camp. While ideas for voluntary transfer were a staple of Zionist discussions in the 1930s and 1940s, and while there existed, as we shall see below, groups interested in carrying out a large-scale expulsion of Palestinians, there was by no means unanimity about the matter among the Zionist leadership, and much of what came to pass was carried out, in fact, without government approval and contrary to the wishes of many ministers.

A much better and more sociological explanation is provided by Uri Ben-Eliezer, who identifies the social actor responsible for the expulsions: the generational group of the young military commanders analyzed in Chapter 3. Ben-Eliezer argues that the formative experience of this group was the Arab rebellion of 1936–1939, which coincided with their reaching young adulthood, and the Jewish response to it, which evolved from a defensive posture to an aggressive offensive one. In the crucible of the armed conflict, they developed a militaristic worldview – a belief that political problems could and should be solved through the use of force. This is why this group was inclined to expel the Palestinians. But Ben-Eliezer also explains why it was possible for them to do so. He argues that they managed to forge an implicit alliance with a faction of the political leadership of the labor movement, especially Ben-Gurion. The latter was interested in co-opting the younger generation because he feared they might become political challengers and because he could use them in his struggles against other factions within the leadership. Co-optation was the only possible strategy, since at this point the leadership lacked the coercive institutions of a state and relied on voluntary submission to enforce its authority.

The terms of the bargain were roughly this: Ben-Gurion would adopt the militaristic worldview of the younger generation and would accept the idea that political problems could be solved through the use of force; in return this generation would submit without challenge to the authority of the leadership. They would even accept Ben-Gurion's intervention in military decision-making. This bargain evolved over a long time and was only truly sealed during the war, as late as May 1948. This was the context for the formulation of the notorious Plan D and the massive wave of expulsions that followed in its wake. There is no point in looking for a smoking gun, said Ben-Eliezer, because the younger generation was already inclined to expel the Palestinians, and the very essence of the bargain was that no explicit instruction would be needed. Ben-Gurion's famous wave toward the East – signaling approval for an unspoken suggestion, "Let them leave" – captured this bargain well.[11]

This is a reasonable account, as far as it goes. It ignores, however, the complexity of the formative experiences of the young commanders and thus tends to naturalize their trajectory. As we saw earlier, whether they grew up within the separatist sector or in a mixed environment like Alon, they all shared the experience of the agonistic in-between sphere, where they struggled with Palestinian youths but also perceived a certain proximity to them, emulated them and even formed acquaintances. Their formative experiences with respect to the Palestinians were, therefore, contradictory. Rather than the expulsions being "explained" by such experiences, they might be seen as a way of resolving the contradiction inherent in the life experiences and worldviews of these individuals, a sort of "existential decision," an internal splitting, which, once taken, throws them to one side and accounts for all past experience as "leading" to it. It is not difficult to recognize moments of such fateful decision-making in the trajectories of the young commanders. The young Alon left alone in the family farm, after his father took ill, sold it without permission and joined a kibbutz (i.e., the separatist sector). Dayan, too, after he was injured and deemed out of circulation, left the family farm and joined the ranks of the dominant faction in the labor movement.[12] The social principle underlying such decisions by the young commanders was always the same: to extract themselves from the limited and contradictory milieu of their upbringing and become oriented to significant others in the separatist sector, where most symbolic and political capital was concentrated.

Even once those decisions were taken, however, the trajectory of the young commanders remained indeterminate, at least for some while. On the basis of their formative experiences in the in-between sphere, they claimed the status not only of activist military commanders but also of experts on Arab affairs. Dayan, for example, served in 1945 and 1947 as the officer in charge of Arab affairs at the Haganah General Staff and organized networks of informers.[13] Alon, the reader may recall, commanded the unit of *mista'ravim*. One could imagine an alternative trajectory, in the course of which they would have become allied to the political leadership as advisers on Arab affairs. That is, they would have realized the social principle implicit in their trajectories – movement toward the core of the separatist sector – but occupied there a similar in-between, dare we say "hybrid," sphere of mediation. In this position, I would argue, they would have been much less likely to opt for wholesale expulsion, since they would have had a vested professional interest in the maintenance of their networks and the objects of their expertise.

As I will show later in this chapter, a marginal position in the field of orientalist expertise typically predisposes one toward solutions that would make orientalist expertise obsolete in the long run, whereas a more central position predisposes one toward solutions that envision a lasting role for orientalist expertise. It is significant, therefore, that the positions of expert or adviser on Arab affairs were monopolized by the Arabists. It tilted the trajectory of the young commanders in a more strictly military direction.[14] Later in their careers, they found all sorts of justifications and post hoc accounts for this arbitrary fact of trajectory adjustment – most famously, in his 1956 eulogy on the grave of Ro'i Rothenberg, Dayan challenged his fellow Israelis to recognize "in all its brutality, the destiny of our generation," namely, to fight and to expel, to recognize that they were faced with a tragic choice between two equally valid rights[15] – but we need not follow them in this direction. What I would like to do is less to "explain" the expulsions, in the sense of locating them within a certain master narrative, than to sharpen the question about them, to isolate the fact of the expulsions, in all their brutality, as a naked question mark.

There is one more modification I would like to add to Ben-Eliezer's account: as Ben-Eliezer himself notes, not everybody was expelled, and whole villages managed to stay put. Especially if they surrendered without a fight, reports Morris, they were more likely, though by no means certain, to remain in their homes.[16] This fact points to the existence of other factors besides the alliance between the young commanders and Ben-Gurion that were necessary for the expulsions. Ben–Eliezer gives us a clue, since he argues that the success of the coalition between the young commanders and Ben-Gurion depended on its ability to impose a *militaristic definition of the situation* on the other actors involved, namely, a definition according to which the situation was one of "war," implying that political problems were to be solved by force of arms and that the situation was one of conflict between a "state" and its "enemies," those who were outside it or whose expulsion was desirable.

The point is that they were not always able to impose this definition, not in all battles, not with respect to all villages. It is possible to analyze the conquest of each specific village as a sort of game of communication in which the warring sides do not clash merely at the physical level but also (though not necessarily) at the symbolic level, each attempting to impose its own definition of the situation. The initial bombardment by the attacking forces, therefore, was not meant only to soften the target but also to signal that "this is war." If the defenders decided, for example, to evacuate the women and children, they would concur in this definition and reinforce it. This is why such evacuation tended to end in expulsion of the inhabitants and the complete destruction of the village, whereas if the women and children remained in the village even during the battle, many times (though by no means always), expulsion did not follow directly upon conquest. Additionally, in many battles there were messengers going back and forth between the warring parties, facilitating a more complex game of communication and opening more possibilities for the defenders to define the situation as something other than war. The main point is that if the villagers managed to surrender without a fight (not a small feat in itself), and a few hours passed, they sometimes succeeded in changing the definition of the situation from "war" to "occupation" and even into a relationship of "government" or "policing" (i.e., the relationship between a state and its [recalcitrant] subjects). In these cases, it became more difficult to expel the inhabitants, though by no means impossible, as the evidence shows.[17]

I emphasize this point, because in this sense, and in this sense only, one can talk about a certain compatibility of interests being created between the villagers and the experts – not because the experts were more "moderate" than the military commanders but because they were, like the villagers, interested in changing the military definition of the situation in order to obtain a certain degree of authority. If these struggles are understood, as some have suggested they should be, as struggles between "moderates" and "hard-liners" over whether to expel or not, they may indeed appear as completely insignificant and somewhat bewildering. By the very nature of the dominant coalition, the experts were shut out from most of the decisions – since they were taken under the pretext of war – as their own complaints show. More importantly, it is wrong to think that Sephardi notables, Arabists, and Foreign Office officials invariably attempted to protect Palestinians from expulsion.

On the contrary, many times they encouraged and advocated it. In fact, the first to suggest that certain Arab villages should be completely erased and their inhabitants expelled was no less than Eliahu Elishar, leader of the Sephardi community and later author of such books as *Living with Palestinians*![18] This and other interventions by notables, Arabists, and the like should be understood as claims for expertise, claims that their knowledge and advice were relevant to the conduct of the expulsions and should be taken into account. Typically, to make such claims, the experts needed to change the definition of the situation from war to something else – neighborly relations, retaliation, even government – and the grain of truth in viewing the experts as "moderates" is that, to enforce a changed definition of the situation, they needed to create an alliance with the villagers. They could do so even in the course of battle if they were called upon to mediate in the game of communications, as sometimes happened, or if a village surrendered without a fight and was occupied. This was the secret of their "moderation." It also means that the expulsions depended on a certain balance of power on the Jewish side, a balance of power that could be exploited and disrupted by a well-calculated resistance on the part of the villagers themselves.

In the early phases of the war, Arabists and notables still acted and advised in much the same way as they did before. They did not define the situation as war but kept referring to it as "disturbances" (*me'oraot*), thereby linking it with the events of 1920, 1929, and 1936. In accordance with this definition of the situation, they recommended reacting in ways that would not disturb the delicate balance of "neighborly relations" with the Palestinians, an area in which they claimed special expertise. Their expertise permitted them to distinguish, as Danin put it crudely, between "good and bad Arabs" and to direct retaliatory attacks so that neighborly relations would not be harmed – according to the complex logic of vengeance, punishment, and deterrence they had developed earlier. This way of thinking is precisely what led Elishar to demand that certain villages be erased and their inhabitants expelled. The villages chosen should be few and restricted to those whose inhabitants were known to have participated in attacks on Jews. He justified such actions as "teaching a lesson to border communities and other villages."

In short, the purpose of expulsion was not to get rid of the Palestinians altogether but precisely the opposite – to act in a way that would put an end to the cycle of violence and reconstitute the balance of neighborly relations by punishing only the guilty and setting an example calculated to intimidate those who had not yet joined the action. At this early stage, even the representatives of the younger generation, like Dayan, accepted this definition of the situation. Similarly, in late 1947 Danin was still instructing

Haganah commanders that in case of disturbances they should not "harm the fellahin and their villages unless [they have] clear information that the village (and not an individual or several individuals from it) took part in the attack. Such [indiscriminate] punishment right away will only deliver the villages over to the extremists." In effect, the Arabists had a vested interest in defining the conflict as "disturbances," since in this way they could easily justify the utility of their expertise. They promised that if Haganah forces avoided excessive force and miscalculated attacks and were guided by the criteria set by the Arabists as to whom to expel and whom may stay, the disturbances would be contained and escalation avoided.[19]

Institutionally speaking, however, the Arabists and the notables were no longer in a position to enforce such claims. The Arab intelligence branch did not have a direct channel to field commanders, nor any formal authority to instruct them, and it was bypassed by the combat intelligence officers of the brigades in the field – partly because they got information directly from scouts and *mista'ravim*. This is one example of how the war disturbed the existing equilibrium in the field of orientalist expertise. Instead, the leaders of the Arab branch, Danin and Palmon, together with other Arabists and notables, met regularly with Ben-Gurion as his group of advisers on Arab affairs. It was an informal group, however, without clearly defined mandate or authority. Typically, Ben-Gurion wanted to know from them what the Arabs were thinking about this or that turn of events, not how the Jewish forces should act. Quite naturally, he was forced to listen to their advice in this regard, but it is clear that they had very little control over events in the field.

At the same time, they were still notables and influential people in their own localities and regions, and in this capacity they could still act, on a local basis, to mediate between the warring sides. In some areas, they even formed joint Arab-Jewish committees to maintain neighborly relations. Elsewhere, they negotiated truces with Arab villages, or received and interpreted their writs of surrender. They mediated between Palestinian notables and the Jewish commanders and acted to protect business interests they had in common with Palestinian notables, as in agreements negotiated to suspend combat during the harvest season or for the sake of the citrus export trade.[20]

This does not mean that the Arabists and the notables acted only to moderate the actions of the combat units. Their expertise and their role in the communication game with the villagers were used also to facilitate belligerent results – conquests and expulsions. During the battle over Haifa, for example, the Jewish commander did not suspect that the Palestinian defenders were about to collapse. The very idea seemed "fantastic" to him. It was only through the mediation efforts of one Jewish lawyer, who had many Palestinian clients and friends, that he learned of their wish to surrender, and the whole battle was suddenly cast in a different light. In addition, the Arabists used their networks of informers not only to gain information but also to spread rumors and threats, thereby achieving the evacuation of many villages without a fight. The most spectacular case occurred in April and May of 1948 in the upper Galilee. Alon, who commanded the Jewish forces, tells how he "assembled the Jewish *Mukhtars*, who had ties in the Arab villages, and asked them to whisper in the ears of their friends that a huge Jewish reinforcement was on its way . . . and to advise them as friends to flee." After the event, he noted with grim satisfaction that "the only common action Jews and Arabs took together was the evacuation of the Arabs."[21] But one could look at this story also the other way around, namely, that even the supreme act of separation, expulsion, required the mediation of Arabists and notables, who drew on their network ties across the boundary between Jews and Arabs – who acted, that is, within the no-man's-land where separation itself was invalid.

A sort of crisis occurred in January 1948. The Arabists and the notables felt overtaken by events. They complained to Ben-Gurion that their advice was not being heeded, that many friendly villages had been attacked and the inhabitants expelled without provocation, and that many of their friends and informers had suffered and disappeared. In general, they argued, the indiscriminate nature of Jewish attacks was making the situation worse and turning all the Arabs into enemies. Ben-Gurion listened and agreed to convert his informal group of advisers into a formal Committee on Arab Affairs. They also formed a Committee for the Protection of Arab Property. Additionally, it was agreed that the rank and file of the Arab intelligence branch would be appointed as advisers on Arab affairs to the brigade commanders. But none of this was effective. The Committee on Arab Affairs lacked any authority to issue directives. It merely appended its comments to Haganah directives after the event, as the commands were already on their way to field commanders. The Committee for the Protection of Arab Property was unable to block the rampant looting and confiscation, and in May 1948 Danin resigned from it. By that time, he had already become converted to the idea of transferring the Palestinians and making sure they could not return. Finally, the brigade commanders were told that the advisers' mandate was "only to advise, and the authority to decide is in your hands alone." In reality, the brigade commanders tended to ignore the advisers.[22]

With the declaration of statehood, the institutional position of the Arabists and the notables changed once more. From advisers, they became officials and officers. The Committee on Arab Affairs became the Ministry for Minority Affairs, and most of its staff came from the ranks of the notables and the Sephardi leadership. At its head was appointed Bekhor Shitrit, a Sephardi native of Tiberias and a former magistrate. The Committee for the

Protection of Arab Property became a department within this ministry, but within weeks it was shut down, and its powers were transferred to the newly created office of the Custodian of Absentee Property. The latter remained completely outside the purview of either the notables or the Arabists. The Arab intelligence branch was dissolved, and its leaders, Danin and Palmon, moved to the newly created Middle East Department of the Foreign Office, joining their former adversaries, the students. The rank-and-file field officers were drafted into the new Intelligence Service of the IDF, into the military government in the newly conquered Palestinian areas, and into the General Security Service (GSS). There they were joined by some of the *mista'ravim*. Again, none of them were in a position to influence the extent or nature of the expulsions, which were now taking place in the midst of battles between regular armies. Consequently, many of them were converted to the idea of population transfer and numbered among the strongest advocates of blocking the return of refugees.[23]

Nonetheless, once the battles subsided, they all tried to influence the course of expulsions and demanded that the Ministry of Minority Affairs or the Foreign Office be given authority to supervise the steps taken. As before, their claimed expertise consisted in distinguishing between different types of Arabs – those who were "bad" and must be expelled versus those who were "good" and should be allowed to stay. First, there was the vexed and painful matter of the Arabists' networks of informers, friends, and clients. Not only had IDF conquests threatened to completely dismantle these networks and render them irrelevant, but many individuals were expelled who earlier had assisted the Arabists in procuring information or organizing land purchases. Second, and more significantly, there was the matter of villages and towns that had been under Jewish control from the very beginning or had managed to surrender without a fight. The Ministry of Minority Affairs claimed that these were under its jurisdiction. The Palestinians within the areas of Jewish control were no longer the "enemy" but "minorities" within a sovereign state. The issue of their expulsion became a matter of formulating proper minority policy.

The Foreign Office, for its part, demanded a say regarding the expulsions, because what happened to the Palestinians had a bearing on the new state's relations with religious and ethnic communities outside it, especially Christians and Druze. According to the foreign minister, Moshe Sharett, this was an important "test for our capacity to rule the Arab minority," and he suggested permitting the return of a few refugees "to improve our relations with the minorities." The Arabists, for their part, began converting the logic of retaliation into considerations of good *government* vis-à-vis the military tendency to sweep whole areas clean of Palestinian villages. On the one hand, there was the old notion that a good ruler must act justly so as to inspire loyalty. The Jewish forces "must appear before the Arabs as a governmental power acting forcefully, but also with justice and honesty." Hence, only those who were guilty and dangerous must be expelled, and this must be done with the utmost precision, to avoid the perception of arbitrariness. On the other hand, there was the idea of "divide and conquer," a policy that would grant favorable treatment to certain groups (e.g., Christians, Druze, and Bedouins) in order to capture their loyalty while at the same isolating the more dangerous and numerous Muslim majority. This called for a less specific expulsion policy based on global distinctions between worthy and dangerous populations.[24]

Clearly, these two versions of what good government might be and how the expulsions may be conducted reflected the different claims to expertise of the Arabists and the students (now officials at the Foreign Ministry). Although they both criticized the indiscriminate expulsions conducted by military commanders, they put forward different and sometimes conflicting principles of discrimination. Thus, when Ya'akov Shimoni, a former student and Jewish Agency official now at the Middle East Department of the Foreign Office, visited the area of the Upper Galilee, he complained that, despite the recommendations of the Foreign Office, the treatment of the population was "haphazard and different from one place to another." The field commanders did not have clear instructions, "no clear line as to how to deal with the Arabs in the occupied territory – whether the inhabitants should be expelled or remain in their place; whether they should be treated harshly or leniently; whether Christians should be favorably treated or not; whether the Maronites should receive special treatment; whether the Metualis should receive special treatment, etc." Clearly, he had in mind a discriminating policy that favored Christian minorities over Muslims and was disappointed with the inconsistency with which it was carried out. But during an earlier inspection, the Arabists had precisely the opposite reaction. They thought that the distinction between Muslims and Christians was far too general and did not distinguish among those who were the real culprits and those who were innocent. As one of them reported, "I saw actions of purging Muslims, and a much more lenient treatment with respect to Christians and Druze. . . . I saw faces of wanted Christians and Druze, who were not only walking freely in the village, but were also gloating at the Muslims who were expelled and their property was falling apart." From the Arabists' point of view, a much more detailed and discriminating form of knowledge was needed to rule the villages, while the more global policies of the Foreign Office would only achieve the opposite of what they set out to do – the guilty would remain behind and continue to endanger the state while the rest of the villagers would become hostile toward an arbitrary and unjust governor.[25]

Similar disagreements took place with respect to the question whether some of the refugees should be allowed to return, and if so, whom. Here again the distinction between hawks and doves is useless. The Arabists would recommend the return of certain refugees, but the Foreign Office would resist mightily; the Sephardi leadership at the Ministry of Minority Affairs would look favorably on some return scheme, but the Arabists would veto it; and so on. All of them, however, complained that the prime minister and the military commanders were not sensitive to the benefits that could accrue to the state from a discriminating policy of partial return.[26]

These disagreements were soon to grow into a full-fledged struggle over administrative jurisdiction in Arab affairs and the relevance of different forms of expertise. The different interpretations of good government were continued in the framework of a struggle over the proper expertise needed to administer the Palestinians who remained under Israeli control. The dispute about returning some of the refugees turned into a general debate about the management of the border zone and the phenomenon of infiltration. All these struggles took place, we must remember, in the context of the continued dominance of the coalition between Ben-Gurion and the young military commanders. Even once the war was over, this coalition perpetuated the military definition of reality by means of the notion of the "second round," namely, the prediction that the Arab states were preparing to attack again and that the armistice agreements provided merely a lull in the conflict. The experts had to maneuver within the boundaries of this military definition of reality and only occasionally and hesitatingly challenged it.

The Struggle over the Management of the Border Zone

By now the division of labor seems self-evident: Arabists, with their more localized and folksy expertise, deal with the Palestinians inside the state, but for dealing with the Arab states on the other side of the border, a different sort of expertise is called for, more technical, distant, and abstract and involving electronic surveillance, intelligence research, and Middle Eastern studies. The historians of Israeli intelligence have determined that the uneducated Arabists were simply not up to the task. Not only had their networks of informers collapsed because of the massive expulsions, but once skirmishes between neighboring communities were replaced by war between organized armies, the information supplied by informers was of little value. Moreover, the devices for electronic surveillance that were rapidly being developed proved to be a far superior means of gaining information on Arab armies.[27] Put differently, the irrelevance of the Arabists is presented as an inevitable result of the 1948 war and the establishment of the state. The war separated Jews and Palestinians and drew impenetrable borders between them. Across these borders, the relationship was between states and regular armies, and this rendered Arabist expertise obsolete.

But this is an anachronistic argument, which tells the story backwards, explaining the process by its outcome. The war did not fully separate Jews from Palestinians, because in the volume of the armistice line there appeared a new hybrid – the Palestinian infiltrator. Already during the war, and especially during the various ceasefires, military decision-makers were faced with the problem of how to deal with Palestinians who were trying to cross the frontlines back to their villages or in order to harvest their fields. This problem did not disappear with the end of hostilities. Many of the refugees, especially in the West Bank, lived in very harsh conditions practically a stone's throw from their previous homes and fields. Some tried to return to their homes; some tried to rejoin families from whom they were separated, or at least to visit their relatives; some tried to work in their fields; some were driven by hunger to steal; some were smugglers; and others, no doubt, crossed the armistice lines intending to take revenge upon the Jewish settlers. The fuzziness of the situation was increased by the fact that in many areas the armistice lines were not actually marked on the ground (and on the maps they were drawn with a "thick pencil"). Thus, a shepherd leading his flock to graze or a peasant working in his fields could easily find himself in potentially disputed territory. Moreover, the movement of Palestinians was not all in one direction. Some Palestinians within Israel had fields or property on the other side of the border, some would journey to the border to meet with family members whom the war had thrown on the other side, and once they were in no-man's-land, it was difficult to say where they had come from and where they belonged.[28]

The specter of these so-called infiltrators hovered over Israeli policy throughout the first decade of the state's existence. At issue were weighty fears about the return of refugees, which could undo what the war had accomplished. At the same time however, at issue was also the very technique of producing the appearance of the state as a sovereign entity exercising its authority over a clearly defined territory and population. On one side of the border, the infiltrators were refugees and enemies. The relationship between them and the state was clear (i.e., clearly antagonistic). On the other side of the border, the infiltrators were indistinguishable from the "present absentees," the internal refugees who were to be citizens of the state. Again, the relation between them and the state, at least in theory, was clear (i.e., clearly inclusive). But within the volume of the armistice line, they and their relationship to the state remained undefined.[29]

The struggle over the management of the border zone involved two coalitions, each proposing a different solution to the problem of infiltration and, in essence, advocating a different method to produce the "effect of the state."

On the one side were Arabists and the moderates in the Foreign Office; on the other side were academically trained officers in the research branch of military intelligence, aligned with the activists in the General Staff and the Defense Ministry.[30]

For the Arabists, the problem of infiltration and the fuzzy and complex situation along the armistice lines were not altogether different from the problems with which they dealt before the formation of the state: managing neighborly relations in frontier areas distant from central authority. Consequently, it is impossible to maintain the argument that Arabist expertise was made obsolete simply by the war. Indeed, many of the rank-and-file Arabists who were drafted into the intelligence service of the new IDF served in the border zone as special operations officers, recruiting and operating informers and agents on the other side of the border. Others served in the military government (and the GSS), which in this period was specifically entrusted with the task of supervising the border areas and fighting against infiltration. In this role, they deployed the same sort of expertise as in the prestate days: They made distinctions between various types of border-crossers, for example, between "smugglers" and "infiltrators"; they recruited some of those as informers, promising them, as in the past, that the information they supplied would be used to calm tensions and improve relations along the armistice lines; they still negotiated truces (*sulha*) between Jewish and Arab communities across the armistice lines; they still directed retaliatory attacks, carried out by a special unit composed of "minorities" (Bedouins, Druze, and Circassians) and commanded by an experienced Arabist, according to the tried-and-true principles they have formulated earlier; and they still used the village files for these purposes.[31]

In this, the Arabists were supported by the Foreign Office. Some of the top Arabists, after all, moved to the Foreign Office after the Arab intelligence branch was dissolved. Moreover, the minister of foreign affairs himself, Moshe Sharett, considered himself an Arabist of sorts. He grew up in a Palestinian village, spoke fluent Arabic, and had Palestinian friends. Most importantly, however, this was a coalition in which the Foreign Office attempted to co-opt Arabist expertise in order to bolster its case for "moderation." Sharett was locked in a bitter political struggle against the activist faction. He was concerned that its hard-line treatment of the infiltrators (which involved, as we shall see below, indiscriminate retaliatory attacks) would hurt Israel's image abroad, play into the hands of Arab propaganda, harden the Arab position toward Israel to the point of escalation, and rule out the possibility of peace negotiations. Sharett's officials, in the Middle East Department of the Foreign Office, had additional reasons to recruit the Arabists to their cause. As we shall see below, the activist faction cultivated the research branch of military intelligence, and its academically trained officers were fast becoming the dominant players in the intelligence community, undermining the authority of both Arabists and the officials in the Foreign Office, and placing a stranglehold on the resources and information flowing to them. Co-opting the Arabists, therefore, had numerous benefits: First, their expertise contained the promise of a quiet and moderate solution to the problem of infiltration. Second, the Arabists enjoyed an aura of experience and toughness, which the Foreign Office lacked, and could thus remove from it the stigma of weakness and lack of realism. And third, there was already an established division of labor between the Arabists and the former students, the division between political and security intelligence created in the early 1940s. It was precisely this division of labor that was threatened by the rise to prominence of the research branch of military intelligence.[32]

In 1953, after several failed and particularly bloody retaliatory attacks by the IDF, an official in the research division of the Foreign Office prepared a memorandum on "ways of fighting infiltration" in which she recommended all the tried-and-true methods of the Arabists: developing neighborly relations between Israeli and Arab *mukhtars* across the border; exploiting existing enmities between Arab clans; using paid agents to charge that the infiltrators were really smugglers who were violating the Arab boycott of Israel; and conducting retaliatory attacks by "bands of Israeli infiltrators... Jews and minorities... who should appear to be 'privately' organized and unconnected with the Israeli government... [and] should carry out burglaries and robberies... on the Arab side of the border. Rich and influential Arabs should be targeted." The memorandum suggested that these bands would be organized by the special operations officers of military intelligence, many of whom were Arabists. It was obvious that the implementation of these suggestions would require the sort of detailed and precise knowledge, based on intimate familiarity with the realities of the border zone, that only the Arabists possessed. The suggestions echoed an earlier suggestion by the leading Arabist, Josh Palmon, to organize and lead a force of Druze and other minorities to combat the infiltrators: "They... would be allowed to rob the infiltrators.... They are expert smugglers and know all the trails."[33]

It is possible to summarize these recommendations in this way: Controlling infiltration would require the sort of detailed knowledge that could serve to distinguish between the various types of border-crossers, their motives, their intentions, their family ties, their position within the villages, and their alliances and enmities. And it would also require the expertise to act within the border zone and exploit its multiple and cross-cutting alliances in accordance with local rules. Only experts possessed with such qualities would be able to determine who really belonged on this side of the border and who belonged on the other side (i.e., to purify the infiltrator hybrid). Since obtaining the necessary knowledge would require someone to become embedded in the no-man's-land and act within it as if the border did not exist, the state must contract the job out to extra-state agents. The state cannot appear to be meddling on the other side of the border or endorsing the existence of hybrid, cross-border entities and individuals.

This is the arrangement that Arabists proposed to the state elites: The Arabists would reside within the no-man's-land and would take it upon themselves to supervise the border zone. In order to control the infiltrator hybrid, they would create a new type of hybrid – the mixed bands of Jews and minorities who would operate on both sides of the border – but the Arabists would serve as a buffer between the state and this new hybrid. In this way, the state could appear as a sovereign and authoritative entity strictly demarcated from society. In short, to produce the appearance that the state possessed a sovereign external boundary, it was necessary to build a network that crossed, and thereby fuzzified, the internal boundary between the state and society, and in order to reconstitute the internal boundary, it was necessary to position the Arabists in a strategic node of this network, in a sense to make them shoulder (and embody) all the contradictions and ambiguities of the fuzzified borders.

On the other side, however, there was a no less formidable coalition, led by the activist military elite in the General Staff, many of whom were drawn from the young military commanders who conducted the expulsions. The means they chose to deal with the problem of infiltration reflected their military definition of the situation and their ethos of separatist settlement. The most important of these was the creation of "security zones" running all along the borders of the country. Within these security zones, the military was permitted to evacuate and demolish Palestinian villages and to impose movement restrictions. Although these security zones were typically not demarcated on the ground, they could sometimes extend as deep as sixteen miles inward. According to the instructions given to the military, anybody who was found crossing the border or who lacked a special permit within a certain distance from the border (in some cases as deep as five miles inward) was to be shot or arrested. Put differently, since it was difficult to determine the human boundaries – whether the infiltrator was a citizen, an enemy, or something in between – the physical border was fuzzified (or thickened) to create an area in which the state was permitted to arbitrarily determine these distinctions and, because these areas overlapped the areas where most Palestinians lived, treat all Palestinians as a "dangerous population."[34]

The gaps in the outer perimeter of these security zones were plugged up by a second device: *haganah merhavit* (regional defense), namely, the use of semicivilian, semimilitary border settlements to supervise the border and block infiltration routes. Experienced settlers were recruited by the army, originally on a voluntary basis and later on a paid basis, to supervise and defend an extended perimeter around their settlements and participate in identifying and pursuing infiltrators. Eventually they were given the rank of "area commanders," and their salary was split between the Treasury and the Jewish Agency. The army negotiated these terms with the Agricultural Center affiliated with Mapam (a left-of-center party) and the Settlement Department of the Jewish Agency, affiliated with Mapai (the dominant party). The Settlement Department also hired its own guards to perform an essentially similar role. Some settlements were planted purposefully on known infiltration routes in order to block them. Others were asked to extend the cultivation of their fields into the no-man's-land in order to plug it up and prevent land grabs by refugees, or to "determine the border." Since the armistice lines were fuzzy, it was useful to have a "test on the ground" to try to demarcate the borders of the state. If such a test – from the plowing of a field to shooting above the head of a passerby – went unchallenged, the border was drawn de facto. If, on the other hand, an "incident" developed, especially one with a few casualties, the U.N. inspectors were forced to intervene and adjudicate in the matter, and the border was drawn de jure. Put differently, *haganah merhavit* meant that the internal boundary between state and society was fuzzified in order to produce the appearance that state was an externally bounded sovereign territory and even to extend its boundaries when possible.[35]

Finally, because inevitably this semicivilian bulwark along the border suffered losses in clashes with infiltrators, the third plank in the activists' program consisted of retaliatory attacks across the border. Up till 1953, these were still guided by the complex logic of revenge, punishment, and deterrence devised by the Arabists in the 1940s, and the Arabists were still consulted about planning these attacks and determining their targets. The aspect of punishment was prominent, though somewhat modified. Since the information was less specific than in the past, the tendency was toward collective punishment of this or that village without truly discriminating between the guilty and innocent. But there was also an aspect of indirect deterrence, teaching in this way a lesson to other villages, and even revenge, since the government and the army rarely admitted their responsibility and claimed that the attacks were conducted by vigilantes.

All this changed after the Kibbya attack. On the night of October 14, 1953, a paratrooper unit commanded by Ariel Sharon attacked this village, which was just across the border on the Jordanian side, and blew up most of the houses with the inhabitants still inside. At least seventy villagers, including women and children, were killed. The condemnation by the international community was particularly harsh, and the damage to Israel's international status so severe that the IDF General Staff decided to switch to a method of pure and openly declared deterrence: to attack only military and police units and compounds without trying to look for any culprits – and to do so openly. Through this change of method, the activists sought to achieve two main goals: The first (declared) goal was to minimize the number of civilian casualties. The second (less obvious) goal was to provide retaliatory attacks with a new rationale, as means of exerting pressure on Arab states to better supervise their "own" side of the border.

What happened in reality, however, was that the retaliatory attacks, rather than deterring infiltration, escalated the conflict at the border zone into a small-scale war between regular armies. This result too was welcomed, at least by some of the activists, as useful: "One has to play with fire, to put out the fire," said the commander of the research branch of military intelligence. Moreover, the attacks did not reconstitute a clearly defined border. They are better understood as reconstituting the internal boundaries of the state – this was the purpose of the new policy of openness and publicity. After *haganah merhavit* had subcontracted the defense of the state to its citizens, retaliatory attacks reconstituted the effect of the state, because through them the state appeared to be "defending its citizens." Yet, retaliatory attacks had another, perhaps unintended, consequence: they fuzzified the external border once more and turned it into an ever-extending frontier. Although the border between the state and other states was barricaded from the outside in, from the inverse direction, inside out, it became highly permeable, a lawless frontier where Israeli soldiers and civilians moved rather freely. It is well known that retaliatory attacks inspired a whole cult of crossing the border and visiting forbidden sites on the other side.[36]

Combined, these three measures rendered Arabist expertise irrelevant. There was no need for detailed distinctions between different types of border-crossers – they were all to be shot. From the point of view of pure deterrence, it was immaterial who the perpetrators were, what villages or kinship units they belonged to, or what their motives were. Pure deterrence was guided by purely military considerations: tactical surprise (which by its very nature led to choosing targets contrary to the logic of punishment), terrain, and behaviorist deterrent effect (speed of reaction, extent of damage, etc.). In the small-scale war that erupted along the border, the army needed not Arabist expertise but combat intelligence – topography, number of enemy soldiers, their location and equipment, their training, and so on. Some of this intelligence could be provided by informers and agents, but generally it was more effectively produced by electronic surveillance. No wonder, therefore, that Arabists and the Foreign Office tended to criticize the policies of indiscriminate shooting of infiltrators and especially indirect deterrence and then pure deterrence. They pointed out the international outrage and the damage to Israel's image; they bemoaned the hardening of the Arab position toward Israel in their wake, the scuttling of peace efforts, and the danger of escalation; and they offered instead the use of their own services and the principle of discriminating, covert punishment.[37]

But the edge of their criticisms was blunted by the ally of the activists – the research branch of military intelligence. When military intelligence was first reorganized in 1949, after the war, it did not have a research branch. Its organizational structure was created by former British military officers, who sought to "professionalize" the intelligence service and were primarily concerned with limiting the freedom of intelligence officers to evaluate and interpret information. By "professionalism" they meant that the intelligence officers should concentrate on strictly military technical detail and avoid interpretation, particularly the assessment of political factors, which should be left to military and political decision-makers. Hence, they did not separate research from information gathering but created a central combat intelligence branch, which was entrusted with both gathering and evaluating information on Arab armies, and surrounded it with several auxiliary branches each dealing with a distinct topic (topography, the Arab press, embassies, etc.).[38]

Nonetheless, already in 1950, an informal division of labor began to develop within military intelligence: Arabists, who were "practical people . . . who knew how to operate agents and make things work," dealt mostly with information gathering and covert operations, whereas "academically oriented personnel," who "tended to think more," concentrated on research. The chief proponent of this division was the deputy commander of military intelligence, Yehoshafat Harkabi, who held a master's degree in oriental studies from the Hebrew University and had trained in the school for diplomats run by the Jewish Agency. He attracted a following of "West-European-born and especially German Jews . . . from the academic world." In 1953, when Harkabi took over the position of commander of military intelligence, he reorganized it around an administrative separation of the research and information-gathering branches.[39]

With the separation between research and information gathering, the academics finally managed to impose the philological modus operandi they had acquired in the course of their studies. Harkabi's first step, when he was appointed deputy chief of the service, was to initiate work on a voluminous compilation and assessment of all data on Arab armies, termed "All Contingencies" (*Mikre Ha-kol*), in anticipation of an all-Arab war against Israel. In a sense, it was the equivalent of the concordance of ancient Arab poetry produced by the Institute of Oriental Studies. It was an authoritative document that summarized all known data, indexed and cross-referenced so they were easily accessible. It was similar to the concordance in yet another respect: it was meant to provide an "objective" foundation for subjective interpretation. Harkabi reports that it included not only analyses of various contingencies but also "political background and the first rudiments of strategic assessment." Harkabi enjoined research officers to "not only count how many tanks the enemy possesses . . . but also to understand his way of thinking, so as to accurately anticipate his actions." Clearly, the academics were reconstituting the whole philological hierarchy of apprentice, pedant, and interpreter, relegating the Arabists to the position of apprentices and demanding for themselves the privilege of interpreting the data and seeking the subjective intention behind it.[40]

This was also the basis of their alliance with the activists in the General Staff. The activists supported them in their struggle against the Arabists and approved the reorganization of military intelligence. They also showered resources on the new research branch and promoted it – particularly against the Foreign Office – to become the central office for the whole Israeli intelligence community. Information gathered by all the various branches of intelligence – the information-gathering branch, the Research Department of the Foreign Office, the Mossad, the GSS – flowed to it, and it became the sole agency entrusted with formulating the annual national intelligence assessment.[41]

In return, the research officers concurred in the military definition of reality of the activists and provided the necessary expertise to complete and extend their method of producing the effect of the state. To begin with, they displayed a marked disinterest in the problem of infiltration – essentially relegating it to the military government and the police – and concentrated instead on the military danger of a "second round," an attack by the Arab states, or the political danger of international pressure to push Israel back to the borders mandated by the 1947 U.N. General Assembly decision. Their only contribution to the debate about infiltration was to compile statistics on cases of infiltration and plot them on a graph to figure out their rhythm, when and where they increased or subsided, or to classify them by their consequences – murder, burglary, and so on. The goal was to see whether retaliatory attacks had an impact on the "rate" of infiltration and whether the rate and type of infiltration could be shown to correlate with the interests of Arab leaders. Such graphs could be presented to the U.N. observers to back Israel's complaints. Their chief value, however, was not in what could be *done* with them as in what could *not* be done, not so much in what they *told* but in what they were *silent* about. They constructed infiltration as a distant and inscrutable object of knowledge, almost like a natural phenomenon or a fertility rate. The knowledge produced by the Arabists, about motives, social ties, and so on, was "black boxed" by such graphs, captured and digested as "data," and its producers and their expertise disappeared from view.[42]

More importantly, as they abstracted from the data and sought the subjective intention behind it, the research officers constructed the image of a strategic decision-maker on the other side of the border responsible for all the various local attacks. They used the graphs to claim that the rate of infiltration rose and fell with the interests and intentions of Arab leaders. In this way, the research officers provided three essential services to the activists. First, they reinforced and rationalized the logic of retaliation as pure deterrence. Since it was possible to trace the "intention" behind diverse local attacks, incidents, and accidents to a central decision-maker, it was possible also to rationalize the attacks on army bases and police stations as exerting pressure and producing effects on this decision maker. But since in reality the attacks did not curb infiltration but on the contrary led to escalation at the border, the second service provided by the research officers was to affirm and reinforce the idea of the "second round" and the military definition of reality. This is exactly what "All Contingencies" did, beginning with the assessment that the Arab states were preparing to a start a new war in order to destroy Israel. This assessment provided an explanation why the retaliatory attacks seemed to be failing and did not produce the desired calm in the border zone. The answer was simple: the Arab states had already taken the strategic decision to engage Israel in a second round and so were not going to let the pressure subside. It was possible, therefore, to rationalize the escalation as preemption – better to begin the second round earlier, on Israel's terms. It was the head of the research branch, indeed, who coined the paradox of playing with fire in order to put it out.[43]

There was no need, therefore, to pay attention or deal with the messy and hybrid realities of the border zone, because the coming war would sweep it clean and push the border further outward. Here was the third service the research officers provided to the activists: producing the "effect of the state." It was almost as if by projecting the image of a strategic decision-maker on the other side, they conjured up "the state" as its mirror reflection on this side, which appeared as an organized and cohesive actor whose actions were rational and effective. At the same time that the external border was fuzzified, subcontracted, extended, and thickened into an arbitrary frontier, at the same time that events within the border zone escalated into small-scale war, the interpretation of intentions abstracted the state and detached it from the web of social relations to reconstitute its effect.

As I emphasized earlier, this was not a premeditated conspiracy between the two allies. The interpretation of intentions originated, as I've shown, in the philological (and archeological) training of the research officers, while their allies, the activists, originally tended to think more like the Arabists, whose expertise they imitated and with whom they cooperated in attempting to manage the Israeli-Arab hybrid, as we shall see below. The research officers and the activists found each other because the research officers struggled against the Arabists in order to impose their own form of expertise as prototypical whereas the activists struggled against the moderates of the

Foreign Office, and a structural homology was established between these two struggles. Only after they found each other could the interpretation of intentions be deployed to translate and align the interests of the two sides and cement the coalition between them.

In this struggle, the activists were victorious. What was the social significance of their victory? The crucial point is that the foreclosed alternative, the Arabist proposal on how to resolve the problem of infiltration, did not make a strong distinction between what was inside the state and what was outside it. No matter the location, the solution involved dealing with "Arabs" and required the same type of expertise. The expertise of the research officers, on the other hand, was limited to the Arab leaders, regimes, and armies on the other side of the border. The significance of their victory, therefore, was that the cognitive territory of the Orient was split into two, as if a separate jurisdiction of "intelligence" had been cut out and entrusted to the research officers and was kept strictly separated from knowledge and expertise pertaining to the Palestinians inside the state. As we shall see below, this latter province became the specialized jurisdiction of the Arabists. It follows that the fundamental basis upon which this division of labor was erected, and with it the whole jurisdictional rearrangement of types of expertise and forms of discourse, was the exclusion of the infiltrator-refugee hybrid.

This division of labor was due not to the needs imposed by a new objective reality but to the fact that the coalition of Arabists and the Foreign Office was defeated in its bid to manage the borders and produce the effect of the state. There was also another consequence of this defeat: the Foreign Office gradually lost all influence on the evaluation and assessment of intelligence, which became the monopoly of the research branch of military intelligence. The Middle East Department of the Foreign Office simply became another subservient subcontractor of military intelligence, providing it with "data." As Ezra Danin complained, "It seems to me that the Middle East Department does not exist at all. The Foreign Office relies on military intelligence for knowledge and analysis. To my mind, there could not be a greater mistake." The research unit at the Foreign Office, as well, was ineffectual. It was a "penal colony" where people were sent after completing their term abroad and before they were assigned with another job.[44]

In response, some of the officials in the Foreign Office left their positions and returned to the Hebrew University. The rest retreated to the auxiliary interpretation of their expertise: *hasbara*. If by reading Arab newspapers and other published sources, compiling and analyzing them, they could no longer claim to be doing intelligence research, or "political intelligence," they could still construe it as *hasbara*, in the sense of combating Arab propaganda. Their research and their files would serve to "arm [the state] ... with weapons in written form" (*kley neshek she-bekhtav*), to justify and explain Israel's position on matters such as the problem of the refugees, infiltration, the status of Jerusalem, and so on. Indeed, in 1953, just as the research branch of military intelligence was formally created, the Foreign Office created a separate department for *hasbara*. Among its many tasks, it produced highly polemical pamphlets based on the Arab press, compiling translations of articles or reproductions of caricatures and sometimes juxtaposing them with Israeli or Western materials in such a way as to debunk specific Arab claims and bolster Israel's case on the world stage. It was symptomatic, therefore, that the same rearrangement and division of labor based on the exclusion of the infiltrator-refugee hybrid also created during these same years "the problem of refugees" as an object of Israeli *hasbara* discourse. There, in the province of *hasbara*, the refugees were destined to reside for many years, until the Oslo Accords and the creation of the Palestinian Authority.[45]

The Struggle over the Management of the Palestinian Minority

On July 19, 1950, at a meeting of the committee coordinating the various government bodies dealing with Palestinian affairs, participants were alarmed by reports of "Arabs who are converting to Judaism with the aim of getting favorable treatment. . . . After considering the matter, the committee decided to . . . act so that rabbinical institutions in Israel will not perform such conversions before consulting with the relevant government bureau." The matter of Arabs who converted to Judaism abroad was also discussed, and it was agreed to check immediately if it would be possible to prohibit their entrance to Israel. Finally, the committee also discussed the matter of Arabs who changed their names into Hebrew names and requested the adviser on Arab affairs at the Prime Minister's Office to verify that their old surnames would appear in small print on their ID cards.[46]

What a distance separates this meeting from the young Ben-Gurion's naïve belief that Palestinian peasants were the descendants of the ancient Jews and that Zionism should seek to emulate and assimilate them! The internal boundary between Jews and Arabs was now problematized, and within its volume there appeared another hybrid, the "Israeli Arab." And just as happened with the dubious infiltrator, it became a sinister specter – the Arab who can pass as a Jew – not so much because these fears were realistic but because at stake was again the very technique of producing the effect of the state. On one side of the internal boundary, the Palestinians were a "hostile minority," a "fifth column," an internal enemy, in short, "Arabs." On the other side, they were citizens of the Jewish state, that is, "Israelis." But in between, they and their relationship to the state remained undefined (unless one subcontracted the rabbis to define it). The real problem was how to produce the effect of the state. How could the relationship between the Palestinians and the state be something different and separate from the control exercised by one group in society over another? It fell to the experts, once again, to propose alternative means of, if not defining, at least managing and negotiating this relationship, a thankless and doomed endeavor:

Only a handful of the state's captains have ever imagined the possibility of constructive educational activity to find an ideational and cognitive basis that would allow the Arabs in Israel to develop for themselves a clear and logical consciousness justifying the fact that they were, at one and the same time, Arabs who cherish their culture and tradition, but also loyal citizens of the state of Israel. In such circumstances, the burden fell on the experts – the Arabists. They were required to find positive and logical solutions in the absence of a clear policy line. They did the best they could, but mostly they have become . . . perplexed guides for captains lost in the fog.[47]

It is common to depict the struggle over the management of the Palestinian minority as taking place between a hawkish, security-oriented approach and a dovish, liberal one. Occasionally it was also construed as a jurisdictional struggle between ministries.[48] But this is a very partial view. In fact, the opposition between hawks and doves does not adequately differentiate between the various participants of this debate, because, first, security ranked high on everybody's agenda, and, second, nobody's "liberalism" went so far as to espouse a significant form of political autonomy for the minority. The range of options on this dimension was simply too narrow to provide for much contrast. Instead, I would like to suggest that the main difference between the protagonists was in the techniques they offered to manage the internal boundary between Jews and Arabs and to purify the Israeli-Arab hybrid. The interministerial struggle, for its part, while it was real and significant, is also not satisfactory as an explanation. To take it to be a sufficient explanation is to depict the conflict as purely instrumental and to treat how the protagonists positioned themselves with respect to one another as purely random. Instead, I would argue that position within the field of orientalist expertise (which includes institutional affiliation) provides a much better principle of explanation for how the protagonists positioned themselves and how they formed alliances.

There were four suggestions on how to overcome the ambiguity of the internal boundary between Jews and Arabs. Two of these sought to eliminate the boundary altogether, either through population exchange or through assimilation. The other two sought to preserve the boundary but immobilize all movement across it, either through the granting of substantial religious and cultural autonomy or through direct control and supervision of the minority.

Population exchange was the preferred option of the activist military elite. Beginning from the premise that "every minority should be regarded as potentially hostile" and taking into account "the existence of a neighboring state with aggressive tendencies, having mutual ties, such as culture, religion, race or nationality with the minority" and the "concentration of [the] minority group . . . along the national boundary," they concluded that "elimination of the presence of the minority," especially through population exchange, was the "best" option. The population exchange envisioned, modeled on the Greek-Turkish example, would have involved transferring the remaining Palestinians to the surrounding Arab states and in return absorbing Jews who resided in Arab countries. The idea was to reach a situation where the distinction between inside and outside, enemy and citizen, would be clear-cut and the state would appear as a clearly defined sovereign entity, delegated its authority through a clearly defined relation to a purely Jewish nation. The state would sacrifice nothing, neither its external borders nor the internal boundary between state and society. The only price would be a permanent military definition of reality: "The treatment of minorities . . . is a military problem, even in peace times." The activists spoke as military experts, but as we saw earlier, they also made auxiliary claims to some expertise in Arab affairs. Based on their youthful experiences in the agonistic in-between sphere, they presented themselves as similar to the Arabists in possessing insight into the mentality of the Palestinians, especially the peasants who were uprooted from their land. Dayan, for example, claimed to understand, even empathize with, the implacable "hatred that consumes and fills [their] lives." He warned Israelis that it was useless to think that the refugees would ever give up the desire for return and revenge. The tragic "destiny of our generation" demanded, therefore, that its members harden their hearts and do what was necessary to guarantee the security of the state, even if that meant expelling more Palestinians, something that Dayan was busy doing in 1950 as commander of the southern front. His tragic narrative aside, here was a clear case where a marginal position in the field of orientalist expertise was translated into a proposal that would, in the longer term, eliminate the need for orientalist expertise altogether and thus turn the tables on the dominant factions in the field. Moreover, as I've argued earlier, the tragic narrative was a means of rationalizing post hoc the arbitrary manner in which these individuals resolved the contradiction inherent in their life experiences and worldviews. Indeed, Dayan was not alone. Transfer was supported, for similar reasons, by many in the military and political elite, and at their biding various plans were drawn up to encourage, peacefully or through force, Palestinian emigration. Although they kept hoping that a new war would permit them to solve this problem once and for all, they were not idle in the meantime. As late as October 1950, they were still transferring out of the state the populations of towns and villages that were too close to the border.[49]

But without war, with the Arab states uninterested in population exchange, and with a major international outcry over the forcible expulsions (an outcry they had feared would occur), the activists did not really have a solution to the problem of the Palestinians who remained within the borders of the Jewish state. Meanwhile, the status of these Palestinians remained undetermined, especially the internal refugees who were cut off from their former homes and lands. Alexander Dotan, an official at the Department for International Institutions at the Foreign Office and chairman of the advisory committee on the refugees, suggested a different way of eliminating the internal boundary, namely, to "integrate the Arabs in the state by opening the gates of assimilation before them." Unlike other measures, this would be a "final solution,"; that is, it would completely erase the internal boundary between Jews and Arabs and allow the state and the nation to overlap.[50]

There were several striking features to this suggestion. First, even though his preferred means of erasing the boundary were cultural and not coercive, Dotan justified his proposal by reference to security considerations. After touring the Palestinian villages under Israeli rule and being particularly impressed by the plight of the internal refugees, he warned that the present policy was turning the Palestinians into "a persecuted and exiled national minority that identifies with the Arab nation" and suggested assimilation as a way of combating this "security threat." As I noted earlier, the distinction between hard-liners concerned about security and liberals concerned about civil rights does not hold water. Additionally, Dotan supported the use of harsh means against those "who are not willing or are unable to adapt to the state" (i.e., those who would not assimilate). They should be "resolutely combated."[51]

Second, even though the end goal of his proposal would have meant that expertise in Arab affairs was no longer needed, at least not within the state, Dotan, like Dayan, needed to present himself as possessing such expertise to justify his proposal and convince others of its feasibility. Unlike Dayan, he did imitate not the Arabists but the academic orientalists. He learned literary Arabic and received basic academic orientalist training at the Hebrew University. He proclaimed that the historical record shows "that assimilation has always been, from antiquity till now, a rather regular process in the Middle East," drawing on the image of the Orient as carnival.[52] At the Foreign Office, Dotan was employed in various jobs relating to *hasbara* in Arab affairs, and he prepared propaganda pamphlets based on clippings from the Arab press. His case, therefore, confirms the pattern I identified earlier: Actors whose position in the field of orientalist expertise was fairly subordinate and precarious, such as the activists (who were "second-rate Arabists") and the *hasbara* officials (who were "second-rate academic orientalists"), opted for solutions that eliminated the internal boundary and with it also the need for orientalist expertise, at least in the long run.

Dotan did not envision a long process of assimilation. For his proposal to be attractive to decision makers, the unity and normality of the state had to be achieved in short order. Note that Dotan spoke about assimilation and not conversion. This was no scheme to convert the Palestinians to Judaism. In fact, he said very little about religion, probably because this was, of course, the Achilles' heal of his program: Although he depicted the elimination of the internal boundary as bringing the *Palestinians* into the state, in reality it meant that *both* Jews and Palestinians had to be assimilated – both had to be dragged kicking and screaming into secular, liberal modernity. This was to be a total cultural revolution, since Dotan seemed to be aiming at a civil Hebrew nation where religion was not state business but a matter of personal choice. In fact, Dotan considered the task of assimilating the Palestinians to be no different from the task of absorbing the Jewish immigrants from Arab countries and to require the same means, a concentrated dose of *hasbara*, in the old sense of the term. To achieve assimilation, he explained, would require

a general assault on the Arab minority both by the state and by the secular Jewish public in the country . . . [and] the creation of a secular Jewish cultural mission. The mission's role would be to act as the messenger of the Jewish people and Israeli progress in the Arab village. . . . Special seminars in this mission will train Jewish instructors to work in the Arab villages just as this is done in the immigrant camps [*ma'abarot*] and the new settlements and in the missions to the Indian villages in Mexico. . . . Such a mission, which would dwell in the village, which would occupy itself with teaching Hebrew in the school and coaching the youth, with agricultural instruction, with social and medical assistance and social guidance, which would act as a natural mediator between the village and the authorities and the Hebrew public, and which would know all that takes place in the village and its vicinity from the security point of view – such a mission could effectively influence all village affairs and completely transform it within a few years.[53]

In order to eliminate the internal boundaries between Jews and Arabs, therefore, Dotan needed to fuzzify the boundaries between the state and society. He cautioned that no party political activity would be permitted in the missions, but he clearly did not envision them as purely state institutions. The Palestinians could not be commanded to assimilate, they had to be persuaded and indoctrinated by individuals who indeed saw this as their "mission." The "secular Jewish public," for its part, could not be commanded to undertake such a task. They had to perceive it, of their own free will, as their duty, that supreme Zionist paradox of "the duty of volunteering" (*ha-hova she-bahitnadvut*). To achieve assimilation, therefore, the power of the state had to be merged, cross-bred, with the pastoral power of the Zionist church.[54]

Dotan's proposal caused much outrage and ridicule among the experts. Even one of his colleagues at the Foreign Office, Shimoni, thought that it was a "shocking document" and that the idea of the missions seemed hopelessly impractical. This is also what Josh Palmon, the adviser on Arab affairs to the prime minister, thought: "The idea to send Jewish missionaries to the Arab villages – a government cannot do something like this, and such private organizations do not exist."[55] But this was only a half-truth. There *was*, in fact, such a "private" organization that had representatives in each Palestinian village and town; an organization with a thoroughly Zionist, modernist, secular outlook; an organization that provided ideological guidance and cultural instruction (e.g., *hasbara*) and whose members, while paid, did have the sense of performing "the duty of volunteering." Moreover, as the adviser on Arab affairs to the prime minister and thus in charge of coordinating the activities of all the different agencies dealing with the Palestinian minority, Palmon met regularly with the representatives of this organization and entrusted them with important tasks. This organization was the General Federation of Labor, the Histadrut.

Ostensibly an association of trade unions, in many respects an arm of the dominant political party, the Histadrut was always something more than either. It was called "a state within a state," but it is better characterized as existing within the volume of the boundary between the state and society (and party). During British rule, the Histadrut worked hard to separate the Jewish and Palestinian economic sectors, and after the formation of the state, it changed course and acted as an auxiliary arm of the state to reintegrate the Palestinians within the Jewish economy, though in a subordinate status. The leaders of the Arab Worker Department of the Histadrut met regularly with the adviser on Arab affairs and with the military governors to coordinate their policies. Already in 1949, they together drafted an action plan to integrate the Jewish and Palestinian economies, which the Histadrut was to execute on behalf of the state. The employees of the Arab Worker Department of the Histadrut, who were recruited from among the political activists mentioned in Chapter 3 and increasingly included Jews who emigrated from Arab countries, would probably have not condoned Dotan's proposal, but in a sense his vision was an extreme logical extrapolation of what they did in practice.

First of all, as Dotan did, the action plan justified the economic integration of the Palestinians as promoting security. It was meant to "assist the struggle against those elements in the Arab public who oppose, either in principle or in action, the state of Israel, its security and development." For these reasons, the Arab Worker Department pushed the Histadrut to accept Palestinian workers as full members, and in 1953 some of its employees resigned in protest because their proposal was not accepted, and the Palestinians were only made members of specific trade unions (full membership was extended in 1959). The Palestinian laborer was thus the first candidate to become part of the secular, Hebrew, assimilated nation envisioned by Dotan. Ever since, he has also haunted the Israeli imagination as the quintessential Israeli-Arab hybrid, the figure of the Palestinian-passing-as-Jew. Recall how in A. B. Yehoshua's novel *The Lover*, Naim, an adolescent Palestinian boy working for an Israeli mechanic, decides to stroll down the main street of Jewish Haifa. To his surprise, but also to his great satisfaction, he discovers that nobody can tell that he is not Jewish.[56]

More importantly, the premise of the action plan was that modernization and development would turn the Palestinians into loyal and assimilated citizens. This was the bargain that the Arab experts of the Histadrut offered to the state elites: all economic, social, and even cultural matters relating to the Palestinian minority would come under their jurisdiction, as the state would subcontract to the Histadrut the implementation of economic and social policy. It is important to understand that the activities of the Histadrut were by no means limited to Palestinian workers but encompassed the whole economic, social, and cultural life of the minority. Already the action plan noted that the chief arena for the Histadrut's work would be the villages. Throughout 1950, the employees of the department visited all Palestinian villages under Israeli rule and together with local representatives prepared detailed reports that covered all social groups in the village, including employers and landowners, and all aspects of village life, including fertility and mortality rates, the water supply, the mosque and the cemetery, health, education, and so on. On the basis of these reports, and in coordination with the development authority at the Prime Minister's Office, the Histadrut embarked on a campaign to develop the Arab sector and promote producer and consumer cooperatives. The Histadrut also developed an extensive network of cultural activities in the villages, such as movies, clubs, sports, lectures, and libraries, seeking to promote "understanding and friendship" between Palestinian and Jewish youths, women, workers, and so on (i.e., *hasbara*). In return for this extensive jurisdiction, the Histadrut and its experts would manage for the state the fuzzy and ambiguous internal boundary, which the Palestinians were slowly, in single file as through a metal detector gate, encouraged to cross. Put differently, the integration of the Palestinians as citizens was granted, yet suspended until some future point in their "development," when the Histadrut and its experts would confirm that the Palestinians had become "modern." The Histadrut and its experts would serve as an "accelerating, guiding, involving, defending and cultivating factor [in the process of integration] . . . while protecting it from possible deviations." They would instill the proper attitudes, guide those inclined to develop, and report the deviants; they would serve as mediators between the Palestinians and the institutions of the state and the market. As one historian said, "The Histadrut saw itself in these years as representing the Arab public, and as the most appropriate body to organize it." This was by no means merely a cynical plot to control and manipulate the Palestinians. The experts at the Arab Worker Department, especially at its economic desk, were leftists who believed that their mission was to integrate the Palestinians into the state and create equality between Jews and Arabs. This is why some of them resigned in 1953 when the Histadrut declined to accept the Palestinians as members.[57]

Nonetheless, the experts of the Histadrut worked hand in hand with the military government and with the Office of the Adviser on Arab Affairs to the Prime Minister. Whenever "security" was at issue, they could be counted on to rally to the cause and reinforce the internal boundaries. In the summer of 1952, for example, there was an emergency meeting of the Arab affairs experts of Mapai and the Histadrut. There was a revolution in Egypt, and they were worried about "possible nationalist fervor among the Palestinians." They recommended expediting and reinforcing Jewish settlement of the Galilee, where most Palestinians were concentrated. Jewish settlements should be planted as a wedge between Palestinian villages as well as around Nazareth so as to prevent any Palestinian claims based on territorial contiguity and to rule out all talk of separating the Galilee from Israel. At the same time, they also recommended that Jews not be settled inside Palestinian villages and towns, only alongside them, to avoid friction. "In retrospect," wrote one of the participants,

this meeting of the Arabists of Mapai and the Histadrut seems to me to have been their finest hour. Despite our close ties to the Arab population, and despite our daily efforts to create a positive atmosphere of understanding and co-existence between Arabs and Jews in Israel, we understood the need to reinforce Jewish settlement in the Galilee, and in this way to shatter the false hopes of the extremists among Israeli Arabs that the Galilee would some day be cut off from the state of Israel.[58]

Although he worked with the Histadrut and coordinated its activities with those of the other agencies dealing with Palestinian affairs, Palmon, the adviser to the prime minister, did not share its vision of integration, even suspended until some time in the future. In an interview many years later, he gave the following explanation:

I was against integrating the Arabs into the life of the state. . . . This country is built as a mosaic of communities. Each community constitutes one stone in the mosaic, and its borders are delineated. You blur the boundaries between the stones, and you have blurred the whole picture. This is not good. It is better to have separate development.

The separation prevented the Arabs from integrating in Israeli democracy, but they did not have democracy before either. They never had it: they did not miss it.[59]

Already during the war, many Arabists had moved to positions in the military government, created in August 1948 to deal with the occupied Palestinian population. It was a natural transition to switch from being an adviser to brigade commanders to handling the affairs of the people in the area conquered by a brigade. Palmon, at the Foreign Office, continued to advise the prime minister on the matter of the Palestinians and was the inspiration behind the decision, in 1949, to dismantle the Ministry for Minority Affairs and instead create Arab affairs departments in all the relevant government ministries. Palmon himself was appointed to the new position of special adviser on Arab affairs. Reporting directly to the prime minister, he was entrusted with coordinating the policies of these departments as well as the other agencies dealing with matters pertaining to the Palestinian population: the GSS and the military government, where many rank-and-file Arabists now worked; the police; the Histadrut; the custodian of absentee property; the JNF, and so on. The new structure imitated British colonial practice.

The establishment of the position of adviser on Arab affairs was the most important achievement of the Arabists in their struggle to concentrate authority over the Palestinian minority in their hands. While the executive authority of the adviser's position was rather ill defined, the adviser and his assistants enjoyed a great deal of power and influence, absent from the positions held by Arabists during the war. The adviser, besides reporting to the prime minister, was his sole representative in his role as chairman of the Central Committee for Arab Affairs. In reality, this made for a rather loose coordination, and Palmon later unsuccessfully attempted to centralize the structure, but this was not the main significance of the role played by the Arabists.[60]

Throughout its existence, the military government, along with the Arabists has been consistently criticized for playing a politically partisan role, acting as vote getter for Mapai, the dominant party. Many years later, Palmon replied to the critics by asserting that "minority policy was not meant to bring votes for Mapai but for Ben-Gurion's rule. At least this is how I perceived it at the time." An astonishing statement, as Ben-Gurion was Mapai's leader, but it contains an important grain of truth. In accordance with the practices they had developed since the 1940s and with the claims they began making during the war, the Arabists saw themselves as experts in *governing* the rural Palestinian population. This was the essence of the bargain they offered to the state elites: The Arabists would receive jurisdiction over all aspects of policy with respect to the Palestinian minority, and in return they would deploy an art of government that would gradually dispense with the more coercive aspects of military rule – Palmon was advocating their suspension already in 1952 – and yet would maintain the internal boundary intact and prevent any movement across it.

Arabists not only would provide the rhetoric (e.g., the claim that the Palestinians "don't really miss democracy") but more importantly would organize a system of segregation, control, and co-optation to secure the consent of the ruled on the basis of a knowledge of their mentality. Hence the reference to Ben-Gurion's rule: Good government was not democratic but paternalist. It vested authority in a single strong father figure – first, the military governor, then Palmon himself, and finally the supreme governor, Ben-Gurion – who would act with justice and prudence, equitably dispensing punishment and reward where they were due: "We must treat this minority in an egalitarian way, as long as this does not seriously injure the security of the state and Jewish settlement. If the Arabs will use the chance given to them and adopt the formula for their lives as a minority in Israel, they would be better off and so would we."[61]

At the same time that they would concentrate authority and vest it in a single person, the Arabists would organize the segmentation of the population, first along ethnic and denominational lines – Druze, Christians, Circassians, Bedouins, and so on – and then also within each village along *hamula* lines, as they had learned to do during the 1940s. In this way, they would create a vertical relationship between each *hamula* and the governor rather than horizontal ones among *hamulas*. And anybody daring to oppose the Arabists would have to reckon with their considerable networks of informers and collaborators in the villages as well as with the Arab departments of the various ministries, which were capable of firing and blacklisting any Palestinian official, intellectual, or public worker with the laconic justification of "security considerations." Justice, consistency in the application of commands, divide and conquer, a distinction between "good" and "bad" Arabs, the creation of economic dependency, intimidation when necessary – these were the ingredients of good government.

Good government meant that the Palestinians were neither integrated nor expelled. Although not averse to the possibility of population exchange in the future, the Arabists agreed with the Foreign Office that this could only be done in the framework of peace agreements with the Arab states. Meanwhile, "the problem of the Arab minority is a problem without solution." The Arabists did not pretend to solve the problem but purported to act as "custodians" over the "minority" population, with the jurisdiction to determine, in each specific case, the balance between security considerations and a liberal approach. Equity and justice were to be administered "as much as was feasible, up to some ill-defined 'red line' – ill-defined because it was liable to be drawn as the result of specific developments and events that could not be foreseen."[62]

The Arabists saved their most scathing remarks for Dotan's assimilation proposal. This was an "impossible and unrealistic magic bullet." The Palestinians simply would not be interested, at least not in a genuine way. "We are not a big and strong enough attracting force to cause voluntary assimilation . . . and I do not believe in coerced assimilation," Palmon said. Moreover, as experts in handling the no-man's-land between Jews and Arabs, the Arabists warned, in terms reminiscent of the critique of the *mista'ravim*, of the dangers it held for those who would enter it and act within it. "The Jewish missionaries to the Arab villages," Palmon said, "will either be mocked in the Arab village, or they will become similar to Arabs [*Yista'arvu*], and become involved in *hamula* conflict [*fasad*], smuggling, etc." The Arabists implied that this had already happened to Dotan himself, who was misled by the villagers and "became a victim of a double conflict [*fasad*] – among the residents themselves, and between them and the various officials on the ground – a conflict which is, probably, an inevitable part of reality in the Arab landscape."[63] In short, the twilight zone between Jews and Arabs was dangerous, and those who were not familiar with it could easily fall to the other side without even noticing it. Arabist expertise, on the other hand, protected its possessors from such dangers. They were the only ones capable of safely residing within the no-man's-land and supervising it.

With respect to the Histadrut's more modest ideal of integration, the Arabists were less categorical. They looked favorably on the work that the Histadrut's activists were doing in the villages, especially because it assisted in combating the growing influence of the communists. But they insisted that control over the internal boundaries remain strict and be kept in their hands. For example, when the Histadrut began registering Palestinians as members of its trade unions, the military government insisted that registration take place in the villages and would not issue permits for the villagers to journey to the Histadrut's offices in the (Jewish) cities. This considerably slowed the registration drive, to the great consternation of Histadrut officials.[64]

The Arabists thus seemed to offer the state the best deal. They would do both things at once: preserve the internal boundaries and secure the consent of those shut out on the other side. The price to be paid, however, was a substantial fuzzification of the state, since the internal boundary between Jews and Arabs, which was impenetrable from one side, was highly permeable from the other. The area on the other side of the internal boundary, administered by the military government, became the playground of all sorts of social and political actors, and the boundary between the state and society, which was none too stable within the Jewish sector, completely disintegrated on the other side. Or at least so it seemed to contemporaries.

In the collective imagination, the internal boundary did not remain stable, it thickened and became a no-man's-land where all was permitted and the unthinkable happened: "Government officials, who reside within the perimeter of Arab villages in order to perform their official roles impartially and without connection to their personal views – use their position for purely party political action. Officials of the Labor Ministry – members of Mapam – help the communists; 'military governors' – members of Mapai – create their own institutions, and the emissaries of the Ministry of Religious Affairs encourage the religious circles and the church. The Minister of Minority Affairs himself has nothing left to do but to sip coffee with a few notables."[65] Inevitably, as we shall see in Chapter 5, the Arabists, who were already occupying a somewhat ambiguous position between Jews and Arabs, were swept up in this projection, enveloped within the boundary they were meant to supervise, as they predicted would happen to Dotan's emissaries. They became identified with the no-man's-land and its dangers. As if by producing the effect of the state, they were infected with its fuzziness.

Finally, there was also the option of autonomy. Much has been made of the conflict between the "moderate" minister of minority affairs, Bekhor Shitrit, who championed autonomy, and the "hard-liner" Palmon, who insisted on security and control. In reality, their positions were not all that far apart. Bekhor Shitrit was not altogether the dove he is depicted as. The autonomy he suggested was not political autonomy but quite limited cultural and religious autonomy. Unlike Palmon, who was not exactly the hawk he is purported to be, Bekhor Shitrit never suggested something as radical as abolishing the Arab departments of the various ministries.[66] I would argue that the real distinction between them, and between the options of autonomy and control, was not between a security-minded approach and a liberal one but between two different claims to expertise and two different methods of managing the internal boundary and producing the effect of the state.

There were actually two groups who championed some sort of limited autonomy. One consisted of Shitrit and many of the employees of his ministry, who were notables, mostly of Sephardi extraction. They claimed that because they were orientals and natives of Palestine themselves, they should be entrusted with managing relations with the Palestinians. As one of them stated, "It is unthinkable that people who have not yet acclimated themselves to the environment and do not yet understand the essence of the problem, will try to solve this question." Their position was that the newly arrived Ashkenazi Jews did not possess the skills or the experience to deal with such a delicate question as rule over an Arab minority. Shitrit was the one who proposed that a Ministry of Minority Affairs be created and that he be entrusted with leading it. He "conceived of the Ministry as a place where the *Sephardi* population would realize its comparative advantage: knowledge of

Arabic and solid working relations with the Arabs in the private sector and in formerly-British controlled institutions such as the police." The Sephardi experts would "advise the other ministries about Arab affairs, observe how the actions of these ministries affect the Arabs or other minorities, and act as a go-between where necessary."[67]

Shitrit envisioned the Sephardi experts playing a role of mediation and representation. The ministry's role would be to "rehabilitate and promote the relations with the minorities." The Sephardi experts would serve as "a fitting link between the Arab population and the newly formed institutions of the Jewish state." They would instruct the minorities about their rights and responsibilities in a democratic state, convey the will of the government, and serve as the "mouthpiece" of the minorities. Moreover, they would also mediate between the minorities and the Jewish majority. One of their tasks would be to educate Jews, especially the newly arrived immigrants from Europe, that Arabs deserve to be seen in a positive light. In short, they were to use their experience to establish the same sort of respectful yet guarded coexistence that they had enjoyed as notables, and they were to act as the paternalist patrons and protectors of the minorities, which they always thought of in the plural, as in Palmon's "mosaic of communities."[68]

The second group envisioning some form of autonomy were academic orientalists, inside and outside the government. The director of the Department for Muslim Affairs at the Ministry of Religious Affairs, for example, was Professor Hayyim Ze'ev Hirshberg, an expert on the history of Jews in Muslim countries. Although he clashed with Shitrit over who should have control of the Muslim *waqf* funds, he agreed with him that some limited form of religious and cultural autonomy should be extended to the minorities. (*Waqf* is a religious endowment, typically landed property willed by individuals to a mosque or Muslim religious institution, and the income from the endowment is to be used solely for the needs of the institution.) Similar views were espoused by Yehouda Leib Benor, assistant general director of the Ministry of Education, an Egyptian Jew educated in London, and by Goitein at the Hebrew University. Their broad academic knowledge of the intricacies of Islam and Arab culture, they argued, made them much more suitable than the uneducated Arabists, or even the notables, to formulate the state's policy with respect to cultural and religious affairs. Hirshberg stressed this point in an internal government memorandum in which he insinuated that Palmon, the adviser to the prime minister, could not read literary Arabic, did not understand the intricacies of Islamic law, and therefore failed to understand or respond correctly to petitions by Muslim judges (*kadis*). Moreover, the European-trained academics presented themselves as better equipped than the Arabists "to teach a lesson to the community about the administration of government according to Western standards – that is to say, education for independence and responsibility."[69]

The autonomy they envisioned was quite limited: Muslim communal autonomy in the selection of local *kadis*, local education committees at the villages, and so on. The most far-reaching proposal was Shitrit's suggestion to have general elections for a supreme *kadi* who would serve as a court of final appeal for the other *kadis* and to give local religious committees control of the *waqf* funds. All such measures were justified in a similar way: The Palestinians ("Arabs" was the word typically used) were not one national group but a mosaic of various religious, cultural, and ethnic groups. They were "minorities," in the plural. A good minority policy should prevent their crystallization into one group, which would be dominated by the Muslims and by Arab nationalist sentiment. What better way to maintain the mosaic than to exploit the already existing religious and cultural fissures between the groups and their natural inclination toward denominational self-organization? Giving them limited autonomy would not be injurious to security. The comparative record of secular or non-Muslim states such as Turkey and Bosnia-Herzegovina (a province in the Austro-Hungarian Empire) showed that it was possible to grant cultural and religious autonomy to Muslims without encouraging political dissent. Treating all of these groups as equally dangerous was foolish and likely to be a self-fulfilling prophecy. Suppression was just as dangerous as autonomy, but the latter had the advantage of "interesting [the minority] in the state in which it lives by giving it full opportunity for progress."

On the other hand, the advocates of limited autonomy cautioned that the policy of assimilation was impossible owing to the deeply religious nature of both Jewish and non-Jewish populations (Hirshberg, Benor, and Goitein were observant Jews). To these considerations, one must add that Israel's minorities policy would have a direct effect on the treatment of Jews living in Arab countries – to whose study Hirshberg and Goitein dedicated their lifework and whom the Sephardi leadership saw as its natural wards. If the Palestinians were mistreated, the Jews would suffer. An enlightened policy that made "the non-Jewish citizens partners in our political, social and economic life, without minting them into one minority bloc, and without granting broad autonomous rights, except in matters of religion and culture," would set a positive example to the Arab states about how to treat the Jews.[70]

Finally, their vision of autonomy held potential appeal to state elites because the academic experts and the Sephardi notables promised that they would be able to align themselves with and foster the modernizers among the minorities and encourage them to create change from within, thus permitting the state to remain formally aloof from the communities, which would handle their own affairs. Hirshberg spoke about the modernization of the *shari'a* (Islamic law) from within, and Benor boasted of his own influence on the modernization of Palestinian education under the British Mandate. The shock of 1948 and the isolation from other Arab states had rendered the minorities, especially those in the Arab villages, into "raw material, from which it is possible to form different shapes." In this context, the best strategy would be to "let the powers of development and assimilation have their influences – and several negative phenomena will stop by themselves."[71]

It is important to recognize that although the Sephardi claim was based on longstanding social ties between Jewish and Palestinian notables, and although Shitrit enjoyed personal popularity among the Palestinian population, his intention in creating the Ministry of Minority Affairs was to centralize these ties and affections and vest them in one, clearly delimited government authority. He was a stickler for the rule of law. The same was certainly true for the academic orientalists. The main point of the autonomy proposal was indeed to prevent any fuzzification of the boundaries between state and society – to avoid, for example, a situation in which the state would be perceived as playing the role of a religious authority or as taking sides in religious and cultural disputes – so that the state would appear before the eyes of the minorities as a separate and self-contained entity, an attractive emblem of modernity and rationality. Additionally, the academics and the notables pointed to their credentials and knowledge in making the case that this could be done without damaging or fuzzifying the internal boundaries between Jews and Arabs: Their expertise would permit them to act on the minorities from a distance and gently cultivate and encourage the positive tendencies that would develop spontaneously among the minorities themselves.

Some forms of local religious autonomy were indeed made into law, especially in matters of marriage and divorce (the reasons for that, however, may well have had to do with internal Jewish politics, especially the wish to avoid creating an institution of civil marriage). On the whole, though, the notables and the academic orientalists were defeated by the Arabists, or they were co-opted, as happened also to the Histadrut's activists. The military government remained intact. The *waqf* funds were appropriated by the custodian of absentee property, and the state used the money for its own purposes. *Kadi* appointment legislation was held up till 1961, and even later the process was tightly controlled by the Adviser's Office. Arab education was tightly controlled by the GSS and the Arab Department of the Education Ministry, which dictated the curriculum and fired teachers or principals whom they considered disloyal to the state. The Histadrut's efforts to "modernize" the villages had to take a backseat to the Arabists' system of encouraging internal factional conflicts. As I have tried to show here, the Arabists' victory was due not only to their emphasis on "security" considerations but also to the fact that their expertise was congenial to the dominant technology of state building in this period. Their proposal for how to supervise the internal boundary between Jews and Arabs was the one that offered the most latitude for practices that fuzzified the boundary between state and society, exactly what the notables and the academic orientalists sought to curb.

What was the significance of the Arabists' victory? First, as I explained earlier, it reinforced the emerging division of labor and the rearrangement of jurisdictions, according to which knowledge about the Arabs outside the state (i.e., "intelligence") was separate from knowledge about the Arabs inside the state (i.e., "government"). Second, the Sephardi leadership emerged as the main loser from this division of labor. Just as Arabist expertise did not make a strong distinction between what was inside the state and what was outside it, so Sephardi expertise (and to a large extent also the expertise of the academic orientalists) did not make a strong distinction between the knowledge necessary to manage and integrate the Palestinian minority and the knowledge necessary to absorb Jewish immigrants from Arab countries. Both were relatively heterogeneous "oriental" populations whose needs, or the religious and cultural differences among them, were not familiar to the Ashkenazi leadership. Both needed somebody who could explain to them their rights and duties in a familiar language, represent them in their dealings with the government, and act as their patron. As we shall see, the defeat of the Sephardi leadership in the struggle over the management of the new immigrants from Arab countries meant that the cognitive territory of the orient was sliced once more: A new and hermetic division was drawn between the jurisdiction of knowledge necessary to govern the Arabs and the jurisdiction of knowledge necessary to absorb the Jews from Arab countries.

The Struggle over the Absorption of the Arab Jews

I will not deal fully here with the manifold struggles that took place in these years over the absorption and management of the immigrants from Arab countries. Much of what transpired, especially the party political struggle, is not directly relevant to my purpose in writing this book. I will concentrate, therefore, on only a few aspects of this complex topic, those that are pertinent to my main interest, namely, how expert jurisdiction was reapportioned in these years.

The first point I would like to highlight is that the immigrants were constructed as Jewish–Arab hybrids. Here is a typical example: On November 3, 1955, in a speech to the parliament, the Prime Minister Ben-Gurion argued that IDF retaliatory strikes across the border were necessary because in their absence the "injured border settlers" themselves would take the law into their hands and carry out "revenge attacks across the border." He went on to say, "Thousands of these settlers come from the East, where the people are educated in the *Kom* – the custom of revenge through 'an eye for an eye' – and revenge attacks by them could turn into a wild spree and bloodbath among innocent civilians on both sides of the border."[72]

Why do I say that these claims contributed to the construction of the immigrants as hybrids? First, because they were manifestly false. No immigrant settler had ever crossed the border on a revenge attack. We know, and Ben-Gurion knew, that the worst bloodbaths were perpetrated by "special" army units and that the handful of vigilantes who crossed the border were either rogue army officers, typically native born, or veterans of the extreme right-wing underground organization Lehi. Ben-Gurion was being duplicitous, as he had been in the past, in order to absolve the state of responsibility for past and future atrocities.[73]

Moreover, the idea that the new immigrants from Arab countries shared the culture of Palestinian peasants was also wrong. Hardly any of them were peasants in their countries of origin. Most were urbanites – merchants, artisans, shopkeepers, and workers – and many were Western-oriented. There was little in common between, say, Iraqi merchants from Baghdad and Palestinian peasants.[74] But the unnecessary embellishment, the reference to the *kom*, taken from the fable book of Orientalism, is telling. Ben-Gurion was depicting the new immigrants as too close to the Arabs, as straddling the cultural boundary between Jews and Arabs, and through a leap of analogical reasoning befitting a mythmaker he deduced that they would also violate the physical borders of the state. In essence, he constructed them as Arab-Jews, an ambiguous hybrid challenging the state's integrity and character.

Another reason I say that the immigrants were constructed as Arab-Jews is to avoid being misunderstood as claiming that there was really such a single group, *mizrahi* Jews, and that they were really hybrid Arab-Jews. There are indeed some among the critics of Zionism who hold this view. Ella Shohat argues, for example, that Middle Eastern and North African Jews shared the culture of their Arab neighbors and that they identified themselves as an integral part of an Arab civilization. For this reason, she claims, they were perceived as threatening by state elites and the Ashkenazi public, and for this reason they suffered discrimination. She adds that the category of *edot ha-mizrah* (oriental ethnicities) was invented in an attempt to deny and censor the Arab nature of the new immigrants. Moreover, this is also why the new immigrants were sent to settle in the periphery of the country, close to the external and internal borders, in a sort of divide-and-conquer policy meant to create enmity and friction between them and the Palestinians.[75]

I think what happened was much more complex than suggested by this account. First of all, the category of *mizrahi* Jews was too eclectic and too heterogeneous – as we saw, it was put together as a matter of expediency, for sheer numerical reasons – for someone to summarize what was common to it using such a simplistic formula as "Arabness." Persian Jews, Indian Jews, Sephardi Jews from Greece and Turkey, none of them could be considered Arab, yet they were all part of the initial category.

Second, even among the Jews residing in Arab countries, there were many who did not identify themselves as part of some purported common Arab culture but defined themselves in opposition to Arab culture. Not unlike many contemporary Arab intellectuals, they were Westernizers and identified with the West.[76]

Third, as I argued in the previous chapter, rather than being a form of self-designation, a means used by the Jews of Middle Eastern and North African countries to identify themselves, the category of hybrid Arab-Jew reflected how they were *perceived* by the Zionist emissaries and officials who met them. Their being perceived in this manner, however, stemmed from the external point of view of the emissaries (for members of Iraqi society, for example, Iraqi Jews were not "Arab-Jews," they were "Jews" plain and simple).[77]

It follows that I disagree with Shohat on another count. I do not think that Zionism denied and censored the Arab origins and culture of the immigrants and that this is the significance of the category of *mizrahi* Jews.[78] Given that the hybridity of the immigrants was constructed, the only point of such denunciation is to garner for the critics the prestige of denunciation, to turn them into representatives of a silenced and repressed group. The relationship between Zionism and *mizrahi* Jews was far more complex. Zionism invented the category of *mizrahi* Jews as hybrid Arab-Jews. Unlike the Sephardi hybrid, for whom hybridity was a form of self-understanding and self-presentation, the hybridity of *mizrahi* Jews was imposed on them. By the same token, Zionism marked the *mizrahi* hybrid from the very beginning as an object for a discourse of purification, a discourse that would separate within the new immigrants what was essentially Arab and what was essentially Jewish. Not to "deny" their Arab nature, mind you, but on the contrary, to isolate it, highlight it, study it, and use it over and over again in order to give form to the paradox of the boundary and to make sense of all the inevitable contradictions of the Zionist project – all the enumerable times when its strict separations threatened to dissolve into the twilight of the no-man's-land. Denial was just one strategy within this discursive complex and not necessarily the most important one.

As Yehouda Shenhav has shown, ever since Zionist leaders identified Middle Eastern Jews as the object of a plan for massive immigration, they displayed a highly ambivalent attitude toward them. On the one hand, the immigrants were Jews, our own, they were to be liberated, and in them lay the hope of building a Jewish state. On the other hand, they were no different from the Arabs, alien, and their incorporation threatened to distort the very character of the Zionist project. This is why the religiosity of Middle Eastern Jews was highlighted and problematized. It became their entry ticket into the Zionist mainstream, the only way for them to prove that they were "really Jews." By the same token, however, the religiosity of Middle Eastern Jews also marked them as inferior and backward (i.e., the entry ticket was issued "on notice," upon the condition that they modernize).[79] This ambivalence was accentuated when the new immigrants began arriving in their thousands after the formation of the state. One can find Zionist leaders characterizing the immigrants as "primitives," "ignorant," "lacking any Jewish roots," "violent," and "lazy" and worrying aloud about the "oriental danger," about the resulting deterioration in the "overall cultural level of the state." But at the same time, one can also find them waxing poetic about the "ancient Hebrew beauty" and the "fierce love for the holy country" of the Yemenites, or about the "rich fountains of pioneering spirit, of heroism and productivity," that the Jews of North Africa or Persia or Egypt harbor.[80]

Beyond the ambivalence, there was also real confusion about who exactly belonged to this category of *mizrahi* Jews. For example, it is possible to interpret the Jewish Agency's decision to form a department for "Jews of the Middle East," as excluding from this category Sephardi Jews and perhaps the Jews of North Africa, Central Asia, and India as well. Mapai, on the other hand, had a more inclusive department for "oriental ethnicities" (*edoth ha-mizrah*), but its leaders agonized over whether the Sephardi Bulgarian and Greek Jews should be included under its mandate. Mapam, a left-of-center party, apparently felt that other distinctions should be emphasized, and it formed a department for "oriental ethnicities and Yemenites." Throughout the whole period from 1942 to 1953, there was an intense debate about the differences between these various groups, about which ones presented more fitting "human material" for pioneering settlement, and all sorts of speculations about their racial makeup, ancient origins, and level of civilization, but at the same time there was a strong sense that the groups belonged together because they all were different from the Ashkenazi and European Jews and thus posed different problems.[81]

We should not dismiss these debates about classification as an insignificant historical curiosity. At stake in the question of classification, I would argue, as indeed in the whole problem posed by the hybrid nature of the new immigrants, was again the matter of the internal boundary between state and society. As one of the ministers in the first government confessed, he was "afraid to speak about the matter of oriental ethnicities . . . since soon, with the increasing immigration, we will have to speak about Ashkenazi ethnicities" (*Ha-edoth Ha-Ashkenaziot*).[82] If the various immigrants were being lumped together as *mizrahi*, and treated differently from the European immigrants (as the one million plan mandated), wouldn't it seem that the state was nothing but the domination of one group over another? But if they were not lumped together, how could an effective policy of absorption be formulated? How would it be possible to draw the boundary between state and society, to separate the state from the European, Ashkenazi group, without thereby undermining the "cultural level" of society?

As they could never arrive at a single, definite classification of the new immigrants, the quandary haunted decision makers throughout this period, primarily because in actuality there were all sorts of local decisions and unplanned processes that marked the new immigrants as different and initiated a process of ethnicization that led, in later years, to the crystallization of the *mizrahi* category. In particular, there was an ongoing process of spatial segregation, as the new immigrants from Arab countries were sent to settle the border zone or were to be found squatting next to the Arab ghettos in the mixed cities. One can find, in the files of the Jewish Agency and the protocols of cabinet meetings from this time, all sorts of justifications given by decision makers explaining why certain groups, for example, Kurdish Jews, were to be sent to settle the border zone – because they were hard working and brave fighters. Even so, I think that spatial segregation was less the result of an overall policy coordinated from above and more a reflection of the differential power of various groups to resist or subvert state plans. In other words, spatial segregation reflected the unfortunate fact that the state was not quite separate from the "Ashkenazi ethnicities."

Not only immigrants from Arab countries were sent to settle the border zone. Initially, at least, there were an equal number of European immigrants sent there. Over time, however, there were two complementary and mutually reinforcing processes that changed the picture. First, from the very beginning, many of the settlers of the border zone – among them large numbers of immigrants from Arab countries – resisted their forced settlement by deserting their towns and villages and migrating back to the cities of the coastal plain. Yet there were always some who were unable to resist, because they lacked connections to the state elites or their families were too big to be mobile. Both of these causes were more prevalent among the immigrants from Arab countries – the state elites were European born themselves, and many of the European immigrants, who were Holocaust survivors, arrived as singles. It was easier for the authorities to restrict the mobility of these weaker groups through a variety of coercive means: threatening that if they moved to the cities, they would be denied food stamps; confiscating their identification cards; assessing a fee for leaving; denying them permits for residence and employment in the cities; even setting up police roadblocks on the roads leading from the borders back to the coastal plain. These coercive tactics were not altogether different from the movement restrictions that the military government imposed on the Palestinians, their neighbors in the border zone. Additionally, the situation of those who were left behind worsened because the *kibbutzim* and *moshavim* in their vicinity, which were well connected to the state elites, appropriated most of the formerly Palestinian land that could be cultivated.[83]

Second, especially after 1953, as Aziza Khazzoom showed, there was a marked bias against Jews from Middle Eastern and especially North African countries, who were roughly 30 percent more likely to be sent to development towns.[84] Another way of looking at it is that educated "oriental" Jews had about the same chance of being sent to development towns as uneducated Ashkenazi Jews. One might speculate that by 1953 the processes of selective out-migration and marginalization noted above had already made it clear that the border zone, especially the development towns, were not the site of pioneer distinction they purported to be but a stigmatized periphery that was fast becoming identified as "oriental." Hence, the bias in assignment became pronounced, exactly at the time that the number of immigrants from Asian and African countries overtook the number of European immigrants.

In the mixed cities, the immigrants resisted the plans of the government and the Jewish Agency by squatting in abandoned Palestinian houses. Here, again, differential power and connections to state elites determined that the stronger groups occupied the best houses in the better parts of the city and were able to resist any attempts to remove them, whereas the weaker groups had to be satisfied with squatting in partly ruined houses in the least desirable parts of town, namely, next to the Palestinians. It was typically the case that after the cities were occupied by the IDF, the Palestinians who remained behind were forcibly concentrated in one place, a sort of Arab ghetto. Next to them now sprouted concentrations of impoverished Jewish families, typically immigrants from Arab countries. In Haifa, for example, the Palestinians were moved to the Wadi Nisnas neighborhood, and within a few months an immigrant slum, mainly inhabited by North African Jews, sprang up in the adjacent Wadi Salib neighborhood. Similar slums emerged in Jerusalem along the no-man's-land separating the Israeli and Jordanian halves of the city, as well as in Jaffa and Lod next to the Palestinian ghetto.

At the beginning of the chapter I emphasized that the attempt to purify the Israeli-Arab hybrid led directly to the creation of the *mizrahi*, or Arab-Jew hybrid, and the two remained intimately intertwined. The attempt to erect a strict internal boundary separating Jews and Arabs by means of forcible residential segregation ended up producing a "third space" in which the *mizrahi* category took shape and that was perceived by contemporaries as scandalous, as a sort of no-man's-land in which Jews and Arabs mixed and mingled. Thus were created those notorious places synonymous in Israeli collective consciousness with *mizrahi* identity and *mizrahi* protest: pockets of concentrated poverty associated with symbolic and physical proximity to the Palestinians on the margins of the internal and external borders, such as Wadi Salib, where antiestablishment "riots" erupted in 1959, and the Jerusalem border neighborhood of Musrara, whence emerged the Israeli "Black Panthers" movement. Put differently, it was not that the new immigrants were sent to the border (internal or external) *because* they were *mizrahi Jews*, or Arab-Jews, they *became mizrahi*, in the sense this term is used today, because they were sent to the no-man's-land along the external and internal boundaries and because, unlike stronger groups, they remained stuck there.[85]

The officials dealing with the absorption of immigrants knew a great deal about what was taking place along the internal and external boundaries, and their reports reflected a sense of dismay and failure. The files of the Department for Middle Eastern Jewry of the Jewish Agency are full of reports about visits to concentrations of poor immigrants from Arab countries. The officials expressed shock at the living conditions and viewed the proximity to Palestinian concentrations as a scandal, explicitly connecting this proximity to the deviant behaviors they observed – crime, prostitution, and child neglect. They described Lod's old city as a "lair of criminals," "a dangerous center for the spread of sexual diseases," "a cancerous tumor . . . spreading and shaking the body [of the city of Lod]," attracting all sorts of shady characters. In short, when the internal boundary between Jews and Arabs widened into a no-man's-land populated by the *mizrahi* hybrid, it was perceived as a source of pollution. Around it emerged a discourse of moral panic, which was sometimes clothed in a semiscientific jargon of public hygiene (and even "mental hygiene"). In this way, the no-man's-land and the hybrids residing in it were marked as in need of urgent purification. The officials also reported an endless litany of complaints by Middle Eastern Jews about discrimination: discrimination in the granting of permission to leave the absorption camp, discrimination in the allocation of housing, discrimination in the granting of approval for squatting, insensitivity toward their peculiar needs, and so on. They warned that "the inevitable result is: crystallization of prejudices and turning what was originally a suspicion of ethnic discrimination into unshakable certainty, and from this follows a deepening of the chasm between the ethnicities."[86]

The typical response of the absorption functionaries and the state elites to this growing sense of failure was equivalent to Dotan's suggestion to assimilate the Palestinians, and it suffered from similar problems. Their response was to reject the classification into groups altogether, to say, with Ben-Gurion, that "a Yemenite Jew is not Yemenite for us. He is a Jew; he is a human being like us. A Yemenite Jew is first of all a Jew, and we want to turn him as much as possible, as fast as possible, from a Yemenite to a Jew who forgets whence he came, just as I have forgotten that I am Polish." This formulation was not just a summary of the "melting pot" ideology, it also sought to rescue the state, to reconstitute the effect of the state, because it mandated that the only legitimate relations were between the state and individual citizens, that is, Jews who forgot whence they came. Just as it was for Dotan, however, this arrangement could work only on the condition that the individuals "adapt to Israeli reality, Israeli freedom, Israeli equality, Israeli heroism, Israeli society and culture."[87]

Herein lay the problem, the same as with Dotan's suggestion, because this magic word – "Israeli" – could neither undo the realities of ethnicization on the ground nor overcome the lack of agreement even among the absorption authorities on any of these issues. It was an empty word. This was demonstrated beyond doubt by the failed experiment of the "Supreme Committee on Culture," which Ben-Gurion and his cultural intelligentsia created in 1951, hoping it would provide authoritative definitions of what an "Israeli style of life" would mean, what values and norms should be imposed on the new immigrants, how the Hebrew language should be spoken, and so on. To their surprise, most of the distinguished members of the committee – intellectuals, professors, and representatives of various movements – completely rejected this task as impossible and artificial and as ignoring Jewish tradition and religion.[88]

Without a cultural and linguistic consensus, it was impossible to define a necessary and unequivocal linkage between the individual and the state, and the functionaries in charge of the absorption of immigrants were reduced to uttering imaginary formulas in which the "spirit of the state" pulled itself out of the marsh by its own hair and all by itself produced its own effect:

What would be the bridge upon which we could come to the Yemenites and they could cross over to us? Based on my intimate knowledge of these affairs, I say that this bridge is the allure of the state . . . only one language is agreeable to them and they understand it and this is the language of the state. . . . When I come before them . . . I come before them with the state on my lips. And then I do not feel any barriers between them and me. I say: the bridge of the state is the only bridge, infallible bridge, and it is capable of turning the Yemenites into citizens of the state.[89]

While the absorption of immigrants was typically managed and controlled by the functionaries of the Jewish Agency and contested fiercely among the political parties, the sense of failure and crisis created an opportunity for various groups of experts to intervene. They provided explanations for the failure to absorb the immigrants from Arab countries and asserted that their expertise could be used to amend the situation. They also addressed the crisis of the state and described how it would be possible to reconstitute its boundaries. One such group was composed of Sephardi notables and activists, assisted to some extent by academic orientalists. This was roughly the same group discussed earlier, who pushed for some forms of limited cultural and religious autonomy for the Palestinians.

Even before the formation of the state, the Sephardi leadership laid a claim to represent Jews residing in Arab countries who were being persecuted, to be their "mouthpiece, because we are closely tied to these brothers in family ties." At the time, the Zionist leadership encouraged them to represent these Jews. The Jewish Agency did not want to appear as protecting the status of Jews in other countries while demanding that they be permitted to immigrate to Palestine. Once the state was formed, the Sephardi elite continued its advocacy on behalf of Jews persecuted in Arab countries. They called on the authorities of the state to act immediately to bring these Jews to Israel, and they proposed various schemes of population exchange in which Palestinians would be traded for Jews. But they also began to criticize the absorption of these immigrants. They warned that "mistakes" were being made and, in particular, that the authorities were not fully aware of the differences between the various groups. For example, Iraqi Jews were a completely different "human material." They were "traditional" (i.e., religious). They were "deeply rooted in Iraq and their economic situation was good." They would make "great demands," and thus their absorption could not be handled as in the past. The absorption authorities must "understand their customs and ways of life, which are different from the customs and ways of life of the rest of the oriental ethnicities."[90]

This analysis was seconded by academic orientalists, who argued as well that in order to deal with "the problems of the ethnicities immigrating to Israel from the countries of the Muslim Orient . . . one must first understand the economic, social, political and cultural background of this vast and important area." They also granted to the Sephardim the same sort of middle position between East and West as in the prestate era, noting that they "stand between the two major sectors [of the Jewish public] . . . the one originating from Western countries and the other originating in oriental countries" and implying that they could mediate between the two.[91]

The Sephardi elite offered to mobilize the Sephardi public, "without any party political bias," to ease the burden of the absorption institutions and also to lead an effort, together with other oriental Jews, to facilitate the absorption of the immigrants: "Knowing their needs, their language, their customs and their manners – will make it much easier to integrate them among us and will dissolve the disagreements that lately have so aggravated the relations between the oriental immigrants and the rest of the public."[92]

The few employees of the Department for Middle Eastern Jewry who themselves were Sephardi or of Middle Eastern extraction were making similar recommendations. Time and again they called for an absorption regimen that was more modulated, less bureaucratic, and adapted to the needs and capabilities of each specific group (as distinguished by country of origin). Time and again they recommended that more aid workers and instructors be drafted from among the immigrants themselves so that each group would be educated by their own members – people of the same country of origin or at least of a similar cultural background. There was even some coordination between the officials and the Sephardi notables, as when the Sephardi leadership of Safed enlisted the help of Sephardi employees at the Department of Middle Eastern Jewry to support their bid to have North African immigrants sent to their city, because "the great Sephardi past of the city . . . [would] make it suitable for the absorption of oriental immigrants."[93]

The bargain that the Sephardi leadership was offering to the state elite, therefore, was rather simple, and it was similar to the offer they made with respect to the Israeli-Arab hybrid, since they understood the problem of the absorption of immigrants as akin to the problem of the Palestinian minority: They would be put in charge of absorbing the immigrants from Arab countries – or more precisely, their expertise would be recognized as the relevant expertise for dealing with the absorption of these immigrants – and they would thus gain real influence on the management of absorption. The similarity in their traditions and customs would allow them to attend to the specific needs of each group and thereby reduce tensions. Moreover, since they were acting as state officials, the state would no longer seem to be the domination of one group over another. Put differently, they presented their hybrid status and their middle position between East and West as an asset that the state could use, both in relation to the immigrants and in relation to the Palestinians. There was very little chance, however, that their offer would be taken. Control over absorption was fiercely contested among the various political parties, since it was perceived as a key to gaining the votes of the immigrants. A Sephardi political party ran in the first elections and joined the coalition government. The Sephardi notables were clearly making a bid to become recognized as the representatives and paternalistic protectors of the rest of the "oriental ethnicities," and therefore they were dangerous. The state might no longer be perceived as the control of one group by another, but it would become a bifurcated state, split between equally balanced Sephardi and Ashkenazi political estates.[94]

There was, on the other hand, another group of experts who were more successful than the Sephardi notables in gaining jurisdiction, not so much over the actual absorption of immigrants from Arab countries, which was highly politicized and contested, but over the types of knowledge deemed relevant to their absorption. These were sociologists and psychologists. They presented themselves as purely technical experts, without political ambitions, and thus did not threaten other political actors. At the same time, however, they offered a powerful discourse to purify the *mizrahi* hybrid and reconstitute the appearance of the state as an objective entity, separate from society and acting in its name. The purification inhered, first and foremost, in the disciplinary division of labor, since the absorption of the Arab-Jews was to be detached from the inclusive cognitive territory of the orient and become the sole jurisdiction of the social sciences, limiting the jurisdiction of orientalist expertise to Arabs per se. Moreover, the discourse of the social scientists purified the Arab-Jew hybrids because it presented the matter of their absorption as part of the general field of "social problems" and "modernization."

On August 23, 1949, the Department for Middle Eastern Jewry of the Jewish Agency hosted a meeting of the agencies and institutions dealing with research on the absorption of immigrants. Among those invited were sociologists, statisticians, psychologists, psychiatrists, and medical doctors, representing, respectively, the Hebrew University, the Institute for Research on Public Opinion and the Central Bureau of Statistics, the Committee for Mental Hygiene, and the Ministry of Health. Orientalists were not invited to this meeting. It was decided to launch three studies of the immigrants from Arab countries: a demographic survey, a sociological observation of immigrant families, and a psychiatric study of their mental health. In December 1949, the sociology department of the Hebrew University, in association with the Department for Middle Eastern Jewry, began an "inquiry into the conditions of absorption of immigration . . . with a special emphasis on distinguishing between different types of immigrants according to their origins and cultural environment." This research was led by the young sociologist Shmuel Noah Eisenstadt.[95]

Two years later, the editor of the social science journal *Megamot* (Trends), the psychologist Carl Frankenstein, initiated a discussion among sociologists, psychologists, social workers, and philosophers about the "problem of ethnic differences" with the practical intention of providing educators and social workers with guidelines for dealing with new immigrants from Arab countries. It is noteworthy that orientalists again were not asked to participate in this debate.[96]

Clearly, "social problems" were not the affair of orientalists, and their expertise was not deemed relevant. The expertise offered by both Eisenstadt and Frankenstein was technical. They took little interest in the background of the immigrants and were more concerned with defining the general form to which they should conform. They both understood this form to be *differentiation*, a differentiated personality and a differentiated role structure. In this sense, the position they were seeking to carve out for themselves in the field of orientalist expertise was parallel to Ben-Gurion's position in the political or ideological field.

One starts with the norm as an unmarked universality, defined in exceedingly abstract terms – Israeliness, modernity, stable social relations, normal mental development, the capacity for abstract thought, differentiation. It is impossible to define this norm in substantive terms, unless by the fact that it is identified with the Ashkenazi public or a portion thereof. This means that the norm is defined negatively, through identifying the "others" who are not part of the Ashkenazi public and who are thereby defined as a problem from the point of view of integration and absorption into this norm. For example, the immigrant children from Arab countries are defined as a social problem because their grades at school are typically lower than those of European children. They are not less intelligent, explained Frankenstein, but they lack "powers of abstract critical thought," which are characteristic of Western-modern differentiated thought processes and therefore are prerequisites for integration in "our society." This failure is caused by a certain cultural pattern, the "oriental mentality" of the society in which they were raised, but it can be overcome with the correct application of scientific psychological principles to education work. Difference, therefore, is marked not as something irreducible but as something to be overcome. The Yemenite will become "a Jew who forgets whence he came."[97]

Eisenstadt's book on the absorption of immigrants, for example, began with two chapters on the "general trends of modern Jewish migration" and on the "Yishuv" (the name typically used for the prestate Jewish community in Palestine). Then followed a separate chapter on the "Oriental Jew in Palestine," which made it clear that oriental Jews were not part of the "general trend," that the "general trend" was European, and that the "Yishuv" was a society built by European Jews, while the Oriental Jews marked a deviation from this norm: "In this chapter we are concerned with those groups within the *Yishuv* which have not displayed the complete transformation and institutionalization so far described." They were not differentiated but concentrated in rather narrow occupational strata, and they practiced endogamy. Moreover, Eisenstadt performed, in the field of expertise, the same exclusion that Ben-Gurion instituted in the political field. Not only were Sephardi Jews not recognized as having any special expertise relevant to the problem of absorbing the immigrants, they were themselves identified as part of the "problem of ethnic differences." He did not assign them a middle position between East and West but included them resolutely among the oriental Jews as evincing similar signs of backwardness, lack of differentiation, and the resulting social disengagement: "symptoms of the lack of integration and tension specific to immigrants . . . unstable social relations and deviant tendencies . . . juvenile delinquency, criminality, instability of family life, etc."[98]

Both Eisenstadt and Frankenstein nonetheless took a dim view of the existing policy of absorption and the functionaries implementing it. The forces that created ethnic differences, they noted, were unconscious rather than conscious. Hence, absorption policy had to be evaluated not from the point of view of its *content*, such as the messages of unity one would like to convey, not on the level of *hasbara*, but with regards to its *form*, what it conveyed to the immigrants implicitly through its practices and social organization; how it interacted with their unconscious; and what unpredictable consequences flowed from it. For example, superficially it may seem that the immigrants were responsive to *hasbara* and ideological instruction. They may have imitated the habits, ideas, and values of the absorbing group, as instructed. This, however, would not be a fully conscious form of adaptation but one motivated by unconscious fears and a weak ego. Such "superficial and external imitation . . . will not lead to real change, but to disintegration of the personality and its collapse."

Here was the same theme we encountered earlier with respect to the Sephardim, namely, that imitation was superficial and did not amount to real internal change. Now, however, this theme is harnessed to provide an explanation for the immigrants' tendencies to "deviance" and "anomie." But whereas the point of the earlier critique was to purify the Sephardi hybrid by showing that he was really and primarily oriental, now it is purified by reference to a universal model of the personality, compared with which it is found wanting. By the same token, the critique of superficial imitation was also mobilized to expose the superficiality of the old Zionist practices of *hasbara* (in the old sense) and ideological education as well as their incapacity to really absorb and integrate the immigrants. Here was a claim, therefore, to take over these practices, to rearrange them in accordance with sociological and psychological concepts, and to submit their practitioners – the absorption officials, teachers, and instructors – to the superior authority of sociologists and psychologists: "The educator, who seeks to create unity by imposing the cultural patterns of his own group, must understand the mental structure of the other ethnic groups . . . in order to know how to change it."[99]

Eisenstadt, for his part, criticized the excessive politicization and bureaucratization of absorption. Politicization meant that there were too many different agencies dealing with the immigrants and that there was no proper coordination between them. The result is that the immigrants develop a "heightened consciousness of the lack of structure and instability of Israeli reality." This problem was minimized, however, if the immigrants were organized into small cohesive groups, typically of the same country of origin, and settled in small agricultural villages (*moshavim*). Government policy there tended to be more coordinated, and it gave the immigrants "the sense of entering a single, obligatory social reality"; that is, the *moshavim* were places where it was possible to create the appearance of the state as an objective entity separate from society and its conflicts. It is noteworthy that Eisenstadt mentions that the same level of coordination as in the *moshavim* was achieved only in "a few institutions in Ramle." Ramle was a formerly Palestinian town where the military government took it upon itself to handle the affairs of both the remaining Palestinian population and the new immigrants. Eisenstadt recommended the *moshavim*, however, also because in his mind this form of absorption imitated the "normal" pattern set by the earlier pioneers and thus would cause the immigrants to adjust to the prevailing norms of voluntarism and contribution to society. Frankenstein, too, thought that "the adaptation of the primitive person to a society at a higher level of differentiation depends on whether he can exist within a framework of life that is familiar to him . . . like the small community, work in a personalized economic setting, etc."[100]

Bureaucratization, for its part, created overdue dependence. It meant that the immigrants were "educated into a maximum of irresponsibility towards the [state] institutions . . . and their only independence was the independence to exploit these institutions." Again, this could be ameliorated to some extent by settling the immigrants in *moshavim*. The cooperation and moderate degree of self-government practiced there would teach them the values of self-reliance and contribution to society. Bureaucratization, however, also meant that a wide gap separated the lives of the immigrants from the lives of the functionaries, who were their only window onto "Israeli reality." It was a rigid separation of roles, which did not permit true differentiation and adaptation. Hence, Eisenstadt suggested breaking down the bureaucratic separation between immigrant and functionary. Similar to Dotan's idea of missions, he recommended that officials and teachers live among the immigrants. They should teach less and spend more time on "social activities." Here too was a claim that the practices of *hasbara* and ideological education should submit to social scientific principles. Teachers and officials should be "trained in the special social and psychological problems of absorbing immigration, and especially specialize in the various forms of intensive social work. . . . They should have a thorough and general social understanding of the problems" (i.e., not a narrow bureaucratic or political party view).[101]

Thus, Eisenstadt's and Frankenstein's strategy in the field of expertise paralleled Ben-Gurion's strategy in the political field: to combat the bureaucracy and maintain the ethos of volunteering while at the same time elevating the state (and their own charisma) above party politics. They offered their expertise as a tool for realizing this project, as an extension of the state that would permit it to act "from a distance" among the new immigrants, without the dangers of politicization and bureaucratization. Sociological and psychological expertise translated the problem of ethnic differences into an objective ladder of differentiation (i.e., modernization) and thus purified the Arab-Jewish hybrid, separating within it what was backward, undifferentiated, and "primitive" (i.e., "Arab") from what was progressive, creative, genuine, and dynamic (i.e., "Jewish"). In later years, Eisenstadt's students fanned out among the distant and poor *moshavim*, studying their small group dynamics, assessing their interaction with state institutions, evaluating their degree of integration with society, and scoring them on the ladder of modernization. Similarly, generations of social workers and educators trained by Frankenstein spread through the slums, studying "neglected youths," assessing their family dynamics, and explaining their failure at school, and they too scored them on the ladder of differentiation. The Arab-Jews became "*mizrahi* Jews," the object of social scientific and psychological knowledge. Neither the Sephardi elite nor the orientalists were able to contest the dominance of this form of expertise.

Summary

The main point of this chapter is that alongside the demographic and territorial transformation of Mandatory Palestine wrought by the 1948 war and its aftermath, there was a transformation and redivision of orientalist expertise. Although much has been written about the first transformation, hardly anybody has noticed the second one. Further, much that has been written about the demographic and territorial transformation has failed to appreciate the extent to which it was incomplete, the extent to which the attempt to draw sovereign boundaries between Jews and Arabs and separate them as much as possible led to the emergence of three types of hybrids, which have continued to haunt policy ever since. I have also sought to show that the second transformation – the division of jurisdiction over the Orient between various forms of expertise – was in direct proportion to the incompleteness of the first one. The experts have been mobilized, and willingly have offered themselves, to manage and purify the hybrids. The main causal force producing this new division of expert labor was the struggle between various groups of experts and the interest of state elites in harnessing them to produce the effect of the state.

In these struggles, the main losers were the Sephardi leaders, who were pushed to the margins of the field of orientalist expertise. From the margins, they continued in later years to challenge the established authorities of the field and demand a role suited to their expertise. Typically, however, they claimed the least coveted and least defended role of *hasbara*.

For the officials in the Foreign Office, the victory of military intelligence and their own relegation to the role of *hasbara* caused them deep disappointment. Gradually, they split into two groups. Roughly half of them remained in the Foreign Office, the other half went back to the Hebrew University, finished their studies, and in due course became professors. The second generation of Israeli orientalists finally came into their own after their detour to the Jewish Agency and the Foreign Office. But if anyone had expected them to finally break the boundary instituted by their professors between the study of historic Islamic civilization, which alone qualified as "science," and more modern and more practical preoccupations, he or she would have been disappointed. When they returned to the Hebrew University, they were entrusted with the task of creating a new "Department of the Contemporary Middle East." To the surprise of their former mentors, they objected to this name, which they viewed as reflecting a nonrigorous and nonacademic approach, and instead settled on the "Department of the Middle East in the Modern Era." By this they meant the study of the Ottoman Empire. The boundary work of their mentors, between "science" and "practice," remained intact, only shifted a little in time. The study of the Ottoman period was "scientific" because the relevant state archives had been opened. But the Ottoman period itself was perceived as a period of "decline," one that paled in comparison with the golden age of the Arab caliphate.

Moreover, the new department could only grant bachelor's degrees, and those who wanted to obtain a Ph.D. needed to study ancient Islamic history. Maybe it was that the philological *habitus* proved too strong to overcome. No less important was the fact that they were now disconnected from the networks through which flowed current information about contemporary developments. As we shall see in Chapter 6, only by plugging back into these networks, under carefully controlled conditions, was the third generation of Israeli orientalists capable of creating expertise in commentary and analysis of contemporary events in the Middle East. It is possible to speculate, however, that there was also another reason behind the second generation's avoidance of more contemporary and practical concerns: a genuine sense of having been burned once, in the Jewish Agency and the Foreign Office, and a reluctance to repeat the experience. They decidedly joined their mentors in the ivory tower: "Tempting voices beckon to the historian of modern times from beyond the borders of science, and he must use all his powers to overcome his instinct . . . the instinct of hasty assessment . . . the instinct of easy synthesis and superficial generalization."[102]

But in one respect at least they did not follow their mentors. Whereas their professors were obsessed with the historical affinities between the Islamic and the Judeo-Arab civilizations, they restricted themselves to the study of the Arab world and abandoned the study of Jewish history to the field of Judaic studies. And whereas their professors were enthralled by their encounter with the first communities of Middle Eastern Jews who immigrated to Palestine, especially the Yemenites, and dedicated many studies to their dialect, folklore, and religious tradition, they completely avoided the study of the *mizrahim* and did not involve themselves in the debates about the absorption of immigrants. Arabs, not Jews, were their province.

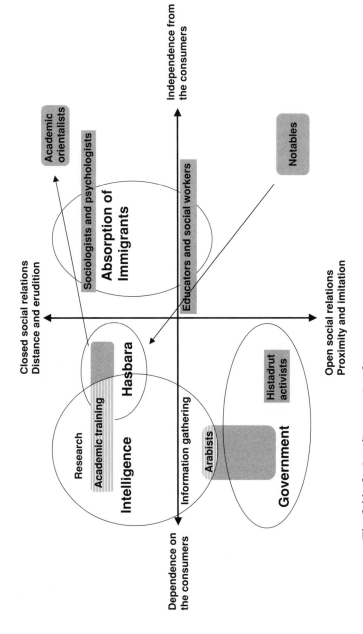

FIGURE 4.1. The field of orientalist expertise after 1953.

This division of jurisdictions was the decisive discursive fact, and it had far-reaching consequences. The second generation of Israeli orientalists, it is true, did not yet see their role as "studying the enemy." They claimed that the value of orientalist scholarship lay in "humanistic education" and its result, "self-knowledge of man and his society." But even this noble goal was envisioned through a relation of *analogy* between Jews and Arabs, not their synthesis – in other words, from the other side of the boundary separating different jurisdictions:

We, like the scientists in the West, approach the study of the Middle East as a world that is different from our own in its history and culture . . . this situation permits us to maintain a distance from our object of study, the distance necessary for scientific work. . . . [Nonetheless] I dare say that it is possible for us to benefit from studying our neighbors' deliberations, who like us are between the hammer of Western civilization and the anvil of their ancient religious tradition.[103]

By 1953, the field of orientalist expertise had been completely transformed, as shown in Figure 4.1. Four different jurisdictions were differentiated – intelligence, government, *hasbara*, and the absorption of immigrants – each controlled by a different group with a different form of expertise, and each organized around the purification of one of the hybrids. The expertise necessary to speak about Arabs outside the state was separated from the expertise necessary to speak about the Arabs inside the state, and both were separated from the expertise necessary to deal with the Arab-Jews. Thus passed away the liminal territory of the Orient, where the transmutation of identities could be performed, and its place was taken by the buffer zones of separatism.

CHAPTER 5

The Discourse about the Arab Village

In the Hebrew textbooks they still tell stories about the little
village. There is a question there: "what work do the people of
your village do?" And the correct answer is still: agriculture.
—Sayid Kashua
Arabs Dancing

IN THIS CHAPTER, I focus on the jurisdiction acquired by Arabist expertise:
government over the Palestinian citizens of Israel, monitoring the internal
boundary, and purification of the Israeli-Arab hybrid. In particular, I argue
that within this jurisdiction *the "Arab village" was constituted as a discursive object*. I would like to briefly explain what this claim means. First, I use the term
"discursive object" to point to the fact that participants in the discourse were
able to refer to the "Arab village" as a *genus* and to be certain that they were
all speaking about the "same thing." Discourse always involves rules for identifying what is similar and what is different.[1] These rules could have defined
similarity "below" or "above" the level of the Arab village, distinguishing
units of analysis by ethnicity, region, religion, mode of cultivation, size, or
what not. But this is not what happened. In the second part of this chapter,
I show that there are two specific discursive features – the analysis of the
space of the village as composed of a traditional "core" and a more modern
"periphery" and the analysis of the social structure of the village as divided
into warring *hamulas* – that served to demarcate the Arab village as a *sui
generis* social and spatial entity from all that surrounded it and permitted the
participants in the discourse to believe that they were all talking about the
"same thing."

Second, by saying that the Arab village was *constituted* as an object, I do
not mean to say that it was merely "constructed," that the discourse was in
some sense "false," and that the village or the *hamula* did not really exist.
The village qua discursive object is, in fact, an ongoing, though precarious,
accomplishment of practices that isolate its physical structure, arrest and redirect the dynamics of settlement within it, demarcate *hamula* struggle from

its connections to other political and economic struggles, upset and readjust the balance of power between *hamulas*, and indeed also name and analyze the resultant features as components of an organic system. Put differently, the village is a real entity exactly because it is a discursive object, not despite the fact that it is. From my point of view, there is no distinction or contradiction between discourse and reality, nor between discursive relations and social or natural relations. In fact, in the first part of this chapter I show that the qualities that constitute the Arab village as a discursive object emerged within the jurisdiction of government, as the achievement of practices of land confiscation, land planning, and the cultivation of *hamula* struggle implemented by the Arabists within the framework of the military government.

It follows, therefore, that the discourse about the Arab village is nothing but a continuation, in another form and by other agents, of the military government and the practices of the Arabists. Nonetheless, the emergence of this discourse is significant, because it took upon itself the task of purifying the Israeli-Arab hybrid and supervising the internal boundary at exactly the moment when Arabist expertise was in crisis. It is not coincidental, I believe, that this discourse emerged right as the military government was being dismantled. In the third part of this chapter, I analyze the discourse about the Arab village to show how it works to purify the Israeli-Arab hybrid by continuously separating what is modern and Western, and thus the external influence of Jewish-Israeli society, from what is traditional and oriental, and thus the internal essence of the "Arab village."

By saying that the discourse about the Arab village functions as a mechanism of purification, I mean to indicate that the more significant effects of this discourse have to do not so much with the villages themselves as with the internal boundary between Jews and Arabs. As I show in the first part of this chapter, an unintended consequence of the Arabist method of purification and supervision was that Arabist expertise itself became identified with the excesses and scandals of the border zone. The visible symptoms of this contamination were the rumors, fears, anxieties, and criticisms that focused on the military government. From this point of view, the dismantling of the military government and the constitution of the Arab village as a discursive object were intimately connected as two tactical moves within the same strategy. This strategy withdrew the Arabists to behind the scenes and limited their visibility. It meant that a greater distance was created between the experts and the hybrids, and it relegated the task of purification to a scientific discourse of "modernization."

In the fourth part of the chapter, I draw certain parallels between the Arab village and the Jewish "development town." They are both purification devices that construct their objects as hybrids – Israeli-Arab and Arab-Jew – halfway between tradition and modernity, East and West. In this way, they legitimate and reproduce this cultural hierarchy by inscribing it in the very landscape of Israel as part of the spatial taken-for-granted experience of every Israeli. This is why, when these purification mechanisms falter, the result is experienced as so threatening. In the fifth and final part of the chapter, I argue that contemporary developments – the urbanization of the villages and the growing political sophistication of their inhabitants – have undermined the objectivity of the village and that the response to this situation has been symptomatic: a retreat to the 1948 problematic of the "internal enemy" (i.e., a renewed and explicit focus on the unresolved problem of the Israeli-Arab hybrid). More than anything, this response is evidence that for thirty-five years the discourse about the Arab village worked to dissolve this problem – to purify the hybrid – but that it can do so no more. The owl of Minerva flies at dusk.

The Military Government and the Objectification of the Arab Village

To some extent, the four competing approaches analyzed in Chapter 4 – transfer, assimilation, autonomy, and control – each played some role in the operation of the military government. During the first decade of its existence, the military government still oriented itself toward the task, specified in its mandate, of attempting to push or encourage Palestinians to leave the country. An internal memo of the military government specified that in the case of war one of its roles would be to "encourage and make it possible for certain parts of the population to move to neighboring countries." During their regular meetings, the military governors frequently mentioned either concrete steps they took to encourage such out-migration or policy proposals directed toward the same end. They also mentioned that they got "clear . . . directives . . . to try to minimize the size of the population."[2]

At the same time, the military government cooperated with the Histadrut and the relevant government ministries to develop the villages and integrate their inhabitants, at least formally, within the official life of the state. Military governors debated, for example, whether it would be wise to require of the villagers to celebrate the Day of Independence (which marked the victory over the Palestinians themselves) and to raise the Israeli flag. They worked closely with the Ministry of the Interior to set up municipal councils, with the Ministry of Education to implement the law on compulsory education, and with the Ministry of Agriculture to plan crop distribution.[3] The military government also took an active role in setting up local religious councils and encouraging local autonomy in religious and cultural matters.[4]

Nonetheless, the dominant approach taken by the military government was the fourth one – to establish a system of control over Palestinian villages – in keeping with the dominance of Arabists in its highest ranks as well as in the Adviser's Office and with the relative monopoly of Arabist expertise over the jurisdiction of government. From the outset, the military governors were instructed to appoint a local dignitary as village *mukhtar*, just as the British colonial administration had. The *mukhtar* was answerable directly to the military governor and nobody else. Among his tasks were "keeping the peace in the village, reporting to the representative of the governor information about the property of absentees, about infiltrators, about people who possess weapons ... helping the authorities and the representative of the governor in the fulfillment of their duties such as collecting taxes."

Moreover, the *mukhtar* was to serve as the governor's eyes and ears in the village, and his authority was delegated by the governor. "Any resident of the village must assist the *mukhtar* in the fulfillment of his duties, if he so commands. Disobeying such a command will be considered an offense." The institution of the *mukhtar* was the source of endless clashes between the governors and the Ministry of the Interior, which wanted to see a local municipal council installed in the villages. Typically, the governors stalled, or they made sure that the council was appointed rather than elected and was still controlled by their trusted *mukhtar*. The *mukhtar* was an essential link in the chain of paternalist government, but Arabist expertise mandated even closer relationships of supervision. Officers at a lower rank than the governors were appointed as "regional representatives of the military government" and required to reside in the area under their supervision: "The representative must stay in the area and it is preferable that he will live in the area.... He must be required to be in the area not only during regular office work hours ... Continuity of work and continuous supervision on the ground [is essential]." These representatives were in close contacts with the *mukhtars* and kept an eye on them. They kept a "record of sins" in which were noted the names and addresses of offenders and their punishments. In many respects, they were similar to the *intendants* of the French ancien régime in its later days. One of their chief roles was indeed to organize taxation, but they were also entrusted with the less differentiated "police" task of supervising, reporting on, and coordinating any aspect of village life that was deemed relevant to the security of the state. The areas under the control of the military government were not administered as occupied or lawless territories, and hence "in order for the military government to execute the security policy," it was necessary to concentrate in the hands of the representatives "full jurisdiction over the actions of all state institutions and civilian services ... as well as over the protection of rights, the satisfaction of needs, and any action to advance the Arab population." In short, supreme governmental authority in all matters, civilian as well as military, as well as "paternal" guardianship, was concentrated in the hands

of the governor or his representatives. In some areas, for example, in the
south of the country, the governors reported that "governmental institutions
hardly exist, and the existing institutions rely on us more than we rely on
them."[5]

It is very clear from the files of the military government that although the
military governors and their representatives deployed this formidable power
to achieve various ends, they gave primacy, and this is how they interpreted
their charge, to the task of protecting the internal boundary between Jews
and Arabs and immobilizing as much as possible any movement across it.
This was how they sought to purify the Israeli-Arab hybrid. We already seen
that they debated the problem of Palestinians converting to Judaism, and
indeed they required the Population Registry Bureau of the Ministry of the
Interior (which contained a subdepartment for the registration of minorities)
to report to them "all cases of conversion." They also did not look favorably
on requests by *kibbutzim* to host and organize groups of Arab youths for the
purpose of pioneer settlement outside the area of the military government.
They thought that "there was something wrong in this." Most importantly,
they supervised the internal boundary by organizing and enforcing spatial
segregation. The Israeli-Arab hybrid was to be purified primarily by keeping
Arabs and Jews strictly apart from one another and pronouncing any mixing
as suspect from a security point of view.[6]

As mentioned earlier, the areas of the military government were declared
special security zones, and the movements of Palestinians inside and outside these areas were restricted by means of the notorious "permits regime."
Special permits from the military governor were required for transit within
the security zone as well as for entry and exit to and from it. In this way,
the military government supervised the internal boundary between Jews and
Arabs. The permits regime was also used to limit the access of Palestinians
workers to the labor market and thus prevented them from competing effectively with the new Jewish immigrants. But the permits regime did more.
It effectively fixed the residence of Palestinians in the villages, since the area
under the jurisdiction of the military government was divided and subdi-
vided into smaller and smaller zones, residence in which was the basis upon
which the military governor issued employment permits and marriage cer-
tificates, dispensed food and clothing coupons, and allowed the delivery of
mail and the procurement of organized transportation. Movement between
these zones, and thus effectively between villages, required special permits
and these were doled out gingerly. Thus, the Palestinian population was kept
rural and fixed to villages. The usual pattern of migration from villages to the
cities was interrupted. This also led to a dramatic reduction in the number
of intervillage marriages. It was the first necessary step in the constitution of
the Arab village as object.[7]

Not only were the Palestinians fixed to the villages, the villages themselves were "folded back" upon themselves, frozen in time and space, and forced to appear to the naked eye as what the Arabists continuously said they were – traditional "Arab" villages, densely overpopulated and spatially underdeveloped. The expertise of the Arabists, after all, was in understanding and controlling the rural population, and they had a vested interest in keeping the Palestinians rural (both to protect their position in the field of orientalist expertise as well as to protect the state's "security"). This was also how they promised to purify the Israeli-Arab hybrid and produce the effect of the state: The rural nature of the Palestinians guaranteed that they were essentially different from the Jewish population and therefore would not seek to integrate with it or assimilate into it. Further, their rural nature guaranteed that they were traditional and therefore needed paternalist government rather than democracy.

The spatial structure of the village was fixed, frozen, and folded back upon itself mainly through the confiscation of Palestinian lands. From 1948 to 1953, Palestinian villages lost most of their land through a series of laws empowering the state to take over the property of "absentees" or to expropriate private land for a variety of public purposes, from the creation of security areas to agrarian reform. The military governors and the adviser on Arab affairs were regular members of the Supreme Expropriations Committee, which coordinated the confiscation drive, and the military government was entrusted with carrying it out. The rationale for the confiscation drive was identical with the reasons routinely given to explain why the military government was necessary: its purpose was to consolidate state control over large areas that were overwhelmingly populated by Palestinians and close to the border. Decision makers worried that such Palestinian territorial blocks "might be used in the future as a basis for separatist claims or at least for claiming the Galilee as an autonomous district."

Typically, the hinterland surrounding Palestinian villages was confiscated to block their tendency to spread outward until they approached one another to form a single territorial block or even a city. In order to drive a wedge between them, Jewish settlements were planted on the confiscated lands, particularly in areas where previous Jewish settlement was sparse or nonexistent. One of the tasks of the military government was to assist in the establishment and maintenance of these new Jewish settlements. Because the process of planting these settlements was long and arduous, however, and because in reality the settlements were far fewer than were needed to keep watch on even a fraction of the land, the military government became a sort of "custodian" of state lands meant for future Jewish settlements. This custodianship was tantamount to a policy that always sought to keep the Palestinian villages in check and to prevent their spatial development. A host of delay tactics were used for this purpose, such as systematically denying building permits and proceeding at a deliberately slow pace in drawing up official zoning plans for the villages. At the same time, a great deal of the routine activity of the military government involved monitoring of state lands and removing "unauthorized" squatters or shepherds from within their perimeter as well as identifying and destroying illegal construction – in short, making sure that the villagers did not encroach on the confiscated lands earmarked for Jewish settlement.[8]

The combined effect of confiscation of landed property, tight control over the issuance of building permits, and zoning restrictions meant to block urbanization produced a distinctive spatial structure, which as we shall see in the next section was identified by geographers as characteristic of the "traditional" Arab village undergoing a slow modernization process and as fundamentally different from the spatial structure of the fully modern Jewish settlements. Invariably, the effect was to fold the spatial structure of the village back upon itself, freeze its "traditional core," and populate its periphery with hybrid forms of illegal construction.

These spatial measures were supplemented by the sociopolitical effects of the Arabists' art of government, which sought to cultivate internal *hamula* struggle within the villages and to block all forms of cross-village or national political organization. Like land confiscation and spatial segregation, this government strategy folded the Arab village back upon itself and produced the appearance of a traditional social structure hopelessly stultified by its own divisions and conflicts. It purified the Israeli-Arab hybrid by underscoring the essentially rural and traditional nature of the Palestinians and their need for paternalist government. Elections and modern municipal government, it was intimated, made up a superficial layer of imitation resting on this more decisive essence, and one should not accord them much importance.

From the very inception of the military government, the Arabists advised the Population Registry Bureau of the Ministry of the Interior to include information about *hamula* membership in the official population registry, next to the regular entries marking each Palestinian citizen's name, date of birth, residence, and so on. This information was partly gleaned from the old village files compiled by the Arabists before the formation of the state and partly provided by the *mukhtar*. The military governors typically appointed as *mukhtar* an elder understood to be at the head of a *hamula*. In this and myriad other ways, they could favor one *hamula* over another; encourage competition between them to win such favors; and, most importantly, increase the power and prestige of such elders and guarantee that other residents had no choice but to obey "their" elders and act as members of a *hamula* – since this was the only way to gain permits and public service jobs, for example.[9]

My point is not that *hamula* conflict was invented by the Arabists but that they shaped it in accordance with their distinctive worldview and art of governing the villages. It is better to think of *hamula* conflict not as a self-contained institution but as one phase of what was a more or less flexible and loose dynamic of alliance formation, which generally tended to spread beyond the village as protagonists sought allies in other villages, in the cities, and in the state administration and eventually formed nationwide coalitions. There is much evidence that under British rule, for example, the dominant pattern of political organization and conflict among Palestinians linked such *hamulas* – which are better viewed not as kinship units per se but as alliances knit together by the language of kinship – into ever-widening networks of national political organization.[10]

The military government, on the other hand, methodically encouraged *hamula* segregation by supporting relatively weaker *hamulas*. Thus it weakened the strong *hamulas*, which represented supra-village alliances, and created an artificial balance of power within the village. In this way, it effectively changed the rules of the game: Power was now granted to those *hamulas* that kept their politics and alliances at the village level. At the same time, the Arab departments of Mapai and the Histadrut organized local *hamula* electoral lists to run in municipal elections and mobilize votes for Mapai in the national polls. Moreover, the military government resolutely combated all attempts to form national-level political organizations, especially by the Communist Party. Anybody who opposed these new rules of the game had to reckon with the wrath of the military governors, the Adviser's Office, and the Arab departments of government ministries, which controlled appointments for all official and professional jobs. These worked together with the General Security Service (GSS) and received information from the *mukhtars*. They could dismiss any Palestinian candidate for an official position (even a teaching position) with the laconic justification of "security considerations." They regularly used this power to ensure that non-*hamula* elements could not join municipal coalitions or hold municipal offices.[11]

This tactic of divide and rule deployed by the Arabists produced a distinctive social and political structure, which, as we shall see in the next section, was identified by anthropologists, orientalists, and political scientists as characteristic of the traditional Arab village undergoing a process of political modernization. Thus, in a sense, the foundations for constituting the Arab village as a discursive object were laid by the Arabists, because their practices produced the Arab village as a social institution and a segregated physical structure.

Yet, in direct proportion to the objectification of the Arab village, the authority of the Arabists had eroded and become subjective. The unintended consequence of the Arabist method of purification and supervision was that

Arabist expertise itself became identified with the excesses and scandals of the border zone. The governors and the representatives of the military government, after all, resided in the areas under their jurisdiction. They supervised the internal boundary from close range, making sure it was impenetrable from the inside out. But their very existence there meant that the internal boundary was highly permeable from the outside in, thus giving rise to a thickened no-man's-land that threatened to engulf Arabist expertise and sully it.

A meeting of the military governors on December 12, 1951, captures the dilemmas they faced as well as their sensitivity to the fact that, in the public's eye, they were increasingly being identified with the scandal of the border zone. The question they discussed was this: How should they respond to requests from officers who had recently retired from the military government and now wanted to reenter the areas under its jurisdiction as civilians in order to lease land or to conduct business?

One of the governors defended such requests. These people, he said, meaning some of the rank-and-file Arabists, had dedicated their lives to the Zionist cause, so much so that they had never bothered to acquire an occupation. Now that they had left the service, they were encountering difficulty finding work in the private sector. In the course of their service they had indeed gained expertise in Arab affairs, but on the Jewish side of the internal boundary there was no demand for such expertise. Their requests, therefore, should be granted.

Another governor disagreed. Public opinion was likely to condemn the governors if they granted such requests. There were already too many rumors about corruption within the ranks of the military government, and the governors should try to avoid even the appearance of anything unsavory. Another governor chimed in and confessed that "in these matters, we are already committing serious crimes." Yet another, sensing that a negative verdict was gaining support, asked that the decision be postponed because he had already let in some of these veterans. He testified that they were useful people, both from the business point of view and "from the point of view of their conduct with Arabs." Finally, the governors decided on a compromise: "The military government does not look favorably upon the entrance of officers retired from the military government to conduct business with the Arabs in its areas, but it would neither discriminate in their favor nor against them."[12]

What was the issue here? Clearly there was the specter of corruption. The whole country was under an austerity regime, which gave rise to a thriving black market. The strict segregation of the Palestinian population meant that a lot of money could be made by selling black market goods across the internal boundary. To do so, however, one needed good connections in the military government, which granted the necessary permits for entry and exit. Indeed, even Mapai's senior expert on Arab affairs warned that the military government was being "infiltrated by black market elements" and that there were some functionaries who abused their authority for economic gain.[13]

But the matter of corruption was but one aspect of a more general problem. The Arabist bargain with the state elites, after all, was that in return for jurisdiction over the Palestinian minority, the Arabists would keep the internal boundary intact. By the very nature of their expertise, they staked their own persons, their agility, and their honesty and honor as warranty that the boundary would remain intact. No one else but they could move across the internal boundary without damaging it and without falling prey to the lure of the other side. They were still certain of their capacity to do so, which is why the representatives of the military government were instructed to reside in the areas under their jurisdiction. But what would happen if they left the no-man's-land, went back to the Jewish side for a while, and then returned? How many times should they be allowed to do so? At what point did they cease to be trustworthy? If as veterans they could leave and return at will, the boundary would no longer remain intact. Not only would it become permeable from the outside in, but it would also "thicken" into a no-man's-land inhabited by shady characters, hybrids who moved back and forth across the internal boundary and carried back into the metropolis the dangerous habits and excesses permissible on the other side. This dilemma is typical of colonial societies. British crime literature, especially the Sherlock Holmes genre, is replete with the image of the sinister secrets of colonial life coming back to Britain to haunt its gentlemen.

The governors' concern for public opinion is evidence that, already by 1951, Arabist expertise was being compromised and contaminated. As the years passed, things became worse and worse. The Arabists were becoming scarcely distinguishable from the hybrids they were meant to supervise and purify. The visible symptom of this contamination was the ever-growing body of rumors, fears, anxieties, and criticisms that focused on the military government. The criticisms arrived from various quarters: from the Palestinian population itself and its political representatives; from left-wing Jewish politicians; from journalists in search of a sensationalist scandal; from academically trained orientalists who were eager to point out errors made in the treatment of the minority; and, finally, even from within the ranks of the military government itself and from among the Arabists. The military government was accused of being politicized and of organizing votes for the dominant party. As we have already seen, there were rumors about corruption and abuse of power for economic gain. There was also the accusation that the military government acted to underdevelop the Palestinians and prevented their integration within the state. More than anything, the critics decried the powers of arbitrary punishment possessed by the military governors and their representatives and condemned the myriad injustices that they perpetrated on the Palestinians. This meant, argued the critics, that the military government was in fact achieving the opposite of what it was supposed to do: Rather than providing security and keeping the minority in line, it was gradually alienating the Palestinians and turning them into enemies of the state.[14]

What animated all these criticisms and lent them force was the image of the military government as scandalous. The military government was characterized as a "huge prison" for the Palestinians, not only in the sense of an area of restricted entry and exit but also in the sense of an area outside the law rife with corruption and arbitrary punishment. It was imagined as an area outside Israeli society into which were channeled all its illicit and ugly impulses – its alter ego. A sensationalistic novel written by a veteran of the military government, *The Ugly Governor: The Truth about the Military Government*, captured this image well. The actual "truths" told by this book were not all that important, and they were certainly not novel. There was nothing in the book that was not said by the critics time and again. The packaging, however, was telling. The author promised to tell "the truth about the military government." The publisher announced that "for the first time, the censors allowed to depict the military government as it is in reality, and to publicize all the true facts. This book will cause a scandal." Most importantly, the front cover of the book was designed to convey the image of scandal and sensation: it was completely black, while the subtitle – "The Truth about the Military Government" – appeared within a shining star of whiteness. This design implied that the military government was symbolically included within the "apparatus of darkness," a term invented by the critics in this period to refer to the security services; yet it also implied its opposite, that the scandalous actions of the military government would be brought into the light and exposed.[15]

The initial response of the military governors to these criticisms was to try to reform the military government from within. For example, in reaction to the accusation of politicization, they debated among themselves the possibility of periodically moving the representatives of the military government from place to place because "the representatives were directly involved in the conduct of the elections, and this hurts the [military] government. Working in the [military] government creates the lure of corruption."[16] Breaking the attachment to one place was meant to minimize the opportunities for corruption but also to rescue the representative, the Arabist, from being mired in the border zone and identified with it. Similarly, in response to the accusation that they were underdeveloping the villages, the military governors sought to promote, together with the Ministry of the Interior, the formation of local municipal councils. The main objective was to disaffiliate themselves somewhat from the *mukhtars* and the *hamulas* and avoid being identified with them. The actual functioning of these local councils was of much less importance to them. Most councils were appointed rather than elected and still represented a balance of power between *hamulas*. Others had to be forcibly disbanded because they had begun to veer into dangerous nationalist territory. All in all, by 1961 there were only eighteen functioning councils.[17]

These initial steps indicated the direction that the Arabists eventually took. Their response came in the form of a tactical shift that withdrew the Arabists to behind the scenes, limited their visibility, and thereby increased the distance between the experts and the hybrids. This is how, I believe, one should interpret the "abolition" of the military government in 1966. As some Palestinian critics argued at the time, the military government was not so much "abolished" as made invisible. Its authority was passed to civilian bodies, especially the police, the GSS, and the Office of the Adviser on Arab Affairs, but these continued using the same practices, and the military exerted a strong influence on their decisions.

More importantly, by no means did the "abolition" of the military government mark the end of spatial segregation or the cultivation of *hamula* struggle. The permits regime remained in force for at least two more years. The designation of Palestinian-dominated areas along the border as special security zones was only revoked in 1972. As the military government was being disbanded, a special Committee for Population Dispersion was formed, composed of the general managers of relevant government ministries and led by the former chief of the GSS, to deal with the "increased possibilities for mobility of the minority population." At the same time, the Office of the Adviser on Arab Affairs coordinated the activities of newly formed regional security committees, composed of army officers, police officers, GSS operatives, and functionaries of relevant government ministries. These committees were established in order to maintain close supervision and "custodianship" over state lands, as the military government had done earlier, and they too saw their charge as protecting and maintaining spatial segregation. For their part, the police and the GSS took over the networks of informers and collaborators in the villages and continued to use them to supervise the Palestinian population and cultivate *hamula* struggle. The Arab departments of the various ministries remained in place, and the Adviser's Office continued to coordinate their activities, which included the blacklisting of any Palestinian suspected of nationalist tendencies. Finally, the Labor Party (Mapai's successor) continued to organize local *hamula* lists to run in municipal elections and relied on *hamula* leaders as part of its electoral machine.[18]

The abolition of the military government should be understood, therefore, as a tactical move within a larger strategy. The Palestinian critics were correct to note that it merely made power less visible and thus was probably meant to deflect criticism. Boimel argues convincingly that, by the mid-1960s, state elites had reached the conclusion that the military government was no longer necessary as a deterrent and was probably counterproductive because it caused dissension within the Jewish public. Its functions of supervision, segregation, and co-optation could be continued by less visible means.[19] It is significant, however, that although many of the same policies were continued, the abolition of the military government did mean the discontinuation of the position of representative of the military government — that is, the residence of the Arabists among the population on the other side of the internal boundary. This means that, at least in part, the abolition of the military government was a tactical move in response to the image of "scandal" and to the ambiguity that became attached to the figure of the Arabist, and it was motivated at least in part by the professional interests of the Arabists. With this tactical move they sought to save their position and authority within the field of orientalist expertise and to protect their claim to manage the jurisdiction of "Israeli Arabs" on behalf of the state. This move involved increasing the distance and reducing the association between the experts and the hybrids.

From this point of view, the emergence in these same years of an academic discourse about the Arab village was not accidental, even though it was unplanned. When we put side by side the emergence of this discourse, the abolition of the military government, and the withdrawal of the Arabists behind the scenes, it is possible to understand all three as corresponding and complementary tactical moves within the same strategy. At the same time, it is important to note that this was a "strategy without a strategist." Although it was a smoothly functioning apparatus of discourse and practice whose various parts were well coordinated, there was no archplanner and no intentional and conscious conspiracy to construct it.[20] This strategy is better understood as a series of tactical moves between which strategic correspondence was gradually established by virtue of the fact that they were undertaken by actors who had a similar set of predispositions and who gradually taught each other to speak the same language, the language of the discourse about the "Arab village." Additionally, the strategic correspondence between the various tactical moves was established because they were all undertaken within the preexisting jurisdiction of government over the Israeli Arab hybrid, the boundaries and parameters of which were already well established and clearly defined.

The Arab Village as Discursive Object

In the space of one year in the mid-1960s, two seminal doctoral dissertations were published reporting studies conducted in the villages of the "small triangle" in the coastal region. Abner Cohen, who in the 1950s worked there as school superintendent for the Arab Department of the Ministry of Education, published his *Arab Border Villages* in 1965; Subhi Abu-Gosh, a Palestinian, completed his dissertation on *The Politics of an Arab Village in Israel* in 1966, just as the military government was being disbanded.[21] In a rare moment of simultaneous discovery, both dissertations reported a similar finding (despite the fact that they observed two different, in fact quite dissimilar, villages), namely, that despite the efforts at modernization and their inclusion within the Israeli system of local administration, the social organization of "Arab villages," as the authors called them, was still dominated by the traditional *hamula*, and their politics were still mostly a factional struggle between *hamulas*. The authors differed, however, in their interpretations: Abu-Gosh thought that the *hamula* system was a simple residue of past traditions, whereas Cohen argued that it was revived by the villagers as a response to modernization. According to Cohen, the *hamula* system tended to disappear during the British Mandate period, but the villagers revived it as an adaptation strategy in response to the crisis of their inclusion in a Jewish state.[22]

As can be seen in Figure 5.1, within the space of a few years after their dissertations were published, the number of scholarly publications about the "Arab village" written by Israeli academics multiplied exponentially.[23] In essence, a new interdisciplinary field of study had begun to coalesce around

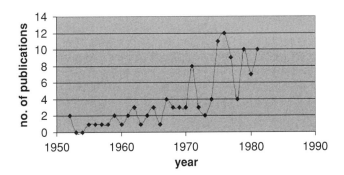

FIGURE 5.1. Publications about the Arab village, 1952–1982. *Source.* Data from Sammy Smooha and Ora Cibulski. *Social Research on Arabs in Israel 1948–1982: Trends and an Annotated Bibliography,* vols. 1–2 (Haifa: University of Haifa, The Jewish-Arab Center, 1989).

the Arab village, combining the contributions of anthropologists, political scientists, geographers, and orientalists. Most importantly, as we shall see, most of these new studies continued to affirm the importance of the *hamula*.

This exponential rise in the number of publications clearly had to do with the growth of the university system in Israel: Tel-Aviv and Bar-Ilan universities were formally established in 1955–1956 but were accredited and began to expand only in 1960.[24] Haifa and Ben-Gurion universities were established even later. It stands to reason that as the number of academic appointments grew, the number of publications would grow as well. Indeed, there was a similar growth in publications about other aspects of Palestinian life in Israel, in particular, publications about education and intergroup relations.[25] Nonetheless, this is not a sufficient explanation. When the universities were first created, they did not establish new departments for anthropology, geography, or *mizrahanut* unless they could count on recruiting appropriate staff for them. Where did the new academics come from, and why did they have expertise in the Arab village? I would argue that the rise of a discourse about the Arab village is at least partly explained by the existence of the military government and its demise in these years. First, the military government supplied the new discourse with its *object*, with the Arab village as a stable spatial and social entity understood to be *sui generis*. Second, the military government also supplied the new discourse with its *subjects*, that is, with academically trained personnel who were nonetheless similar to the Arabists in that they could claim hands-on knowledge of village life.

By enforcing spatial segregation, the military government was actually undermining the reproduction of Arabist expertise. If Jews and Arabs lived completely separately, how would it be possible to grow a new generation of experts who had firsthand knowledge of Palestinian life and networks of Palestinian acquaintances? The military government had to grow its own experts, and for that purpose it could typically count on two alternative sources of recruits: Jewish immigrants from Arab countries, who spoke Arabic, though not the Palestinian dialect, as their native tongue,[26] and high school graduates who took intensive courses in Arabic and Middle Eastern history and culture. Together, these two groups contributed the bulk of new recruits into the military government, but the military governors were particularly interested in the high school graduates, who were Ashkenazi, educated, and upper class. In May 1950, they met with the principal of Haifa's Ha-Re'ali gymnasium – an elite school that employed academic orientalists as teachers in a special track devoted to Arabic and Middle Eastern history – and discussed an intensive summer field camp they were about to set up in the areas of the military government. The students were to "learn the problems of the Arabs and assist the governors." The principal was enthusiastic and explained that in recent years the school sought to reshape students' training "away from academic problems to matters having to do with reality." The military government promised to provide the students with an instructor, to organize *hasbara* sessions, and to provide for room and board – though one of the governors suggested that the students could support themselves by teaching Hebrew to the Palestinians. The emphasis was to be on face-to-face daily contacts with Palestinians, immersion in order to acquire first-hand knowledge of their dialect, customs, and so on. From then onward, the graduates of Ha-Re'ali and similar high schools with oriental studies tracks were regularly recruited into the military government until it was abolished.[27]

At least some of the academic scholars who wrote about the Arab village and other matters having to do with the Palestinians under Israeli rule acquired their expertise in this way: from a high school track in Arabic and Middle Eastern studies into the military government or the Office of the Adviser on Arab Affairs, where their outlook and expertise received a particular inflection, a particular bias in favor of close observation, daily contacts, and hands-on knowledge of village life. Then, when the military government was disbanded, some moved to the academy, especially to the disciplines of anthropology and geography.[28]

When I say that the abolition of the military government and the emergence of a discourse about the Arab village should be viewed as two corresponding tactical moves within the same strategy, I also mean to point to the formation of a hybrid Arabist-academic form of expertise within the military government and its migration to the academy. It is not surprising, for example, to discover that Baruch Gitlis, the author of the exposé mentioned earlier about the military government, was one of these scholars. A representative of the military government, he was also a graduate of the Institute of Oriental Studies at the Hebrew University. The critique of the military government coming from within its own ranks was typically produced by these part-academics, part-Arabists, because the critique pointed in a direction that favored the assets they possessed and corresponded to their *habitus* – the withdrawal of the experts further away from their subjects and into the academy.

Having arrived there, they quickly turned the Arab village into the center of a burgeoning cottage industry of anthropological, political science, and geographical studies. As I explained earlier, the Arab village could serve as the productive center of this industry because it was constituted as an object by the military government and thus could be treated by participants in the discourse as the "same thing," as identical to itself and different from its environment. First, the conflict of *hamulas* was analyzed as the unique and essential quality of "village politics," which marked it as sharply different from modern "material" and "rational" politics:

In village politics the interests of the individual are subordinate to the interests of the *hamula*. The interests of the *hamula* (which are essentially non-material and relate primarily to its prestige in the village) are very much bound up with the chairmanship of the local council . . . [that] symbolizes authority and prestige.[29]

Hamula struggle is thus *sui generis* and manifests the unique essence of the village as a locus of rural-traditional identity. To constitute it as an object meant to demarcate it from wider, more "modern" conflicts, such as class conflict between peasants and agrarian lords or party conflict over national leadership. As I argued earlier, *hamula* conflict is better seen as one phase in a wider dynamic of alliance formation that tended to spread beyond the village to encompass these wider conflicts. It was only due to the policies of the military government that it remained confined to the village. Consequently, in the discourse about the Arab village, *hamula* conflict and party or class conflict would appear opposed to one another as inside and outside, "core" and "shell," essence and appearance. This opposition served as a ready-made rebuttal to any explanation that sought to relate events in the village to the actions of the state. Such explanations were "superficial" and did not uncover the more "basic" underlying process:

Many of the villagers, perplexed by this condition, tend naturally to relate this to the plane of village-state relations. In this way, they tie problems arising from a complicated basic process with superficial political interpretations that seem to explain difficulties and provide an outlet for perplexity.[30]

Analogously, the spatial structure of the village, the product of confiscation and segregation, was analyzed as exhibiting a "traditional pattern of settlement," sharply distinct from the modern organization of physical space discernible in the Jewish sector. This pattern, it was argued, reflected in spatial terms the traditional social structure of the village divided into *hamulas*:

On the basis of these studies it is possible to present a general model of the traditional Arab village in Israel. . . . The structural units making up the village were hierarchized: the smallest structural unit is the house – accommodating the nuclear family. The second unit is the courtyard – holding together several families of a patriarchal household. . . . The third unit is the neighborhood, a combination of several yards. Socially, a "neighborhood" is a "*hamula*." One neighborhood or more make up a village.[31]

As with *hamula* conflict, spatial organization was constituted as an object by marking a line that separated essence and appearance. At the "core" of the village the geographers identified a traditional pattern typical of the Arab village, a "model of primitive planning" characterized by high density, winding and narrow streets, houses and yards surrounded by high walls touching one another, and so on. They argued that this traditional pattern had endured over the centuries despite myriad infinitesimal changes to the spatial layout of the village. This core is distinguished from the new neighborhoods that surround it. While *in* the village, the latter are no longer *of* the village but represent the effect of outside forces:

Most Arab villages contain an old, traditional village core. This densely-populated core in the center of the village developed slowly through time and its structure is adapted to the traditional needs and livelihood of the inhabitants. . . . In most of the villages today, the traditional village core comprises only a portion of the built-up area. The current alignment of the village consists of new neighborhoods surrounding the core.[32]

Thus, the academics took over the object constructed by the military government as the unquestioned datum of their research, the taken-for-granted background against which they marked change and difference. In this way, they reproduced the village qua discursive object and lent it the legitimacy of science. But they did something more, since by contrasting the traditional village with modern Israeli society and by analyzing the changes in the former as the influence of the latter, they worked to purify the Israeli-Arab hybrid.

The Purification of the Israeli-Arab Hybrid

The metaphor of the traditional "core" signifies a specific relation between tradition and modernity: the village is portrayed as an island of tradition amidst a roaring ocean of progress, represented by the "modern" Israeli society and state:

The political process in the Arab village in Israel has been undergoing significant changes under the impact of modernization. The introduction of new political institutions into village life, in conformity with the general policy of the state to develop a modern local administration instead of the traditional *Mukhtarship*, has changed the focus of local politics.[33]

This is an interesting and paradoxical relationship. As the quotation above shows, the village is portrayed as being penetrated by modern practices that transform it. That is, it is passive. At the same time, however, the passivity that allows it to be so easily penetrated and developed is also depicted as "retarding change," an obstacle to modernization. Tradition quickly succumbs before modernity, it is merely a "subjective factor," and yet it remains as an ineradicable residue that "detracts from the development of the village."[34] The words used – "retard", "detract," "subjective" – seem to indicate that, from the point of view of participants in the discourse, traditional elements constitute temporary obstacles on the road to modernization. But when the whole of this discourse, its repetition and accumulation over thirty-five years, is taken into account, it becomes clear that a more permanent relationship is at stake. Over and over again the complaint is repeated that even though the encounter with "modern" society has produced distinct changes in the Arab village, its traditional social organization still endures and delays moderniza-tion: "While political practices characteristic of modern societies have been adopted, traditional norms have not been abandoned altogether."[35] In fact, some even speculate, as Cohen did, that tradition is reinforced *not despite* the contact with modernity but *because* of it, as a reaction: "Contact with a Western society, such as the Jewish one," may sometimes "cause closure and maintenance of traditional social institutions and frameworks."[36]

This traditional organization is infallibly represented in this discourse by the *hamula* system. Participants in the discourse warn that it is "important not to exaggerate the significance of all these changes, because for the time being the foundations of social structure are still intact. The transition is not sharp. It is not easy to define the degree of change." Observers who "mistakenly" consider the modernization of the Arab village "as about to be completed" are misled by "external signs that are not always a faithful reflection of the internal system of relations." Although there is change, the internal system of relations is still "subject to the laws of gravity of an ancient social tradition. The power of the traditional social frameworks is most evident during a period of elections or a blood feud between *hamulas*."[37]

It is precisely this combination of modernization from without and the stubborn resistance of the *hamula* system from within that are responsible for the hybridity of Israeli Arabs, for the fact that they are always halfway between their backward brethren in the Arab countries and their progressive Jewish compatriots. Modernity comes from without, and running against native institutions it can produce only halfway houses, piecemeal change, and hybrid forms. Thus, when one attempts to introduce "municipal gov-ernment," which "is a form of administration that has developed in the west over centuries," into the Arab village, one has to accept all sorts of compro-mise half-measures because one is planting the institution "in a different soil ... [that] has not yet modified its fundamental character, despite the changes it had undergone."[38]

Since the *hamula* system is embedded in the spatial structure of the village, the confrontation between modernity and tradition is also inscribed in the geography of the village. Specifically, it is responsible for the hybrid form of a "semi-modern neighborhood model." This model combines the effects of urbanization and modernization that were absent from the "traditional neighborhood model," but it also evinces the stubbornness of tradition in the form of *hamula* organization and a corresponding distribution of land. These delay the transition to a "modern neighborhood model."[39]

The discourse about the Arab village is thus a mechanism that purifies the Israeli-Arab hybrid. It may be true, as Amnon Lin complained, that there never existed a clear policy, never a "clear and logical consciousness," that could resolve the hybridity of Israeli Arabs – their awkward status within the state, their "double loyalty." But the discourse about the Arab village permitted at least a working consensus. One must recognize that from the point of view of state elites there was a great deal of utility in preserving the status of the Palestinian citizens of Israel as hybrids, between citizens and enemies, between the village and the city, between modernity and tradition. In this way it was possible to use them, for example, as itinerant and commuting laborers from whom it was possible to squeeze surplus value without the danger of provoking class conflict; or it was possible to use them as an organized group of voters that nonetheless forever remained disconnected from the centers of influence; or it was possible to use them as risky citizens, as a "dangerous population," with respect to which it was possible to embed mechanisms of surveillance and control into the very fabric of legal discourse (as in the case of the Emergency Security Regulations). In order to produce all these utilities, however, in order to continue to mobilize these Israeli-Arab hybrids, it was necessary to also have a mechanism that purified them. This was precisely the role of the discourse about the Arab village. It analyzed the Israeli-Arab hybrid into its components and distributed these components on a temporal dimension. On the one side were democracy, municipal government, universalism, meritocracy, the labor market, the nuclear family, and urban society and its temptations – in short, "modernity," identified with Jewish Israeli society. On the other side was the village, with its gerontocratic-patriarchal structures of rule, with the particularistic attachment to the *hamula*, the clan, and the extended family, but also with its communal values and sense of belonging – in short, "tradition," identified with the Arab village:

Their home is in the village, and to the village they return . . . carrying with them influences they have absorbed in the city, which they radiate onto the whole of the Arab rural population.[40]

The village could stand as shorthand, a metonym, for the whole Palestinian population, its "traditional core," its true essence, purified of external, Western influences. Take for example the little pamphlet issued by the Office of the Adviser on Arab Affairs titled *The Arab and Druze Settlements in Israel*. Despite the fact that the pamphlet included articles about Palestinian cities, towns, the Bedouin, and so on, for its cover was chosen a drawing of a "typical" Arab village nestled on the hillside, with ancient domed houses and a peasant plowing the land using an ancient plow. The whole of the Arab and Druze settlements were self-evidently represented by this scene of peasant life. Twenty-five years later, the geographers who edited *The Arab Settlement in Israel* chose a slightly modified simile, an aerial photo of a village (probably in the West Bank) sloping from the hillside. And this at a time when at least 88 percent of the Palestinians in Israel lived in urban or urbanizing settlements (those with more than 2,000 inhabitants)![41]

At the same time, whatever is modern – and this could be almost anything that the social scientist values as positive, because the contrast between modernity and tradition is a flexible formula, able to be applied to almost any opposition – comes from outside, invades the village from all sides and changes it, but the difference between the two is never abolished. Modernization is always put off until some uncertain future time, and hybridity is transformed into a quantitative difference, a matter of arriving late and needing to catch up.

For thirty-five years this diagnosis was repeated, and the same recommendations accumulated, never deviating from the accepted formulas implied by the metaphor of external modernity and a traditional core, never abandoning the initial dimension charted by Abu-Gosh's and Cohen's opposing interpretations of the *hamula*. Some have argued that previous modernizing policies did not go far enough and recommended therefore enhanced and better-planned modernization. Others, on the contrary, have attributed the incompleteness of modernization to the stubbornness of tradition and recommended adjusting development plans so they take it into account. If modern agricultural technology did not manage to rescue the village from poverty, enhanced modernization in the form of industrialization was suggested, or, on the contrary, agricultural cooperatives based on traditional communality. If officially appointed *mukhtars* proved to be corrupt, they should be replaced by an elected municipal council, or forms of internal traditional control over them should be encouraged. If there was illegal construction, planning for nuclear families was the suggested solution, or adjusting construction to the needs of traditional *hamulas*.[42]

One is struck by the truly Sisyphean character of these recommendations. The never-ending travails of Sisyphus did not, of course, have anything to do with the stubborn nature of the stone he was pushing but with his doom, his own nature, so to speak. Similarly, I would suggest that the repeated lament over the failure of modernization cannot be explained merely by the actual delay in the development of the Arab village. Instead it should be grasped as stemming directly from the structure of discourse: Precisely those features that are perceived as blocking modernization are the features that constitute the Arab village as an object (the spatial structure, the struggle of *hamulas*). That is, the conditions that allow orientalists to speak about the "same thing" also supply them with a permanently flawed, permanently suspended object.

Moreover, this Sisyphean lament should not be seen as a failure of discourse itself, an empty gesture, because it was highly productive. It achieves two things at one and the same time. First, it purifies the Israeli-Arab hybrid. The failure of modernization guarantees that discourse continually separates within this hybrid what is modern, and therefore the influence of Jewish society, from what is traditional, hence its own Arab essence. Purification is not, and can never be, a "solution" to the problem posed by hybridity, not a "solution" in the sense of "dissolution," as Lin wanted, because it works concurrently and complementarily with the mobilization of hybridity for various purposes. It permits the continuation of various practices that subsist on this hybridity – for example, the development of a weak labor force commuting from the villages to the cities but never settling there, or the various arrangements for organizing and buying the votes of the villagers, or the whole security apparatus that replaced the military government and developed practices for supervising and controlling risky citizens (including leftist Jewish activists) – because it prevents the two sides of the antinomy from infecting one another.[43] Wherein lies a second achievement of the discourse about the Arab village, a second service it performs: by purifying the Israeli-Arab hybrid, it also protects the boundary and distance between object and subject, between the village and the social scientists, who study it from their vantage point in "modern" Israeli society. The experts are withdrawn, far away from the hybrids and the border zone, relatively immune to their dangers.

From now on, to study the Arab village, to speak the truth about it, the experts would have to place themselves not in the intermediate zone between Jews and Arabs – as did the prestate Sephardi authors who wrote about the fellahin, or as did the Arabists – but squarely within a modern, Western Israeli society.

From this respect it can be said that contact between the Western and industrialized Jewish society and the traditional rural Arab society has brought about the very rapid changes that have taken place.[44]

This is why the discourse must repeat itself. Not in order to objectify the Arab village – this had already been done by the military government – but in order to objectify the distance between the experts and the hybrids, and with it also the internal boundary between Jews and Arabs. Hence the "abolition" of the military government and the emergence of a discourse about the Arab village appear as two corresponding tactical moves within the same strategy. The internal boundary between Jews and Arabs has remained intact, and movement across it, at least from one side, has remained extremely difficult.

But Arabist expertise, which originally was contaminated by its efforts to supervise the boundary, has been strung out into a new, partly invisible, and more flexible network. The supervisory and coercive functions of the governors' and representatives' positions receded into the shadowy folds of the state apparatus, while the discourse of purification was undertaken by academics. Indeed, over time, the academics came to replace the Arabists in the senior and visible position of the adviser on Arab affairs to the prime minister. After the Arabist Shmuel Toliedano finished his term in 1977, his place was taken successively by three academic experts with Ph.D.s, two of whom specialized in the Arab village – Moshe Sharon, Yosef Ginat, and Yitzhak Bailey.

On the other hand, these academic experts displayed certain characteristics that demonstrated their similarity to and continuity with the Arabists, or more precisely they demonstrated that this form of expertise developed within the jurisdiction originally occupied by the military government and defined by its differentiation from intelligence, *hasbara,* and the absorption of immigrants. First, most of them had served in the apparatus of the military government and its kindred agencies. Indeed, oftentimes they began their academic research while serving there and utilized the unique access to research sites and informants thus afforded them. Second, whether anthropologists, geographers, or orientalists, they had a decided preference for ethnographic observation and close, hands-on knowledge of village life. Unlike Middle Eastern studies, which I discuss in the next chapter, the discourse about the Arab village was a form of expertise that developed within a colonial-type encounter. Finally, they professed to have "friends" and acquaintances among the Palestinians, particularly in the villages, and to be in conversation with them. This was certainly a byproduct of their previous work in the supervisory agencies, as well as of the ethnographic nature of their research, but it also demonstrated that they needed to compete with the old Arabists in order to usurp their position and thus needed to assume a similar role as mediators between the Jewish public and the Palestinians. Therefore, despite now residing in the academy, every now and then, to prove their worth, they had to leave their comfortable offices and patrol the internal boundary, make quick incursions to the other side, and come back with reports about what they had seen with their own eyes.[45]

The Village and the Development Town

As a mechanism of purification, the Arab village is analogous and complementary to the Jewish "development town." The original master plan drawn by the planning division of the Prime Minister's Office in 1949 was intended to create small to midsize towns on the periphery and populate them with new immigrants. The planners envisioned these towns – small and well-designed regional centers serving surrounding agricultural communities – as an antidote to the social ills bred by the large megalopolis. They were inspired, in equal measure, by the Soviet experiment of constructing industrial towns and planting them on the periphery of the USSR; by the British Labor government's project of surrounding London with new satellite garden cities; and by the German "theory of central places," which extolled the virtues of the small-scale city or town. The size of the new towns (20,000 to 50,000 residents) and their design (which included division into self-contained neighborhood units, or "eggs") were carefully calibrated to produce an intimate environment, one that would "be exempt from the disorientation, alienation, social injustice . . . and other urban malaises associated with the cosmopolitan city." Incidentally, the planners also recommended settling new immigrants in abandoned Palestinian villages. They were highly critical of the standard practice of the Settlement Department of the Jewish Agency, which preferred, wherever possible, to erase abandoned Palestinian villages and settle immigrants in new, makeshift communities. They thought that the demolition of the old Palestinian villages damaged "the landscape and historical heritage of the country."[46]

The original vision notwithstanding, the ambition to plan and install from scratch a whole new form of urbanism has unfortunately proven to be an example of hubris. The new peripheral towns became pockets of concentrated poverty that were completely dependent on the center for investment and jobs. They could not serve as commercial centers for the agricultural communities around them because the latter – *kibbutzim* and *moshavim* – already had a well-organized marketing network of their own. They could not become centers of agricultural production themselves because the *kibbutzim* and *moshavim* had already managed to usurp most of the formerly Palestinian land around them. They could not become industrial centers because most investment continued to go to the central cities, where the infrastructure was already developed. This situation led to the same process of selective out-migration as in the border settlements; that is, those who had more resources and connections managed to get out, while those who did not, many of them immigrants from Middle Eastern and North African countries, stayed behind, locked into a cycle of poverty engendered by peripheral location, low-paying jobs, and social isolation. To this one must add the fact that from 1953 onward the absorption authorities directed Jews from Middle Eastern and especially North African countries in greater proportions to the development towns. Consequently, the new towns became coded as "*mizrahi*."[47]

Very early on, as the planners were confronted with the perverse consequences of their experiment, they began to refer to the new towns as in need of "development." That is, these towns were to be included in specially designated development zones that were to receive special government attention and resources. In 1955, the Ministry of the Interior created the new position of advisor on development towns, which in short order became a whole department within the ministry.[48] From then on, the new towns were universally known as "development towns," and the term quickly lost its technical-neutral connotation. It became attached to the coding of these towns as "*mizrahi*" and served to associate *mizrahi* identity with a low score on the modernization scale; thus, in one of those familiar cases of technical doublespeak, the term "development" came to stand for its opposite – backwardness. This meant that development towns became potent spatial devices of purification. They complemented the purification discourse of the social scientists, who won jurisdiction over the Arab-Jewish hybrids in the early days of the state. The very term "development town" served to indicate that the immigrants from Arab countries were backward and that they needed to become Westernized before they could be integrated into Israeli society. Sociologists, psychologists, social workers, planners, anthropologists, and geographers studied the development towns in order to explain the causes of the backwardness of their residents. They never wearied of emphasizing that the "oriental" heritage of the residents did not prepare them properly to be integrated into a "Westernized" society such as Israel, and they prescribed various means of accelerating their integration and pushing them in the direction of development and modernization. Just as with the Arab village, the hybrid was stretched and suspended over a temporal dimension: always pushed forward in the direction of Ashkenazi modernity, always hindered and delayed by its backward, traditional Arab origins.[49]

The same analysis holds also for the *moshav olim*, the semi-cooperative agrarian settlements created especially for the new immigrants. Here was another spatial purification device deployed by the discourse about the absorption of *mizrahi* Jews. The various immigrant agrarian settlements were studied by sociologists and anthropologists hired by the Settlement Department of the Jewish Agency to assist the planners and advise them on how to resolve practical problems. Similar to the discourse about the Arab village, the social scientists bemoaned the failure of modernization (which they identified with the model of the cooperative *moshav* developed by the socialist labor movement) and attributed this failure to the cultural heritage of the immigrants from Arab countries as well as to the struggle between *hamulas* in the settlements, a struggle that they too conceptualized in isolation from and in opposition to class and party political struggles. The theme of the struggle of *hamulas*, in fact, was developed during the same years in two parallel tracks – with respect to the Arab village and with respect to the *moshav olim* – and the participants in both tracks even cited one another.

To be more precise, the sociologists and anthropologists who studied the *moshav olim* cited their colleagues, the experts about the Arab village, but not vice versa. But this was not pettiness on the part of the latter, since, as I explained in the introduction, these two discourses perform different roles: the discourse about *mizrahi* Jews needs the discourse about the Arab village in order to constitute its subjects as Arab-Jewish hybrids, while the discourse about "Israeli Arabs" does not require such assistance. It is premised on the objectivity of the Arab village, which is guaranteed by the mechanisms that control and monitor the internal boundary. Thus, it is possible to say that the Arab village, the development town, and the immigrant *moshav* complemented each other as parallel and mutually supportive arms of the Israeli border regime.[50]

Yet, especially after the 1967 war, development towns also became sites of resistance to Ashkenazi hegemony and to the purification discourse. The economic prosperity that followed on the heels of the war, along with the incorporation of another captive Palestinian population into the Israeli labor market, gave many of the residents of development towns the necessary boost to climb up the occupational ladder and consequently the economic resources to escape the cycle of poverty associated with peripheral location.[51] With rising economic status came a certain political assertiveness and growing electoral clout. Protest against discrimination in the allocation of resources, against their exclusion from political influence, and against their forced settlement on the periphery became standard operating procedure for politically ambitious residents, and while such protest rarely became radical, it turned development towns and their residents into vital political resources.

Moreover, development towns also became sites where a *mizrahi* ethnic identity could be asserted and mobilized as a political resource, as evidenced by the obligatory visit every candidate for the premiership had to pay to the *Mimuna* (festival of spring) celebrations in one of the development towns. Thus, a space had been opened up in Israeli culture where one could assert *mizrahi* identity as genuinely Jewish, as an integral part of Israeli identity, and yet this space remained limited to the local and the folkloric. It was a space at the periphery rather than at the center. The struggle of development town residents thus served merely to confirm the social logic within which *mizrahi* identity is recognized as "low" culture, backward and inferior to the dominant discourses of the government, academia, and the intellectuals.[52]

If one would like to understand (and thus maybe upset) the set of relationships that are capable of turning such resistance into an affirmation of the status quo, one has to take into account the Arab village. Its unchallenged objectivity, constituted by a scientific discourse speaking from within the truth, means that it represents the Orient as absolute negativity, as exterior to the one who speaks about it. It is no accident, then, that this discourse began to disseminate just at the time when talk about the "melting pot" began to be challenged by the struggles of development town inhabitants. As the purification device of the development town faltered somewhat, the objectivity of the Arab village continued to guarantee that the essential underlying structure – with Orient and Occident opposed to one another as past and future, as obstacle and destiny – would remain intact.

There are two ways in which the Arab village provided this guarantee. First, in order to speak about the Arab village, as we saw before, in order to be "within the truth," one had to speak from a position within a modern, Western Israeli society that observed the village from without. And this was true even for *mizrahi* social scientists, like Sami Smooha, who has played an important role in exposing the social division, in his terms, between the "dominant Ashkenazi minority" and the "subordinate Sephardi majority." When, on the same page, he writes about the Palestinians, he slips into the author's position prepared for him in advance by the discourse about the Arab village and describes Jews as "generally Western and democratic" in comparison with the Palestinians.[53]

Discourse does not impose itself on its subjects; it lures them. It possesses the power to co-opt speakers and turn them into subjects because it gives them the possibility of being "within the truth," which is a form of social power. This can be the case even if one is a Palestinian citizen of Israel. Different groups among the Palestinians mobilized the discourse about the Arab village, especially the theme of *hamula* conflict, to challenge the veteran leadership or to distinguish themselves as more modern and developed than other Palestinians. This strategy is evident, for example, in a story by Sayid Kashua. In this subversive fantasy, an unexplained military blockade is suddenly imposed on the Palestinian villages and towns within the green line. Under the pressure of this blockade, the young protagonist's semi-village–semi-town is forced into isolation and self-sufficiency, as if it returned to its ancient essence as an Arab village. Indeed, the protagonist, who lived outside the village for many years and was forced to return to it recently, "discovers" and reports that underneath the modern patina of administrative institutions everything that takes place in the village is still dictated by *hamula* struggle.[54]

The second and more important way in which the Arab village guarantees the separation between Orient and Occident, between Arabs and Jews, and makes it self-evident is by virtue of its objective spatial reality, which gives a concrete body, a concrete materiality, to the discourse of modernization and purification. In a variety of ways, the discourse of modernization and purification had been inscribed onto the physical landscape of the state of Israel, and its separations and oppositions had become part of the spatial background knowledge (in the phenomenological sense) at the disposal of any Israeli, part of what is taken for granted and natural. We are a long

distance now, an irreversible distance, from the prestate discourse that identified Palestinian peasants as the embodiment of biblical customs and types
and that analyzed the space of the village as a mirror in which Jews could
learn to recognize their own ancient, typical self. We are a long distance
now even from the planners' wish to settle Jewish immigrants in abandoned
Arab villages and their concern to preserve these as an organic part of "the
landscape and historical heritage of the country."

There were many reasons the preferred choice was to demolish the villages
rather than preserve them – Arabists and military commanders considered
it a way of demonstrating to the refugees that nothing was left for them to
return to; surrounding *kibbutzim* and *moshavim* wanted to take control of
village lands and did not want immigrants to be settled there and compete
with them; planners considered the hilltop location of many of these villages
as unnecessarily cumbersome – but regardless of the reasons, the consequences for physical landscape were far-reaching. Not only were the traces
of Palestinian presence erased as much as possible, but Jewish and Palestinian
spaces were sharply demarcated and differentiated from one another. They
could be adjacent and even touching and yet embody completely different principles of organizing space, heterotopias with respect to one another.
An early photograph of Kisalon, the first *moshav olim*, shows two rows of
one-story prefabricated houses strewn along a dirt road (Fig. 5.2). It is like
a sketch, a hurried drawing of an eastern European "street village," a village that developed along a thoroughfare over many years, only in this case
the houses were planted first and the road was traced between them. Another characteristic spatial form is the circular model made famous by aerial
photos of Nahalal, the first *moshav*, like a marvelous sketch of a modernist
utopia, self-contained, arrayed against its environment (Fig. 5.3). It became a
canonical model for many other settlements, especially those in the territories
occupied after 1967, flexibly adapted to follow the contours of hilltops and
mountainsides. Then there were the famous *homa u-migdal* (wall and tower)
settlements, like "dimensionless points" strewn over a map, with invisible
lines connecting them to form a strategic deployment.[55]

Had the immigrants been settled in the abandoned Palestinian villages, or
had the remaining villages not been constituted as *sui generis* "Arab villages,"
Jewish and Palestinian rural spaces would not have become so sharply demarcated. As it is, however, the Israeli landscape has been produced as a spatial
simulation of the narrative of modernization. Movement in space, from the
periphery to the center, is also movement in time, from past to future, from
backwardness to progress. The traveler in Israel no longer sees the "land that
was" – the Holy Land of the pilgrims or the Palestinian spaces that have
been erased, and even the orthodox settlers have fled to the hills of the West
Bank in order to find there anew (and lose again) what the Israeli spatial

FIGURE 5.2. Moshav Kisalon in its first year. *Source.* Rafi Segal and Eyal Weizman, eds., *A Civilian Occupation: The Politics of Israeli Architecture* (New York: Verso, 2003).

FIGURE 5.3. Aerial photo of Nahalal. *Source.* Moshav Nahalal official website, http://www.nahalal.org.il/on.asp.

regime consumed – but is ushered along a distinctive route, starting from the hypermodern urban agglomerations of the coastal plain and ending with the vista of an "Arab village" somewhere at the furthest ends of the country, its traditional "core" perched on a hilltop, visible from the highway winding below. And in between are the intermediate spaces, approaching one another and yet completely heterogeneous: the "semimodern neighborhood type" on the outskirts of the village, sloping down the hill and into the plain, as if attempting to swarm it; the "street village" *moshav*, which recalls the eastern European Jewish town but is typically inhabited by *mizrahi* Jews; or the development towns, which in their clumsy attempt to simulate communities, with their "neighborhood units" consisting of large tenement buildings constructed using prefabricated materials, evoke the nightmarish memory of a different kind of modernity, the Stalinist one. This whole simulation revolves around the Arab village, which anchors and orchestrates its movement, thus naturalizing and reproducing the social and cultural divisions between Jews and Arabs and between Westerners and orientals.

The Return of the Internal Enemy

Of late, however, this simulation no longer seems as well anchored and stable as in the past. For, truth must be told, from the moment the military government was lifted, processes were set in motion that began to undo the objectivity of the Arab village. From 1966 to 1978, Palestinian society underwent a process of rapid urbanization, so that, by 1986, 45 percent of the Palestinians lived in towns with more than 10,000 inhabitants (though these were still officially classified as "villages"). Over 90 percent currently live in settlements with more than 2,000 inhabitants.[56] Yet the mechanisms of denial still continued to work for a while. In 1984, for example, as its population passed 22,000, Um-al-Fahem was still officially classified as a village, while a geographer timidly dared to raise the possibility that it might be something else altogether.[57] But denial could not be maintained indefinitely, and in due course its place was taken by two opposite reactions. On the one hand, some attempted to normalize the delayed and incomplete urbanization by comparing it with the transformation of rural sectors in other countries and by attributing it to general processes such as the rise of "late capitalism."[58] On the other hand, some engaged in shrill alarmism and analyzed the changes not as urbanization but as a process of covert autonomization, the formation of territorial blocks, and a challenge to Israeli sovereignty:

From the point of view of sovereignty, we have lost control in the Galilee, and in Wadi A'ra and in the security zone [in the Negev]. . . . Wadi A'ra is gradually turning into a fundamentalist Palestinian metropolitan area . . . A'rabe – each time they move and extend its boundaries . . . And the Jew what does he do? The Jew builds a road that goes around Nazareth to get to Tiberias, and in this way a "mini-Palestine" is being defined. And this is the situation today from Dir Makhsur to Sha'ab, and between Sakhnin and Dir Khana. . . . The Arabs build illegal buildings, and just ahead of the elections we draw for them a new residential zone, larger . . . and all that was illegal becomes legal.[59]

To my mind, there is no better evidence for the role played by the discourse about the Arab village in purifying the Israeli-Arab hybrid than the fact that, as the village begins to lose its objectivity, the focus of the debate shifts, as if it leapt backward almost fifty years, to the original problematic of the Israeli-Arab hybrid. With the shift in focus return all those anxieties that surrounded the hybrid and that were submerged and calmed for fifty years by the discourse about the Arab village. The specter of the internal enemy has returned, and with it also renewed debates about the advantages and disadvantages of population exchange, autonomy (cultural or territorial), and assimilation:

I think it is important to signal to the whole world, to the Arabs in the territories and to Israeli Arabs, that a one-sided transfer is out of the question. If the Arabs talk about [us] relinquishing Gilgal [a settlement in the occupied territories], or about evacuating 120,000 Jews, or all the Jews residing in the territories – we should tell them: "would you like an exchange?" This means that Sakhnin and Tayibe and Um-al-Fahem [Palestinian towns within the Green Line] will have to be uprooted as well. . . . I suggest to put reciprocal transfer on the public agenda. . . . There is space for exchanges.[60]

The same discursive shift is evident also with respect to the *hamula*. The objectivity of the Arab village was partially undermined because the *hamula* is no longer what it used to be. Urbanization and proletarianization; the effects of the 1967 war and the rise of Palestinian nationalism; the rise of a new, more assertive leadership; the Islamic revival; and, no less importantly, the transformation of party politics within the Jewish sector itself – all these have undermined the grip of the supervisory apparatus on village politics.[61] A clear signal came in 1976, when the Tracking Committee (Va'adat Ha-Ma'akav), composed of "village" mayors, organized demonstrations to protest the confiscation of Palestinian lands. The killing of several protesters by the police consecrated this day as the first "land day," and it has been marked every year since with demonstrations and protests. At the time, the experts and policy-makers were completely taken by surprise. Denial, once again, worked for a short while. The protests, the claims of unequal treatment, and the resistance to government plans, the experts reasoned, were evidence that the Arab village was not sufficiently modernized and that there still persisted "traditional rural values" that conflict with the "progressive norms of the Jewish city."

In short, not the confiscation of their land nor their status as second-class citizens is what led the Palestinians to revolt; rather, their "frustration and bitterness . . . reflect a severe crisis of values caused by oscillating between influences of the traditional-conservative culture, on the one hand, and those of the modern-western culture, on the other."[62]

In due course, however, the mechanisms of denial began to falter. Their place was taken, once more, by a debate that reaches back to 1948 and explores once again the same approaches that were debated then. Again, one side is optimistic, seeing in the events a "normalization" of the situation, an opening for assimilation: "Today, it is easier to be an Israeli-Palestinian. The Israeli Arab is no longer submitted to a daily loyalty test to the state of Israel, he is no longer under the daily magnifying glass of the government, the authorities, the police, the GSS, or who knows who. A lane was opened for a more thorough and more profound internalization of Israeliness." The contradiction between nation and state "is going to be resolved," provided that equality can be achieved. If the Jewish public is unwilling to grant equality to the Palestinians, then "autonomy is really a good solution."[63] Others return to various "divide and conquer" proposals, championing the Druze, the Bedouin or the Christians.[64] But over the whole debate hovers the specter of the internal enemy, represented most forcefully by those who point to the emergence of a "Palestinian political establishment" and warn Israelis to stop "evading the issue" and face the harsh reality. They adopt the old tone of the Arabists, implying they can see behind the Arab charade while the optimists and the "beautiful souls" are misled by pleasantries and appearances:

When dealing with Israeli Arabs we must remember that there is a cultural, religious, national and ethnic gap between us and them, in the sense that their language is full of insinuations and hints, and things are said gently, mildly and pleasantly, and it is easy to be misled. They speak about equality, but behind the word equality there is actually a cruel struggle over the same piece of land. . . . First, they say, we shall renovate the ruined mosque, then we shall only sleep in it from time to time, then we shall only build a square next it, and clean the area around it, then we shall only conduct weddings there – and so on and so forth, little bites in the "Salami method," and everything is done by means of wonderfully cultured and civilized speech, pleasantly . . . while they serve you plentiful food, Baklava and Coffee.[65]

By no means do I wish to argue that these are the only, or even the dominant, voices among the experts. The last three authors quoted – Israeli, Lin, and Sofer – all occupy fairly proximate and somewhat subordinate positions in the field of orientalist expertise. They are similar to the old Arabists in combining a certain degree of dependence on the consumers (Lin has worked in the political apparatus all his life, Israeli spent part of his career in the army, and Sofer is an adviser to the Labor Party) with a certain measure of openness in regard to social relations and knowledge (Sofer and Lin boast of Arab acquaintances and friends, and Israeli is of *mizrahi* origins). Their subordinate position in the field of orientalist expertise accounts for their hawkish views, while experts who are differently positioned tend to be more dovish. My point, however, is different. Regardless of their position and their views, all the experts tend to agree that "an inevitable historical process is taking place here, and the problem is that Zionism did not find an answer to the matter of Israeli Arabs."[66] We can put the matter differently: from the moment that the objectivity of the Arab village began to dissolve, the problem of the Israeli-Arab hybrid – which the discourse was supposed to purify – was raised anew and suddenly assumed enormous proportions. This fact demonstrates that the discourse about the Arab village is no more, and in its stead the "account of 1948" has been reopened: Who are the Israeli Arabs ("an ambiguous entity almost by its very nature")? Where do their loyalties lie? What could be the nature of their affinity to a Jewish state?[67]

CHAPTER 6

Military Intelligence and Middle Eastern Studies

It is possible to say that this is a sort of indicator. The failure of vision and barrenness of thought of the leadership are in direct proportion to the rise in the power and importance of "intelligence and assessment agencies." . . . And even though we are not dealing here with astrologists, but with intrepid and opinionated generals, who convey their assessments with semi-scientific terminology – of late it seems that they fulfill for us the same divinatory function. Maybe there is one difference: the astrologists are a little bit less sure of themselves.

—Doron Rosenblum
Haaretz, June 25, 2004

THE MAIN ARGUMENT of this chapter is that within the jurisdiction of intelligence – that is, the supervision of the external boundaries of the state – there took shape a new form of orientalist expertise common to both military intelligence research and the new discipline of "Middle Eastern studies," especially as practiced in institutions such as the Dayan Center (formerly the Shiloah Institute) at Tel-Aviv University, the Truman Institute at the Hebrew University, and the Institute for Terrorism Research at the Interdisciplinary Center in Hertzeliya.[1] Moreover, this new form of expertise plays a crucial role in shaping the dominant definition of reality through which Israelis perceive themselves and the Middle Eastern world around them.

I would like to explain briefly what I mean by this argument and what its significance is. By "form of expertise" I mean neither a property of an individual nor even of an organized group (a profession), neither a given body of knowledge nor an acquired skills set. I believe expertise should be analyzed as a network connecting individuals found in different positions and with different skills as well as devices, resources, demonstrated effects, models, and arguments. It is possible to diagram this network along five dimensions. First, there is the relation between those who are empowered to speak as experts and those who produce knowledge but cannot speak, humans as well as nonhuman devices. An excellent example of such a relation is the division, described in Chapter 4, of military intelligence into research and information-gathering branches. I show in this chapter that the expertise of research officers is not a quality they possess by virtue of their education or their skills but inheres in the fact that they managed to position themselves at what Latour calls an "obligatory point of passage" in the network, a point through which must pass all the different flows of information arriving from agents and informers, aerial photos, monitors of the Arab press, electronic eavesdropping, military attachés, and foreign intelligence agencies.[2]

The second dimension is the relation between those empowered to speak as experts and those who listen to them, their clients. In the case I am dealing with here, this is a sensitive and delicate system of relations, because among the clients are some of the most influential and powerful individuals in Israeli society, namely, the top political and military decision-makers. This fact carries with it certain advantages, since such powerful individuals are capable of providing the network of expertise with abundant resources, and indeed they have compelled all the other intelligence agencies to report to the research branch of military intelligence. On the other hand, there are distinct disadvantages and dangers: the politicians and the top brass are impatient clients who tend to usurp for themselves the right to speak as experts and in many cases limit and minimize the experts' freedom of speech. Precisely because they are positioned at an obligatory point of passage, a bottleneck mediating between the men of power and the production of knowledge, the researchers at military intelligence are especially vulnerable to the danger that their clients will appropriate their assessments and present them as if they were the product of their own thinking. In the second part of this chapter I show that the experts have responded to this danger by creating research institutes like the Dayan Center, which function as a sort of a liminal protected space between the academy and the state. Although these institutes have remained affiliated with the research branch of military intelligence and continue to enjoy the information flowing to it, they also constitute an arena within which the experts can socialize with the men of power without losing control over the dissemination and attribution of their assessments.

A third dimension of the network of expertise is the relation between those empowered to speak as experts and those about whom they speak. Put differently, the network of expertise involves a set of alliances or manipulations meant to secure from those about whom the experts speak a set of performances predicted by the experts.[3] The reader might wonder how could this be true in the case of intelligence. After all, intelligence officers attempt to collect and analyze information that the other side attempts to hide. How is it possible to talk about an alliance, partnership, or a network connecting the two sides? Without denying these obvious facts, I would argue that the image of intelligence work as "passive" – as consisting of monitoring, collecting pieces of information, and combining them into a full picture – is false. In Chapter 3, we saw that this image originated in the struggle between the academic experts and the Arabists, in the victory of the former and the constitution of the jurisdiction of intelligence in accordance with the principles of distance and erudition. After all, if the Arabists had won, it would have not seemed so strange to argue that intelligence involves a set of alliances and ties with those about whom the experts speak – their informers and acquaintances. This argument could easily be applied, for example, to the construction of the Arab village as an object of discourse, described in the previous chapter.

My point is that the network comprising intelligence expertise includes "active" elements that serve to form ties with the adversary (however incomplete and unsatisfactory these may prove to be, as shown by intelligence failures and strategic surprises). That is, intelligence assessments are involved in a certain game of communication with the adversary. They are not simply the opinion of the intelligence community about what is likely to take place, but also and inescapably a "message" to the adversary. It is from this point of view that one should consider the relations between intelligence officers and political and military decision-makers; the relations between intelligence officers, academic commentators, and journalists; and the public status of the Annual National Intelligence Assessment produced by the research branch of military intelligence. All of these are essential components of the network comprising intelligence expertise, and they enable the experts to involve the other side in a game of communication, of sending and receiving messages, a game that routinely tends to confirm the assessments and interpretations that guide the encoding and decoding of messages.

A fourth dimension along which it is possible to analyze the network of expertise consists of the accounts and interpretative tools that the participants use in order to make sense of their positions and of the ties between them. What transforms a tie into a more or less stable alliance is the interpretation, which, as Latour puts it, "translates" the interests of the different participants and creates between them a certain level of correspondence and coordination. The alliances composing the network shared by researchers in military intelligence and the Dayan Center are based on a very specific account, according to which their role is to divine the other side's intentions on the basis of the information provided to them. As I showed in Chapter 3, the origins of this account lay in the philological *habitus* of the academic researchers, and thus it is a self-serving account; it is their claim to social recognition and prestige. In this chapter, however, I emphasize two other aspects of this account: first, the way in which it serves to translate and coordinate the interests of the various participants in the network of expertise (the gatherers of information, the researchers, the decision makers, even the adversary), and, second, its role as a specific worldview, as a dominant cultural lens through which Israelis perceive the Middle Eastern world around them. The interpretation of intentions conjures a world of leaders, decision makers, whose intentions are clearly defined (though possibly hidden) and whose jurisdictions are clearly demarcated, and it excludes the hybrids, the infiltrators and the refugees, from this world.

This is, in a sense, the fifth dimension of the network of expertise. It should be analyzed also with respect to those who are excluded from it and about whom no one speaks. As we saw in Chapter 4, the whole jurisdiction of intelligence came into being on the basis of the purification and exclusion of the infiltrator-refugee hybrid. The network of intelligence expertise is based on this exclusion, because the devices of manipulation it deploys – the intelligence assessment as a message to the adversary – do not work on the hybrids. Hence it is impossible to translate their interests, to form alliances with them, or to secure from them the performances of interest. Precisely for this reason, as we saw in Chapter 4, the research officers defined the jurisdiction of intelligence as applying solely to the Arab regimes on the other side of the border and confined the refugees within the jurisdiction of *hasbara*. Even after 1967, when the refugee camps in the West Bank and Gaza came under Israeli rule, military intelligence refused to deal with collecting and analyzing information about them (though the research branch did create a desk dealing with the PLO) and left this role to the GSS and to the experts advising the military government in the occupied territories.

For this reason, the experts who worked in *hasbara* or in the military government could use the silenced voice of the refugees as a resource in order to occasionally challenge the dominance of military intelligence and to try to change somewhat the structure of relations in the network of expertise. They endeavored to speak for the refugees and explain to the Israeli public and decision makers what the refugees "really" wanted and what their position was with respect to Israel. Among these challenges, the most successful was the interpretation of the Palestinian covenant developed by Yehoshafat Harkabi. It blended seamlessly the various goals of intelligence, *hasbara,* and diplomacy and became a canonical scheme for domesticating the refugees and tying them (though quite loosely) to the network of intelligence expertise. At the conclusion to this chapter I argue that the Oslo Accords and the creation of the Palestinian Authority meant that it was no longer possible to continue to exclude the infiltrator-refugee hybrid from the jurisdiction of intelligence. The refugees have returned, and correspondingly, the network of intelligence expertise has been forced to inch closer to its alter ego, *hasbara*, from which it has attempted to separate itself for the past 50 years.

"This Funny Word": The Interpretation of Intentions and the Construction of the Network of Intelligence Expertise

Shortly after its inception in 1953, the research branch of military intelligence became the most influential and prestigious of the intelligence branches in Israel, and in 1957 it was entrusted with formulating the Annual National Intelligence Assessment. This status did not accrue to the research branch because it was able to successfully predict the actions of Arab states and armies. On the contrary, the years from 1953 to 1973 were full of intelligence blunders, for many of which the research branch was responsible, while the more noted intelligence successes were typically the result of the ingenuity and efficiency of other information-gathering agencies or the seizure of a wealth of Arab classified documents following military victories.[4]

I would suggest, rather, that the prestige and influence of the research branch were acquired through alliances and ties that were negotiated by its top officers and that positioned it at an obligatory point of passage within the network of intelligence expertise. The character of its position at an obligatory point of passage is evident in four aspects. First, the administrative division between the research and information-gathering branches placed the research branch at the top of the internal hierarchy of military intelligence and forced all the other branches and agencies – electronic reconnaissance, monitors of the Arab press, secret agents, aerial photography, field intelligence, and military attachés – to send their reports to the research branch, where they were collected, archived, and digested into summaries and assessments. Typically (though not universally), only the summaries and assessments, not the raw data, were disseminated to decision makers.

Second, in short order all the other nonmilitary intelligence agencies – the Mossad, the GSS, and the research department of the Foreign Office – were also subordinated to the research branch of military intelligence and were required to pass to it the information they collected, but the latter was not obligated to repay them in kind. If in the early 1950s the Israeli intelligence community was composed of a multiplicity of competing agencies that did not always share their information with the others and that occasionally clashed over the correct interpretation of the information, by the end of the decade the situation was completely changed, for the research branch of military intelligence had gained a decisive advantage over all the others, especially in terms of the privileged access it enjoyed to the top military and political decision-makers. This is the third aspect of the research branch's position at an obligatory point of passage: the research branch was entrusted with formulating the Annual National Intelligence Assessment, while the degree of freedom of other intelligence agencies to interpret the information they collected was correspondingly and increasingly narrowed.

Finally, the research branch was granted the authority to specify to all the other intelligence agencies (military as well as civilian) what information it needed them to obtain. In this way, the latter were turned into apprentices, in a sense, of the research branch. That is, the research branch occupied an obligatory point of passage not only with respect to the flow of information from the bottom up but also with respect to the flow of commands and specifications from the top down. The final blow came in the early 1960s, when the head of the Mossad, Isser Harel, an influential cadre who was closely allied with a faction within Mapai, the dominant party, and who resisted mightily the efforts to subordinate his agency to military intelligence, was forced to resign and replaced by the commander of military intelligence at the time. For a brief period, his replacement occupied both posts at once, and then he became the head of the Mossad full time. He immediately began to fill the top positions in the Mossad with retired military intelligence officers and formalized the division of labor between the two so that the research branch alone had the authority to determine intelligence needs.[5]

It is possible to consider these developments from a slightly different angle: in order to present themselves as credible allies of state elites, military intelligence researchers needed to extract themselves and their discourse from the no-man's-land surrounding the external borders (i.e., to distance themselves from the hybrids and from the realities on the ground), but by the same token they also needed to present themselves as intimately acquainted with everything that took place on the other side of the border (i.e., to maintain proximity to the hybrids). In order to accomplish both contrary goals, their strategy was to weave a hierarchical and extensive network, tying together various information-gathering agencies and reaching all the way into the border zone. Within this network, they themselves were positioned at an obligatory point of passage, far from the border zone, untarnished by association with the hybrids. The network they created channeled all the information to a central office far away from the points of contact with the border zone.

In order to weave this network, however, and to capture the obligatory point of passage within it, the researchers needed the support of the top political and military echelons. They needed ties to influential decision makers as well as insight into their way of thinking and an ability to adapt assessments to their needs. The crucial alliance between the research branch and the military and political elite was forged by the top officers of the research branch, individuals who were typically parachuted to their positions as part of their military careers; who previously served in the Operations Branch of the General Staff, sometimes as personal assistants to the chief of staff; and who were later, after they finished their stint in intelligence, promoted to even higher positions in the defense establishment.

The status and connections of these individuals, the social proximity between them and the top military and political decision-makers, guaranteed that the latter would listen to the assessments of the research branch and treat them seriously. No less importantly, it guaranteed that the research assessments, for their part, were attuned to the operational and strategic mode of thinking of the upper political and military echelons and were formulated in a language familiar to the decision makers and according to criteria they recognized as important. Consequently, the intelligence research assessments gradually acquired the wider format of strategic analysis, eventually including not only an evaluation of the adversary's capabilities and intentions but also information on the IDF's own forces and an analysis of its possible operational and political goals, something that the top research officers, who came from the operations branch of the General Staff, were eager and more qualified to provide.

Put differently, this alliance was crucial for the rise of the research branch because of the pattern of *generosity* it established. Research assessments were not formulated in autonomous closure, in an erudite and obscure language, but through exchange with an important group of decision makers. They were adapted so they could be grafted directly onto the operational and strategic discourse of the defense establishment, consequently enjoying wide circulation and increasing influence. The alliance between the research branch and the top political and military decision-makers also meant that the latter made sure that the other intelligence agencies would remain subordinate to the research branch – which later was upgraded into a research division – and that they showered resources on it and on the intelligence corps in general. This is an important point. While most of the investment went into sophisticated equipment for the information-gathering branch, it still served to increase the prestige and influence of the research branch, because the latter's position at an obligatory point of passage allowed it to appropriate and black-box, so to speak, the achievements of information gathering and to attribute them to the value added by research assessments.[6]

All these network features – the alliance with the top political and military echelons, the position of the research branch at an obligatory point of passage, and the capacity of the researchers to appropriate the achievements of information gathering – depended on the particular way in which the researchers understood and presented their role, namely, their claim to deduce from the information the intentions of Israel's adversaries. The interpretation of intentions served to translate and coordinate the interests of the various actors participating in the network. With respect to the information-gathering agencies, the claim to interpret intentions meant that there was always a marked distance between the information and its meaning, so that the value added by research would be especially high while the achievements of information gathering would be obscured. As one of the commanders of the information-gathering branch complained, the category of intentions – "this funny word," as he put it – empowered the researchers to appropriate the work of information gathering because it minimized their dependence on the data and permitted them to interpret it idiosyncratically:

> The information, which constitutes the intelligence service's sole right for existence, is captive to the choices, instincts and whims of the evaluators, who are the sole spokespersons for the whole elaborate intelligence system.[7]

Despite these complaints, the relations between the research and information-gathering branches remained stable and productive over many years, not only because of military discipline but also because the interpretation of intentions, just as it subordinated one to the other, also created a certain correspondence between the interests of the two sides. As in the Institute for Oriental Studies at the Hebrew University, the hierarchical relation between research and information gathering was interpreted in epistemological terms. The production of knowledge was depicted as a pyramid within which the subordinate position of the apprentices, the operatives collecting the information, was necessary if the details were to be pieced together into a complete picture.

The interpretation of intentions also served to strengthen the alliance between the research branch and the top political and military echelons by endowing the ties between them with a specific meaning and establishing a certain division of labor that both sides understood. The interpretation of intentions is a form of discourse in which the researchers take it upon themselves to represent this or that enemy leader in simulations and, in General Staff or Cabinet meetings, to clarify how he might think, what considerations he might take into account, and how is he likely to act:

> Asad is a cool, realistic and calculated leader. . . . Syria will not go to war alone. Asad is afraid that the IDF will get all the way to Damascus. War is simply out of the question, and Syrian troop deployment stems probably from fears about an Israeli attack.[8]

The organizational structure of the research branch was shaped in accordance with this form of discourse and served as an additional factor that bolstered the researchers' claim to interpret the intentions of enemy leaders. The research branch was divided into desks, each dedicated to a specific Middle Eastern country (or several neighboring countries), and each desk was divided into a section that researched enemy armies and a section that studied "political and social processes." This structure meant that the desk and section chiefs, to whom was channeled all the information pertaining to enemy leaders and military commanders, were the natural candidates to represent these in simulations, war games, or General Staff meetings. By its very nature, the division into desks, each led by a career research officer whose tenure in the position was very long, created an artificial scarcity of actors capable of interpreting the intentions of a given enemy leader and representing him.

At the same time, it made it possible for desk and section chiefs to become identified with "their" enemy leader and to present themselves as intimately acquainted with his personality, mentality, and way of thinking. It is told about the chief of the Jordanian desk that he knew the comings and goings of King Hussein's court by heart, even though he never visited it; that he could recognize from photos the faces of all the dignitaries and advisers who visited King Hussein; that he used to fly the Jordanian flag every morning and celebrate King Hussein's birthday every year; and that he was so identified with the king as to be "personally angry" at him when Jordan (against the officer's prediction) joined the 1967 war.[9] Thus, at the same time that the network woven by the research officers depended on the exclusion of the Arabists and on creating as wide a distance as possible between the experts and the hybrids, it also included auxiliary devices that allowed the researchers to present their knowledge as based on proximity and imitation, precisely the claim made by the Arabists. This residual and auxiliary form of proximity was necessary to enable the researchers to persuade the top military and political decision-makers that their expertise was authentic and that they could perform the task allotted to them.

I do not think, however, that we can explain the emergence and prominence of the interpretation of intentions simply by referring to the researchers' interest in securing recognition and prestige. Rather, the claim to interpret intentions originated in the encounter between the philological *habitus* of the researchers, as institutionalized in the administrative division between information gathering and research, and their need to connect with the operational-strategic thinking of their allies – that is, in an encounter between and mutual adjustment of supply (of skills and predispositions) and demand (for specific discursive products). Moreover, the claim to interpret intentions was reproduced over time because it endowed this encounter with meaning and translated the interests of the two sides. Operational-strategic thinking demanded that someone be able to represent the enemy leader in simulations, while the internalized philological *habitus* allowed the research officers to identify this demand as the ascent to the next level of the philological hierarchy – the position of the speculative interpreter – a move they internalized in the course of their studies as well nigh the *raison d'etre* of their careers. They were conditioned to desire the attributes of this position, the "brilliance" that marked the speculative interpreter's advantage over the pedant and the increased capacity to obscure their reliance on the work of the apprentices:

An intelligent evaluator is not interested in merely reporting or summarizing information. . . . He exists to apply his creative analytical powers . . . to build a conceptual architecture – an integrated, almost global assessment.[10]

It follows that the interpretation of intentions is crucial to the functioning of the network of intelligence expertise. It cannot be proscribed simply by instructing the research officers to be more careful about what they say, or even by explicitly prohibiting them from interpreting intentions. After the fiasco of the 1973 war, in which the research branch insisted to the very last moment that Egypt and Syria did not intend to go to war, a committee of inquiry instructed the research branch to carefully separate the assessment of intentions from factual information about capabilities and to concentrate on the latter. Nonetheless, not much has changed since. The research branch was never able to implement this recommendation, and when a decade had passed, Ehud Barak, then commander of military intelligence, announced in a programmatic article that "reality forces us to return to reliance on the integration of facts about the technical deployment of the enemy with an understanding of the overall context for such deployment and an assessment of the enemy's intentions." There were two reasons for this return: on the one hand, the researchers had internalized the interpretation of intentions as the prize they were conditioned to desire; on the other hand, this form of discourse grafts itself productively and with ease onto the operational-strategic thinking of the decision makers and intuitively makes sense to them – those who "make decisions" tend to understand the world around them as the product of decisions.[11]

The claim to interpret intentions serves also to translate the interests of the adversary, of enemy leaders, and to tighten the ties connecting them to the network of intelligence expertise. To grasp this point, one must realize that the Annual National Intelligence Assessment is not simply the opinion of the intelligence community about what is likely to take place in the Middle East. It is a political speech act, one that is central to the Israeli political system.[12] The National Intelligence Assessment is submitted to the government once a year, and the next day the main points are reported in the media. Throughout the year, politicians leak intelligence assessments to the press, and they are of course free to report only what suits their interests. In response, top intelligence officers have joined the game of selective leaks and developed their own set of give-and-take ties to military correspondents, who can then boast of reporting the views of "senior intelligence sources."[13] Moreover, because the research branch possesses a near monopoly over the supply of assessments (and because its officers can leak their assessments directly to the press), even when political and military decision-makers are interested in the supply of specific assessments and recommendations different from those voiced by the research branch, they are forced to avoid, as much as possible, overt conflict with the research branch. Supply and demand must coincide. The result is a process of negotiation in which official policy and intelligence assessment are slowly adjusted to one another, facilitated by the social proximity between the commanders of military intelligence and the political hierarchy. There were, of course, notorious cases in which an open controversy erupted between the research branch and certain decision makers, but the status of these events as "scandals" shows that they are the exception that proves the rule. Both sides were damaged by the controversy and attempted to return things to normal as soon as possible.[14]

It follows, therefore, that intelligence assessments are not merely predictions about what may happen but policy tools, messages directed at the adversary and calculated to elicit certain performances. When this network of relations is interpreted using the language of "intentions," the ties binding it are made stronger. The intelligence assessment is at one and the same time the lens through which the enemy's actions are viewed as indicating certain intentions; a message to the other side that their intentions have been exposed (as well as a message to the Israeli public or the international community that the other side has such intentions, i.e., *hasbara*); and the interpretation guiding Israeli policy in reaction to these intentions. Raymond Cohen demonstrated how this mechanism worked in 1986, when tensions between Israel and Syria escalated to the brink of war: The research branch interpreted Syrian maneuvers as indicating aggressive intentions. Its assessment was leaked to the press so as to warn the Syrians that the game was up. The Syrians, however, understood these leaks as a different kind of message, a threat possibly indicating an Israeli intention to attack. As a result, they mobilized their forces. Israel responded in kind, and the resulting dynamic of escalation validated the original assessment.[15]

Although Cohen sought to warn against the dangers of escalation inherent in such assessments, I think this is not necessarily the most important point. The opposite scenario was just as likely: the Syrians might well have cancelled their maneuvers in order to avoid escalation. This was exactly the performance that the assessment was intended to elicit. In this case, the assessment and the reaction to it would have been presented as a success because the adversary's intentions would have been "foiled." Put differently, the assessment acts to narrow the Syrian range of maneuvers so that most "responsible" and predictable reactions to it end up by validating the original assessment. As I emphasized in Chapter 4, the point is that in order to create the effect of the state, Israeli policy requires credible partners on the other side of the border, and the interpretation of intentions assists in tying such partners to networks of stable and predictable effects because it conjures the image of a decision maker, a strategist, who is responsible for everything that takes place on the other side of the border. As one research officer wrote, "A system of checks and balances was thus created between Israel and Syria. . . . At the end of the day, this system rests on two pillars: [Syrian] President Asad and Israel's total deterrent capability."[16]

The network of intelligence expertise created by the research officers and their partners is powerful and pervasive. Within it they hold a strategic position of great influence and prestige, which enables them to shape the dominant definition of reality through which Israelis perceive the world around them. As Cohen put it, "Whenever you find consensus among ministers, high-ranking officers – even military correspondents – about a certain Middle Eastern issue, chances are that it derives from an assessment by military intelligence."[17]

Nonetheless, there are also certain distinct disadvantages attached to the position of research officers. The proximity they enjoy to the high echelons of the defense establishment limits in certain respects their independence and personal prestige. First, they are typically so closely allied to certain decision makers, and their assessments are so inextricably mixed with political considerations, that they easily are drawn into the struggles among the political elites and invariably accused of political bias. As we saw in Chapter 4, for example, the struggle between Ben-Gurion's activist faction and Sharet's moderate faction was also conducted as a proxy fight between the research branch of military intelligence (representing the first) and the research department of the Foreign Office (representing the second). Later, in the early 1960s, when Ben-Gurion found himself opposed by a dominant faction within Mapai (composed of Levi Eshkol, Golda Meir, and Pinhas Sapir), their struggle erupted into the public sphere through a dispute between the research branch of military intelligence (which supplied assessments supporting Ben-Gurion's position in the struggle) and the Mossad (which was closely aligned with the dominant faction in Mapai) over the assessment of Egyptian plans to build long-range missiles.[18]

Second, research officers are directly subordinate to the commander of military intelligence, who is directly subordinate to the chief of staff and the minister of defense. Their very position at the bottleneck of the intelligence network means that it is easy for their superiors to appropriate their assessments and to present them as the product of their own independent reasoning. "The opinion of research" is typically presented to the government by the commander of military intelligence (sometimes accompanied by the director of the research branch), who thus has license to ignore, distort, or appropriate the opinions of individual researchers. Put differently, the research officers are vulnerable because they do not have control over the dissemination and attribution of their discourse, and from the moment that their analysis is put on the page or voiced in front of their superiors, it is easy prey.

But the vulnerability of the research officers is greater still. Even if they could attain some measure of control over the dissemination and attribution of their discourse, such control would be, by definition, too dangerous for them to wield. There is no better way to malign an intelligence officer and undermine her authority than to argue that she is presenting only her personal assessment and to insinuate that she is promoting a particular political viewpoint (an easy task due to the inescapable proximity of intelligence research to politics). The capacity to attribute discourse to a distinct author – which is a *sine qua non* in the academic game – would be the kiss of death in the game of intelligence assessments. From the moment that a particular intelligence officer becomes identified with a specific assessment or interpretation, the authority of the latter is undermined, and she herself becomes vulnerable to accusations and insinuations.[19]

The main power that the research officers wield, therefore, is not the capacity to create a monopoly over their discourse but rather the opposite, the capacity to be generous (in Nikolas Rose's sense) and allow their discourse to insinuate itself into the judgment of their superiors almost without notice. Put differently, what from one angle could be seen as their weakness – their inability to protect their assessments from being appropriated by their superiors – could be seen from another as the very mechanism of their own power, the very means by which their assessments became influential. As one veteran instructed younger officers, "If you were right in your assessment and your clients adopted it, very often they will turn it into their own property, as if it derived from their own logic, and your part in it will be forgotten. You should consider precisely this situation to be an ideal accomplishment."[20]

Yehoshafat Harkabi recalls that when he served as the commander of military intelligence, he used to prepare a daily intelligence report for the prime minister in which he included not only information received that day but "basic facts, attempting to create an awareness and sensitivity of the decision-maker to the specifically Middle Eastern aspects of the topics handled by military intelligence." Although successful, his efforts also demonstrated that the flipside of influence was loss of control over the attribution of discourse: every time he presented the prime minister with an intelligence assessment, reports Harkabi, he would discover that the latter has already arrived at the same conclusion earlier, "by virtue of his keen historical sensibility."[21]

The Protected Space of the Shiloah Institute

The annexation of the Shiloah Institute by Tel-Aviv University in the early 1960s must be understood as a complementary event within the overall process that began with the creation of the research branch of military intelligence – that is, as a necessary offshoot of the network of intelligence expertise. The main contribution of the Shiloah Institute lay in the fact that it was a place where the discourse of the experts could be protected from appropriation by their clients and attributed to them without fear. The Shiloah Institute is a liminal institutional setting, a protected space between the university and officialdom. It is a space controlled by the experts, a space into which they occasionally invite their clients, the men of power, to present them with their assessments, pump them for information, and enjoy the prestige that proximity to power brings.

The organizational structure of the Shiloah Institute, which in 1983 was transformed into the Dayan Center, and the patterns of expert labor within it imitate the mode of production of intelligence knowledge that was institutionalized in military intelligence. Additionally, it benefits from a supply of classified information passed to it by the army, as if it was a sort of auxiliary research arm of military intelligence. Such trust is probably facilitated by the fact that many of the experts working in the Dayan Center served in the research branch of military intelligence and still perform their reserve duty there.

The major point, however, is that the networks that are woven within this protected space and that connect the experts with their clients are not premised on relations of hierarchy and authority, as in military intelligence, but on patterns of academic sociation and cooperation. Thus, the experts at the Dayan Center enjoy at least some of the attributes of the position secured by the research branch of military intelligence – proximity to decision makers, ability to appropriate and black-box the work of information gathering – and yet maintain control over the dissemination and attribution of their own discourse. In short, they have managed to strike a balance between dependence and independence, closure and generosity. Therefore, in Figure 6.1, I put the Shiloah Institute at the center of the field of orientalist expertise.[22]

The Shiloah Institute was established in 1959 as a joint endeavor of the Foreign and Defense ministries, the military, the Hebrew University, and the Israeli Oriental Society. It was originally envisioned as an "independent" research agency serving the Foreign Office and other state agencies and providing them with information and research on "contemporary problems of Arab countries" as well as "informing the rest of the world about Israel's views about the region." It was staffed by career officials from the Foreign Office and some doctoral students from the Hebrew University. Their work included editing the official journal of the Israeli Oriental Society, *Ha-Mizrah Ha-Hadash* (The New Orient), as well as preparing the annual *Middle East Record* (*MER*), which compiled information from open sources on all significant events in the Middle East in a given year.

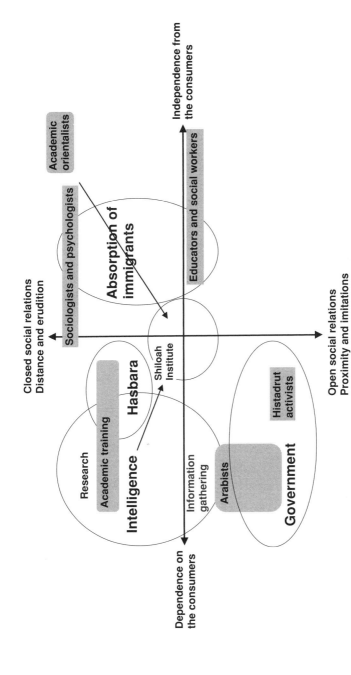

FIGURE 6.1. The field of orientalist expertise after 1965.

A young nontenured lecturer at the Hebrew University, Shimon Shamir, came up with the idea of having the university annex the institute. After the Hebrew University authorities declined his initiative, he wrote a memo in December 1965 to the administration of Tel-Aviv University, established just a few years earlier, and recommended that it annex the Shiloah Institute. He emphasized that the institute "is already well-known in professional circles around the world . . . it possesses a large number of archival materials . . . and it is guaranteed the support and cooperation of the state in the professional sphere, as well as in funding, and in collecting materials to be used for research." Tel-Aviv University seized the opportunity, agreed to place the institute under its auspices, and appointed Shamir as its director and as chair of a new department devoted to the history of the modern Middle East. He brought with him a few young doctoral students and nontenured lecturers from the Hebrew University. Thus, the social actors responsible for the annexation and redesign of the Shiloah Institute were, as in the prestate period, a group of young scholars who encountered mobility barriers within the Hebrew University. Unlike the older generation, however, this group no longer faced a strictly split field.

First, the administration of the newly created Tel-Aviv University, intent on recruiting allies to support it in its struggle against the more established Hebrew University, was already modifying the accepted boundaries. Its strategy was to strike alliances with powerful state agencies by offering them departments and programs tailor-made to their needs, such as a department of labor studies, intended to secure the support of the General Federation of Trade Unions, and a department devoted to military history, created with support from the army. The Shiloah Institute fit within this strategy and indeed secured the continuing support of the foreign ministry, the military, and other state agencies in the form of funds, personnel, and archival materials.

The other cause of change in the structure of the field, as represented in Figure 6.1, was the network of expertise developed by the research branch of military intelligence, which could now be extended to bridge the chasm between practical and academic research. One former research officer, Itamar Rabinovich, having obtained a Ph.D. in Middle Eastern studies from UCLA, now joined Tel-Aviv University and became Shamir's second-in-command. Another former officer, Yitzhak Oron, having served as director of the institute before it was annexed to Tel-Aviv University, remained on board for the first few years to assist in the transition. One could say, therefore, that Tel-Aviv University's annexation of the Shiloah Institute was facilitated by a unique interlocking of interests between the authorities of the university, high-ranking officials and officers at the Foreign Office and military intelligence, and a group of young academics whose mobility was blocked or at least delayed at the Hebrew University. They were all interested in breaking the monopoly of the orientalists at the Hebrew University, who were strictly opposed to any links between academic historical research and intelligence research on current affairs.[23]

Once in Tel-Aviv University, Shamir and his colleagues shaped the Shiloah Institute as a liminal institutional setting located between the academy and officialdom. From it they wove a social network that connected the experts with their clients, not through relations of authority, but through four forms of intellectual sociation taken from the academic world:

1. *Research teams.* Military intelligence officers and state officials were invited to become guest researchers, who reside for a year at the institute and make use of its research facilities. For example, in the first three years of the institute's existence, guest researchers included the head of the Jordanian desk in the research branch of military intelligence, a high-ranking Mossad official, three Foreign Office experts, a member of parliament, and an official in the Office of the Adviser on Arab Affairs.[24] The guest researchers were asked to participate in the institute's regular teamwork, preparing the annual publication *Middle East Contemporary Survey* (*MECS*), which replaced the earlier *MER*. They also published their independent research in the institute's monograph series.

2. *Committees.* Military intelligence officers and state officials were also appointed to the permanent research committee of the institute, responsible for approving research grants, selecting guest researchers, deciding on team projects, and so on. The first research committee included a former commander of military intelligence, a former military intelligence and Mossad officer, two Foreign Office experts, and a member of parliament.[25] In 1983, the Dayan Center was established to provide a more comprehensive organizational framework, and it encompasses the Shiloah Institute and various auxiliary documentation and fund-raising units. This reorganization did not lead to any fundamental change in the pattern of relations between the experts and the state, and the same professors who controlled the Shiloah Institute, Shimon Shamir and Itamar Rabinovich, continued to control the Dayan Center. At the same time, the creation of the Dayan Center did express the growing prestige and influence of the experts as well as their increasing international connections. Essentially, the center served as a budgetary unit that managed the endowment donated to the Shiloah Institute in that year and the increasing flow of grants and funds resulting from the connections and efforts of the leading professors. An international

advisory board was created, and among its members were financiers, such as Edmond de Rothschild and Edgar Bronfman, as well as important personalities from the world of foreign and security affairs, such as James Schlesinger, Cyrus Vance, and Alexander Haig.

3. *Conferences.* The Shiloah Institute sponsored conferences and panel discussions on topical issues of the day, to which were invited military intelligence officers, state officials, and high-ranking politicians as speakers, commentators, and honorary guests. A few random examples: A conference in January 1986 on "The Iranian Revolution and the Islamic World" included the participation of Yitzhak Rabin (then an opposition member of parliament) and the Adviser on Arab Affairs to the Prime Minister, a public debate in December 1987 about the first intifada included the participation of the Adviser on Arab Affairs to the Prime Minister and a former commander of military intelligence, and a 1987 seminar on "The Middle East Twenty Years after the Six-Day War" included the participation of two Foreign Office officials and another former commander of military intelligence.

4. *Edited volumes.* The Shiloah Institute also published edited volumes comprising articles written by academics, military intelligence officers, state officials, journalists, politicians, and so on. One example is the volume titled *The Decline of Nasserism*, edited by Shamir. This volume was dedicated to the memory of a former commander of the research branch of military intelligence. A former commander of military intelligence wrote the introduction. The volume included contributions from twelve academics, ten "researchers in public and state institutions," three journalists, and two members of parliament.[26]

These forms of sociation constructed the institute at once as a protected space within which it was possible to protect the discourse of the experts from appropriation by powerful clients and as an interface with the official world, allowing the experts to create a "fellowship of discourse" with men of power. Thus, in comparison with the situation of the doctoral students in the prestate period, these forms of sociation were doubly advantageous: The experts were not confined to an ivory tower and could enjoy all the benefits accruing from proximity to officials and politicians (influence, prestige, resources, and classified materials), and they were not exposed to the dangers of crossing over into the official world and losing control over their discourse.

From its inception, the Shiloah Institute regularly recruited its personnel from among individuals who served in the research branch of military intelligence and who typically still do their reserve duty there.[27] Moreover, the organizational structure of the institute imitates, to a large extent, the mode of production of intelligence knowledge as institutionalized in military intelligence:

1. *Teamwork and desk organization.* Horizontally, the Shiloah Institute was divided into "desks," each dedicated to an Arab state or group of states, as well as specialized desks for "superpowers in the Middle East," "inter-Arab relations," and "Israeli-Arab relations." A senior researcher, who specialized in the relevant country or topic, headed each desk. As in military intelligence, the work of the desks and the information and analyses they produced were to be coordinated through regular meetings of the senior researchers. The final product of this teamwork was the annual publication of the institute, the *MECS*, which aimed at providing full coverage of Middle Eastern events. It was organized in two parts, mimicking the structure established by *All Contingencies* for the Annual National Intelligence Assessment as well as replicating the desk structure. The first part was composed of country surveys, and the second of several synthetic treatises on "inter-Arab relations," "the Israeli-Arab conflict," and so on. This model of teamwork, and the ambition to offer as wide a coverage as possible, dictated the institute's recruitment policy and the selection of topics of specialization by the junior researchers. Thus, the institute was able to imitate the pattern established by military intelligence, where researchers in charge of a particular desk are apportioned the task of representing the perspective of a particular Arab leader, in whom they specialize.[28]

2. *Hierarchical division of labor between research and information gathering.* Vertically, the institute was shaped as an organizational hierarchy, at the foundation of which was an "information center," the functional equivalent of the information-gathering branch of military intelligence. A non-faculty full-time staff member was appointed to run this center, whose task was to organize the work of research assistants in collecting and archiving information about events, personalities, and so on, mostly from open sources such as the Arab press. In 1972 alone, they produced 25,000 cards cataloguing new items of information. Later, the card index became a computerized database. This database was not simply an archive (many of which exist in the university) but also, as Rabinovich put it, a "distribution center" that "distributes daily lists of the new items of information catalogued, so they could be used by people who are interested in this material." The use of the code word "distribution center" is telling, as precisely such a center was established in military intelligence just a few years earlier, in 1967.[29] Because the database functioned as a distribution center, the work of the assistants was made immediately available to the senior researchers.

The format of the institute's publications also reflected this hierarchical division between information gathering and research and between apprentice, pedant, and interpreter. The main work done at the institute was the compilation of concordances and surveys directly based on the data collected by the research assistants. The most important publication was the *MECS*, which summarized the major events in a given year and also included abstracts of diplomatic documents, trade agreements, and so on. The senior researchers prepared the *MECS* in their role as pedants. In the same role they also contributed to the survey series published by the institute – short summaries of significant developments, almost without any interpretation. The research assistants were also employed in preparing the institute's series of research and instruction tools, such as bibliographies, indexes, abstracts of articles about the Middle East, and books containing "basic data about the modern Arab press." All these concordances and research tools served as a continually updated resource for the senior and guest researchers as they wrote monographs to be published in the institute's monograph series. Typically, these monographs cited the *MECS* and the survey series profusely but went beyond them to provide explanations, assessments, and interpretations.

This hierarchical structure was conserved and reproduced by differential patterns of employment and promotion. Although the department of Middle Eastern studies employed only a small number of teaching assistants (e.g., thirteen in 1971), the information center employed roughly twice as many research assistants (twenty-five in 1971).[30] Many of these research assistants were students who, as "apprentices", also worked on their master's theses and doctoral dissertations and eventually graduated and took academic positions. But at least half never advanced beyond the master's level and remained employed at the institute for many years as nonfaculty research staff. They were sometimes promoted within the institute, from research assistants to "researcher." In other cases, students found employment in the various intelligence agencies.[31] This was especially true for women, who had less chance of completing their graduate studies and obtaining a tenure-track academic position than their male colleagues. Of the eighteen assistants about whom I have career information, between 1967 and 1989, nine never obtained a Ph.D., and seven of these were women. Of the nine who obtained a Ph.D., with an average time of 11.5 years from the beginning of employment to the awarding of the degree, only three were women.[32]

Since it was shaped as a liminal space between the academy and the state, mimicking the organization of military intelligence, and since the latter's research officers could move into this space either at the end of their service or for a short period as guest researchers, the Shiloah Institute became in essence an integral part of the network of expertise created by the research officers, a sort of an auxiliary arm specializing in "basic research." Indeed, the intimate ties with military intelligence benefited the institute, as Shamir promised in his memo, by ensuring a direct flow of classified and nonclassified information collected by military intelligence. According to the Bulletin of the Faculty of Humanities, the information center at the Shiloah Institute contains "a large collection of middle eastern newspapers and archival material from the archives of several institutions within Israel and outside it" – a euphemistic way of referring to, among other items, Syrian, Egyptian, Jordanian, and Palestinian documents captured by the army during Israel's wars and used by the institute's researchers in preparing their monographs.[33] Additionally, institute researchers have been able to "pump" the guest researchers and lecturers who hail from the intelligence community for classified information.[34] Finally, many of the senior researchers have served in military intelligence as their reserve duty and have been able to use some of the classified information they encountered there in their academic publications.[35] It follows from all this that the Shiloah Institute, and the Dayan Center after it, functioned within Tel-Aviv University as a sort of semisecretive enclave, the access to which was restricted to those with the proper security clearance. Some of the texts produced within this enclave, including master's theses and doctoral dissertations, were themselves semisecretive and not accessible to the public. Because they contained classified information, they could be read and judged only by professors who themselves belonged, in one way or another, to the network of intelligence expertise and had received the necessary security clearance.

The reader may justly argue that there is nothing surprising or shocking about this aspect of the Shiloah Institute. The academic space is only ostensibly governed by principles of free access. In reality, access is restricted to sites within it in a graduated manner, from classrooms, which are accessible to anybody; through offices, dorms, and libraries, which require a university ID for entrance; to laboratories that manipulate dangerous materials, utilize very expensive devices, or engage in security-related (e.g., nuclear) research and are off limits to laypeople and academics not engaged in the work being done there. All this is true, but the principle of exclusion and restriction upon which the Shiloah Institute was premised seems to me quite different. The institute excluded, in advance and with no recourse to appeal, a whole category of citizens defined by the state as "dangerous" – that is, Palestinian citizens of Israel.[36] The Shiloah Institute was, therefore, an auxiliary arm of the network of intelligence expertise and of the State of Israel also in another sense: it reproduced and thereby also reinforced the whole system of divisions and exclusions that manufactured the effect of the state out of the oxymoron "Jewish and democratic" and that constructed Palestinians as second-class citizens, at once included and excluded. If we add to this the fact that relatively few of the institute's researchers were of *mizrahi* origins – especially in comparison with the Department for Arabic Language and Literature at Tel-Aviv University, for example – then we get in one place, within the enclave of the Shiloah Institute, the whole hierarchy of the Israeli social order converted into epistemological categories – Arabs excluded, *mizrahi* Jews at the bottom or excluded.[37]

Let us return, however, to the experts at the Shiloah Institute and its later incarnation as the Dayan Center. Within the protected space they created, they could now associate with the men of power, the politicians and the army commanders, and learn from them their language: the diplomatic language that is used to formulate messages to enemy leaders, the military language of simulations and the analysis of intentions. The proper use of this language cannot be acquired merely by reading texts. According to Wittgenstein, in order to master the rules of a particular language game, one must become immersed in the form of life that endows it with meaning. Indeed, for the academic experts to become interpreters of intentions, they had to learn the rituals and conventions of the official form of life. Only through the silent and embodied agreements that these rituals convey is it possible to grasp the meaning of official modes of speech. Hence, the importance of the protected space of the Shiloah Institute. For the academics of the Shiloah Institute, who typically were only junior officers in military intelligence, it afforded the opportunity to acquire invaluable experience, to observe firsthand how the politicians and the commanders behave and speak, to imitate and rehearse the conventional rituals of the official form of life, and to become well versed in its intricacies. Indeed, this is precisely what the first director of the Shiloah Institute recommended to the experts: "The researcher of political intelligence must gain experience in the life of political practice . . . in order to try to understand 'what really happened' . . . we need to try to understand 'how things really get done.' The best way to gain such understanding is to participate in the doing. . . . One way in which the researcher of political intelligence could learn is by participating in the decision making process of his clients. . . . Participating in negotiations . . . working for the diplomatic service . . . "[38]

The Orientalists' Debate

None of what I have said up till now should be taken as indicating that I think that the experts – especially those at the Dayan Center – are necessarily highly influential individuals to whose words the men of power listen carefully. As I explained earlier, intelligence expertise is not a quality of an individual or even of a group of individuals but is a network of ties woven between agents who occupy different positions. To analyze it, one must take into account not only the experts who speak but also the direct producers of knowledge (humans as well as devices), the clients who use it (especially politicians and the top military brass), those about whom knowledge is produced (especially enemy leaders), and the interpretations that all the various participants in the network give to the ties between them and that serve to translate and co-ordinate their interests. Power and influence produced by this network are not the property of this or that individual, not even of those who occupy an obligatory point of passage (as we saw, there are clear limits to their ability to control the attribution and dissemination of their discourse), but they belong to the network as a whole and to the discourse that it produces and dissem-inates. Unlike the military intelligence officers, the experts at the Dayan Center do control the attribution and dissemination of their discourse, but by the same token this feature of their position also limits their influence, and for two reasons: First, the men of power, especially the politicians, are not in-terested in sharing the limelight with them. Second, the more the academic experts do enjoy the glare of publicity, the more vulnerable they become, easy targets for the criticism that they are responsible for political or military failures or that their assessments and interpretations are politically biased. For these reasons, they tend to accept the view that their role in the network is to do "basic research" or "didactic intelligence" and to provide the decision makers with "wide and deep background" about things like "personality, leading group, movement, ideological current, political school, moods, how we are perceived by the other."[39]

The leaders of the Shiloah Institute became acutely aware of these lim-its in the aftermath of the Yom Kippur war (October 1973), following the publication of the report of a committee of inquiry appointed to investigate the intelligence blunder preceding the war. On the one hand, this was a time of opportunity for the experts, because the committee faulted the research branch of military intelligence and called for the creation of alternative as-sessment agencies involving the academy. On the other hand, if the experts attempted to take advantage of the opportunities, they stood in danger of becoming themselves engulfed in the acrimonious public debate and of los-ing the neutral status they strove so hard to attain. In fact, the community of academic experts was not exempt from the public debate and mutual ac-cusations. Their rivals at the Hebrew University perceived an opportunity to settle their accounts with the upstarts from Tel-Aviv, who before the war received much more attention from the press and were even invited to testify before the Security and Foreign Affairs Committee of the parliament.[40]

The majority of the participants in a conference titled "The Goals of the Arab Struggle against Israel in the Wake of the Yom Kippur War," which

took place on the Hebrew University campus in 1974, offered scathing criticisms of their colleagues from Tel-Aviv. In particular, they faulted what they
described as the unwarrantedly optimistic assessments issued by the Shiloah
Institute before the war. Amnon Cohen, a professor at the Institute for Oriental Studies opined that he was glad "to hear that we have other voices in
the academic community." Among the Jerusalem scholars, none was more
vehement in his attack than Yehoshafat Harkabi, the former commander of
military intelligence and now a professor at the Hebrew University. He demanded, in a widely read newspaper opinion piece, to start a "national soul
searching" and claimed that the intelligence blunder was caused by illusions
that were cultivated by "politicians, commentators, journalists, academics
and intellectuals." He toured the country and gave lectures in which his
accusations became more specific and personal: the experts at the Shiloah
Institute, he argued, were responsible for the blunder, because they lulled
the Israeli establishment into a false sense of security by focusing on the
more congenial opinions of Arab moderates. For their part, the leaders of
the Shiloah Institute, Shamir, Rabinovich, and Haim Shaked, did not remain silent. They gave a collective interview to the same newspaper, under
the headline "The Orientalists' Debate," in which they accused Harkabi of
dishonesty and of introducing a polemical and one-sided "new style . . . to
the professional sphere; and it is possible to doubt the impartiality of this
critique."[41]

   In order to understand the causes and character of Harkabi's attack, one
must go back to the 1960s, when, after he was fired from the position of commander of military intelligence, he served as the director of the Department
for Strategic Planning at the Defense Ministry and was simultaneously working on his doctoral dissertation at the Hebrew University. Harkabi collected
an enormous number of Arabic books, articles, pamphlets, and documents,
some of which were captured during the 1967 war, and in them he sought
to trace the logic and internal cohesion of what he called "the Arab position
in the Israeli-Arab conflict." He argued that

any conflict is a struggle between opponents, each of whom has a position in the
conflict, that consists of the sum total of his opinions about the conflict, his emotions
regarding [the conflict], and is expressed through his policy. From this point of view,
the conflict is in a sense a debate between these two positions.

With the term "position" he sought to denote an "ideational framework that
includes [the Arabs'] thinking about the conflict," defines their goals, and
dictates their actions.[42] Even though Harkabi claimed he took the concept
of "position" (or "attitude"; this is the same word in Hebrew, *emdah*) from
the field of cognitive psychology, it is not difficult to trace this definition to

Harkabi's philological training at the Institute for Oriental Studies as well as to the interpretation of intentions à la military intelligence.

Nonetheless, Harkabi's move involved a challenge to the dominant position of the research branch of military intelligence and the Shiloah Institute. In a sense, he sought to shift the balance of power within the network of intelligence expertise and to create a sort of "supercenter" dealing with what he called "strategic research." Strategic research would include not only intelligence and Middle Eastern Studies but also military history, operations research, system analysis, strategy, research on Israel's foreign policy, and analysis of conflicts. He claimed that Israel was lacking "a scientific understanding of the conflict" and that such "scientific analysis of the conflict might actually help to clarify political and party political disagreements among us, and might actually help to bring opinions and hearts closer together" – a clear insinuation that military intelligence was too politicized.[43]

Harkabi's arguments in the debate had two layers. First, on the substantive level, he argued that the experts of the Shiloah Institute, especially Shamir, contributed to the atmosphere of complacency before the war, because they focused on what was said by Arab moderates and deduced that Arab hostility toward Israel was waning and the time was ripe for negotiations. He insinuated that they were politically biased. Shamir was a well-known dove and aligned with the moderate left. Second, on the methodological level, Harkabi noted that the experts of the Shiloah Institute tended toward a "deep" interpretation of intentions. They did not remain at the manifest level of what the text actually said in plain words but speculated about latent intentions and unconscious possibilities that somehow underlay the text. He argued that Shamir and his colleagues ignored what the Arabs said in public about their intention to start a war and instead speculated that the decline of pan-Arabism and the strengthening of the specifically Egyptian component in Egypt's national consciousness and policy would lead Egypt to adopt a more pragmatic attitude toward Israel.[44]

We should understand this methodological critique as reflecting Harkabi's relatively marginal position in the network of intelligence expertise. He was no longer at the bottleneck of intelligence assessment, and most of his work before the war was in the field of *hasbara*, either internal instruction for the IDF Education Corps or external polemics for the Hasbara Department of the Foreign Office.[45] For this reason, he essentially retreated to the position of a pedant and to a literal reading of the text, valuing above all fidelity to the text:

The approach that this paper takes involves a close and detailed examination of the significance of how political decisions are formulated – the simple meaning of the text. While it is possible to criticize this approach for being "misplaced literalism," i.e. for attributing a strict meaning to words that was not present in the minds of their speakers when they used them. . . . It seems to me that this is a false criticism. . . . We do not possess the sort of x-ray machine that would permit us to penetrate the "soul" of the PLO and examine its thoughts, and consequently we can judge its positions only by what it says and does.[46]

He objected to the tendency to underestimate the significance of "extreme Arab expressions against Israel" and to argue on the basis of a "deeper" figurative interpretation that they are "merely expressions of emotionalism, and need not be taken seriously." Such a tendency, he warned, reflected "lack of interest in Israel in Arab developments in the sphere of ideas, and especially lack of interest in the possibility of using these developments in the international political struggle." This is simply "to misunderstand a basic issue: namely, that the conflict between us and the Arab states is conducted . . . most of the time . . . through a competition over international public opinion." By "using materials taken from the dialogue that the Arabs carry out among themselves," it is possible to "refute the logic of the dialogue that they attempt to carry out with the rest of the world. . . . The intentions and weaknesses of the Arabs' positions become manifest precisely in the course of the debates that they conduct among themselves."[47] Clearly, Harkabi sought to revalorize the work of *hasbara*, but this does not mean that he wanted to give it pride of place above intelligence. His intention was to reintegrate intelligence with *hasbara* and diplomacy as part of a global "scientific analysis" of the conflict.[48]

In their response to Harkabi, the leaders of the Shiloah Institute concentrated on the first, substantive level of his criticism. The reason is clear: not only did he argue that they were wrong in their assessments, Harkabi also threatened to destroy the status they worked hard to create for themselves, because he suggested that academics should not be exempted from the fate that befell the military intelligence officers responsible for the blunder, who were demoted or asked to resign. Put differently, Harkabi displayed utter disregard for what they attempted to create in the protected space of the Shiloah Institute, that is, the status of experts who are not part of the official hierarchy and whose discourse cannot be evaluated by external criteria, since it deals with "basic research" or "didactic intelligence." They were worried less by the unlikely prospect of being summoned before the committee than by Harkabi's attempt, in a sense, to erase the distance between different positions within the network of intelligence expertise. Harkabi's attack threatened to bring down the walls of the Shiloah Institute, the protected space they erected precisely because they wanted to create a context in which their interpretations and commentary could be grafted onto the official discourse and nonetheless would be accumulated as the private property of the expert, without being polluted by proximity to the politicians and their actions. For this reason, their reaction was swift – their collective interview was published only one week after Harkabi's op-ed piece – and scathing. They insinuated that Harkabi himself was responsible for the intelligence blunder, both because his writings tended to underestimate the strength of the Arabs and their readiness for war and because he was much more influential than they were. But the main thrust of their response was to define the proper rules of use of basic academic research: What is permissible to do with it and what is not? Who can repeat it, add to it, or dispute it, and when and in what context?

Our academic role is to analyze processes and provide the most complete picture. Afterwards, it is possible to use this for better or worse – depending on the user's intent. The easiest thing, and probably the most malicious, is to take things that were said before the war and to say after it that they caused the blunder. . . . This form of critique will hang as Damocles' sword over serious academic activity in this field. If we will not be able to analyze things as they are, and worry whether individuals may use them as they please – this is the beginning of the degeneration of the profession.[49]

Shamir explained that he was misunderstood: he had indeed pointed out that Egypt was undergoing a process of de-Nasserization and a strengthening of the specifically Egyptian component of its identity vis-à-vis the Arab one, but this did not mean that all the conclusions, "which were not mine," followed. Rabinovich, for his part, stressed that they were engaged in "basic research," something different from both practical intelligence and *hasbara*: "As researchers, our role is to analyze, and not to educate or direct; to asses, without making recommendations that have a direct operative political application. As researchers our role is not to tell the government what to do." As an example, he noted that when he was summoned to testify before the Security and Foreign Affairs Committee of the parliament, the questions put to him were analytic, not practical. The utility of expert discourse, therefore, is didactic, and such discourse should not be confused with either operative recommendations or a political opinion. When he appeared before the committee, he felt that the MPs understood this much better than Harkabi:

This phenomenon, when people dig into what others say, could destroy research. People will avoid voicing their analysis and assessments. . . . After all, anything I may say about Syrian policy from 1967 to 1973 could be diverted to political purposes by somebody. And yet we still hope that we can conduct the debate matter-of-factly and analyze Arab positions in a balanced way.[50]

In short, the response of the leaders of the Shiloah Institute to Harkabi's attack was to perform boundary work, to attempt to separate the "academic role" of the experts from the "political uses" of their discourse. It was also a fairly obvious message to their competitor that he was undercutting his own status as well. Harkabi's next article, two weeks later, was much more conciliatory. It was titled "For a Personal Soul-Searching," and in it he admitted his own failures. But he also agreed that he went too far with his critique because "a balanced consideration will show that the direct influence on decision-making by those called orientalists in this country was minimal. This holds both for me and for my opponents."[51]

When it came to Harkabi's methodological critique, the experts of the Shiloah Institute were less inclined to respond. They typically attempted to present Harkabi as an Arabist or an old-style orientalist. *Mizrahanut*, they argued, suffers from bad public relations. The public thinks that this field deals with

the secrets of "Arab mentality," as if it is an occupation for those who possess some occult wisdom. . . . Unfortunately, there are those who feed this image. Their writings are full of quotations from Arab texts that purportedly reflect the inner recesses of the "Arab" soul, his twisted personality and his perversions. In recent years, our profession has began to be perceived as esoteric. As if through texts open to orientalists alone, it is possible to find the key to the "hidden intentions" of Arab policy. . . . About the blunder of 1973, we are told by many that our mistake lay in the fact that we did not understand Arab mentality and the logic of the Egyptians, which is different from our own. Well, the decision-making process in Egypt is logical, and the decision to go to war followed rationally from Egyptian interests. These interests, above all else, we must understand and analyze.

But this depiction of Harkabi was misplaced. He too distinguished himself from the Arabists and old-style orientalists. Many Israelis, he said, including orientalists, underestimated the soul-searching that the Arabs did after the 1967 war, and that is why they were surprised. They thought that the Arabs were not rational, but the Arabs debated the conflict in a rational way.[52]

Harkabi's critique, in a sense, drew an analogy between the approach of the Shiloah Institute and the notorious "conception" that led military intelligence to ignore the signs indicating war. The analogy was not at the substantive level (since the "conception" was based on an analysis of the technical military conditions necessary for Egypt to go to war)[53] but at the methodological level – the same "deep" interpretation of intentions that ignores clear signals sent to it by information gathering (or the text), the same hubris of the "intelligent evaluator" and his "architectonic concept." In actuality, the two sides in this controversy shared a similar methodology. They both had acquired the philological *habitus* under similar circumstances – in military intelligence and under the authority of the professors at the Institute for Oriental Studies – and they both participated in the network of intelligence expertise that was premised on the exclusion of the Arabists. The difference between them was merely a matter of location within the network itself rather than a question of method or skills. Harkabi's attack was formulated from the point of view of the pedant, who mistrusts the speculative excesses of the interpreter. For this reason, the Arabists who commented on the debate were critical of both sides. Both, they argued, did not really understand "Arab mentality" and lacked the necessary familiarity with and immediate proximity to their subjects:

Harkabi analyzes the data at his disposal, in the form of Arab newspapers, literature, reports, political declarations, decisions of certain conventions, etc. His assumption is that one should accept what is said as concrete intentions and one should not entertain illusions, based on a gap between declarations and intentions. Shamir, on the other hand, assumes a gap between two levels: the declarative-ideological level and the concrete-operative level. . . . The problem is that there are no parameters with which to measure the gaps between words and intentions and deeds, but the lack of such parameters should not lead us as well to ignore the existence of such gaps. . . . Words and ideas on one level, deeds and reality on another. Indeed, there is no measuring rod with which to measure the gaps. Maybe intuition and practical experience could supply what is lacking. But in order to get these, theoretical research will not suffice. Maybe these scholars need to descend from the heights and move among the Arab population. Then they will acquire experience and sharpen their intuition through direct contact with the members of this society.[54]

The reader will probably not be surprised to learn that the writer was a veteran Arabist and military governor. He was also a graduate student in sociology at Tel-Aviv University; that is, he was among those who tried to synthesize the Arabist art of government with the social sciences, especially ethnography. Precisely because the network of intelligence expertise relied on the exclusion of Arabist expertise, he could identify what was common to the two rival sides and point out what was arbitrary about their claims. Hence also his sardonic recommendation that they should descend among the common people and "sharpen their intuition" there.

The concept of "intention" or "position," around which the debate revolved, has meaning only within the network of intelligence expertise, and only because this network involves ties to those who listen to and use the experts' commentary as well as ties to those about whom it is pronounced. If the interpretation of intentions possesses a certain validity and stability, albeit rather precarious, it is only within the game of communication between decision maker, expert, and adversary. This point is illustrated by the following story. In September 1976, the commander of military intelligence approached the experts of the Shiloah Institute and asked them to formulate indicators that could be used to determine whether the Arab states were interested in peace or not. Together with officers from the research branch, the staff of the Shiloah Institute formulated two questions: Is there a change in the public Arab declarations regarding Israel? Is there a normative change in the underlying Arab position with respect to peace with Israel? By October 1977, they had arrived at the conclusion that no significant change in the underlying Arab position was pending. Six weeks later, Anwar al-Sadat, Egypt's president, arrived in Jerusalem for a dramatic visit, which initiated the peace process between Israel and Egypt. As the president's plane entered Israeli airspace, the army's chief of staff, armed with the assessments of military intelligence, was still arguing that this was a "trap."[55]

I have recounted this story here not in order to poke fun at the experts' blindness. This story is important because it demonstrates three points. First, despite Harkabi's attack, the academics at the Shiloah Institute had managed to create for themselves a privileged position within the network of intelligence expertise, as members of a sort of auxiliary center for basic research. Even the research branch of military intelligence now delegated tasks to them and consulted them. The second point is that academic expertise and intelligence expertise were identical, part of the same network. The "indicators" developed by the Shiloah Institute's experts were shaped in accordance with the internalized predispositions of the philological *habitus*. They were composed of two stages — information and assessment, pedant and interpreter, overt declaration and underlying intention. The third point is that the concept of "intention" or "position" is a product of this network, and its main function is to translate and coordinate the interests of the participants in the network. This concept completely loses its validity when one of the participants in the network seeks to disturb the system of relations within the network and change it in a fundamental way — as did Anwar al-Sadat, for example.

Despite the failure of their assessment — and this was not the only failure they had — the experts at the Shiloah Institute had achieved their goal. Within the walls of their protected space, the alchemy took place, a result that had evaded their predecessors, the doctoral students of the Institute for Oriental Studies. Because they were now able to associate with decision makers and convey to them their assessments, they became influential. They accumulated both the social capital of well-placed connections and the symbolic capital of being "in the know." But because such association took place within the protected space of the Shiloah Institute, the experts maintained control over the dissemination and attribution of their discourse, and their academic standing was not affected. On the contrary, their connections meant that they enjoyed many of the resources mobilized by the network of intelligence expertise, such as classified documents, information, and funds, and they could convert these into the capital of scientific prestige and academic power. They became department chairs, deans, rectors, and presidents of universities.

They were rewarded with prestigious and endowed chairs. In time, they were able to convert this capital once again and cross over into the official world. But unlike their predecessors, the doctoral students, they did so from a position of strength. They did not endanger their academic standing, nor did they need to climb the long ladder of official tenure. Rather, they were appointed to influential and sensitive posts by the topmost political decision-makers. Indeed, because they had already practiced and rehearsed the rituals of the official form of life within the Shiloah Institute, and because, as one of them testified, the teamwork practiced at the institute was no different from the conducting of business by diplomatic delegations, they found the transition rather natural – except for, as this academic noted ruefully, the necessity to appear before TV cameras and microphones.[56]

Who Believes in the Palestinian Covenant?

Harkabi's attack, therefore, did not undermine the position of the Shiloah Institute, nor did it lead to a fundamental change in the structure of relations in the network of intelligence expertise. Nonetheless, the polemics did have some important consequences, at least in terms of what took place at the immediate margins of the jurisdiction of intelligence. The crowning achievement of Harkabi's oeuvre was the analysis of the Palestinian Covenant. Soon after the second version of the covenant was drafted during the meeting of the Palestinian National Council in July 1968, Harkabi translated the document into Hebrew and attached it as an appendix to an article he published in a major Israeli daily on November 21, 1969. At the same time, he prepared an annotated version of the covenant, replete with his own commentary and explanations, for the Hasbara Center. It was a masterpiece of pedantic literal interpretation.

The covenant, according to Harkabi, was a "coherent and well-drafted doctrinal document." Each and every word in it was carefully chosen, since it was meant to express the "central idea" of the Palestinian national movement. "The covenant is . . . the doctrine of the Palestinians." (Harkabi uses here the noun *Torah*, a word that has weighty connotations in Hebrew, as it specifically denotes the five books of the Pentateuch and more generally the whole of the sacred texts and their study.) For this reason, one must treat everything it says with complete seriousness and not dismiss it as a "bargaining trick, an opening gambit in negotiations," nor as an "emotional, psychological matter." That is, in the analysis of the covenant there is no place for "deep" and sophistical interpretation. Nonetheless, when analyzing the covenant one must remember that "in the matter of the conflict, the Arabs tend to speak in an algebraic language whose underlying terms mean the destruction of Israel, but without saying so explicitly. . . . Their aim is to present a pragmatic line and create the impression of moderation." It is it not possible, therefore, to read the covenant without the annotation and clarification provided by the pedant, who translates its language and explains the significance and derivation of the terms it uses. Harkabi's conclusion was that "the covenant completely rejects Israel's existence and institutionalizes this rejection . . . in an ideational framework." The rejection of Israel is the basic idea of the Palestinian national movement, "and it is very hard for a national movement to change the basic idea of its conception." For this reason, "the claim that the PLO holds as a bargaining chip the possibility of a change in its position is a false claim," a "political myth."[57]

In order to understand the context for Harkabi's intervention, we must recall that the jurisdiction of the network of intelligence expertise was limited to Arab regimes and leaders, and even after the 1967 war, when the vast refugee camps of the West Bank and the Gaza Strip came under Israeli control, military intelligence refused to deal with collecting and assessing information about them. The result was that a certain no-man's-land, a sort of unoccupied interstitial domain, was created in between the jurisdictions of intelligence, government, and *hasbara*, and immediately a struggle arose between the experts as to who was to occupy it. The first to enter it were Amnon Cohen and David Farhi, young doctoral students at the Institute for Oriental Studies at the Hebrew University. After the war, then Defense Minister Moshe Dayan (who in the 1950s was enrolled as a bachelor's student at the Institute for Oriental Studies) pressured the Hebrew University authorities to "lend" Cohen and Farhi to the unit of the Adviser on Arab Affairs in the newly formed military government in the territories. The two, who had served in military intelligence earlier, consulted with their teachers and received their blessings. Unlike the earlier military government over the Palestinian citizens of Israel, the military governors in the occupied territories were not Arabists but career army officers, many of whom did not even speak Arabic (though there were exceptions, like Zvi Al-Peleg and Yosef Luntz). Behind this staffing policy was Dayan's intention to bypass the Arabists in order to implement a wholly new policy in the occupied territories, a policy that was diametrically opposed to what the Arabists implemented with respect to the Palestinian citizens of Israel – open bridges between the West Bank and Jordan, economic integration of the territories with Israel, minimal interference in the everyday lives of the inhabitants.

Dayan justified his preference for the young doctoral students by saying that the Arabists mostly had expert knowledge about the rural Palestinian population and an understanding of the common people, whereas in the occupied territories "we are dealing now with a different type of Palestinians, an educated political elite – and we need Israelis who speak its language." Military intelligence, for its part, refused to allocate any of its officers to become military governors. It was principally concerned with events on the other side of the new borders and did not accord much importance to the collection of information in the occupied territories. Nor was it particularly interested in the opportunity for its research officers to gain firsthand experience of the Palestinian residents. Expertise in Arab affairs, therefore, was not placed in the hands of the governors but was concentrated in the auxiliary unit of the Adviser on Arab Affairs. The adviser was defined as "an Arabist who is attached to the governor and informs him about the mood of the local population." The adviser's role, therefore, was not to govern the population but to represent it, to speak for it, and to coordinate the necessary contacts between the governor and the local leadership. Additionally, the adviser was to advise the governor and assist in decision making and policy formation. Later, Farhi was appointed adviser on Arab affairs to the defense minister himself, a position that chiefly involved the coordination of policy in the occupied territories and that, after Farhi's tenure, was occupied by other orientalists from the Hebrew University – Amnon Cohen and Menahem Milson.[58]

Suddenly, there was an opening for a new-old type of expert – neither an Arabist who specializes in the villages, nor an interpreter of the intentions of leaders and regimes, but someone capable of moving among the educated elites and representing them (as Eliahu Sasson and the doctoral students at the Jewish Agency had sought to do before the formation of the state). Neither a governor, nor a researcher, but an adviser. A new position was created that, within the network of intelligence expertise, would have been previously impossible: a position whose responsibilities included representing the refugee-infiltrator hybrid and speaking in its name, explaining to the Israeli public and decision makers what the Palestinians wanted:

It is difficult to speak in generalizations, but let's try to construct a synthetic type of the Arab person in the territories, a sort of collective personality: he would like the name "Palestine" to be represented at the table, where the fate of the Palestinians will be determined, but they definitely do not want that the Palestinian representative will aspire to the destruction of Israel. . . . They want a Palestinian state alongside of which Israel will exist within the 1967 borders. . . . More importantly: this collective Arab person is completely unwilling to agree that the East Bank, the Jordanian Kingdom of today, is not part of the Palestinian motherland. . . . Of course, the Arabs of the West Bank and Gaza want to live under an Arab rule, and not a Jewish one. But they will not give up Jordan and they do not want to be disconnected from Israel.

Interviewer: There is therefore, an irreconcilable opposition between them and the PLO and Yasser Arafat?

Farhi: Yes, definitely, he does not represent them.[59]

On the other hand, those who filled this position were each associated with a particular decision maker – Farhi with Dayan, Amnon Cohen after him with Ezer Weitzman, and Milson after them with Begin and then Sharon. Further, because each had only one client, the market situation, so to speak, of this adviser was such that, more than being an adviser, he was the spokesperson and messenger of this decision maker. The way Farhi represented the Palestinians, as willing to exist alongside Israel, wanting to maintain their ties with Jordan, and opposed to the PLO, corresponded in every detail to Dayan's policy, which included economic integration of the territories with Israel, relative tolerance for expressions of extremism (a "let them talk" policy), and open bridges with Jordan (through which, his critics argued, the influence of the PLO seeped into the territories). The important point is, therefore, that the structural characteristics of the position of the advisers – proximity and immediate contact with the residents of the territories, status as a representative of the residents, the need to adapt the supply of advice to the policy demands of their powerful clients – meant that their style of interpretation was radically different from Harkabi's. Unlike him, they did not pay much attention to the declarations and documents of the Palestinian organizations.

"It is of course much easier," explained Farhi, "to analyze the political position of the PLO, because this is an organization . . . possessing means of expression, institutions, doctrinal documents, official spokespersons." The problem, however, is that "despite the fact that people tend to assume that the Palestinian organizations are the sole true official representatives of the Palestinians . . . this is not so in reality." Despite the fact that they identify verbally with the PLO, in actuality the residents of the territories are moderate and pragmatic. The radical pronouncements are nothing but a tactical maneuver following from a "cold political calculus." It follows, therefore, that one should analyze, not texts, but what the residents of the territories really truly feel and think. One needs to deal with "a much more amorphous reality, that is undocumented . . . a reality that is difficult to measure." Literal interpretation and fidelity to the text are unsuitable for this task, which requires a much "deeper" sort of interpretation: "Since the Six-Day War, young Farhi has learned to read the pages of the lives of the Arabs in the West Bank, and he understands well the visible lines, and especially the invisible lines, whose secrets are difficult to decipher." Put more cynically, the expertise of the advisers consisted in their ability to report firsthand on what the Palestinians "really" felt and thought. If such feelings and thoughts were directly transparent in what the Palestinians said publicly, there was little need for their expertise. The more they reported attitudes and thoughts that differed markedly from what the Palestinians said publicly, the greater the value added by the experts.[60]

A different attempt to enter and occupy this interstitial domain was made by Shimon Shamir of the Shiloah Institute. Immediately after the 1967 war, he teamed together with an economist and an anthropologist to conduct re-search on a refugee camp in the vicinity of Ramallah. In this three-pronged study, Shamir was in charge of analyzing the political attitudes of the refugees. He and his students conducted interviews with residents of the camp. He criticized the "existing literature" because it identified the attitudes of the refugees either with "official declarations made by the spokespersons of Palestinian organizations" (Harkabi's approach) or with the attitudes of "in-tellectuals and other elite groups from among the refugees who reside in the cities" (Farhi's approach). Unlike these approaches, he explained, he would like "to learn something about the positions of refugees in the camps, as they are expressed by the refugees themselves." That is, social science methods were used to mobilize the refugees as a resource that would permit Shamir to challenge the other experts and to claim for himself the role of representing the refugees and reporting to the Israeli public what the Palestinians wanted.

He warned, however, that "attitudes can be understood correctly only on the basis of deep knowledge of the society under study and of the cultural norms, political problems and social contexts in which they are expressed." What the respondents said could not be interpreted literally. For example, while interviewing camp residents, "we heard certain opinions when we talked in private with one person and other opinions, sometimes the opposite ones, when we spoke with the same people in the presence of others." The claim to interpret was based, therefore, on the "contradictory layers" in the attitudes of the refugees, on the fact that they were "ambiguous and included many internal contradictions." Like the advisers, Shamir found a large distance between the rigidity of public ideology and the flexibility of everyday behavior, but unlike them he confirmed that the refugees did express "deep emotional identification with the PLO ... as an authentic expression of Palestinian identity and a source of pride for all Palestinians." His conclusion was that it would be possible to examine "the operational attitude" of the refugees "only in relation to concrete proposals ... and it is quite possible to imagine a situation in which many refugees will display attitudes that are different from those expressed today on the formal level as the consensus of the whole refugee public."[61]

The third competitor seeking to represent the infiltrator-refugee hybrid was Harkabi. He was joined by other experts from the Hebrew University, especially Emmanuel Sivan and Yehoshua Porath. This group was closely aligned with the Foreign Office and with everything related to *hasbara*. In 1972, they were among the founders of the Mount Scopus Center for Re-search on the Arabs of Eretz Israel and on Arab-Israeli Relations. This center worked together with the Foreign Office to publish a series of translations from the Arabic, titled *Arabia and Israel [Arav u-Israel]*, in which "naturally a large part is taken by the issue of the conflict." The first editor of the series was

Hrakabi, and Sivan and Porath were on the editorial board. Together with the short-lived Hasbara Ministry, they also published the *Jerusalem Quarterly*, edited by Sivan. During the same period, the Truman Institute – of which the Mount Scopus Center was a research unit – began to provide regular briefings and seminars for the consular staff of foreign embassies in Israel. The instructors included both Foreign Office officials and the academic staff of the Truman Institute. As materials, they used collections and anthologies of the writings of Israeli orientalists, especially from the Hebrew University, which were used also to train Israeli diplomats how to present matters regarding the conflict "in their communications with foreign parties."[62]

Despite their ambition to align Middle Eastern studies with the discipline of history in order to extract it as far as possible from its problematic political role, and despite their honest attempt to achieve this ideal in their writings, neither Sivan nor Porath were able to disconnect their work from the context of *hasbara* – that is, from the context of a polemical encounter with the objects of their study. The introduction to the second volume of Porath's magnum opus on the Palestinian national movement, begins with a sharp attack on Palestinian historiography. He accuses Palestinian historians of being apologetic and ignoring the facts, and he claims that in this respect they are no different from, in fact are direct descendents of, the authors of classical Islamic historical literature. Sivan, for his part, specialized in "listening to radical Islam," not only to decipher its motivations and nature but to unmask it as a dissembler, as talking the language of democracy only for Western ears, while in reality its plans were nondemocratic. Many other Israeli experts have continued on Sivan's path, including Martin Kramer or Yitzhak Reiter.[63]

The fact that they were aligned with the Foreign Office and with *hasbara* meant, however, that they were relatively marginal to the network of intelligence expertise, and for this reason they tended to adopt the posture of the pedant and the ethic of fidelity to the text. Consequently, they typically adhered to Harkabi's interpretation of the Palestinian Covenant. From Harkabi's point of view, research on the attitudes of the refugees was superfluous. It is much more significant to study the "attitudes of leaders who direct the affairs of the state ... or the platforms of publicly influential organizations." He was not impressed with Shamir's finding that the refugees tend to be more flexible in everyday behavior and in private conversations. He drew precisely the opposite conclusion from this finding:

Some Israelis who recently conducted conversations with Arabs in the territories have gotten the impression that oftentimes Arabs will express themselves much more moderately in private, while when more Arabs join the conversation they express a much more extreme attitude. This is very important evidence. The very fact that when they are in a group they consider it imperative to repeat the extreme versions shows that this is the prevailing attitude among their public.[64]

The competitors had a chance to debate their opposed views in the conference organized by the Mount Scopus Center in April 1974, titled *The Goals of the Arab Struggle against Israel*. Shamir was not present, but most of the participants referred to his arguments, either explicitly or implicitly. Emmanuel Sivan began the debate by underlining and reiterating the importance one must accord to official speech and official texts, arguing that if one reads them rigorously and pays close attention to their context, it is possible to use them to understand the speakers' intentions and predict their actions:

Some here will probably raise the following objection against [what I said]: Sadat said this or that. So what? . . . In a state where the degree of free expression is minimal, and where the ruling elite is very small . . . in such a situation there is enormous significance to what the speaker says.[65]

Porath followed in the same vein: "It is possible to argue that all this talk is not representative; it is merely a particular manner of speaking; others speak differently. Well, they may speak differently, but they do not write differently."[66] In other words, both Sivan and Porath articulated a position very close to Harkabi's approach (literal interpretation). The advisers, on the other hand, warned that it is dangerous to accord too much significance to the written, formal, word. One must also take into account "the spoken word" and rely on direct personal impressions. If one talks to the Arabs, Amnon Cohen reported, one learns that there is a wide gap between what is written, or even said, and a much deeper layer of identity:

On the face of it, the facts show that after the Yom Kippur War there is more "Palestinian talk" and more pronouncements in this spirit among the residents of the territories. The question is what is the significance of this fact. It does not necessarily mean, as some people here think, that these were dormant feelings that now for the first time could be expressed. It is no less possible that what we see here is an almost unconscious utilization, among the greater part of the public, of the conjuncture in which it becomes possible that Palestinian identity might be the best path or the best horse to ride from an international and inter-Arab perspective, and so for now it is useful to do so. I said unconscious, because I believe it was an unconscious response.[67]

A bit later Cohen said that Sivan and Porath's arguments seemed "as if they came out of Harkabi's school of ideas, and as such I was disturbed by the attempt to present certain extreme expressions, certain hostile slogans, as if they were the sum total or even the majority . . . one should not consider them a decisive factor, nor even a principal factor." Beyond what is written, there are also "small external details," such as the way that Sadat begins his speeches. From details like this it is possible to learn about what was left unsaid.[68] Cohen was assisted here by an unexpected ally – orientalists of the older generation, experts on classical Islam, especially the speculative interpreters among them. They, too, were uncomfortable with literal interpretation. One reported on the debriefings of Arab prisoners of war she conducted for the army after the 1967 war (several other professors from the Institute of Oriental Studies participated in these). It was possible to see, she said, that even in matters of religion, presumably the closest to their hearts and their identity, the Arabs "say one thing and do another."[69]

In his response, Sivan attempted to find a compromise acceptable to his critics. He sought to put the emphasis on what was common to all of them rather than what separated them – what was shared between the *hasbara* approach of literal interpretation and the intelligence research approach of deep interpretation but set these approaches apart from the approach of the Arabists. At the same time, he also confirmed that academic expertise and intelligence expertise were in fact one and the same thing and that both had their common origins in philological training:

The bitter fact is that in order to analyze human intentions, at least from the methodological aspect, we must start with their verbal expressions. Later, we need to check the degree of correspondence between verbal expressions and behavior. But we cannot assume that verbal expressions are completely disconnected from behavior, especially not when we have a pattern.... I do not accept the claim that this is a conception taken from somebody's school of ideas. This is simply the historical methodology we possess.... our approach is in fact the royal highway of historical research with philological roots, which for better or worse dominates *mizrahanut*, and for that matter also most work in the field of strategic intelligence. This is really what lies at the root of [this debate].[70]

Well spoken! Unfortunately, there is a wide gap between "human intentions" (indeed, an essential element of any interpretative act) and the concept of intention around which the debate revolved – that is, what did the Arabs or the Palestinians "really" want? What was their true and final attitude with respect to Israel?[71] This concept was responsible for the aporia of the text, for the constant pendulum movement between the various interpretative strategies that were used in the debate. As regards this concept, the reader should recall the admonishment by Israel's first foreign minister, Moshe Sharet, quoted in Chapter 3:

Is there in the [British] Ministry of the Colonies some kind of box, and inside it a piece of parchment, and on it is written all that Britain would want in Palestine? Does the Minister of the Colonies himself know what Britain might want in a few years in Palestine . . . ? Absolutely not. For [the British], in the given situation there are certain things that are fixed, and many others that are not fixed.

Similarly, Uri Bar-Yosef said the following about the 1973 Yom Kippur war:

> It is difficult to determine with certainty when exactly the Egyptian decision to go to war was made. . . . The difficulty . . . stems from the fact that Sadat, as he himself admits in his memoirs, even after he already decided to go to war, was still looking for a political alternative that will allow him not to realize his decision. . . . The Egyptian decision to go to war was made in the course of a long and drawn out process, so that it was possible to retreat from it almost at any stage.

Or in the words that the Egyptian writer and Nobel Prize winner Naguib Mahfouz puts in the mouth of an Egyptian café habitué, "If the future will prove that Israel is a good state, we will live with it in co-existence, and if it turns out that the opposite is true, we will eliminate it just like we eliminated the crusaders' state in the past." Everything that we know about humans – leaders as well as ordinary people – shows that they are fickle and, more importantly, that regardless of whether they have "good" or "bad" intentions the probability that their conduct will be guided by such intentions is low. What is much more likely is that their so-called intentions will be used by the actors later to justify what happened. They are interpretative resources, "accounts," by means of which people give meaning and direction to their conduct a posteriori.[72]

Nonetheless, Sivan's response was important, because it was a sort of compromise between the *hasbara* approach of literal interpretation and the intelligence research approach of deep interpretation. It was, in fact, a compromise acceptable to Harkabi as well:

> The only way to discover their position, therefore, is to check what they say and what they do, and to examine how consistent they are in their pronouncements and in the relation between saying and doing. If . . . there is a difference between their deeds and their words, this is significant evidence about how coherent their position is . . . or it demonstrates that there are changes and developments [in their position].

This compromise made it possible, on the one hand, to connect the interpretation of the Palestinian Covenant with the network of intelligence expertise and, on the other hand, to exclude the advisers and the Arabists from the network. This for two reasons: first, because one deals only with "leaders or influential organizations" whereas the refugees themselves remain beyond the pale; second, because Harkabi had already agreed with the researchers of the Shiloah Institute that neither they nor he possessed much influence over decision makers. That is, he joined in their boundary work between academic research and politics, something that the advisers, by the very nature of their position, could not do. Harkabi's version of the interpretation of the Palestinian Covenant became a major asset of the network of intelligence expertise. It became the preferred method of supervising the margins of the network, namely, the refugee-infiltrator hybrids, because of the facility with which it could quickly discount everything it did not know about them.[73]

How could one, therefore, examine "the relation between saying and doing"? The Arab regimes, as we saw, were tied to the network of intelligence expertise, and it was possible to act on them from a distance, to send messages and conduct experiments. But how would it be possible to do the same with respect to the Palestinians? In his "national soul-searching," Harkabi drew the necessary conclusion from this quandary: Israel's stated position that it will not negotiate with the PLO is mistaken. It suffers from the absence of a scientific and well-reasoned approach to the conflict. The PLO, after all, was playing a smart game and had made its position ambiguous, as Harkabi showed in his interpretation of the covenant, and so the world thinks that it had already recognized Israel. For this reason, if Israel agrees to negotiate with the Palestinians and demands that they state explicitly that they recognize Israel's existence, their game will be up, they will be exposed, because such recognition "contradicts the principles of the PLO as they appear in their national covenant." If they will agree, very good – there will be peace. "If they will refuse, as I tend to think, we will benefit." The gap is so great that it is unlikely there would be an agreement: "A flexible and sophisticated position will assist us to stand steadfast and upright in the difficulties and trials that are still waiting for us."[74]

It is common knowledge that during the 1970s Harkabi transformed himself from a hawk into a dove and became one of the first Israelis to meet with PLO moderates. But these categories – hawk and dove – only prevent us from grasping what really took place. Harkabi's transformation was not the result of disenchantment with the state's (and his own) ideology and of taking a hard look at reality (as his supporters on the left would say), nor was it a failure of nerve and a wild goose chase after the false hope of peace (as his critics on the right would say). Harkabi first and foremost had a professional interest, so to speak, in negotiating with the PLO. In order to stabilize his position as an expert, in order to tighten the ties that connected the interpretation of the Palestinian Covenant with the network of intelligence expertise, he needed to find of a way to tie the Palestinian leaders and organizations to the network. Diplomacy was nothing but one more device to be placed at the disposal of the interpretation of intentions, just as *hasbara* was nothing but one goal that could be achieved through it. The promised integration of the three – intelligence, *hasbara*, and diplomacy – and thus stronger ties to the network of intelligence expertise, was inherent in the schema of "unmasking."[75]

The Discourse of Commentary

The preceding has dealt with the network of intelligence expertise itself, and I considered the discourse that this network produces – the interpretation of intentions – only in terms of its role as translating and coordinating the interests of network participants. Now I would like to describe this discourse in terms of the definition of Middle Eastern reality that it produces and disseminates. The first property of this definition of reality is that only Arab regimes and leaders participate in it. The subject of this discourse is the "modern prince," whether a leader, a party, an organization, or a regime. This is attested by the importance accorded to the genre of political biography in the writings of the Dayan Center experts. Almost all of them have written, at one point or another, the biography of this or that Arab leader, and almost all of them are known to specialize in at least one Arab regime. They typically do not, on the other hand, write in any serious way about the economic policies of Arab states, about their demographics, or about social classes and processes.[76]

This lack, which the experts are painfully conscious of and ritually be-moan, stems from the fact that the goal of their discourse, the crowning achievement to which they aspire, is to provide an *internal* explanation for the policies and actions of Arab leaders or regimes. Even when they consider economic or demographic data, these are typically gleaned from secondary sources and are meant to serve as background for the actual interpretative act. This explanation is "internal" in the sense that policies and actions are made sensible and accountable by relating them to the intentions, motivations, ideology, or plans of the Arab regimes and leaders themselves. The goal of this discourse is to reconstruct the collective or individual subject that is hiding behind all the different actions, events, words, and policies undertaken and that integrates them into a cohesive whole – namely, the basic intention of the leader or regime; the internal logic of these actions, events, words, and policies; or the central idea guiding them (what Harkabi called "position"). The task is quite simply to provide "overt intelligence" (and in hindsight), to predict and explain political or military action on the basis of the information that could be gleaned from the speeches, writings, and official declarations of the leader or regime. This goal necessitates that the latter will be depicted as a "riddle," as a distant and foreign other with whom it is impossible to converse:

Saddam Hussein and his regime are still a riddle. This book attempts to unravel this riddle, not by using secret documents or classified intelligence, but by using open, yet the richest of sources: political discourse, as it appears in Hussein's speeches, in declarations and official documents, in journalistic commentaries and in books. This method affords a double advantage: it uncovers the deepest historical, political and ideological layers at the basis of the *Ba'th* regime, which dictated its actions and trapped the regime and Iraqi society within them. It opens up a window for understanding the internal logic that has motivated the senior members of this regime, a logic that oftentimes cannot be grasped by the logic of an outside observer.... Finally, this method provides overt intelligence on the intentions, plans and actions of this regime. By analyzing Saddam Hussein's discourse we realize that he was the main source of leaks about the secrets of the regime: he exposed his plans with regards to Iran, Kuwait, Israel and the West long before he acted on them. In time, talk that sounded to the untrained ear as merely boasting, became real. Saddam Hussein proved that his words must be taken literally.[77]

The second property of this definition of Middle Eastern reality, therefore, is that the environment surrounding Israelis is populated by regimes and leaders who are riddles ("sphinxes" in Maoz's language), because behind everything they say and do there hides a basic intention or a central idea or an internal logic that "cannot be grasped by the logic of an outside observer." Thus, the experts must intervene and write as commentators to elucidate and explicate this logic. In order to do this, the experts rely on the tried-and-true philological modus operandi of comparing texts taken from the same genre or attributed to the same author and searching for telltale omissions or additions, a distinctive style or rhetoric, that can assist them in assigning the text to a particular school, circle, or author.[78] The goal is not simply to determine who wrote the text but to establish it as an "original" text, as Harkabi did, for example, with the Palestinian Covenant – a site where one can learn directly about the basic intention of the regime, whether it was meant to remain secret or is instead an open and official platform:

The October Paper ... reflects the worldview, ideas, policy and ambitions of President Sadat. The paper was presented to the nation in a public speech. After its ceremonial presentation to the public, certain procedures were activated to have it ratified.... After the paper was legitimized in this way it became a basic platform and the intellectuals and the media were instructed to interpret it and disseminate it to the public.[79]

The point of establishing a particular text as "original" is that, from then onward, all other texts can be interpreted on the basis of their relations with it. It can serve to create in other texts a layer of preestablished "telltale signs," namely, expressions and ways of using them that were found in the original text and may suggest how what the text says relates to the original intention. This does not mean that the discourse of commentary is content to always demonstrate that "there is nothing new under the sun." On the contrary, if the commentators insist on arguing that each and every contemporary expression merely repeats and reflects the original intention, then their discourse begins to lose its specific added value and becomes similar to classical orientalism as Said described it – precisely the version of orientalism from which they sought to distinguish themselves. This is why they emphasize that "the Arab world is neither monolithic nor static, and any generalization about its aims and methods may distort the picture more then assist in its comprehension."[80] And they have good reason for such emphasis: the "deviations" from the original text, the changes and modifications, are the fodder upon which their commentary subsists.

From this fact follows the third property of the definition of reality created by the discourse of commentary: the world surrounding Israelis is populated by regimes and leaders whose behavior is determined on a dimension or a continuum stretching from "ideology" to "pragmatism." On the one side of this dimension, one finds the original text as it was established by one of the commentators – for example, the Palestinian Covenant as it was presented and interpreted by Harkabi. Therefore, one finds there also literal interpretation. On the other side of this dimension, one finds the image of the Machiavellian prince, whose preeminent interest is in protecting his domain and guaranteeing the process of succession and who is willing to dissemble and tell lies to achieve these objectives:

By its official declarations, the goal of the regime, which has the status of a national historical imperative, is to realize the idea of greater Syria.... In actuality, none of our authors find evidence that there actually exists a Syrian operational master plan to realize this goal. According to the authors, Syria is motivated by a narrow and limited nationalistic tendency: securing the well-being and welfare of Asad and his men, of the Allawi ethnic group, and of Syria in its current borders, in this order of widening concentric circles.[81]

In short, on one pole of this dimension we find words that are identical with the thing-in-itself, the intention, while on the other pole we find empty words, whose sole function is to hide the real thing. Israelis encounter the Middle Eastern reality around them as an endless flow of discourse that includes both empty words and words that reveal the essence of things. At their side and whispering in their ears, they find the commentators, who purport to assist them in separating one from the other:

There remains one unanswered question, and it is whether the document about imperialism mentioned earlier was a contingency plan kept secret till the time is right to implement it, or whether it was just one more document in a long row of wordy documents, that only by accident reappeared after Iraqi policy has changed. One thing is clear, the document reflected ways of thinking that were so deeply engrained in the Iraqi *Ba'th* that it was easy to harness them anew for immediate political needs.[82]

As the last sentence shows, the category of "pragmatism" is an empty schema whose value is completely determined by its function: to bridge between the two poles, or, in this instance, to allow the commentators to traverse the distance separating ideology from the prince, the original text from its deviations, words that are identical to the thing-in-itself from empty words.[83] There is another such schema, parallel and diametrically opposed, whose function is to lead in the opposite direction, back from the prince to ideology. This schema is the power of rhetoric, or as Benjo puts it, "the double-edged sword of language." In her book, she depicts Saddam Hussein, who was celebrated by his cronies as "the engineer of words," as someone who became trapped in his own discourse, ensnared by the double-edged sword of language, which gradually legitimized actions (such as the invasion of Kuwait) that were contrary to cold political calculation and finally led him to destruction. This schema is very similar to the old orientalist motif of the Arabs as people who are enamored of their own language to the point that they cannot distinguish "between fact and dream and between legend and reality. Whole nations who believe that simply intoning a word, or disseminating it in political discourse or military announcement, is enough to turn it into a substitute for action itself."[84]

The important function performed by these two schemas accounts for the ubiquity of the genre of political biography, because both schemas rely to a large extent on an analysis of the personality of the Arab leader in order to create a flexible mechanism that can alleviate the tension between the original text and its deviations. In that, they betray their origins in the modus operandi of military intelligence, according to which the researcher represents the way of thinking, mood, and considerations of the Arab leader. Thus, the commentators have taught the Israeli public to perceive the reality around them as populated by Machiavellian leaders whose preeminent interest is in protecting their domain and guaranteeing the process of succession and who are willing to dissemble and tell lies to attain their ends. And yet, at the same time, the commentators have made sure to qualify this image and add to their descriptions of the personalities of these leaders precisely those characteristics that would guarantee the continued necessity of textual-ideological analysis.[85]

For years, they have taught the Israeli public to recognize a certain image of the Egyptian leader Nasser, as a meddler and conspirator who coldly calculated his actions in accordance with his interests and yet was overwhelmed by his own rhetoric – the very words he uttered lightly would acquire an independent force and impose themselves on him. Similarly, the commentators turned Hafiz al-Asad, the former Syrian president, into the ideal type of the prince. Countless commentators told the Israeli public that he was a cold and sober leader, a rational and tough negotiator who measured every decision by a calculus of interests and power, that he did not give anything without charging much more in return. Thus, when Asad agreed to meet Clinton in Geneva, the commentators explained that he did so because he was worried about the succession process. No doubt he was the prince defending the interests of his house, for whom pragmatic considerations are more important than any ideology. But when the talks with Syria fell through, just a little bit later, the commentators explained that Asad, however pragmatic, also held steadfast to an uncompromising, extreme Arab nationalist ideology, that he could not give up the role of the Arabs' champion and standard bearer in the struggle against Israel. If one examined what Asad said publicly before the negotiations began, they said, one knew that the negotiations would not work. In the end, his words came back to straightjacket him.[86]

What is the significance of this analysis? As I explained earlier, the concept of "intention" is a device for translating and coordinating the interests of the participants in the network of intelligence expertise, including the interests of the participants in the game of communication between the Israeli leadership and its Arab counterparts. It follows that these various interpretative schemas – ideology, the original text, the prince, pragmatism, the double-edged sword of language – are means by which the products of this communication game are interpreted, legitimized, and purified. The products of dialogue, of give and take between the two sides – a give and take that is often violent or involves the threat of violence – are presented as if they were qualities of only one side in the exchange. In this way, the commentators perform an important service for Israeli decision makers, and a certain profitable exchange is established between them. On the one hand, the commentators endow Israeli policy with the appearance of legitimacy and objectivity – because they focus on the "intentions" of the other side, even on his personality characteristics, and present these as the decisive considerations for shaping Israeli policy. On the other hand, their participation in the network of intelligence expertise – especially the participation of those appointed as ambassadors and diplomats – endows the commentators with the divinatory capacity to interpret intentions, because within the framework of this network an intention is not a subjective and obscure secret but a pragmatic criterion utilized in the course of conducting negotiations for encoding and decoding messages. Contrary to what the Arabists or the advisers said, the interpretation of intentions does not fail to bridge the gap between words and deeds, because it is a dialogic property of the diplomatic language game:

We must consider the negotiations a long-term attempt to try and identify what are Asad's intentions – did he really want a compromise? What were his real terms and red lines? If it will prove impossible to bridge our positions, will he be interested in an interim agreement?[87]

The consequences of this discourse are that Israelis encounter and experience the Middle Eastern reality around them almost always through the mediation of this or that interpretative dispute and through the mediation of the interpretative schemas mentioned earlier. An excellent example is the dispute over the relevance of the Palestinian Covenant. From the early 1970s up till now, almost the whole of the internal Israeli debate about the Palestinian problem was forced to pass through the prism of the interpretative dispute about the relation between the covenant and subsequent Palestinian decisions, statements, and deeds. The political right, for its part, has mobilized commentators who decipher the formal statements of the Palestinian National Council in accordance with the canonical reading established by Harkabi, namely, literal interpretation that completes and explicates what is said only in "algebraic language." They have pointed out all sorts of significant omissions and telltale phrases that constitute evidence, in their eyes, that these statements do not contradict the covenant and continue to be guided by the original intention of the original text:

On the one hand, it is possible to argue that there is here a renunciation of the doctrine of stages, while subordinating it to a political compromise based on the 1967 borders. On the other hand, it is possible to argue the opposite, namely: the compromise based on the 1967 borders is subordinate to the doctrine of stages and is but one part of it. From other parts of the political statement and the declaration of independence it seems that the latter interpretation is the most credible.... The phrase "a just and enduring compromise," that has become an integral part of the conventional diplomatic language regarding the conflict in our region ... is missing from the political statement. It is impossible to assume that this is an accidental omission.... Alongside the apparent recognition of Israel ... the political statement includes also a rejection of its right to exist.[88]

Put differently, this analysis of the Palestinian Covenant and PLO statements, of which the latest practitioner is Benjamin Begin (former Likud MP and son of Menahem Begin, the late prime minister),[89] asks the reader to accept two contradictory arguments: on the one hand, that there exists a covert plan or intention to destroy Israel (the so-called doctrine of stages) hidden behind what is said; on the other hand, that it is possible to uncover this plan simply by analyzing open sources (i.e., what is said does not hide this intention or plan but in fact makes it manifest). The contradiction or tension could be temporarily assuaged, for example, by focusing on the internal Arab debate, as Harkabi suggested, arguing that what the Arabs say among themselves they do not tell the world at large. But this is by no means a universal refuge. The above quotation, for example, refers to an English language text.

Another tactic is to accuse the commentators mobilized by the left (see next paragraph) that they are misleading the public, that, in fact, they are orientalist because they discount what the Arabs say as empty words. In terms of the public status of the commentators (on both sides), their prestige and the importance accorded their analyses, this is a productive tension because it permits them to present this sophistry as a form of expertise that is relevant and important. In terms of the chances for a rational and self-reflexive Israeli political debate, it is a cul-de-sac.

The political left, for its part, mobilizes other commentators, including Harkabi himself and his most devoted follower, Matti Steinberg. They point out deviations from the covenant in statements and decisions issued by the Palestinian National Council, and they deduce from this fact that there is a growing "pragmatism" among the Palestinians and a greater willingness to reach an accord with Israel. They argue that

national movements do not tend to delete sacred formulations and to repent their sins in the public eye, even if their policy has in fact completely changed.... Instead of de jure change they prefer de facto change, namely the way of gradual forgetting and relegating to oblivion. They gradually stop referring to the old formulations, and concurrently adopt resolutions and positions whose significance is contradictory, even though they avoid declaring this explicitly.

It follows, therefore, that it is possible to interpret omissions and deviations as signs of moderation. Nonetheless, Harkabi and Steinberg also prepared an escape hatch for the left:

The practical validity of the covenant has been voided by historical circumstances ... but historical circumstances would also determine whether it may one day enjoy once again the status of a practical guideline. This is a two-way road, and the return to extremism may take place in two main possible scenarios: extremism because of hope: ... if ... the goals [of the covenant] would seem once more achievable. Extremism because of desperation: if [the other side] does not show a willingness to reciprocate, which [the PLO] considers satisfactory."[90]

One may invert this piece of sophistry and turn it back at its formulators: is it the PLO's road that is two-way or is it the lane upon which commentary moves, from ideology to pragmatism and back again? Just as commentators may determine that omissions and deviations are signs of moderation, they may invert course and decide that the omissions and the deviations are nothing but dissimulation, an "algebraic language" behind which hide the extremes of either hope or desperation. I do not wish to argue, of course, that this interpretative seesaw is alone responsible for the political debate and stalemate regarding the "Palestinian problem" in Israel, only that it has forced the Israeli political debate into a prefabricated schema from which Israelis have not yet been able to extract themselves. This schema imposes itself on the participants in the political debate and forces them to require the assistance of commentators or to draw on the established formulas of the discourse of commentary.

In this sense, the Palestinian Covenant is an Israeli document no less, and possibly more, than it is a Palestinian document. It is an Israeli document because Israelis have interpreted and annotated it and written dozens of learned commentaries about it, and also because they used it for their purposes until it became an integral part of the political discussion in Israel. The covenant is like a Talmud page upon which Israeli scholars and politicians have added their annotations – in the margins, below, above, and on both sides – and now their criticisms and their commentaries have become an integral part of the text itself. It is not the "*Torah* of the Palestinians," as Harkabi thought, but the Israeli political Talmud, a source of endless and barren sophistries and scholastic exercises. The covenant holds the truth, not about the Palestinians, but about the commentators and about their claim to speak in the name of the Palestinians and to explain to the Israeli public what they really want. I believe Israelis have paid a dear price, because for many years now they have been listening mostly to the commentators rather than to the Palestinians themselves. The Palestinian Covenant was, and still is, the commentators' mirage, and Israelis would do better to abandon to the commentators the search for a document wherein is written the whole truth about the Palestinians. There are more important and pressing tasks.

The Return of the Refugees

All these properties of the discourse of commentary – the focus on the Arab leader and his construction as a "riddle," the search for an original text wherein could be found his basic intention, the tension between the original text and the deviations from it, the analysis of the personality of the Arab leader between the poles of pragmatism and ideology, the way in which the interpretation of intentions legitimizes and validates Israeli policy, and the two-way nature of the interpretative act – all these acquired tragic dimensions when the al-Aksa intifada erupted in October 2000. Israel's response was guided and validated by an assessment of the situation shared by the research branch of military intelligence, the top commanders of the IDF, the experts of the Dayan Center, and media commentators. According to this assessment, affirmed by the director of the Dayan Center, Asher Susser, among others, the events were directed and orchestrated by Arafat, the prince, whose "strategy . . . is to establish the Palestinian state in a heroic struggle," but he is "hiding his true intentions."[91]

Arafat may have been trying to hide his "true intentions," but the commentators were not deceived. How could they have been hidden, after all, since the commentators argued that Arafat's "true intentions" were identical with those expressed, in so many words and for everyone to see, in the original text, the Palestinian Covenant? They were the same intentions that Harkabi, in his day, had identified. In the words of the commander of military intelligence, "Arafat rejects the approach of two states for two nations. It will not be possible to reach an agreement with him about the end of the conflict, even if Israel will accept the principle and the reality of the right of return, agree to withdraw to the 1967 borders, to the division of Jerusalem and to handing over the sacred sites to Palestinian control."[92]

The gap between words and intentions was filled by commentators who specialized in representing Arafat to the Israeli public – for example, Ehud Ya'ari, who was the commentator on Arab affairs for the state television channel. According to Ya'ari, Arafat was a master strategist who specialized in creating chaotic situations, in raising the stakes and increasing the levels of uncertainty, to the point where he was the only one left standing. Hence, the claim made by the GSS field operatives, who had argued that Arafat did not control the situation in the field, was irrelevant: chaos and lack of control were precisely what Arafat had in mind. This was a situation that he, the master of survival, controlled, at least better than anyone else.[93]

If the reader begins to sense that we are dealing here with a theory that is immune to refutation, one must add that Israeli policy was guided, and continues to be guided, by this theory and therefore also confirms and justifies it in practice. As a former chief of the Palestinian desk in the research branch of military intelligence later said about this theory,

Even the confirmation of this approach in reality does not necessarily prove that it is correct, because from the moment that this approach was adopted by the Israeli political and military leadership it became a self-fulfilling assessment, given that Israel is the stronger side. For this reason, not even Arafat's behavior today can serve as proof for the validity of this conception. Sometimes, because of the status and personal character of the intelligence officer, the rule propounded by one great sociologist holds for him: if people define certain situations as real, they are real in their consequences.[94]

Let us engage in a small thought experiment: let us imagine that Arafat, when he was still alive, gave an order to his troops to cease fire and that the situation in the territories immediately calmed down. The commentators would, of course, have considered this "proof" that he was the one pulling the strings and controlling the situation. And what if the opposite had happened – that is, the violence continued? Well, the commentators would have probably argued that this was the best sort of evidence that their original interpretation was correct and that Arafat could not be counted on. He said one thing and did another, while all the time he continued to covertly strive toward his final objective – the destruction of Israel. Or maybe they would have argued that he too was no longer the master of his own rhetoric, another victim of the "double-edged sword of language."[95] Karl Popper must be turning in his grave, but we are not dealing here with the degree of agreement between hypothesis and reality. We are dealing here with a process, as I explained earlier, in the course of which the intelligence assessment and the policy are gradually adjusted and made to conform to one another. This takes place on the basis of the reciprocal exchange relations between the decision makers and commentators as actualized in the network of intelligence expertise.

What is going on here? As I explained earlier, the network of intelligence expertise is predicated on the exclusion of the hybrids from its jurisdiction. The refugees and the infiltrators were pushed to the other side of the border in order for the interpretation of intentions, together with the doctrine of pure deterrence, to be able to produce the effect of the state. The first conjured, on the other side of the border, the specter of a malevolent master strategist who was pulling all the strings, while the second forced him to play the role that was written for him in accordance with the rules of the game of communication. In this way, the hybrids were chased out of the sphere of intelligence expertise. Even after 1967, as we saw, the no-man's-land into which the refugees were pushed was occupied by the interpretation of the Palestinian Covenant. The latter connected itself to the network of intelligence expertise chiefly on the basis of the fact that it completely ignored the refugees and instead focused on the gap between the words and deeds of leaders and organizations.

This situation was abruptly changed by the Oslo Accords. When the PLO and Arafat returned to the territories, the hybrids and the refugees returned to the jurisdiction of the network of intelligence expertise, and it was no longer possible to ignore them. It is true that the Palestinian Authority was created and that it was required to play the same role earlier imposed on the neighboring states and regimes, but it was not really a sovereign entity in the full sense of the word, as it could not exercise full control over the territory under its jurisdiction, nor enjoy a clearly defined and recognized international status. In short, the Palestinian Authority was a sort of a hybrid itself, somewhere between a state and a nonstate (an organization or party), and the residents who lived under its jurisdiction were all perforce refugees and infiltrators de facto. The Palestinian Authority is a state to the extent that it is expected to achieve a monopoly over the means of violence within its territory (better said, within "area A," which was granted to it, since in areas "B" and "C," the IDF and the settlers possess this monopoly jointly) and to eliminate terrorist activity. It is not a state, however, to the extent that it is prohibited from determining what constitutes an act of aggression perpetrated against it (or even premeditated, as the Bush administration's doctrine of "preemption" permits), an act that would justify violent reaction (or preemption). It is the prerogative of states to determine where the boundary lies between justified and unjustified violence, between self-defense and terror. Being unable to determine this boundary means that the other side can determine it at will. Even the failure of the Palestinian Authority to perform its role as a state – that is, its failure to monopolize the means of violence – can be interpreted by the Israeli side as an act of aggression and as "orchestrating terrorism."

And why was the Palestinian Authority created as such a crippled hybrid? Because the state of Israel itself is a hybrid of sorts. On the one hand, it claims the international status of a sovereign state with clearly defined borders; on the other hand, it continuously extends itself beyond these borders. On the one hand, it is democratic; on the other hand it, is a Jewish state and therefore considers Palestinian women from the refugee camps who marry Palestinian men who are citizens of Israel as de facto infiltrators. The discourse about Arafat and his strategy, the return to the literal interpretation of the Palestinian Covenant, and finally the attempt to build the separation barrier, all these are desperate (and in their consequences also bloody) attempts to purify the Palestinian hybrid and demand that it behave at one and the same time as a state and as a nonstate. They are like semiautomatic spasms of the network of intelligence expertise, when the ties that held it together have been irreparably broken.

The commentators and the intelligence experts who specialized in the intricacies of Arafat's personality have participated in this failed purification campaign. In this respect, Arafat's recent death changed nothing. Maybe the only difference is that the double role played by Arafat, according to the commentators, has now been split between two leaders – Mahmood Abbas and Marwan Barghouti. The first is playing the role of the sober and moderate leader who is intent on peace and who for this reason must achieve a monopoly over the means of violence. The second is playing the role of the terrorist who even from prison continues to covertly pull all the strings and conspires to destroy Israel. We should not delude ourselves: as long as the Palestinian Authority remains a hybrid, part state and part nonstate, any Palestinian leader worthy of the name will have to continue to maneuver between the two poles of "terrorism" and "negotiations" or will have to resign, as Abbas did the first time he served as prime minister.

In the meanwhile, the more they became conscious of the failure to purify the hybrids, the closer the intelligence experts drew to their alter ego – *hasbara*. From the commanders of military intelligence testifying before parliamentary committees, to the learned texts produced by the experts of the Dayan Center, to the daily columns of newspaper commentators, the focus was no longer on analyzing the military capabilities of the Palestinians, nor on the complex set of interests and constraints faced by their leaders, but on documenting the extent of anti-Israeli propaganda in the schools run by the Palestinian Authority, on the content of textbooks, on the denial that the Jewish Temple ever existed or was located on the Temple Mount, on Islamic anti-Semitism, and so on.

The research branch of military intelligence, for example, prepared a "white book" on Arafat intended to be distributed for external *hasbara* purposes. Additionally, the research branch has dabbled in internal *hasbara*, seeking to educate the Israeli public about the true goals of the Palestinian Authority. Beyond the endless leaks to journalists, research officers also compiled a collection of documents confiscated from Palestinian Authority offices and gave them to a journalist to write a book exposing how the Palestinian Authority incited anti-Israeli feelings among its subjects and how it prepared for an armed confrontation with Israel long before the Camp David negotiations.[96]

After all, they were just following in the footsteps of their leader, Israeli Prime Minister Ehud Barak, who had served in the past as the commander of military intelligence. Barak, in his post hoc interpretation of what took place at Camp David, returned to the schema of "unmasking," originally created by Harkabi. The diplomatic overture, he explained, was mainly an intelligence tool, a means of divining the adversary's true intentions. Correspondingly, the goal of the interpretation of intentions is *hasbara* – that is, an unmasking of the adversary before the whole world. I hope the reader will no longer be taken in by this clumsy patchwork of post hoc rationalizations, which, more than it unmasks the true face of the adversary, reveals the fraying of the network of intelligence expertise.

It is important to recall that in the beginning of Zionism there were great longings for the country, which were also in great measure longings for Arab society. In my childhood, we would depict the fathers of the nation, Abraham, Yitzhak, and Yaakov, as Arabs. I do not think this is just a piquant detail. We would dress as Arabs in order to play the role of the fathers of our nation. . . . I comprehend the longing of the Jewish people for *Eretz Israel* also as longing for a simple, rooted existence, that for the Zionists was realized to an enormous degree by the Arab person dwelling in his land. This is how things stood with early Zionism, and the same is true for *Gush Emunim* [the vanguard movement of settlers in the occupied territories], which in many respects is an imitation of early Zionism.

—Rabbi Menahem Fruman
from *The Palestinian Option*

ONE OF MY MOTIVES for writing this book was to challenge the view, which to a large measure is accepted by both the adherents of Zionism and its critics, that cultural separatism was inevitable, as if it was contained in the genetic code of Zionism. From the moment that the first Zionist settlers arrived on the shores of Palestine, we are told, it was ordained that they would distinguish themselves from its inhabitants and separate from them. For this reason, I emphasized in the second chapter that in the period before the formation of the state, the Orient had the meaning of a frontier area, a no-man's-land populated by hybrids, vanishing mediators and hidden Jews, and that Zionist identity was not defined in opposition to it but through a more complex relation of attachment and detachment, affirmation and negation, attraction and revulsion. Consequently, this book, rather than presenting a "post-Zionist" position (in the sense of affirming what Zionism denied and negated), argues that "we have never been Zionist" – that Zionism always included within itself and utilized what it apparently denied and negated and that it could not exist without it. Zionism was never a reality (therefore, there can be no "post-Zionism," as there was no Zionism to advance beyond) but a myth laced with contradictions, a myth that could not serve as a blueprint for anybody's life and that at any given moment had to be invented anew.

For this reason as well, I emphasized in the fourth chapter the contingent nature of the factors that led to the disenchantment of the Orient – the crosscutting struggles, the petty enmities, the contradictory considerations, and undecided dilemmas that led to its dissolution and to the formation of forms of expertise whose raison d'etre was the purification of the hybrids. My goal was not to offer an alternative explanation of cultural separatism but to deconstruct the existing explanations and to disconnect from one another the various components of the master narrative. My goal was to show that all those discourses that today serve to explain and justify cultural separatism themselves owe their existence and justification to the abrupt and violent act of separation – the expulsions, the prohibition against the return of refugees, the military government, the emigration of the Arab Jews and their settlement on the periphery – and to the struggles that followed in its wake. The new forms of rational knowledge – the realpolitik rationality of the network of intelligence expertise, the cultural rationality of modernization discourse – could only come into being on the newly void cognitive terrain created by separation and the dissolution of the Orient. Therefore, they cannot explain separatism; on the contrary, the secret of their own existence is held by the structures of separatism. For this reason, it was necessary in Chapter 4, and in the chapters that followed, to get as close as possible to the individuals involved, as in a movie close-up, when the camera narrows down on the actors, and their movements become clearer, slower, and more pronounced. What is left to do now is to instruct the cameraman to pull back, lift us again to a bird's-eye view of the scene, and change to a panoramic lens.

In the Introduction, I used the term "disenchantment of the Orient" to characterize the overall significance of the change that took place in the social role of expertise in Arab affairs. By no means, however, did I intend to claim that discourses or representations that seek to reenchant the Orient have completely disappeared. Max Weber, as well, when he characterized modernity as disenchanted, did not intend to imply that modernity entails an irreversible secularization process. If this had been his position, there is no doubt that he would have been mistaken. The meaning of disenchantment, in Weber's thought, is that rationality and religion have become disconnected, in the sense that whoever wishes to endow the world with ultimate religious meaning must do so at the price of rationality, while whoever intends to measure their every action by a rational standard must do so at the price of the total and ultimate meaning that religion can give to the world and to human life.

Further, it is possible to interpret Weber's argument in an even more flexible manner, since a person could be rational in the morning and enchanted in the evening. Why not? A scientist when at work, but when at church speaking in tongues. For this reason, the great and inescapable problem of the modern individual is the problem of authenticity, of the fragmentation into different selves each of which belongs to a different and separate sphere of modern life and none sitting easily with the others. Moreover, this problem is not the result of some essential antinomy between religion and rationality, tradition and modernity, but arises from purely social causes, from the fact that the distinction between the various spheres has by now been institutionalized and that countless social actors now possess vested interests in its continuation and in the purification of the hybrids that disrupt its neat divisions. The multiplication and mutual reinforcement of these interests function as a lock-in mechanism. A lock-in mechanism can be said to exist when the ties constituting a specific network have become so numerous and so strong that it is very difficult to sever them and thus very difficult to change the course of the network. The disenchantment of the world, even if it is not irreversible, could still justifiably be characterized as an "iron cage" because the effort required to change it and the associated costs are very high.

Similarly, the disenchantment of the Orient does not mean the elimination of the opposite tendency to reinvent and reenchant the Orient. Especially now, when multiculturalism is an obligatory global ideology, Israeli culture encompasses a large number of discourses and representations that seek to reinvent the enchanted territory of the Orient. There is, for example, the old idea of "integration in the region," into which a new genre of "postmodern" critique is breathing life. The critique is directed at Western culture, which is depicted as "based on an idea of functional hierarchy . . . [in which] human beings are conceived . . . as external observers of the world in a sort of egocentrism and vanity." The original sin of the State of Israel, it is explained, was to "base . . . its orientation on western culture . . . and not . . . on oriental-Islamic culture." And the promise is made that "in order to bring an end once and for all to this terrible conflict, we must recognize that oriental-Islamic culture . . . is not inferior in any way to western culture. . . . If we learn, accept and absorb oriental-Islamic culture, we will be able to continue living here together."[1]

The same theme of integration is given a religious flavor in the activities of Derech Avraham (Abraham's Way), a group consisting of rabbis and Muslim scholars. These scholars emphasize the connection between Judaism and Islam, "a connection . . . that was highly fertile in Egypt and Palestine in the Middle Ages" and that could facilitate the creation of a "proximity between the two religions by being conscious of the affinity between them." The idea of integration, however, is most powerful when it is related not to religion but to the category of *mizrahi* Jews and the theme of returning to the roots of one's identity and thereby also to the multiculturalist agenda of empowering minorities and consecrating otherness as a desirable cultural good. The typical producers and carriers of this discourse are intellectuals and cultural creators whose position is relatively marginal and who seek to challenge the cultural establishment. The typical "consumer base" of this discourse is the educated middle classes: "We are actually Arab-Jews, just like there are Arab-Christians or Arab-Circassians. . . . I am *mizrahi* both because of the origins of my parents and because of the ancient origins of my nation. We should not forget that . . . there is here also an oriental culture with which it is desirable to reconnect. The problem is that this oriental culture had been repressed for years and was considered inferior." Despite the fact that this discourse opposes itself to Western orientalism, the desire to recreate the enchanted territory of the Orient often leads these cultural creators, in a gesture of self-orientalization, back to the same orientalist images developed in Europe: "I spent a long time in the desert . . . and under the influence of life in the desert my work developed naturally towards [my] Middle Eastern roots and the integration between East and West."[2]

And finally there are the settlers. As Menahem Fruman explains in the epigraph to this chapter, precisely those who lord it over the Palestinians also need them in order to shape and produce, as in the early days of Zionism, their biblical Eretz Israel out of the modern realities of settlement, occupation, urbanization, and so on. One might have assumed that the messianic religious faith of at least a portion of the settlers would have protected them from the need to imitate their Palestinian neighbors. But this is a simplistic conception of the nature of religious belief, as if it is an internal essence that requires only itself in order to exist. As a correction to such simplistic images, we should note, as does Gideon Aran, that the settlement movement was animated by a desire to escape from the modernist space I described in Chapter 5 – the space stretching from the hypermodern urban agglomeration of the coastal plain, through the development town, all the way to the traditional Arab village – and to reinvent Eretz Israel (which the modernist space has gradually destroyed) where it was still possible, at the furthest pole of this space, among the Palestinian villages.

Herein lie also at least some of the reasons for the unstoppable spread of the settlement phenomenon. The outposts on the hills are not only part of a rational strategic practice of "creating facts on the ground" pursued with the aim of making their removal difficult and of dividing and isolating the Palestinian population centers from one another. They are also an integral part of a technology of the self wherein they represent "the close connection to the earth and at the same time . . . [the proximity] to God." That is, this is a technology for the production of space, a technology that problematizes and seeks to overcome the loss of authenticity in a disenchanted world by fashioning from the hills the enchanted space of Eretz Israel. For this reason, and despite their racism and hostility, precisely those rooted settlers, the notorious "youth of the hills," the sheepherders who wear only clothes woven from their wool, who handcraft their own goat cheese, who sport biblical-type sandals and huge hand-woven *Kippahs*, precisely they are following in the footsteps of the first Zionist settlers, who observed and imitated their Palestinian neighbors. They are like Ben-Gurion, looking out from the tower in Lydda, or like the members of the shepherds group.[3]

Contemporary Israeli culture, therefore, is saturated with all sorts of projects that aim to reinvent the Orient and endow it once more with enchanted meaning as a space where it is possible to reconcile antinomies, refashion the self, and reconnect past and present, the messianic and the quotidian. The term "disenchantment of the Orient" merely serves to highlight the heavy price, the incredible effort, required of those who would seek to swim against the current and recreate a lost terrain of discourse. Sometimes this means demonstratively giving up the pretension to present the self as a rational speaker – something that is common to the settlers' messianic religious faith, various forms of returning to one's *mizrahi* roots, and New Age philosophy and thus leads to all sorts of surprising combinations between these three tendencies. In other cases, the price to be paid is the necessity of appearing as an inauthentic speaker twice, on both sides of the barricade – this is the typical predicament of *mizrahi* intellectuals. As one of them protested ruefully, "I am being pushed into an impossible corner: I am required to choose between political sanity and ethnic identity."[4]

This price does not reflect, as I emphasized earlier, some essential antinomy between East and West, rationality and irrationality, but is caused by the social phenomenon of lock-in, especially by the fact that countless institutional, professional, and personal interests inevitably were tied to cultural separatism and many people thus became invested in the distinct and continuous existence of different spheres – intelligence, government, *hasbara*, and the absorption of immigrants. Therefore, these interests were also tied to the discourses and purification devices meant to supervise the hybrids and to guarantee that they did not disturb the neat divisions between spheres. Anybody who wishes to speak "seriously" about the conflict, the refugees, the Palestinians or the *mizrahi* Jews, and also to be heard, cannot afford to ignore the existence of the network of intelligence expertise, the discourse about the Arab village, or the sociology of "the problem of ethnic differences." This is because they offer speakers ready-made subject positions, ready-made discursive positions, that with little effort provide them with the gravity, authority, and weight of one who speaks "the truth" and is "in the know." Even before opening one's mouth to speak, one is already supplied with discursive resources, linkages to other arguments, to proofs, to "well-known facts." and to other authoritative speakers. Moreover, even before opening one's mouth, one is already positioned within a Western, modern Israeli society that observes the Middle East, or the Arab village, or the "traditional" culture of *mizrahi* Jews, from without.

Whoever wishes to speak differently, especially whoever wishes to recreate the Orient as an enchanted terrain, must reckon with the fact that against them will be arrayed all the different and crosscutting interests of all those individuals who have learned to relate to themselves by means of the categories of cultural separatism, among which I would include also the category of *mizrahi* identity – after all, who today has a greater vested interest in supervising the boundaries of the *mizrahi* category if not those individuals who have learned to identify themselves as "*mizrahi*" and have turned this identity into the source of resistance practices? Whoever wishes to speak differently must also reckon with the fact that against them will be arrayed all the different and crosscutting interests of the experts whose status and livelihood depend on the continued separation of the various spheres, and also all the different interests of institutions whose raison d'etre is the purification of the hybrids. Moreover, they will also have to reckon with the fact that the sum total of all these interests – in other words, the mechanism of lock-in against which they speak – is intimately connected, in the last instance, to the way in which the effect of the state is produced. This is why whoever wishes to speak differently will be perceived as threatening the state – its borders, its character, its justification, or its very existence. It is much easier, therefore, to continue on the course already established, to build walls of real separation along imaginary internal and external boundaries.

Reference Matter

Appendix: The Main Groups of Experts Listed in the Text

Group	Chapters	Expertise	Organizational/ Institutional Position	Social Origins
Old *mista'rvim*	2	Imitation	Members of Ha-Shomer (founded 1909), a secretive guard and self-defense association	Mostly Ashkenazi Jews, either European or native born, affiliated with the labor movement
Sephardi and other notables	2–4	Mediation, networks of Palestinian acquaintances	Kedma Mizraha (1936–1938), voluntary organization for *hasbara*; Ministry for Minority Affairs (1948–1949)	Sephardi elite; farmers, citrus growers, mayors, and Jewish *mukhtars*
Academic orientalists, first generation	3, 4	Academic credentials, philology	Institute for Oriental Studies, Hebrew University (founded 1926); Brit Shalom (1925–1930), association for promoting Jewish-Arab coexistence	German born and educated

(*Continued*)

(*Continued*)

Group	Chapters	Expertise	Organizational/ Institutional Position	Social Origins
Arabists	3–5	Imitation, mediation, and art of operating informers, government	Haganah Intelligence Service (1936–1948); military government (1948–1966)	Notables and old *mista'rvim*
Students/ officials, second generation of academic orientalists	3, 4, 6	Academic credentials, philology, political intelligence research	Institute for Oriental Studies, Hebrew University (1930s, back in 1953); Haganah Intelligence Service (1936–1945); Political Department of Jewish Agency (1938–1948); Foreign Office (1948–)	Ashkenazi Jews, either European or native born
Labor activists	3, 4	Eclectic	Arab Department of Histadrut	Eclectic, some born in Arab countries
Young military commanders	3, 4, 6	Imitation	Palmach (Haganah shock troops) (1942–1948); IDF General Staff (1948–)	Native born, mostly in labor (i.e., separatist) sector
New *mista'ravim*	3	Imitation	Palmach	Born in Arab countries
Military intelligence research officers	4, 6	Academic training, philological habitus, interpretation of intentions	Research branch of military intelligence	Mostly Ashkenazi Jews, European or native born

(Continued)

Group	Chapters	Expertise	Organizational/ Institutional Position	Social Origins
Academic Middle Eastern studies experts, third generation of academic orientalists	6	Academic training, philological habitus, interpretation of intentions	Shiloah Institute (1965), later transformed into Dayan Center (1983), at Tel-Aviv University	Mostly Ashkenazi Jews, European or native born; some former military intelligence research officers
Sociologists and psychologists	3, 4	Social problems, modernization discourse	Academic departments, advisers to the absorption and settlement departments of the Jewish Agency	Mostly Ashkenazi Jews

Notes

1. The term "Aliya" (literally, "ascension") designates, in Zionist historiography, a distinct wave of Jewish immigration to Palestine and could also be used to refer to a generational unit, the group of individuals who immigrated during this wave. The First Aliya dates from 1882 to 1904.

2. The identification of the above scene as a recurrent literary device is taken from Yaffah Berlovitz, *Inventing a Land, Inventing a People: The Literature of the First Aliya* (Tel-Aviv: Hakibutz Hameuchad, 1996), 113 [H].

3. Jacob Shabtai, *Past Perfect* (Tel-Aviv: Hakibutz Hameuchad, 1984), 173 [H].

4. Shlomo Dov Goitein, "About a Jewish-Arab Symbiosis," *Molad* 2 (February 1949): 259–66 [H]; Yoel Kremer, "Goitein and His Mediterranean Society," *Zemanim* 33-34 (1990): 4–17 [H]; Erich Brauer, *The Jews of Kurdistan: An Ethnological Study* (Jerusalem: The Eretz Israel Institute of Folklore and Ethnology, 1948).

5. Ofra Benjo, *Saddam's Iraq: Political Discourse and the Language of Power* (Tel-Aviv: Kav Adom, 1996), 9 [H].

6. Max Weber, "Science as a Vocation" and "Religious Rejections of the World and Their Directions," in *From Max Weber*, ed. Hans H. Gerth and C. Wright Mills (New York: Oxford University Press, 1948), 129–56, 323–59.

7. I take the inspiration for this inversion from Michel Foucault, *Madness and Civilization* (New York: Vintage Books, 1965). See the excellent exposition in Colin Gordon, "'Histoire de la folie': An Unknown Book by Michel Foucault," *History of the Human Sciences* 3 (1990): 3–26. The first step in the emergence of the modern relation to madness, according to Foucault, was not the formulation of a rational science of mental life but the arbitrary gesture of locking up "unreason" (*déraison*), forcibly differentiating between those who worked and those who did not (including beggars, criminals, runaway kids, and vagabonds) Only later, argues Foucault, and within confinement, there began a process of fragmenting the metaphor of "unreason," and distinguishing within it different forms in accordance

with the needs of confinement. The rational sciences of mental life – psychology and psychiatry – appeared only much later, and it is clear that Foucault considers them to be merely forced interpretations of categories not of their own making, categories formed within the world of confinement.

8. Edward Said, *Orientalism* (London: Penguin, 1978), esp. 201–25. For a similar critique of Said, noting his tendency to present orientalism as unchanging, see Emmanuel Sivan, "Edward Said and his Arab Reviewers," *Jerusalem Quarterly* 35 (Spring 1985): 11–23. For another critique, which focuses explicitly on the problematic distinction between "latent" and "manifest" orientalism, see Homi Bhabha, *The Location of Culture* (London: Routledge, 1994), 71–2.

9. Martin Kramer, introduction to *The Jewish Discovery of Islam: Studies in Honor of Bernard Lewis*, ed. Martin Kramer (Tel-Aviv: Dayan Center, 1999); Bernard Lewis, "The Pro-Islamic Jews," in *Islam in History* (Chicago: Open Court, 1993). Much of the debate revolves around the relation between orientalism and colonialism. Said has depicted orientalism as a form of symbolic mastery over non-Europeans and thus as complementary to the project of attaining military, political, and economic mastery over them. This is why it must reinforce a sharp binary division between East and West. Lewis and Kramer counter that this equation ignores German oriental studies, which had developed independently of a colonial project, and even more ignores the forms of orientalist knowledge developed by Jews, whose status within Europe was not all that different from colonial subjects. Consequently, they rejected the binary division between East and West. See also Susannah Heschel, *Abraham Geiger and the Jewish Jesus* (Chicago: University of Chicago Press, 1998).

10. "The Arab world is not monolithic and not static. Any generalization about its ways and aims may distort the picture more than it would help to understand it." Shimon Shamir, *Egypt under Sa'adat* (Tel-Aviv: Dvir, 1978), 12 [H].

11. A similar critique of both sides in the debate about orientalism and the Jews, and one similarly sensitive to the hybridity of Jewish identity, is articulated by Ivan Davidson Kalmar and Derek Penslar, "Orientalism and the Jews: An Introduction," in *Orientalism and the Jews*, ed. Ivan Davidson Kalmar and Derek Penslar (Waltham, MA: Brandeis University Press, 2005), xiii–xl.

12. Said, *Orientalism*, 7.

13. I owe this observation to conversations with Yehouda Shenhav and Gideon Aran. See also Hannan Hever, Pnina Mutzafi-Heller, and Yehouda Shenhav, eds., *Mizrahi Perspectives on Society and Culture in Israel: A Report on Israeli Patterns of Representation* (Jerusalem: Van-Leer Institute, 1999) [H]; Yehouda Shenhav, *The Arab-Jews: Nationalism, Religion and Ethnicity* (Tel-Aviv: Am-Oved, 2003), 211. On the intimate relation between boundaries and transgression, see Michel Foucault, "Preface to Transgression," in *Aesthetics, Method and Epistemology*, vol. 2 of *Essential Works of Michel Foucault, 1954–1984*, ed. Paul Rabinow (New York: The New Press, 1998), 73. Other scholars have also criticized Said for failing to grasp this essential ambiguity of the orientalist project or have shown how precarious European identity was in the colonies and how it relied on the continuous production and deconstruction of hybridity. See Bhabha, *Location of Culture*, 70–5, 85–6, 112–14; Ann

Laura Stoler, *Race and the Education of Desire* (Durham: Duke University Press, 1995), 95–136.

14. Bruno Latour, *We Have Never Been Modern* (Cambridge, MA: Harvard University Press, 1993). See also Mary Douglas, *Purity and Danger* (London: Routledge, 1966).

15. Ella Shohat, "Sephardim in Israel: Zionism from the Standpoint of Its Jewish Victims," in *Dangerous Liaisons: Gender, Nation and Postcolonial Perspectives*, ed. Anne McClintock, Aamir Mufti, and Ella Shohat (Minneapolis: University of Minnesota Press, 1997), 39–68; Ella Shohat, *The Mizrahi Revolution: Three Essays on Zionism and the Mizrahim* (Jerusalem: Center for Alternative Information, 1999) [H]; Haim Gerber, "Zionism, Orientalism and the Palestinians," *Ha-Mizrah Ha-Hadash* 43 (2002): 27–47 [H].

16. Gershon Shafir, *Land, Labor, and the Origins of the Israeli-Palestinian Conflict, 1882–1914* (Cambridge: Cambridge University Press, 1989); Baruch Kimmerling, *Zionism and Territory* (Berkeley: Institute for International Studies, 1983).

17. The word *mista'ravim* is a Hebrew neologism based on the Arabic word for a non-Arab living among Arabs. In Arabic it carries the distinct implication that one is pretending to be an Arab. My thanks to Rashid Khalidi for this point. About various types of *mista'ravim*, see Joe Lockard, "Somewhere between Arab and Jew: Ethnic Re-Identification in Modern Hebrew Literature," *Middle Eastern Literature* 5, no. 1 (2002): 49–62; Oz Almog, *The Sabra: A Profile* (Tel-Aviv: Am Oved, 1997), 293–4, 305–7, 443 [H]; Gamliel Cohen, *The First Mista'ravim* (Tel-Aviv: Ministry of Defense, 2002) [H].

18. See Timothy Mitchell, "The Limits of the State: Beyond Statist Approaches and Their Critics," *American Political Science Review* 85, 1 (March 1991): 77–96.

19. Amnon Raz-Krakozkin, "Orientalism, Judaism Studies and Israeli Society: A Few Notes," *Jama'a* 3, no. 1 (1999): 34–61 [H]; Sammy Smooha and Ora Cibulski, *Social Research on Arabs in Israel 1948–1982: Trends and an Annotated Bibliography* (Haifa: University of Haifa, Jewish-Arab Center, 1989), 1:20–3.

CHAPTER 1

1. Shlomo Dov Goitein, "The New Orient," *Ha-Mizrah Ha-Hadash* 1 (1949): 1–2 [H].

2. From 1949 to 1977 there were only two articles dealing with Jews: K. Grunwald, "The Jewish Bankers in Iraq," *Ha-Mizrah Ha-Hadash* 11 (1961): 159–65 [H]; Haim Cohen, "Jewish Theosophists in Basra: Symptom of the Struggles of the *Haskala* Generation," *Ha-Mizrah Ha-Hadash* 15 (1965): 401–7 [H]. Additionally, there are a few articles dealing with the negotiations between the Zionist movement and the Arab Nationalist movement and with Israel's foreign policy.

3. For example, the "Index" to *Mizrah u-Ma'arav* 4 (1922) listed eighty articles published that year, of which only two could be said to deal with non-Jewish Middle Eastern affairs.

4. Said, *Orientalism*, 2–3.

5. Said, *Orientalism*, 92–3.

6. Said, *Orientalism*, 68–9. This periodization is admittedly somewhat crude, and it does not take account of changes outside Europe. See the finer distinction between the "Saracen" and "Turkish" periods purposed by Kalmar and Penslar, "Orientalism and the Jews," xxiii.

7. Bruno Latour, *Science in Action* (Cambridge, MA: Harvard University Press, 1988), 198–205, 245.

8. Said, *Orientalism*, 85–7. On British anthropology and its role within the colonial project, see Talal Asad, ed., *Anthropology and the Colonial Encounter* (London: Ithaca Press, 1973). On the emergence of scientific racism in response to the problem of hybridity in the colonies, see Stoler, *Race and the Education of Desire*, 184–90. On the discourse of modernization and development within colonial and postcolonial regimes, see James Ferguson, *The Anti-Politics Machine* (New York: Cambridge University Press, 1990).

9. Said, *Orientalism*, 201–25.

10. Edward Said, *Covering Islam* (New York: Pantheon Books, 1981).

11. Michel Foucault, *The Archeology of Knowledge* (London: Tavistock, 1972), 109.

12. This is not a claim I can substantiate here, since I am only dealing with the Israeli case, but it is supported by the fact that earlier forms of Arab intellectual resistance to orientalism, before this work of disenchantment had been completed, did not begin, like Said, with the discovery that the Orient was imaginary but rather insisted that the Orient's real boundaries lay beyond the Middle East. The real Orient, claimed Taha Husayn, for example, began in India, while the Arabs shared a cultural heritage with Europe. Taha Husayn, *The Future of Culture in Egypt* (Washington, DC: American Council of Learned Societies, 1954).

13. Eli Eyal, "The debate among Orientalists after the Agranat Report," *Ma'ariv*, April 26, 1974, magazine section, 12–13, 37 [H]. Similarly, the only existing study of Israeli *mizrahanut* as a profession was based on a sample population of 39 academic orientalists employed by universities and 76 employed by the IDF or government agencies. The author emphasized that the interviewees agreed neither on the definition of their field nor on who should be included within it. Yom-Tov Eyni, "Professional Aspects of Mizrahanut in Israel" (master's thesis, Tel-Aviv University, 1975), 6–39 [H].

14. Eleanor Rosch, "Principles of Categorization," in *Cognition and Categorization*, ed. Eleanor Rosch and B. B. Lloyd (Hillsdale, NJ: Lawrence Erlbaum Associates, 1978).

15. Max Weber, *Sociology of Religion* (Boston: Beacon Press, 1963).

16. The translation of Weber's sociology of religion into the idea of the "religious field" is in Pierre Bourdieu, "Legitimation and Structured Interests in Weber's Sociology of Religion," in *Max Weber, Rationality and Modernity*, ed. Scott Lash and S. Whimster (London: Allen & Unwin, 1987), 119–36. The idea that certain forms of expertise could derive their power not from mystery and esoteric knowledge but from "generosity" and openness of knowledge is in Nikolas Rose, "Engineering the Human Soul: Analyzing Psychological Expertise," *Science in Context* 5, no. 2 (1992): 351–69.

CHAPTER 2

1. Michael Lewin, "Notes on Trends in the Emergence and Crystallization of a Local Art and Architecture in Palestine," *Katedra* 16 (July 1980): 194–204 [H]. For more on the "oriental" motifs in Jewish architecture and especially in the ceramics dotting some Tel-Aviv houses, see Alec Mishory, *Lo and Behold: Zionist Icons and Visual Symbols in Israeli Culture* (Tel-Aviv: Am Oved, 2000), 96–115, 255–6 [H]. On the inception of Tel-Aviv, perceived as an escape from Jaffa, see Tom Segev, *One Palestine, Complete* (New York: Metropolitan Books, 1999), 183–5. For a definition of Zionism as the attempt to invent a new culture, by rejecting both the culture of origin and the native culture, see Itamar Even-Zohar, "The Emergence and Crystallization of a Native, Local Hebrew Culture in Palestine, 1882–1948," *Katedra* 16 (July 1980): 177 [H].

2. See, for example, Haim Hissin, *Writings of One of the Biluyim* (Jerusalem: Yad Ben-Tzvi, 1990), 51, 94 [H].

3. David Ben-Gurion, "From the Debate: A Conversation with the Members of *Brit-Shalom*," in *Our Neighbors and Us* (Tel-Aviv: Davar, 1931), 183 [H]. All the other quotes are taken from Segev, *One Palestine*, 150–4, 175, 233, 376, 404.

4. Aziza Khazzoom, "The Origins of Ethnic Inequality among Jews in Israel" (Ph.D. diss., University of California–Berkeley, 1998), 35–74; Aziza Khazzoom, "Occidental Culture, Ethnic Stigmatization and Social Closure: The Background for Ethnic Inequality in Israel," *Israeli Sociology* 1-2 (1999): 385–428 [H]; Aziza Khazzoom, "The Great Chain of Orientalism: Jewish Identity, Stigma Management and Ethnic Exclusion in Israel," *American Sociological Review* 68 (August 2003): 481–501; Daniel Boyarin, "The Colonial Drag: Zionism, Gender, and Mimicry," in *The Pre-Occupation of Post-Colonial Studies*, eds. Fawzia Afzal-Khan, and Kalpana Seshadri-Crooks (Durham, NC: Duke University Press, 2000); Raz-Krakozkin, "Orientalism, Judaism Studies and Israeli Society," 34.

5. Khazzoom, "The Great Chain," 485–6; Kalmar and Penslar, "Orientalism and the Jews," xviii.

6. Kramer, introduction to *The Jewish Discovery of Islam,* 5–6, 11, 14–17, 41–3; Mishori, *Lo and Behold*, 20, 24–5, 35.

7. Raz-Krakozkin, "Orientalism, Judaism Studies and Israeli Society," 44–6.

8. Shafir, *Land, Labor, and the Origins*; Kimmerling, *Zionism and Territory*.

9. For the canonical version, see Dan Horowitz and Moshe Lissak, *Origins of the Israeli Polity: Palestine under the Mandate* (Chicago: Chicago University Press, 1978). For a more critical account, see Yonthan Shapira, *Democracy in Israel* (Ramat-Gan: Massada, 1977) [H].

10. On the administration by notables, see Max Weber, *Economy and Society* (Berkeley: University of California Press, 1978), 289–92. Weber usually contrasts the administration by notables with bureaucratic administration by means of officials. The latter work on a full-time basis, they are salaried, and they are appointed on the basis of specialized expertise. Notables, on the other hand, are typically elected or appointed to perform administrative tasks on the basis of their social position as representatives of clans, ethnic groups, religious denominations, etc. They do so as unpaid "amateurs" on a part-time basis, performing their duties as one of several tasks

between which they divide their time. On the politics of notables in the Ottoman Empire, see Albert Hourani, *The Emergence of the Modern Middle East* (Berkeley: University of California Press, 1981). On the British Mandatory government, what it inherited from the Ottomans, and how it organized the relations between governors and notables, see Yaacov Reuveni, *The Mandatory Government in Palestine, 1920–1948: A Political-Historical Analysis* (Ramat-Gan: Bar-Ilan University, 1993), 51–61 [H]; Segev, *One Palestine*, 163–5; Shimon Shamir, "Changes in the Village Leadership of Ar-Rama," *HaMizrah-Ha-Hadash* 11 (1961): 248 [H].

11. Hanna Herzog, *Political Ethnicity: Image versus Reality: A Historical-Sociological Analysis of the "Ethnic" Lists to the Convention of Delegates and the Knesset, 1920–1984* (Ramat Efal: Yad Tabenkin, 1986), 81–119 [H].

12. The concept of "pastoral power" is taken from Michel Foucault, "The Subject and Power," in *Michel Foucault: Beyond Structuralism and Hermeneutics*, ed. Hubert L. Dreyfus and Paul Rabinow (Chicago: Chicago University Press, 1982).

13. *Moshav ovdim* was unlike the *kibbutz* in that land was held as private property and each household produced for its own consumption and profit. It was similar to the *kibbutz*, however, in that productive and distributive infrastructures were shared and, most importantly, farmers worked their own land and would not employ hired labor, certainly not Palestinian.

14. Shabtai Teveth, *Moshe Dayan: A Biography* (Jerusalem: Shocken, 1971), 51 [H].

15. Moshe Smilanski, *Sons of Arabia: Stories and Drawings from the Lives of the Arabs in Palestine* (Odessa: Haylprin, 1911) [H].

16. Teveth, *Moshe Dayan*, 51, 98.

17. Ibid., 51–2, 66–7, 99. Nothing captures the nature of this sphere better than the incident when the young Dayan first acquired his reputation for fearlessness. It was a fight over a piece of land against a neighboring Bedouin tribe. While it was reported in the national press as part of the national struggle, in reality his opponents were friends and acquaintances whom he knew from very early age and who, after a few months, when emotions had calmed down, attended his wedding en masse. Ibid., 137–40.

18. Ibid., 67–8.

19. David Ben-Gurion, "For a Clarification of the Origin of the Fellahin," in *Our Neighbors and Us*, 13 [H].

20. Shlomo Dov Goitein, *Jews and Arabs: Their Contacts through the Ages* (New York: Shocken Books, 1955), 5. A letter from Ben-Gurion to his father captures this opposition between European culture and Bedouin otherness well: "When I was here about 8 months ago – this place was still barren, deserted, strewn with rocks and covered by thorny bushes. Only the sound of an Arab shepherd's pipe carried over the mountains, and in the fields were planted the black tents of *Keidar*, woven of goat hair, and around them the savage Bedouin lay – but when I returned here today from the Diaspora, I found European houses, cultivated fields, the life of Hebrew workers, Hebrew – that means, ours – our property, our labor, our life." David Ben-Gurion, *Letters of David Ben-Gurion*, ed. Yehouda Erez (Tel-Aviv: Am-Oved, 1971), 1:123 [H].

21. The quote is from *In the Land of the Orient*, a travelogue written by Hirshberg in Yiddish for European Jewish readers and cited in Ben-Tzion Dinur, ed., *History of the Haganah* (Tel-Aviv: Maarachot, 1954), 72–3 [H].

22. From a eulogy written by R. Binyamin (Joshua Felman-Redler) at the occasion of the death of Dov Schweiger and quoted in Dinur, *History of the Haganah*, 210. See also Ya'acov Goldstein, *The Group of the Shepherds, 1907–1917* (Tel-Aviv: Ministry of Defense, 1993) [H]: "There is good reason to assume that they joined the Bedouin because of the great admiration the *Shomer* had for them . . . and because of the romantic aura that surrounded the Bedouin, which to a great extent was created by the *Shomer*" (25). As noted, this was a highly masculine and gendered project. At one point, the shepherds even contemplated marrying Bedouin wives, who would be "accustomed to the hard conditions of life." As it happened, some married Sephardi Jewish women, natives of Palestine, whom they believed would be more fitting partners for the nomadic life that was their ideal. In general, women were almost completely excluded from the small circles of the virtuosi.

23. Ben-Gurion, *Letters*, 1:86, 266.

24. Ben-Gurion, *Letters*, 1:143–5, 156. This is the argument of Even-Zohar, "Emergence and Crystallization," 165–89, and Almog, *The Sabra*, 289–94 [H].

25. Michel Foucault, "Technologies of the Self," in *Technologies of the Self*, ed. Luther H. Martin, Huck Gutman, and Patrick H. Hutton (London: Tavistock, 1988).

26. Dinur, *History of the Haganah*, 137–47.

27. Goldstein, *The Group of the Shepherds*, 11–12.

28. Dinur, *History of the Haganah*, 263, 266–7, 288, 362.

29. Yoesf Aharonowitz, quoted in Dinur, *History of the Haganah*, 288.

30. Ben-Gurion, "Origin of the Fellahin," 14. The same point is also made in Yitzhak Ben-Tzvi, *The Populace of Our Land* (Warsaw: Beit Ha-Noar, 1932), 21 [H], and in David Ben-Gurion and Yitzhak Ben-Tzvi, *Eretz Israel: Past and Present* (Jerusalem: Yad ben-Tzvi, 1980 [1918]), 118–19 [H]. This image was used to describe not only Palestine but the Orient in general, as well as oriental Jewry. In his letters to his father, Ben-Gurion uses similar terms to describe the Jewish inhabitants of Jerusalem and Thessalonica. Ben-Gurion, *Letters*, 1:115–16, 176.

31. Ezra Danin, *Zionist without Conditions* (Jerusalem: Kidum, 1987).

32. Goitein, *Jews and Arabs*, 13–14.

33. Amos Oz, *A Story about Love and Darkness* (Jerusalem: Keter, 2002), 41–2 [H].

34. Kremer, "Goitein and His Mediterranean Society," 6–17.

35. I intentionally use the term "Sephardim" and not "*mizrahim*" because in the prestate period it was used far more often. I do not think it is possible to precisely define who the Sephardim were and how they were similar or different from the *mizrahim*. I treat these categories not as real groups but as invented categories, and I investigate not their composition but their discursive function as hybrids. Moreover, as I argue in Chapter 4, the term "*mizrahim*" only became important much later, after Middle Eastern and North African Jews immigrated to Israel and underwent a process of ethnicization, and it was used to denote a different sort of hybridity than "Sephardim" denoted. In between, from the late 1940s to the late 1960s, the term used in common parlance was "*edoth ha-mizrah*" (oriental ethnicities).

36. Yosef Kloisner, "The Eternal Value of the Period of Sepharad," *Mizrah u-Ma'arav* 1 (September 1920): 307–11 [H].

37. Zeev Jabotinsky, "The Jews of the Orient," *Mizrah u-Ma'arv* 1 (September 1919): 59–60 [H].

38. Yoel Yosef Rivlin, "Professor Yosef Horowitz," *Moznaim* 49–50 (1931): 15–17 [H].

39. Eliahu Elishar, "A Palestinian Jew Testifying in Front of the Royal Committee of Lord Peel," in *Living with Palestinians* (Jerusalem: Va'ad Edat Ha-Sepharadim, 1975), 55–6 [H]. See also Hadara Lazar, *In and Out of Palestine* (Jerusalem: Keter, 2003), 55–68 [H].

40. Goitein, "Jewish-Arab Symbiosis."

41. Hana Amit-Kokhavi, "To Know and Understand Our Neighbors: On the Translation of Arab Literature into Hebrew, 1868–2002," *Ha-Mizrah Ha-Hadash* 43 (2002): 213–15 [H]; Liora R. Halperin, "The 'Pioneering Work' of Zionist Arabic Study during the Mandate Period: Zionism in Conversation with Orientalism" (senior thesis, Harvard University, 2004).

42. Max Nordau, "The Arabs and Us," *Ha-Olam* 838, 40 (17.6.1937) [H]; Goitein, *Jews and Arabs*, 19–21. On the other hand, this notion did have some purchase among some of the Zionist leadership. Arthur Rupin, for example, who played a major role in organizing and financing Zionist settlement, thought that Zionism must "integrate itself among the nations of the Orient and create together with them, on the basis of racial similarity to the Arabs and the Armenians, a new cultural unit in the Near East." Another was R. Binyamin, a prominent Zionist essayist, who recommended, in his famous "Arabian Address," intermarriage between Jews and Arabs. Yosef Heller, *From Covenant of Peace to Ichud: Yehouda Leib Magnes and the Struggle for a Bi-National State* (Jerusalem: Magness, 2004), 9–12 [H].

43. Itamar Ben-Avi, "Only Clear Words," *Doar Ha-Yom*, August 8, 1918, 1 [H]. On the political and cultural struggles between the notables, labor, and the writers' group, see Herzog, *Political Ethnicity*; Abraham Cordova, "The Institutionalization of a Cultural Center in Palestine: The Case of the Writers Association," *Jewish Social Studies* 42 (Winter 1980): 37–62 [H]; Abraham Cordova, *Hasolel* (unpublished manuscript, University of Tel-Aviv) [H].

44. See, S. Ussishkin, *Occident in the Orient: History of the Crusaders in Palestine* (Tel-Aviv: Mitzpe, 1937), 3–4, 175–8 [H]. Ussishkin draws an explicit connection between the crusaders and the Zionists and cautions the latter to learn from the demise of the crusader kingdom. It collapsed, he claims, because of mixed marriages and racial miscegenation: "This transformation of a western people into eastern people was unfortunate. Mixed marriages did not bear a successful fruit; the offspring of these misalliances were weaker in body and spirit from their western fathers and eastern mothers. The difficult climate, the many diseases, the permanent fever, the new habits, the assimilation among Greeks and Muslims, all these did not create a new people, strong in body and spirit, but a society marked by all the signs of corruption and degeneration of body and spirit."

45. Yehuda Burla, "The Sepharadim and Our National Revival," *Mizrah u-Ma'arav* 1 (October 1919): 163–71 [H].

46. Elishar, "A Palestinian Jew"; H. Z. Hirschberg, "Editor's Note," in *Zakhor le-Avraham: A Collection of Articles in Memory of Avraham Elmaliah*, ed. H. Z. Hirschberg (Jerusalem: Committee of the Maghrebi Community, 1972), 5–11 [H]; Lazar, *In and Out*, 55–68; Goitein, "Jewish-Arab Symbiosis"; Kremer, "Goitein and His Mediterranean Society"; Rivlin, "Professor Yosef Horovitz," 15–17; Hava Lazarus-Yafeh,

"The Transplantation of Islamic Studies from Europe to the Yishuv and Israel," in Kramer, *The Jewish Discovery of Islam*, 249–60.

47. Ben-Gurion, "Origin of the Fellahin," 15–21. See also Ben-Gurion and Ben-Tzvi, *Eretz Israel*, 198–9, and Ben Tzvi, *The Populace*, 29–39. In voicing this speculation, Ben-Gurion was continuing a long series of similar analyses and claims by earlier Zionist leaders and settlers. Shmuel Almog, "The 'Land to Its Workers' and the Conversion of the Fellahin," in *The Nation and its History*, ed. Shmuel Ettinger (Jerusalem: Zalman Shazar Center, 1984), 170–1 [H].

48. Moshe Dayan, *Living with the Bible* (Tel-Aviv: Yediot Aharonot, 1978) [H].

49. Almog, "The 'Land to Its Workers,'" 172, 175.

50. Yosef Meyuchas, *The Fellahin: The Life of the Fellahin in Comparison with the Life of the Jews in Biblical and Talmudic times* (Tel-Aviv: Davar, 1937), xi–xiii [H]. See also Shlomo Dov Goitein, *Teaching the Bible* (Tel-Aviv: Yavne, 1957) [H]; Moshe Stavski, *The Arab Village* (Tel-Aviv: Am Oved, 1946), 5, 11, 180 [H]; Dayan, *Living with the Bible*, 15; Tuvia Ashkenazi, *The Near East* (Jerusalem: Kedem, 1932), 143–9, 164–5, 178, 184–90 [H].

51. Dalia Manor, "Orientalism and Israeli Art: The Case of Betzalel" (paper presented at the annual meeting of the Association for Israel Studies, Vail, Colorado, May 2002); Dalia Manor, "Biblical Zionism in Bezalel Art," *Israel Studies* 6 (Spring 2001): 55–75; Goitien, *Arabs and Jews*, 77–8, 185, 189; Kremer, "Goitein and His Mediterranean Society," 7; Shlomo Dov Goitein, *Hebrew Instruction in the Land of Israel* (Tel-Aviv: Yavne, 1945) [H]; Shlomo Dov Goitein, "Oriental Studies in the Hebrew University," *Davar,* October 4, 1936, 14 [H]; Mishori, *Lo and Behold*, 80–92.

52. Shenhav, *The Arab Jews*, 73–120.

53. Mishori, *Lo and Behold*, 257, 288.

54. Mishori, *Lo and Behold*, 89–92, 209, 345; Neri Livne, "The Legend of Nimrod," *Haaretz*, February 23, 2002, magazine section, online archive http://www.haaretz.co.il/hasite/pages/arch (no. 796579) [H]; M. Solovitshik, *Treasures of the Bible* (Berlin: Dvir, 1925) [H].

55. He climbs on top of a tower in an ancient fortress outside the Arab city of Ramle: "Who knows, maybe two thousands years ago our heroes fought here with those who stole their country – the eyes are glued to these magical sights all around, the Hebrew heart is overflowing." Or he gazes on the sunset: "The sun is setting – and a wonderful and majestic vision appears in the sky above the sea . . . a vision shown only by the sky above Eretz Israel! . . . What a magical land is Eretz Israel!" Ben-Gurion, *Letters*, 1:79, 89, 115.

56. Manor, "Biblical Zionism," 57–9.

57. See, for example, Moshe Smilanski, *Jewish Colonization and the Fellah* (Tel-Aviv: Mishar u-Ta'asia, 1930) [H].

58. Stavski, *The Arab Village*, 8.

59. Stavski, *The Arab Village*, 8–51, 180.

CHAPTER 3

1. Amit-Kokhavi, "To Know and Understand Our Neighbors," 214–15; Lazarus-Yafeh, "The Transplantation," 250–4, 256–9.

2. Halperin, "The Pioneering Work," 53.

3. Menahem Milson, "The Beginning of Islamic and Arabic Studies in the Hebrew University," in *The History of the Hebrew University in Jerusalem: Origins and Beginnings*, ed. Shaul Katz and Michael Heyd (Jerusalem: Magness, 1997), 575–88 [H]; Lazarus-Yafeh, "The Transplantation," 255; Rivlin, "Professor Horowitz," 15–17; Goitein, "Oriental Studies," 14.

4. Brit Shalom was a movement of intellectuals, some from the Hebrew University and some employed by the Zionist Federation but almost all born in Germany or within the Central European zone of German influence. Among the best known of its members and sympathizers were the philosophers Martin Buber, S. H. Bergman, and A. A. Simon; the historians Gershom Scholem and Hans Cohen; and the Zionist leader Arthur Rupin. Among its members were also a few Sephardi notables. Brit Shalom's program demanded that a greater effort be made to reach a compromise with the Palestinians. Some of its members supported a voluntary limit on Jewish immigration so as to assuage Palestinian fears. Others, later, raised the idea of creating a binational state. The professors of the Institute for Oriental Studies who were also members or registered sympathizers of Brit-Shalom were David Zvi Baneth, Alfred Bonne, L. A. Mayer, Walter Fischel, Shlomo Dov Goitein, Yosef Horovitz, and Max Schlussinger. Aharon Keidar, "The History of *Brit Shalom* in the Years 1925–1928," in *Research Chapters in the History of Zionism*, ed. Yehouda Bauer, Moshe Davies, and Israel Kulat (Jerusalem: The Zionist Library, 1976), 229–30, 235–8, 254, 264–5 [H]; Heller, *From Covenant of Peace to Ichud*, 9–12, 23.

5. Kremer, "Goitein and His Mediterranean Society," 7–10; Goitein, "Jewish-Arab Symbiosis," 261–5; Tamar Herman, "From Brit Shalom to Peace Now: The Pragmatic Pacificism of the Peace Camp in Israel" (Ph.D. diss., Tel-Aviv University, 1989), 148 [H].

6. Keidar, "History of *Brit Shalom*," 229–30, 235–8; Milson, "Beginning of Islamic and Arabic Studies," 578, 580–1.

7. Yoram Sade, "The Academic Group in Brit Shalom and Its Successors: Political and Ideological Behavior in Light of Their Self Image" (master's thesis, Tel-Aviv University, 1976) [H].

8. Moshe Gabay, *Kedma Mizracha, 1936–1939* (Givat Haviva: Institute for Arab Studies, 1984), 13–17 [H].

9. Ibid., 74–5.

10. Ibid., 85–8.

11. Gabay, *Kedma Mizracha*, 27, 65–9; Heller, *From Covenant of Peace to Ichud*, 22. Kedma Mizracha dissolved in 1938, probably because of disagreements about whether to accept the proposal to divide the country into two states, and also because it did not manage to persuade the Zionist Federation to fund its activities.

12. Yoav Gelber, *Roots of the Lily: Intelligence in the Yishuv, 1918–1947* (Tel-Aviv: Defense Ministry, 1992), 161 [H]; Danin, *Zionist without Conditions*, 118–28.

13. Gelber, *Roots of the Lily*, 161, 510–11, 514–15, 520–2; Ian Black and Benny Morris, *Israel's Secret Wars: The Untold Story of Israeli Intelligence* (London: Hannish Hamilton, 1991), 22, 52.

14. Ezra Danin, quoted in Asa Lephen, *The Shai: The Roots of the Israeli Intelligence Community* (Tel-Aviv: Ministry of Defense, 1997), 48–9, 180 [H]. See also Yoav Gelber, "The Formation of Military Intelligence," *Marachot* 294-295 (July 1984): 20–31 [H].

15. Quoted in Milson, "Beginning of Islamic and Arabic Studies," 582–3.

16. Goitein, "Oriental Studies," 14.

17. Tables available from the author.

18. Gelber, *Roots of the Lily*, 86–92; Lephen, *The Shai*, 192, 245.

19. Abraham Cordova and Hanna Herzog, "The Editorial Board of Davar between Ideology and Politics, 1925–1938," *Rivon Le-Mehkar Hevrati* 20, no. 2 (1980): 5–30 [H]; Sarah Ozacky-Lazar, *From a Hebrew Histadrut to a General Histadrut: The Integration of Arabs in the Organization, 1948–1966* (Tel-Aviv: Lavon Institute for the Study of the Labor Movement, 1998), 12–13 [H].

20. For Rabin's experience, see Yitzhak Rabin, *My Father's House* (Tel-Aviv: Hakibutz Hameuchad, 1974), 20–1 [H].

21. Anita Shapira, *Yigal Alon: The Springtime of His Life* (Tel-Aviv: Hakibutz Hameuchad, 2004), 34–8, 42–3, 61 [H]

22. Uri Ben-Eliezer, *The Making of Israeli Militarism, 1936–1956* (Tel-Aviv: Dvir, 1995) [H].

23. For an example of this mode of analysis, which divides experts into those with "orientalist" views and those relatively free of these and thus seeks to explain their actions and attitudes, see Joel Beinin, "Know thy Enemies, Know thy Allies: The Orientalists of *Ha-Shomer Ha-Tzair*," in *Jewish-Arab Relations in Mandatory Palestine*, ed. Ilan Pappe (Givat-Haviva: Institute for Peace Studies, 1995) [H].

24. Asa Lephen, "The Shai: The Paramilitary Intelligence Service," in *Intelligence and National Security*, ed. Avi Kover and Zvi Ofer (Tel-Aviv: Marachot, 1987), 99 [H]; Gelber, *Roots of the Lily*, 510–11; Lephen, *The Shai*, 94.

25. Gelber, *Roots of the Lily*, 515, 525; Yehoshua Palmon, "To Enter the Enemy's Mind: A Personal Point of View," in Kover and Ofer, *Intelligence and National Security*, 282 [H].

26. Palmon, cited in Lephen, *The Shai*, 285 n. 30, and see also 90–3; Gelber, *Roots of the Lily*, 510–11, 516–18, 534, 622; Danin, *Zionist without Conditions*, 154.

27. Milson, "Beginning of Islamic and Arabic Studies," 578–9, 580–1 n. 20, 587; Rivlin, "Professor Horowitz"; Edward Ullendorf, "D. H. Baneth and Philological Precociousness," in *Studia Orientalia Memoriae D. H. Baneth Dedicata*, ed. Edward Ullendorf (Jerusalem: Magnes, 1979), 7–13.

28. Lephen, "The Shai," 100; Lephen, *The Shai*, 48–9; Gelber, *Roots of the Lily*, 513, 523–4; Black and Morris, *Israel's Secret Wars*, 24.

29. Gelber, *Roots of the Lily*, 319, 515, 525; Lephen, *The Shai*, 230, 280 n. 33.

30. Gelber, *Roots of the Lily*, 617–19, 661; Lephen, *The Shai*, 93–5, 194–5.

31. Moshe Sharet, *Political Diary, 1936*, ed. Ahuvia Malkin (Tel-Aviv: Am Oved, 1968), 103, 129–31 [H].

32. Gelber, *Roots of the Lily*, 661.

33. Gelber, *Roots of the Lily*, 683–4.

34. Gerber, "Zionism, Orientalism and the Palestinians, 28–9; Anita Shapira, *Walking into the Horizon* (Tel-Aviv: Am Oved, 1988), 46 [H]; Shimon Shamir, "The Palestinians Are a Nation," *New Outlook* 12, nos. 6-8 (1969): 191–7.

35. On the concept of "point of diffraction," see Foucault, *Archeology of Knowledge*, 65–6.

36. David Ben-Gurion, "Clarifications," in *Our Neighbors and Us*, 180. Similar arguments about the existence of Arab or Palestinian nationalism were voiced by the labor movement's chief expert on Arab affairs and by one of the students: Michael Assaf, *Zionism, Socialism, and the Arab Question* (Tel-Aviv: Ha-Poel Ha-Tzair, 1938), 3–8 [H]; Michael Assaf, *The Arab Movement in the Land of Israel and Its Origins* (Tel-Aviv: Hotzat Ha-Mishmeret Ha-Tzeira, 1947), 32 [H]; Yaacov Shimoni, *The Arabs of the Land of Israel* (Tel-Aviv: Am Oved, 1947), 19–24 [H].

37. Sharet, *Political Diary*, 164–5.

38. Ben Tzvi, *The Populace*, 5–6, 12–13. A similar analysis is presented in Ben-Gurion and Ben-Tzvi, *Eretz Israel*, 119; Yitzhak Ben-Tzvi, *The Muslim World and the Arab World* (Jerusalem: Keren Kayemet, 1936), 13–17 [H]; and Ashkenazi, *The Near East*, 29, 57, 65, 78.

39. Berl Katzenelson, "The Real Content of the Arab National Movement," in *Writings* (Tel-Aviv: Mapai, 1948), 3:187–209 [H]; Assaf, *Zionism*, 21; Assaf, *The Arab Movement*, 67–8; Yosef Waschitz, *The Arabs in the Land of Israel: Economy and Society, Culture and Politics* (Merhavia: Ha-Kibbutz Ha-Meuhad, 1947), 302–3 [H]; S. Amster, *The Face of the Orient: The Problems of Arab Federation, the Great Powers, and Zionism* (Jerusalem: Ahiassaf, 1945), 126 [H].

40. This was because, in the context of the debate about Arab nationalism, the philological analysis of texts and ideas was identified with the position of Hans Kohn, a member of Brit Shalom. It was therefore too far left and too distant from what their superiors were interested in hearing. Hence, the students could not move toward the upper right corner of Figure 3.1 without being perceived as rebellious. See Hans Kohn, *History of the Arab National Movement* (Tel-Aviv: Ha-Poel Ha-Tzair, 1926). The Arabists and the political activists attacked Kohn and derided his attempt to use what they considered to be "Western" concepts that were inappropriate for understanding an "Eastern" reality. Kohn's knowledge, they claimed, was bookish, and he did not understand the "internal-mental, social and cultural condition of the countries of the Orient and their inhabitants." Eliezer Be'eri, "Arab National Consciousness," *Ha-Shomer Ha-Tzair* nos. 15, 16-17, 19 (1943): 4, 7, 12 [H]; Eliezer Be'eri, *The Arabs: A Bibliographical Survey* (Jerusalem: The Jewish Agency, 1944), 21 [H]; Danin, *Zionist without Conditions*, 656. Under this intense pressure, the students did not dare voice any support for Kohn's methods, and they repeated almost verbatim the very terms that were used, just a few years earlier, against themselves: "In Arab affairs one should not accept any written thing as the absolute truth and a living reality; one should not transfer western and European concepts and ways of thinking to the analysis of the Arab world, where reality is very different from the west.... We know very well that the press, the speeches of the politicians, the declarations of congresses, and the decisions of the institutions of the Arab national movement do not represent the opinions of the common public." Shimoni, *Arabs of the Land of Israel*, 240, 272.

41. Danin, *Zionist without Conditions*, 149; Gelber, *Roots of the Lily*, 512–15; Lephen, *The Shai*, 95.

42. Gelber, *Roots of the Lily*, 694.

43. Gelber, *Roots of the Lily*, 329–31; Danin, *Zionist without Conditions*, 160–3; Lephen, "The Shai," 103.

44. Shenhav, *The Arab-Jews*, 33–6.

45. Dvora HaCohen, *The One Million Plan: David Ben-Gurion's Plan for Mass Immigration in the Years 1942–1945* (Tel-Aviv: Defense Ministry, 1994), 9–11, 125–8, 208–9 [H]; Hannah Helena Tehon, *The Ethnicities in Israel* (Jerusalem: Reuvan, 1957), 33, 48 [H]; Herzog, *Political Ethnicity*, 101–2.

46. Shenhav, *The Arab Jews*, 65–72; HaCohen, *The One Million Plan*, 213–15, 312–14.

47. HaCohen, *The One Million Plan*, 63–4, 101–2, 132–5, 208–9, 216–17; S. N. Eisenstadt, *Introduction to the Study of the Sociological Structure of the Oriental Ethnicities* (Jerusalem, 1948) [H]; Carl Frankenstein, *The Abandonment of Youth* (Jerusalem, 1947) [H]; Tehon, *The Ethnicities in Israel*, 7.

48. From an IDF document on the "Art of Hista'ravut," written in 1957 by two former members of Ha-Shachar. Quoted in Cohen, *The First Mista'ravim*, 39. At the end of the book, Cohen compiles a list of all living members of the unit and all those who died during their service. They were all immigrants from Arab countries. Cohen, *The First Mista'ravim*, 392–9.

49. Cohen, *The First Mista'ravim*, 41, 51.

50. Ibid., 148–9.

51. Ibid., 26, 51–2, 95–6, 203–4.

52. Ibid., 35–6, 39–40.

53. On the distinction between scholastic and practical embodied knowledge, see Pierre Bourdieu, *Pascalian Meditations* (Stanford, CA: Stanford University Press, 2000).

CHAPTER 4

1. For the estimate of Palestinians expelled and Palestinians left behind, see Benny Morris, *The Birth of the Palestinian Refugee Problem, 1947–1949* (Tel-Aviv: Am-Oved, 1991), 397–9 [H]. For the numbers of immigrants, see Dvora HaCohen, *Immigrants in a Storm: The Great Aliya and Its Absorption in Israel, 1948–1953* (Jerusalem: Yad Ben-Tzvi, 1994) [H]. About the settlement of the immigrants on Palestinian lands, see Arnon Golan, *Spatial Change as a Consequence of War: The Formerly Arab Lands in the State of Israel, 1948–1950* (Sde Boker: Ben-Gurion University, 2001) [H].

2. Danin, *Zionist without Conditions*, 297–305.

3. Moshe Ar'el, "The Armistice Stage and Its Importance in the History of the State," in *The Foreign Office: The First Fifty Years*, ed. Moshe Yeger, Arye Oded, and Yosef Guvrin (Jerusalem: Keter, 2002), 71 [H]; Benny Morris, *Israel's Border Wars, 1949–1956: Arab Infiltration, Israeli Retaliation, and the Countdown to the Suez War* (Oxford: Clarendon Press, 1993); Hillel Cohen, "The Internal Refugees in the State of Israel: The Struggle for Identity," *Ha-Mizrah Ha-Hadash* 43 (2002): 83–102 [H].

4. Mitchell, "Limits of the State," 77–96.

5. This is the reason there was such a multiplicity of agencies and institutions in this period dealing with various aspects of the "Arab question." Danin complained that there were at least twenty-three such agencies and that, because their jurisdictions and authority continuously changed and overlapped, they continuously encroached on each other's work, without any single center directing their activities or determining overall policies. Danin, *Zionist without Conditions*, 245. The activities of many of these agencies tended to blur the boundary between state and society. See Ian Lustick, *Arabs in the Jewish State* (Haifa: Mifras, 1985), 99–118 [H].

6. On the concept of "translation," see Latour, *Science in Action*, 132–44.

7. Morris, *Birth of the Palestinian Refugee Problem*, 44–9, 53–8, 179–83. In a later article, however, Morris reported finding an explicit order to expel Palestinians during the Hiram operation, that is, during the later stages of the war. Benny Morris, "The Expulsions during the Hiram Operation: Mending an Error," in *Jews and Arabs in Palestine/Israel, 1936–1956* (Tel-Aviv: Am Oved, 2000), 141–8 [H].

8. Quoted in HaCohen, *The One Million Plan*, 31–2, 39.

9. Quoted in Morris, *Birth of the Palestinian Refugee Problem*, 231.

10. Nur Masalha, *Expulsion of the Palestinians: The Concept of Transfer in Zionist Political Thought, 1882–1948* (Washington, DC: Institute for Palestine Studies, 1992), 5–48, 175–8.

11. Ben-Eliezer, *The Making of Israeli Militarism*, 39–41, 95–112, 227–65.

12. Shapira, *Yigal Alon*, 89–90; Teveth, *Moshe Dayan*, 217–43.

13. Teveth, *Moshe Dayan*, 238, 247–52.

14. If my argument sounds far-fetched, let me reply with a minor anecdote: When, in the early 1950s, as a junior military commander who took part in the 1948 war, the young Ariel Sharon decided that a military career was a dead end, he left the army and enrolled as a student of Middle Eastern history at the Hebrew University. Only a chance encounter with a former commander brought him back to the army. For members of this generational group, military career and expertise in Arab affairs were palpable alternatives. Dayan, too, enrolled in the Institute for Oriental Studies at the Hebrew University when his military career seemed uncertain. Teveth, *Moshe Dayan*, 389, 483.

15. Quoted in Morris, *Israel's Border Wars*, 176–7.

16. Morris, *Birth of the Palestinian Refugee Problem*, 300–1; Ben-Eliezer, *The Making of Israeli Militarism*, 263–4.

17. For an oral history account that pays attention to this game of communication, especially to the significance of the evacuation of women and children by the defenders, see Efrat Ben-Ze'ev, "The Palestinian Village of Ijzim during the 1948 War: Forming an Anthropological History through Villagers' accounts and Army Documents," *Ha-Mizrah Ha-Hadash* 43 (2002): 65–82 [H].

18. Morris, *Birth of the Palestinian Refugee Problem*, 53–4.

19. Ibid., 52–5; Danin, *Zionist without Conditions*, 213–15; Gelber, *Roots of the Lily*, 694.

20. Danin, *Zionist without Conditions*, 209–16; Morris, *Birth of the Palestinian Refugee Problem*, 60–3; Shmaryahu Ben-Pazi, "The Impact of Agricultural Seasons on the

Fighting between the Communities" (paper presented at the annual meeting of the Association for Israel Studies, San Diego, CA, May 2003); Golan, *Spatial Change*, 83–5.

21. Morris, *Birth of the Palestinian Refugee Problem*, 113, 168–71.

22. Black and Morris, *Israel's Secret Wars*, 52; Yoav Gelber, *Seeds of a Regular Hebrew Army* (Jerusalem: Yad Ben-Tzvi, 1986), 402–5 [H]; Morris, *Birth of the Palestinian Refugee Problem*, 55–9, 64–5, 188; Danin, *Zionist without Conditions*, 209–16, 220–1, 223–4, 234; Lephen, *The Shai*, 237–40; Golan, *Spatial Change*, 204–6.

23. Golan, *Spatial Change*, 89–91, 208; Alisa Rubin Peled, *Debating Islam in the Jewish State: The Development of Policy toward Islamic Institutions in Israel* (Albany: SUNY Press, 2001), 17–21; Black and Morris, *Israel's Secret Wars*, 55–6; Gelber, *Seeds of a Regular Hebrew Army*, 419–20; Danin, *Zionist without Conditions*, 234; Lephen, *The Shai*, 249, 306–7 n. 7; Morris, *Birth of the Palestinian Refugee Problem*, 124–6, 166–8, 188–90, 204–6, 209, 220–1, 251–2, 321; Intelligence Service 1, Order 53/22 from August 20, 1948, "Regional Intelligence Officers," IDF Archive, 7/2384/1950. To Shitirit's credit, he did argue forcefully in some cases – notably Tiberias – against expulsion. In Tiberias there was an attempt by the Sephardi notables to block the expulsion of the Arab inhabitants and the destruction of the old Arab city center. But they were defeated by a coalition of military officers and Ashkenazi members of the city government. See Golan, *Spatial Change*, 163–5.

24. Morris, *Birth of the Palestinian Refugee Problem*, 58, 134–6, 147–8, 278–9, 288, 483 n. 148; Danin, *Zionist without Conditions*, 220.

25. Morris, *Birth of the Palestinian Refugee Problem*, 270, 301–2.

26. Ibid., 199–205, 209–10, 306, 317–19; Golan, *Spatial Change*, 94, 185.

27. Gelber, *Roots of the Lily*, 613; Gelber, "The Formation of Military Intelligence," 22–5; Gelber, *Seeds of a Regular Hebrew Army*, 420; Hezi Salomon, "The Influence of the Intelligence Services of the Yishuv on Ben-Gurion's Assessment of the Situation, 1946–1947," *Marachot* 309 (July-August 1987): 28–36 [H]; Oded Granot, *The Intelligence Corps*, vol. 5 of *The IDF: Encyclopedia of Military and Security*, ed. Yaacov Eerz and Ilan Kfir (Tel-Aviv: Revivim, 1981), 20–3, 29 [H].

28. Morris, *Israel's Border Wars*, 34–46; Ar'el, "The Armistice," 71; Tom Segev, *1949: The First Israelis* (Jerusalem: Domino, 1984), 37 [H]. In 1952, for example, two Palestinian citizens of Israel were killed by an IDF ambush as they approached the border from within Israel to meet with their relatives on the Jordanian side. A committee of inquiry instructed the army to check whether it is possible to fight infiltration "in such a way that citizens of the state will not be treated in the same way as infiltrators coming from without." Sarah Ozacky-Lazar, "The Military Government as an Apparatus of Control of the Arab Citizens in Israel: The First Decade, 1948–1958," *Ha-Mizrah Ha-Hadash* 43 (2002): 103–32 [H].

29. Adriana Kemp, "Dangerous Populations: State Territoriality and the Constitution of National Minorities" (paper presented at the conference on Boundaries and Belonging, University of Washington, Seattle, September 20–2, 2000); Segev, *1949*, 75. The term "present absentees" refers to Palestinians who remained inside the State of Israel but at the moment of the first population census were not in

their homes. They were counted as absentees, and their property was confiscated. Eventually they became Israeli citizens but were prohibited from returning to reside in their villages of origin.

30. On the split between Sharettt's "moderate" faction and Ben-Gurion's "activist" faction, see Morris, *Israel's Border Wars*, 240–9.

31. Morris, *Israel's Border Wars*, 94, 155, 167, n.170, 204, 214; Black and Morris, *Israel's Secret Wars*, 107, 129; Granot, *The Intelligence Corps*, 29; Yehoshafat Harkabi, *Personal Testimony: The Affair from My Point of View* (Tel-Aviv: Ramot, 1994), 48 [H]; Military Government, *Weekly Security Report, December 27, 1949*, IDF Archive, 293.tzadi.bet.4, 1953/834 [H]. The special operations officers were also recruited from among the *mista'ravim.* Cohen, *The First Mista'ravim*, 360–3.

32. Moshe Sharettt, *Personal Diary, 1953/54* (Tel-Aviv: Ma'ariv, 1978), 1:23–4 [H]; Sharettt, *Political Diary*, 6, 51, 236–8; Granot, *The Intelligence Corps*, 32–4.

33. Morris, *Israel's Border Wars*, 120, 240–50. In fact, the IDF already had a special unit composed of minorities. It was created in 1948 through coordination between the IDF and the Foreign Office, and its commander was expected to regularly report to the Foreign Office because "use of this unit must be considered from both the political and the military points of view." General Staff, *Memorandum*, August 24 1948, IDF Archive, 51/vav/116 1949/6127 [H].

34. Morris, *Israel's Border Wars*, 128–9, 148–53; Kemp, "Dangerous Populations," 7–16.

35. Adriana Kemp, "Talking Borders: The Construction of a Political Territory in Israel, 1949–1957" (Ph.D. diss., Tel-Aviv University, 1997) [H]; Morris, *Israel's Border Wars*, 123–5, 106–7, 127; Ar'el, "The Armistice," 71; Meeting of the General Staff with the Representatives of the Agricultural Center and the Settling Organizations, September 20, 1949, IDF Archive, gimel/1/2/5/110 [H].

36. Morris, *Israel's Border Wars*, 185–90, 196–7, 206, 230; Kemp, "Talking Borders."

37. Morris, *Israel's Border Wars*, 136, 197–8, 228–31, 249–50; Raymond Cohen, "Israeli Military Intelligence before the 1956 Sinai Campaign," *Intelligence and National Security* 3, no. 1 (1988): 100–41.

38. Gelber, *Seeds of a Regular Hebrew Army*, 428, 432; Granot, *The Intelligence Corps*, 17–19; Lephen, *The Shai*, 235; A. Peled, "Intelligence and the Intelligence Officer," *Maarachot* 80 (1954): 50–3 [H].

39. Harkabi, *Personal Testimony*, 50–6; Granot, *The Intelligence Corps*, 33. For example, the first commander of the research branch was a native of Berlin who was then a student of archeology at the Hebrew University. Later, he became one of Israel's leading experts on war in the ancient world. The head of the Jordanian desk at the research branch was German born too. Two more German-born research officers, Gabriel Baer and Uriel Dann, were Ph.D. students at the Institute for Oriental Studies at the Hebrew University. The first became one of Israel's foremost orientalists and president of the Israeli Oriental Society in the 1970s. The second was among the founders of Middle Eastern studies at Tel-Aviv University. Harkabi's chief of staff, as well, was a graduate of the London School of Economics.

40. *All Contingencies: Intelligence Assessment, 1954*, IDF Archive, 39/157/1959 [H]; Harkabi, *Personal Testimony*, 50–6; Granot, *The Intelligence Corps*, 31–4.

41. Gideon Doron, "Israeli Intelligence: Tactics, Strategy, and Prediction," *International Journal of Intelligence and Counter-intelligence* 2 (Fall 1988): 305–20; Cohen, "Israeli Military Intelligence," 100, 103–11; Granot, *The Intelligence Corps*, 32–4.

42. Granot, *The Intelligence Corps*, 47–8; Harkabi, *Personal Testimony*, 94–6. On the notion of "black-boxing," see Latour, *Science in Action*, 130–1.

43. Lieutenant Colonel Mordechai Gihon, *All Contingencies: Intelligence Background*, March 7, 1951, IDF Archive, 103/1953.27; Operations Branch, IDF General Staff, Operation Command "All," February 10, 1953, IDF Archive, 678/1967.15; Morris, *Israel's Border Wars*, 228–31.

44. Danin, *Zionist without Conditions*, 246, 280.

45. Haya Bambji-Sasportas, "Whose Voice Is Heard/Whose Voice Is Silenced: The Construction of the Discourse on the 'Palestinian Refugee Problem' in the Israeli Establishment, 1948–1952" (master's thesis, Ben-Gurion University, 2000), 57 [H]; Danin, *Zionist without Conditions*, 317; Moshe Yeger, *The History of Israel's System for Foreign Hasbara* (Hetzelyia: Lahav, 1986), 43–4 [H]. For a typical example of these pamphlets, see Alexander Dotan, *The Arab War against Israel (as the Arabs Saw it)* (Tel-Aviv: Tversky, 1951).

46. Military Government, *Meeting of the Sub-Committee for Coordination*, July 19, 1950. IDF Archive,1953/834 288 tzadi bet.1 aleph [H].

47. Amnon Lin, *Before the Storm: The Relations of Jews and Arabs in the State of Israel between Hopes and Disappointments* (Tel-Aviv: Karni, 1999), 77 [H]. To properly read this quote, the reader needs to invert the lens of the expert and return every quality attributed to the object back to the scrutinizing gaze. It was not the Palestinians who needed to "develop for themselves a clear and logical consciousness" but the experts. The conjunction of Arabness and Israeli citizenship was oxymoronic not for the Palestinians but for the state. And it was not clear in advance who were going to be the experts entrusted with this task – Arabists, military commanders, academic orientalists, Foreign Office officials, political activists, or Sephardi notables?

48. Elie Rekhess, "Initial Israeli Policy Guidelines towards the Arab Minority, 1948–1949," in *New Perspective on Israeli History: The Early Years of the State*, ed. Laurence J. Silberstein (New York: New York University Press, 1991), 103; Peled, *Debating Islam*, 1–5.

49. General Yigael Yadin, Memorandum to the General Manager of the Treasury Ministry, David Horowitz, *The Absorption of Arab Refugees into Israel from the Security Point of View: Appreciation of the Situation*, September 1949, IDF Archive, 1.2.5/20/1951; Morris, *Israel's Border Wars*, 176–7, 396; Rekhess, "Initial Israeli Policy," 108; Segev, *1949*, 59; Benny Morris, "A Form of Migration in Which Both Free Will and Coercion Are Entangled: About the Transfer of Majdal's Remaining Inhabitants to Gaza, 1950," in *Jews and Arabs*, 149–74 [H]; A. Moll letter to Reuven Burstein, October 25, 1950. Lavon Archive, 219-163-IV [H].

50. Dotan wrote three memos about "The Condition of the Arab Refugees in Israel and Their Problems" (November 9, 1952; November 12, 1952; November 23, 1952). The second one was titled "A Final Solution to the Problem of the Refugees in Israel and a New Policy towards the Arab Minority." Quoted in Bambji-Sasportas, "Whose Voice," 72–5. See also Peled, *Debating Islam*, 101–2.

51. Quoted in Bambji-Sasportas, "Whose Voice," 73.

52. Quoted in ibid., 73.

53. Quoted in ibid., 75.

54. On the "duty of volunteering," see Ben-Eliezer, *The Making of Israeli Militarism*, 98–9.

55. Quoted in Bambji-Sasportas, "Whose Voice," 76.

56. A. B. Yehoshua, *The Lover* (Jerusalem: Schoken, 1979) [H]; Sarah Ozacky-Lazar, "From a Hebrew Trade Union to an Israeli Trade Union: The Integration of Arabs in the *Histadrut*, 1948–1966," *Studies in Israel's Revival* 10 (2000): 389–97 [H]; The Economic Division of the Arab Department of the Acting Committee of the Histadrut, *An Economic Action Plan among the Arab Public in Israel*, June 1950, Lavon Archive, 163-219-IV [H]; Lin, *Before the Storm*, 113–15.

57. Ozacky-Lazar, "From a Hebrew Trade Union," 389–97; Ozacky-Lazar, *From Hebrew Histadrut*, 21; The Economic Division, *An Economic Action Plan*; Moshe Matri, Yosef Eliyahu, and Salem Zoabi, *Report on the Social and Economic Structure Kfar Salem*, July 1950, Lavon Archive, 163-219-IV [H]; Arab Affairs Department of the Acting Committee of the Histadrut, *News on the Activities of the Histadrut among the Arabs* 2 (September-October 1962): 4–5, 15–20, Lavon Archive, 163-219-IV [H].

58. Lin, *Before the Storm*, 116–17.

59. Quoted in Segev, *1949*, 79.

60. Rekhess, "Initial Israeli Policy," 116; Peled, *Debating Islam*, 38, 47–9, 178 n. 25.

61. Palmon, quoted in Bambji-Sasportas, "Whose Voice," 76; Segev, *1949*, 60, 79; Rekhess, "Initial Israeli Policy," 110, 116. The best analysis of Israel's system of control over the Palestinians is Lustick, *Arabs in the Jewish State*.

62. Palmon, quoted in Rekhess, "Initial Israeli Policy," 110; Bambji-Sasportas, "Whose Voice," 76.

63. Palmon, quoted in Bambji-Sasportas, "Whose Voice," 72, 76–8.

64. Ozacky-Lazar, "From a Hebrew Trade Union," 401.

65. Arie Gelblum, "A Journey among Israeli Arabs: The Political Truth and the General Elections," *Ha'aretz*, 1949 [H].

66. Rekhess, "Initial Israeli Policy," 109–14; Segev, *1949*, 60.

67. Eliyahu Elishar, "Jews and Arabs" and "Testimony before the U.N. Commission of Inquiry on the Question of Palestine," in *Living with the Palestinians*, 103, 115; Peled, *Debating Islam*, 19–22, 47; Rekhess, "Initial Israeli Policy," 112–14.

68. Rekhess, "Initial Israeli Policy," 112; Peled, *Debating Islam*, 24.

69. Peled, *Debating Islam*, 26, 36, 41–5, 53–7, 62, 99–102, 193 n. 29; Rekhess, "Initial Israeli Policy," 106; Hayyim Ze'ev Hirshberg, "Problems of the Shari'a in the State of Israel," *Ha-Mizrah Ha-Hadash* 1 (1950): 97–108 [H].

70. Peled, *Debating Islam*, 24, 39, 41, 44, 176 n. 77; Hirshberg, "Problems of the Shari'a," 98; Shlomo Dov Goitein, "The Arab Schools in Israel Revisited," *Middle Eastern Affairs* 3 (October 1952), 272–5; Yehouda Leib Benor, "Arab Education in Israel," *Ha-Mizrah Ha-Hadash* 3 (1951): 1–8 [H].

71. Peled, *Debating Islam*, 42; Hirshberg, "Problems of the Shari'a," 99; Goitein, "The Arab Schools"; Benor, "Arab Education."

72. Quoted in Morris, *Israel's Border Wars*, 192.

73. Sharett, *Personal Diary*, 51.

74. For a detailed account that emphasizes the heterogeneity of the immigrant population, see Khazzoom, "The Origins of Ethnic Inequality."

75. Shohat, "Sephardim in Israel."

76. "I was born in an Arab country to a Jewish minority that worshiped western culture. My father did not consider himself an Arab Jew. He saw himself for some reason as a European." Yitzhak Gormazano Goren, "Preface," *Ha-kivun Mizrah* 3 (October 2001): 1 [H].

77. Shenhav, *The Arab-Jews*, 65–72. The only equivalent construction was, not surprisingly, articulated by the Arab national movement, which considered the Jews to be "Arabs of the religion of Moses." Thus, however much they were opposed to each other, the two nationalist movements concurred in constructing the Jews as hybrid. Purification, however, was already built into this form of hybridization, since secular Arab nationalism recognized many denominations. It thus pronounced the Jews to be really and essentially Arabs.

78. Shohat, "Sephardim in Israel"; Shohat, *The Mizrahi Revolution*.

79. Shenhav, *The Arab Jews*, 25–72. As Hana Herzog argues, the emphasis on religiosity also provided additional legitimation for the distinction between Ashkenazi and *mizrahi* Jews, because there was already an institutionalized distinction between two religious traditions – Ashkenazi and Sephardi. Herzog, *Political Ethnicity*, 169–71; Hanna Herzog, "Penetrating the System: The Politics of Collective Identities," in *The Elections in Israel, 1992*, ed. Asher Arian and Michal Shamir (Albany, NY: SUNY Press, 1995), 81–102.

80. Quoted in Moshe Lissak, *The Great Aliya of the 1950's: The Failure of the Melting Pot* (Jerusalem: Bialik Institute, 1999), 60–5 [H]; Segev, *1949*, 150–62, 181.

81. The files of the Department for Middle Eastern Jewry of the Jewish Agency are full of attempts to classify the new immigrants, comments about the qualities of this or that ethnicity's human material, reasons for treating it differently, and suggestions as to the type of mission with which it could be entrusted. See, for example, Letter from Ezra Mahari, Assistant to Dr. Shlomo Pines at the Middle East Department of the Foreign Office, to Mr. Khalfon, Secretary of the Department for Middle Eastern Jewry, October 13, 1950, Central Zionist Archive, S20/104I [H]; Department for Middle Eastern Jewry, "Report on Visit to an Absorption Camp, June 16, 1949," Central Zionist Archive, S20/104I [H]; A. Khalfon, Secretary of the Department for Middle Eastern Jewry, "About Ways to Absorb the Immigrants from Oriental Countries, December 19, 1948," Central Zionist Archive, S20/104I [H].

82. Quoted in Segev, *1949*, 170.

83. About the settlement of immigrants from Arab countries along the border zone and the struggle over the migration back to the cities, see Adriana Kemp, "'The Migration of Peoples' or 'the Great Fire': State Control and Resistance in the Israeli Frontier," in *Mizrahim in Israel: A Critical Observation into Israel's Ethnicity*, ed. Hanan Hever, Yehouda Shenhav, and Pnina Motzafi-Haller (Jerusalem: Van Leer, 2002), 36–67 [H]. See also HaCohen, *Immigrants in a Storm*, 291–3. About the appropriation of the formerly Palestinian lands by stronger *moshavim* and *kibbutzim*,

see Golan, *Spatial Change*, 174–5, 187–97, 228–64. My thanks also to Emmanuel Marx for his enlightening comments on this issue.

84. Aziza Khazzoom, "Did the Israeli State Engineer Segregation? On the Placement of Jewish Immigrants in Development Towns in the 1950's," *Social Forces* 84, no. 1 (2005): 117–36. I have more to say about development towns in Chapter 5. At this point, let me just note that this category as operationalized by Khazzoom encompasses a significant portion of the distant periphery of the country – but by no means all of it – and also a good chunk of the proximate periphery and semiperiphery, which is less relevant to my overall argument.

85. About the struggle in the mixed cities, see Golan, *Spatial Change*, 54–62, 100, 115–21, 174–5, 228–64; Tamir Goren, "Changes in the Design of the Urban Space of the Arabs of Haifa during the Israeli War of Independence," *Middle Eastern Studies* 35 (January 1999): 115–33. Benny Nuriely's enlightening research on the struggles in Lod shows that some of the inhabitants of these neighborhoods still remember them today indeed as a third space where Jews and Arabs mixed and mingled. They also construct a narrative in which the friendly and neighborly relations between Jews and Arabs in these spaces were a continuation of the pattern of coexistence in the countries from which the immigrants came. From my point of view, it is unimportant whether this narrative is "true" or not. Others among the inhabitants, sometimes members of the same family, tell a diametrically opposite story meant to detach them from any proximity to the Palestinians. The important point, from my point of view, is that *mizrahi* identity, as we perceive it today – especially the double and problematic relation to the Palestinians that is at its core – developed in these neighborhoods, which were perceived and stigmatized by the state institutions, as well as by their own inhabitants, as third spaces, as a no-man's-land between Jews and Arabs. Benny Nuriely, "Strangers in the National Space" (master's thesis, Tel-Aviv University, 2004) [H].

86. Nuriely, "Strangers in the National Space," 85–92; A. Khalfon, "Impressions from a Visit to North African Immigrant Housing in Haifa in December 1948," January 10, 1949, Central Zionist Archive, S20/104I [H]. See also anonymous letter, March 20, 1950, Central Zionist Archive, S20/104I [H]; R. Suzzin, letter to the Department of Middle Eastern Jewry, "Report about Impressions from a Visit to Immigrants Camp Givat Shaul Bet," March 6, 1950, Central Zionist Archive, S20/104I [H]; Department of Middle Eastern Jewry, "Report on a Visit to an Absorption Camp," June 16, 1949, Central Zionist Archive, S20/104I [H]; Department of Middle Eastern Jewry, "Report on a Tour in Ein Kerem Camp," April 11, 1949, Central Zionist Archive, S20/104I [H]; A. Khalfon, Secretary of the Department for Middle Eastern Jewry, "About Ways to Absorb the Immigrants from Oriental Countries, December 19, 1948," Central Zionist Archive, S20/104I [H].

87. Quoted in Lissak, *The Great Aliya*, 68. Another condition was, as Nuriely shows, that they would be separated again from the Palestinians. The Lod municipal authorities tried over and over again, either forcibly or by means of incentives, to relocate the Jews residing in the old city to a separate neighborhood of prefabricated buildings on the outskirts of the town. They eventually managed to carry out this relocation in 1957. Nuriely, "Strangers in the National Space," 94–105.

88. HaCohen, *Immigrants in a Storm*, 145–57.

89. Nahum Levin, an official of the Education Ministry, quoted in Segev, *1949*, 191.

90. Elishar, "Testimony before the U.N. Commission of Inquiry," 114; "Dark Clouds," 121–2; "On the Arab Diaspora: Why Has World Jewry Remained Unmoved," 185–8; "The Debate in the Knesset on the Question of the Arab Jews," 189–92; "Memorandum to the Chairman of the Knesset on the Situation of the Arab Jews," 193–9; and "Eliminating the Iraqi Diaspora," 200–2; in *Living with Palestinians*. See also Shenhav, *The Arab Jews*, 129–30.

91. Tehon, *The Ethnicities in Israel*, 29; Haim Ze'ev Hirshberg, "About the Ethnicities of Israel in the Muslim Orient," preface to Tehon, *The Ethnicities in Israel*, 9.

92. Elishar, "Eliminating the Iraqi Diaspora," 202.

93. Despite their pleas, the director of the absorption department of the Jewish Agency thought that "the information . . . is not serious and not responsible." Most of the houses in the deserted Palestinian quarter of Safed, as well as most of the shops the Palestinians left behind, were given to European immigrants. A. Khalfon, letter to the Absorption Department of the Jewish Agency, February 22, 1949, Central Zionist Archive, S20/104I [H]; letter from Ezra Mahari, Assistant to Dr. Shlomo Pines at the Middle East Department of the Foreign Office, to Mr. Khalfon, Secretary of the Department for Middle Eastern Jewry, October 13, 1950, Central Zionist Archive, S20/104I [H]; Department of Middle Eastern Jewry, "Report on a Visit to an Absorption Camp," June 16, 1949, Central Zionist Archive, S20/104I [H]; A. Khalfon, "Impressions from a Visit to North African Immigrant Housing in Haifa in December 1948," January 10, 1949, Central Zionist Archive, S20/104I [H].

94. The dominant party, Mapai, was willing to accept the existence of a Sephardi electoral list, but only if it would remain under Mapai's influence. If it was independent, it was perceived as threatening Mapai's hegemony. Herzog, *Political Ethnicity*, 113. In Tel-Aviv, for example, the Sephardi notables claimed to represent the immigrants from Arab countries, who squatted in the abandoned Arab villages on the outskirts of the city. They led protests demanding that the city government recognize them as residents and supply them with services. The mayor refused, fearing that they would vote against him in the coming elections. The immigrants then turned against the Sephardi notables. They were not incorporated, and the area became slums. Golan, *Spatial Change*, 110–12.

95. Department for Middle Eastern Jewry, the Jewish Agency, Protocol of a Meeting to Coordinate Research on the Absorption of Immigrants, August 23, 1949, Central Zionist Archive, S20/104III [H]; Department for Middle Eastern Jewry, the Jewish Agency, Report on Research on the Absorption of Immigrants, October 24, 1950, Central Zionist Archive, S20/104III [H].

96. The article that initiated the debate was Carl Frankenstein, "About the Problem of Ethnic Differences," *Megamot* 2 (July 1951): 261–76 [H]. Then came responses by philosophers, sociologists, and educators: E. E. Simon, "About the Double Meaning of the Concept Primitive," *Megamot* 2 (July 1951): 277–84 [H]; Nathan Rotensstreich, "An Absolute Yardstick," *Megamot* 2 (October 1951): 327–38 [H]; Meshulam Grol, "On Human Dignity," *Megamot* 3 (October 1951): 50–64 [H];

Yosef Ben-David, "Ethnic Differences or Social Change?" *Megamot* 3 (January 1952): 171–83 [H]. In turn came a rebuttal by Frankenstein, "On the Concept Primitive," *Megamot* 2 (October 1951): 339–59 [H]. He also provided an editorial "Summary of the Debate about the Problem of Ethnic Differences," *Megamot* 3 (October 1952): 319–29 [H].

97. Frankenstein, "On the Concept Primitive," 353–5; Carl Frankenstein and Gina Orther, "A Method to Improve the Powers of Abstraction in Children of Immigrants from Oriental Countries," *Megamot* 2 (October 1951): 261–76 [H]. That the "normal" is always defined after, and through a contrast with what is identified as the "pathological," was established long ago by Georges Canguilhem, *On the Normal and the Pathological* (Dordrecht, The Netherlands: D. Reidel, 1978).

98. S. N. Eisenstadt, *The Absorption of Immigrants* (Glencoe, IL: The Free Press, 1955), 90–2. The same exclusion of Sephardi Jews was performed also by the historiographical distinction between the "old" and "new" Jewish settlements (Yishuv) in Palestine. Hanna Herzog, "The Concepts 'Old *Yishuv*' and 'New *Yishuv*': A Sociological Approach," *Katedra* 32 (1984): 99–108 [H].

99. Frankenstein, "Ethnic Differences," 270–4.

100. S. N. Eisenstadt, *Progress Report on Research about the Problem of the Absorption of Immigration for the Period of December 1, 1949–March 1, 1950*, Central Zionist Archive, S20/104II [H]; Frankenstein, "On the Concept Primitive," 358–9.

101. Eisenstadt, *Progress Report*, 7–9. I do not wish to say that this sociological critique of bureaucratization was false or unimportant. It was limited, however, to a dominant conception that the social scientists shared with state institutions, according to which the problem of absorbing immigrants was essentially a cultural problem. The assumption was that the immigrants would be absorbed if they became adapted to Israeli culture (and learned Hebrew). The competing view, proposed two decades later by Emmanuel Marx, is that the problem of the immigrants should be understood first and foremost as a problem of creating wider and more complex social networks – something, indeed, that the bureaucracy tends to inhibit. Emmanuel Marx, *The Social Context of Violent Behavior: A Social Anthropological Study in an Israeli Immigrant Town* (London: Routledge and Kegan Paul, 1976).

102. This cautionary note was given at his inaugural address by the first chair of the new department. Uriel Heyd, *The Modern Middle East as a Topic of Research and Instruction* (Jerusalem: Magness, 1953), 14 [H]. Some of their teachers preferred to leave after the formation of the state. In 1957, Goitein left Israel to take up a position at the University of Pennsylvania. He was deeply disappointed with government policy toward the Palestinian minority, with Ben-Gurion's autocratic rule, and with the fact that academic orientalists did not possess any influence. See also Milson, "Beginning of Islamic and Arabic Studies," 582–3, 585 n. 31. For a critique of the orientalist discourse of Ottoman "decline," see Gabriel Piterberg, "The Nation and Its Story-tellers: National Historiography and Orientalism," *Teoria ve-Bikoret* [Theory and Criticism] 6 (Spring 1995): 81–103 [H].

103. Heyd, *The Modern Middle East*, 15. Heyd did suggest that the new department would contribute to the state by studying the history of Middle Eastern Jewish communities, something that might "assist in solving their problems of absorption," but in reality the second generation avoided this thorny and politicized issue and did

not participate in the debate about absorbing the immigrants. See Raz-Krakozkin, "Orientalism," 34–61.

CHAPTER 5

1. On the concept of "discursive object," see Foucault, *Archaeology of Knowledge*, 40–9, 125–7.

2. This argument is made by Yair Boimel, "The Military Government and the Process of Its Abolition, 1958–1968," *Ha-Mizrah Ha-Hadash* 43 (2002): 134, 137–8 [H]; General Staff, Operations Division, Military Government Branch, *The Military Government: Topics for Discussion, January 24, 1951*, IDF Archive, 95/51 20 50/1 81 1955 [H]; Military Governors Meeting, September 27, 1951, IDF Archive,1953/834 133 [H]; Meeting no. 23 of the Authority for the Settlement of Refugees, April 10, 1950, IDF Archive, 1953/834 293 Tzadi-Bet-4 [H]; Letter of Area Commander, Sde Boker, to Block Commander, Be'er Sheba, August 23, 1956, IDF Archive, 1965/1034 946 [H]; Military Governors Meeting, June 6, 1950, IDF Archive, 1955/68 81 Vav/50 [H].

3. This is a good example of the argument I made in the introduction, that the state and the experts at one and the same time construct the hybrids and seek to purify them. The requirement to celebrate the Day of Independence and raise the flag constructs the Palestinians as hybrid Israeli-Arabs who are imitating the practices of the dominant majority. From this moment onward, the experts continuously wonder how to interpret this imitation, whether it is genuine or dissembling. They wonder how much trust one should put in this imitation and what could account for it. In short, they seek for explanations that would purify the Israeli-Arab hybrid they created with their very own hands. Meeting of the Military Governors with the Representative of the Ministry of Agriculture and the Representatives of the Adviser's Office, November 8, 1949; Meeting of the Military Governors with the Representative of the Ministry of Agriculture, June 20, 1950; Meeting of the Military Governors with the Adviser on Arab Affairs, April 11, 1950; Meeting of the Military Governors with the Representatives of the Ministry of Education and the Representative of the Adviser's Office, January 31, 1950; and Ministry of the Interior, Meeting to Discuss Self-Government in the Areas of the Military Government, November 20, 1950, IDF Archive, 1955/68 81 Vav/50 [H].

4. Meeting of the Military Governors, June 6, 1950, IDF Archive, 1955/68 81 Vav/50 [H].

5. Ministry of the Interior, Meeting to Discuss Self-Government in the Areas of the Military Government, November 20, 1950, IDF Archive, 1955/68 81 Vav/50 [H]; *Directive about the Administration of Villages, 1949*, Official Publication no. 1362, 17.8.44, IDF Archive, 1955/68 81 Vav/50 [H]; Memorandum from General Elimelech Avner, Commander of the Military Government, to the Regional Military Governors, "Supply of Services, Taxation and Keeping Order and Security in the Villages in the Occupied Territories," January 28, 1949, IDF Archive, 1955/68 64 Vav/50 [H]; General Staff, Operations Division, Military Government Branch, *The Military Government: Topics for Discussion, January 24, 1951*, IDF Archive, 95/51 20 50/1 81 1955 [H]; Military Governors Meeting, September 27, 1951, IDF

Archive,1953/834 133 [H]; Meeting of the Military Governors with the Adviser on Arab Affairs, December 20, 1949, IDF Archive, 1955/68 81 Vav/50 [H].

6. Office of the Adviser on Arab Affairs, together with Interior Ministry, Population Registry Bureau, Memorandum to the Military Governors, December 19, 1951, IDF Archive, 1953/834 302 Mem-Ayin-2 [H]; Military Government, Meeting of the Military Governors, November 13, 1951, IDF Archive, 1953/834 133 [H]. But they could not enforce the same sort of spatial segregation in the mixed cities. Hence, an important and sad part of the story of segregation and purification, which I will not be able to deal with here, was the fate of the offspring of the few mixed Jewish-Arab marriages. In effect, the purification regime created by the Arabists mandated that the children of mixed marriages were to be treated as Palestinians, not Jews, and certainly not something in between. They could not enjoy what the ancient Roman law called *connubium* – the capacity of fathers from the dominant group to pass their status and privileges to children of mixed marriages (though in most cases the father was Palestinian and the mother Jewish). They could not crossover into the dominant group and in fact suffered the double burden of being perceived as suspect by both sides. For the story of one such person, from the mixed city of Acre, who eventually sued for political asylum in a San Francisco Court, see Sarah Leibowitz-Dar, "Political Asylum? For an Israeli?" *Haaretz*, July 25, 2003, magazine section, 22–8 [H]. For the story of another, who could become "Jewish" only because his parents were separated, see James Bennet, "Between Two Homes and Two Peoples, a Soldier Wanders," *New York Times*, November 9, 2003, A1, A10. About the crucial role of *connubium* in processes of ethnicization and racialization, see Max Weber, "Ethnic Groups," in *Economy and Society* (Berkeley: University of California Press, 1978), 1:385–98.

7. Henry Rosenfeld, *They Were Fellahs* (Tel-Aviv: Hakibutz Hameuchad, 1964), 111–12, 138 [H]; Kemp, "Dangerous Populations," 27, 35–7; Lustick, *Arabs in the Jewish State*, 160–98; Ozacky-Lazar, "The Military Government," 109–11.

8. On the expropriations and the delay tactics, see Ran Kislev, *The Land Expropriation Affair* (Givat Haviva: Center or Arab Studies, 1976) [H]; The Institute for Land Use Research, *Land Expropriation for Public Uses* (Jerusalem: Israel Land Authority, 1976), 4:59 [H]; Lustick, *Arabs in the Jewish State*, 174–87; Sami Smooha, "Existing and Alternative Policies towards Arabs in Israel," *Megamot* 16 (September 1980): 7–36 [H]. Evidence for the routine supervision of confiscated lands can be found in the files of the military government. For example: Military Government (North), *Monthly Summary of Government Activity, October 1963*, IDF Archive, 1965/170 27 Mem-Bet-5 [H]. On the fear of the formation of Palestinian territorial blocks or cities and the policy intended to drive a wedge between Palestinian villages, see Arnon Sofer, "Israeli Arabs: Facts and Trends," in *Israeli Arabs: Where are They Heading? Debate of the Political Circle-Efal with the Participation of Yitzhak Bailey, Elie Rekhess, and Arnon Sofer, April 16, 1994* (Ramat Efal: Yad Tabenkin, 1996), 16–37 [H]; Lin, *Before the Storm*, 116–17; Oszacky-Lazar, "The Military Government," 106.

9. Office of the Adviser on Arab Affairs, *Memorandum to Military Governors, December 19, 1951*, IDF Archive, 1953/834 302 mem-ayin-2 [H].

10. Dan Rabinowitz, *Anthropology and the Palestinians* (Ra'nana: Institute for Israeli Arab Studies, 1998), 104–9, 114–16 [H]; Talal Asad, "Anthropological Texts and

Ideological Problems: An Analysis of Cohen on Arab Villages in Israel," *Economy and Society* 4 (1975): 251–81; Shimoni, *The Arabs of the Land of Israel*, 174–5.

11. Lustick, *Arabs in the Jewish State*, 38–41, 87–91, 93–140, 199–236; Smooha, "Existing and Alternative Policies," 19; Emanuel Kopelevitz, "Changes in the Arab Village in Israel," *Kama* 4 (1952): 203–23 [H]; Lin, *Before the Storm*, 81, 92–7, 111–13. Evidence for such meddling and brewing of conflicts, as well as for actions against the Communists and other non-*hamula* lists, can be found in the files of the military government. For example: Military Government, General Command, Report on the Security Situation in the Areas of the Military Government for the Period from January 1 to January 23, 1950; Military Government, Governors Meeting, March 28, 1950; and Military Government, Meeting of the Secondary Coordinating Committee, April 12, 1950, IDF Archive, 1953/834 293 Tzadi-Bet-4 [H].

12. Meeting of the Military Governors, December 12, 1951, IDF Archive, 834/1953.302.mem-Ain.2 [H].

13. Michael Assaf, "The Bad Legend of the Military Government," *Be-Terem*, May 15, 1953 [H].

14. A good summary of the criticisms leveled against the military government is in Ozacky-Lazar, "The Military Government," 109–11, 115–27. Other sources are Rustom Bastouni, "The Arab Society in Israel," *Ha-Mizrah Ha-Hadash* 15 (1965): 1–6 [H]; Assaf, "The Bad Legend"; Kemp, "Dangerous Populations," 34–40; Boimel, "The Military Government," 136.

15. Baruch Gitlis, *The Ugly Military Governor: The Truth about the Military Government* (Jerusalem: Ogdan, 1967) [H].

16. Military Government, Military Governors Meeting, October 23, 1951, IDF Archive, 1953/834 66 Tzadi-Bet-1-Aleph [H].

17. Moshe Maoz, "Local Government in the Arab Settlements in Israel," *Ha-Mizrah Ha-Hadash* 12 (1962): 233–40 [H]; Shamir, "Changes in the Village Leadership of Ar-Rama," 241–57 [H].

18. Office of the Adviser on Arab Affairs, Prime Minister's Office, Protocol of Regional Security Committee Meeting, October 10, 1966, IDF Archive, 1974/79 215 Karkaot-Klali mem-bet 510 [H]; Office of the Adviser on Arab Affairs, Prime Minister's Office, Protocol of Regional Security Committee Meeting, February 7, 1967, IDF Archive, 1974/79 215 Karkaot-Klali mem-bet 510 [H]; Letter from Y. Hibner, Ministry of the Interior, to the Office of the Adviser on Arab Affairs, January 1, 1967, IDF Archive, 1974/79 331 mem-bet 510 [H]; "Isser Harel to Head a General Managers Committee on Population Distribution," *Haaretz*, March 31, 1966 [H]; Boimel, "The Military Government," 152–5; Kemp, "Dangerous Populations," 14; Lin, *Before the Storm*, 174–6; Ra'nan Cohen, *Kiss of the Tzabar: A Life Story* (Tel-Aviv: Yediot Aharonot, 2002), 62–6 [H].

19. Boimel, "The Military Government," 156.

20. On the idea of a "strategy without a strategist," see Pierre Bourdieu, *The Logic of Practice* (Stanford, CA: Stanford University Press, 1990), 42–51.

21. Subhi Abu-Gosh, "The Politics of an Arab Village in Israel" (Ph.D. diss., Princeton University, 1966); Abner Cohen, *Arab Border Villages in Israel* (Manchester: Manchester University Press, 1965). On Cohen's government job, see Rabinowitz, *Anthropology and the Palestinians*, 93. Abu-Gosh also reported his findings in an official

publication of the Office of the Adviser on Arab Affairs. Subhi Abu-Gosh, "The Integration of the *Hamula* in the Local Council of an Arab Village," in *Arab Society in Israel: Changes and Trends* (Jerusalem: Office of the Adviser on Arab Affairs to the Prime Minister, 1969), 9–20 [H].

22. Abu-Gosh, "Politics of an Arab Village in Israel," 219; Cohen, *Arab Border Villages*, 2–3. Most other orientalists rallied behind Abu-Gosh's interpretation and did not accept Cohen's. The very idea that the *hamula* could be considered somewhat of a "revival" was too radical for them. See, for example, Gabriel Baer's review of Cohen in *Ha-Mizrah Ha-Hadash* 15 (1965): 308–10 [H].

23. The data for compiling Figure 5.1 were taken from Smooha and Cibulski, *Social Research on Arabs in Israel.* I selected all titles that included a reference to villages, villagers, peasants, fellahin, etc. In the period after 1965, there were 104 titles. By comparison, there were only 15 similarly titled texts by a mere seven authors in the period predating the formation of the state in 1948.

24. See http://www.tau.ac.il/tau-archives/toldot.html; http://www.biu.ac.il/General/Hebrew/biu_history.html.

25. Smooha and Cibulski, *Social Research on Arabs in Israel,* 18–19.

26. Abner Cohen, in fact, belonged to this pool of recruits, having arrived to Israel from Iraq in the early 1950s. In A. B. Yehoshua's novel *The Lover,* the Palestinian protagonist refers to the "strange Iraqi Arabic" spoken by the GSS operatives (161). The fact that Iraqi and Egyptian Jews were recruited into the military government and the GSS shortly after their immigration to Israel is mentioned also in David Grossman, *Present Absentees* (Tel-Aviv: Ha-Kibutz Ha-Meuchad, 1992), 96 [H].

27. Military Government, Meeting of the Military Governors with Dr. Kutler, Representative of Ha-Re'ali in Haifa, May 30, 1950, IDF Archive, 1953/834 293 Tzadi-Bet-4 [H]; General Staff/Operations Branch/ Military Government, "Drafting of Orientalists for the Year 1964/1965," IDF Archive, 1970/724 38 Kaf-Aleph-7221 [H].

28. For example, Yoseph Ginat, who served as a representative of the Arab department of the Histadrut in the south. Then in 1975 he completed his dissertation on marriage patterns in the Arab village and was appointed to Haifa University's Department of Eretz Israel Studies. Later, in the 1980s, he returned to serve as the Adviser on Arab Affairs to the Prime Minister. Another example is Aharon Layish, who worked at the Office of the Adviser on Arab Affairs through the 1950s and 1960s but at the same time was a doctoral student at the Institute for Oriental Studies at the Hebrew University. In the 1970s, he too finished his dissertation, on the legal status of Muslim women, and was appointed to the Hebrew University. The career patterns of Moshe Maoz, Emmanuel Marx, and Matti Peled involved similar service in the military government or the Office of the Adviser on Arab Affairs.

29. Abu-Gosh, "Politics of an Arab Village in Israel," 1–29. The same opposition between modern politics and *hamula* conflict, as the essence of the traditional Arab village, is found in myriad works of the period: Gabriel Ben-Dor, *The Druze in Israel: A Political Study* (Jerusalem: Magnes, 1979), 215–16 [H]; Cohen, *Arab Border Villages,* 9–10; Salman Fallah, "Kafr Summayya': A Druze Village in Upper Galilee," *Israel Exploration Journal* 18, no. 1 (1968): 36, 40; Yosef Ginat, *Changes in Family Structure in*

the Arab Village (Ramat-Aviv: Tel-Aviv University, 1976) [H]; Ya'akov Landau, *The Arabs in Israel* (London: Oxford University Press, 1969), 15; Aharon Layish, "Trends after the Six-Day War," in *The Arabs in Israel*, ed. Aharon Layish (Jerusalem: Magnes, 1981), 241–7 [H]; Aharon Layish, "Changes in the Arab Society in Israel," in *The Arab Society*, 1–8 [H]; Maoz, "Local Government," 233–4; Elie Rekhess, *The Arab Village: A Revitalized National-Political Center* (Tel Aviv: Shiloah Center, 1985), 186 [H]; Shamir, "Changes in the Village Leadership of Ar-Rama," 242–7, 257; Shimon Shamir, "Changes in Village Leadership," *New Outlook* 5, no. 3 (1962): 93–112; Benjamin Shidlowsky, "Changes in the Development of the Arab Village in Israel," *Ha-Mizrah Ha-Hadash* 15 (1965): 26 [H]; Benjamin Shidlowsky, ed., *The Arab and Druze Settlements in Israel* (Jerusalem: Office of the Adviser on Arab Affairs, 1969), 22–3 [H]; Ori Shtendel, *The Minorities in Israel* (Jerusalem: Merkaz Ha-Hasbara, 1970), 5–6, 62–3, 65–8 [H]. This trope was by no means limited to apologists of Israeli policies. The discourse of the critics, too, was organized in a similar way. See, for example, Sharif Kanaana, *Socio-cultural and Psychological Adjustment of the Arab Minority in Israel* (San Francisco: R&E Research Association, 1976), 60; Khalil Nakhleh, "The Shifting Patterns of Conflict in Selected Arab Villages in Israel" (Ph.D. diss., Princeton University, 1973), 239–41; Khalil Nakhleh, "The Direction of Two-Level Conflict in Two Arab Villages in Israel," *American Ethnologist* 23 (1975): 497–516; Henry Rosenfeld, "Change, Barriers to Change, and Contradictions in the Village Family," in Layish, *The Arabs in Israel,* 76–103 [H]; Sammy Smooha, *Arabs and Jews in Israel* (London: Westview Press, 1989), 5, 175.

30. Shamir, "Changes in Village Leadership," 112.

31. Ariela Anden and Arnon Sofer, *New Neighborhood Model in Arab Villages in the North* (Haifa: University of Haifa Press, 1986), 7 [H]. A similar analysis of the traditional spatial structure of the village is presented by many other geographers and planners: M. Avitzur, *Taiybe* (Ramat-Gan: Bar-Ilan University, 1976) [H]; M. Avitzur, "Taiybe: Processes of Change," *Hevra u-Revaha* [Society and Welfare] 1, no. 1 (1978): 22–30 [H]; Yoram Bar-Gal and Arnon Sofer, *Geographical Changes in the Traditional Arab Villages in Northern Israel* (Durham: University of Durham Press, 1981); Yoram Bar-Gal and Arnon Sofer, "Changes in the Minority Villages in the Galilee," in *Horizons in Geography* [Ofakim Be-Geografia] (Haifa: University of Haifa Press, 1976) [H]; Moshe Brawer, "The Internal Structure of the Traditional Arab Village," in *The Arab Settlement in Israel: Geographical Processes*, ed. David Grossman and Avinoam Meir (Ramat-Gan: Bar-Ilan University, 1994), 109 [H]; Gideon Golany, "Geography of the Traditional Arab Village of the Village Taiybe Model" (master's thesis, University of Haifa, 1967) [H].

32. Bar-Gal and Sofer, *Geographical Changes*, 1–3 [H]. For a similar opposition between the traditional core and the outlying neighborhoods, see Golany, "Geography of the Traditional Arab Village," 40–57; Brawer, "Internal Structure of the Traditional Arab Village," 103–5.

33. Abu-Gosh, "Politics of an Arab Village in Israel," 219.

34. Bar-Gal and Sofer, *Geographical Changes*, 11.

35. Abu-Gosh, "Politics of an Arab Village in Israel," 219; Abu-Gosh, "Integration of the *Hamula*," 20; Anden and Sofer, *New Neighborhood Model*, 7–9; Isaac Arnon and Michal Raviv, *From Fellah to Farmer: A Study of Change in Arab Villages* (Rehovot:

Settlement Study Center, 1980), 167–8, 196; Bar-Gal and Sofer, "Changes in the Minority Villages in the Galilee," 34.; Golany, "Geography of the Traditional Arab Village," 131–3; Elie Rekhess, "The Intelligentsia," in Layish, *The Arabs in Israel*, 186, 196 [H]; Shamir, "Changes in the Village Leadership of Ar-Rama," 247; Ori Shtendal, *Minorities* (Jerusalem: Hasbara Center, 1972), 5 [H]; Shtendel, *The Minorities in Israel*, 62; Emmanuel Yalan, *The Modernization of Traditional Agricultural Villages: Minority Villages in Israel* (Rehovot: Settlement Study Center, 1972), 59.

36. Layish, "Changes in the Arab Society in Israel," 1.

37. Shtendel, *The Minorities in Israel*, 62. For the same diagnosis, see also Shamir, "Changes in the Village Leadership of Ar-Rama," 247; Abu-Gosh, "Integration of the *Hamula*," 20; Bastouni, "Arab Society," 5.

38. Maoz, "Local Government," 233.

39. Anden and Sofer, *New Neighborhood Model*, 7–9. For a similar analysis, see Bar-Gal and Sofer, *Geographical Changes*, 11; Bar-Gal and Sofer, "Changes in the Minority Villages in the Galilee," 34; Golany, "Geography of the Traditional Arab Village," 131–3; Shtendel, *The Minorities in Israel*, 71.

40. Shtendel, *The Minorities in Israel*, 3–4.

41. Shidlowsky, *The Arab and Druze*; Grossman and Meir, *The Arab Settlement*; Yitzhak Schnell, "Changes in the Arab Village in Israel: Urbanization under Conditions of Marginality," in Grossman and Meir, *The Arab Settlement*, 132–3.

42. Bar-Gal and Sofer, *Geographical Changes*, 10–11; Gabriel Baer, *The Village Mukhtar in Palestine* (Jerusalem: Magnes, 1979), 58 [H]; Arnon and Raviv, *From Fellah to Farmer*, 167–8, 222–3; Michael Brodnitz and Daniel Dominsky, "Industrialization in the Arab Village in Israel," *Rev'on Lekalkala* [Economic Quarterly] 33, 128 (1986): 533–46 [H]; Yosef Waschitz, "On the Problems of the Arab Village in Israel,"*Kama* 4 (1952): 187–202 [H]; Kopelevitz, "Changes in the Arab Village in Israel," 203–23; Anden and Sofer, *New Neighborhood Model*, 33, 65.

43. Emmanuel Marx, on the other hand, recommended network methodology as a way of studying these hybrid phenomena without seeking to purify them. In ethnographic research, this would mean that the ethnographer focuses on an individual or a small group and attempts to chart the network of ties and relations within which they move, ignoring all the accepted distinctions between inside and outside, village and city, tradition and modernity. In this approach, commuting to work is not conceptualized as movement from one society (or sphere) to another but as the weaving of a single social network within which the social world of the commuters is shaped and contained – a fragmentary social reality, devoid of stable and fixed entities. Emmanuel Marx, "On the Anthropological Study of Nations," in *A Composite Portrait of Israel*, ed. Emmanuel Marx (New York: Academic Press, 1980), 15–28; Emmanuel Marx, "The Social World of Refugees: A Conceptual Framework" (unpublished manuscript, revised version of the Refugee Studies Program Second Annual Colson Lecture, Oxford, March 7, 1990).

44. Bar-Gal and Sofer, *Geographical Changes*, 83–4.

45. For a good example, see Sofer, "Israeli Arabs," 17, 29. He is a geographer, but his lecture (to the members of a Labor Party think tank) is peppered with references to conversations he held with "friends in the Arab sector" and with

Palestinian "colleagues." He presents himself as someone who "for 25 years ... has been observing" what is taking place on the ground in the Arab sector and has firsthand knowledge of things that the Jewish public prefers to ignore and evade. He is a lone voice in the desert, and "only the security apparatus, with all its branches, has been [observing] with me."

46. Zvi Efrat, "The Plan: Drafting the Israeli National Space," in *A Civilian Occupation: The Politics of Israeli Architecture*, ed. Rafi Segal and Eyal Weizman (New York: Verso, 2003), 59–76; Golan, *Spatial Change*, 114–15, 245–62. The original vision was laid out in Arye Sharon, *Physical Planning in Israel* (Jerusalem: Prime Minister's Office, 1949) [H].

47. Golan, *Spatial Change*, 173–5, 187–93, 196–7; Efrat, "The Plan," 73–4; Khazzoom, "Did the Israeli State Engineer Segregation?"; Oren Yiftachel, "Social Control, Urban Planning and Ethno-Class Relations: Mizrahim in Israel's Development Towns," *International Journal of Urban and Regional Research* 24, no. 2 (2000): 417–34.

48. Erez Tzfadia, e-mail message to the author, November 20, 2003.

49. Over the years, there accumulated a large body of research and discourse about the development towns, some of which was conducted in the service of the state in order to assist in solving the practical problems of these towns. See, for example, Elisha Efrat, *Development Towns in Israel: Past or Future* (Tel-Aviv: Ahiasaf, 1987) [H]; Center for Research on Settlement, *Development Towns and Their Hinterland*, Settlement and Development no. 11-12 (1968) [H]; Ministry of Labor, Authority for Manpower Planning, *Development Towns in Israel: First Report about Twenty-one Towns* (Jerusalem, 1964) [H]; D. H. K. Amiran and A. Shachar, *Development Towns in Israel* (Jerusalem: Hebrew University, 1969) [H]. Significantly, Amiran was one of the pioneers of research on the Arab village. Brawer, "Internal Structure of the Traditional Arab Village," 100. Another group of studies was conducted within the framework of the Berenstein Israel Research Project, organized by the Department of Anthropology at Manchester University, with the aim of documenting and assessing the great wave of immigration and its consequences. Emanuel Marx, "Introduction," in Marx, *A Composite Portrait of Israel*, 6; Myron Aronoff, *Frontiertown: The Politics of Community Building in Israel* (Manchester: Manchester University Press, 1974); Shlomo Deshen, *Immigrant Voters in Israel: Parties and Congregations in a Local Election Campaign* (Manchester: Manchester University Press, 1970).

50. Many of the studies of the immigrant *moshavim* were also conducted within the framework of the Berenstein project: Shlomo Deshen, "A Case of Breakdown of Modernization in an Israeli Immigrant Community," *Jewish Journal of Sociology* 8, no. 1 (1965): 63–91; Shlomo Deshen, "Conflict and Social Change: The Case of an Israeli Village," *Sociologia Ruralis* 4 (1966): 31–51; Moshe Shokeid, *The Dual Heritage: Immigrants from the Atlas Mountains in an Israeli Village* (Manchester: Manchester University Press, 1971), xvii–xviii, 2–6, 63–4, 68, 217–19; D. Weintraub, "A Study of New Farmers in Israel," *Sociologia Ruralis* 4 (1964): 3–51; Alex Weingrod, *Reluctant Pioneers: Village Development in Israel* (New York: Cornell University Press, 1966).

51. For the changes in the labor market following the 1967 war, see Moshe Semyonov and Noah Levin-Epstein, *Hewers of Wood and Drawers of Water: Non-Citizen Arabs in the Israeli Labor Market* (Ithaca, NY: ILR Press, 1987).

52. On politics and protest activity in development towns, see Amiram Gonen, "The Geography of Electoral Competition between Labor and Likud in the Jewish Cities of Israel, 1965–1981," *Medina, Mimshal u-Yehasim Bein-Leumyim* 19–20 (1982): 63–87 [H]; Lev Grinberg, *Public Activists of the Histadrut and Municipalities: The Ethnic Dimension*, Jerusalem Institute for Israel Research, no. 33 (1989) [H]; Deshen, *Immigrant Voters in Israel*; Erez Tzfadia and Oren Yiftachel, "Between National and Local: Political Mobilization among Mizrahim in Israel's 'Development Towns,'" *Cities* 21, no. 1 (2004): 41–55. I do not want to belittle the struggles of development towns' residents. Nonetheless, it is often the case that resistance embodies a certain objective (mis)recognition and thereby serves to reproduce the relations of domination. The characteristic response of workers to what usually passes as "high art" is to ridicule it and to expose its arbitrary nature, and yet by the same token they self-exclude themselves from the centers of legitimate culture and reinforce the cultural hierarchy. Pierre Bourdieu, *Distinction: A Social Critique of the Judgement of Taste* (Cambridge, MA: Harvard University Press, 1984), 41. Similarly, the protest directed at the center merely serves to reinforce the peripheral status of development towns and of *mizrahi* identity.

53. Smooha, *Arabs and Jews in Israel*, 18.

54. Sayid Kashua, *And It Was Morning* (Jerusalem: Keter, 2004), 115–16, 126–7 [H].

55. Sharon Rotbard, "Wall and Tower," in Segal and Weizman, *A Civilian Occupation*, 42–51; Efrat, "The Plan," 69; Rafi Segal and Eyal Weizman, "The Mountain: Principles of Building in Heights," in Segal and Weizman, *A Civilian Occupation*, 79–97.

56. Schnell, "Changes in the Arab Village in Israel," 132–4.

57. Elisha Efrat, "Um-al-Fahem: A City?" *Haaretz*, October 25, 1984, 9 [H].

58. Schnell, "Changes in the Arab Village in Israel," 129–31.

59. Sofer, "Israeli Arabs," 24–5.

60. Sofer, "Israeli Arabs," 17. This lecture was given in 1994, after the Oslo Accords but long before the beginning of the second intifada. After its eruption, the very same ideas were expressed by former Israeli prime minister Ehud Barak: The Palestinian citizens of Israel are an "irredentist time bomb," they are at the "forefront of the Palestinian struggle.... This fact may require changes to the democratic rules of the game ... in order to guarantee Israel's Jewish character." He also suggested transferring the Palestinian city of Um-al-Fahm and the villages of the "small triangle" to the future Palestinian state – transferring, but not forcibly, only with consent. See Benny Morris and Ehud Barak, "The Camp David Summit and Its Aftermath," in *Camp David 2000: What Really Happened There?* ed. Danny Rubinstein (Tel-Aviv: Hemed, 2003), 120–1 [H].

61. Cohen, *Kiss of the Tzabar*, 63–70; R'anan Cohen, *Entangled in the Web of Loyalties: Society and Politics in the Arab Sector* (Tel-Aviv: Am-Oved, 1990), 52–4 [H].

62. Rekhess, *The Arab Village*; Rekhess, "The Intelligentsia," 186.

63. Elie Rekhess, "Israeli Arabs after the Oslo Agreements," in *Israeli Arabs: Where Are They Heading?* 10–16 [H].

64. Yitzhak Bailey, "Whither Leads Our Road with the Bedouin?" in *Israeli Arabs: Where Are They Heading?* 5–10 [H]; Lin, *Before the Storm*, 154–5; Raphael Israeli, *Arabs in Israel: Friends or Foes?* (Jerusalem: Ariel Center for Policy Studies, 2002), 119–40 [H]. See also the interview with Sofer in Grossman, *Present Absentees*, 147–55.

65. Sofer, "Israeli Arabs," 27–9; Lin, *Before the Storm*, 199–212; Israeli, *Arabs in Israel*, 42–4.

66. Sofer, "Israeli Arabs," 27.

67. Cohen, *Entangled*, 11–14; Grossman, *Present Absentees*, 237–49.

CHAPTER 6

1. In many respects, this is not a new argument, since the practitioners themselves attest to the near identity between intelligence and academic research. According to Yitzhak Oron, the first director of the Shiloah Institute and a former officer in both military intelligence and the Mossad, there is no methodological or epistemological difference between intelligence and academic research and commentary. The only difference is ethical. Intelligence researchers are faced with much greater responsibility, since they are dealing with matters of life and death, and therefore they are deeply committed to intellectual honesty, self-doubt, and modesty. Academics, by implication, are less committed to these values. The greater ethical responsibility of intelligence researchers is reflected in the language they use, which is characterized by much greater value-neutrality and precision. Yitzhak Oron, "Political Intelligence Research: Personal Accents," in Ofer and Kover, *Intelligence and National Security*, 287–91 [H]. Emmanuel Sivan, perhaps the most prominent Israeli expert on contemporary Islam, agreed that the studies produced by the Shiloah Institute were an "academic reflection of the modus operandi . . . of research in a governmental agency." Emmanuel Sivan, "The Decline of Nasserism or the Decline of Orientalism?" *Haaretz*, June 15, 1979, 23 [H].

2. Latour, *Science in Action*, 198–205, 245.

3. This is Latour's most innovative insight. He requires the sociology of science to be "symmetrical" and to analyze the relations between scientists and the "natural" phenomena they study just as they would analyze the relations between the scientists and other "social" actors involved in the process of inquiry – that is, as relations of power, manipulation, and persuasion. Latour, *Science in Action*, 144.

4. Yosef Ben-Zeev, "Intelligence during the 1956 War," *Maarachot* 306–307 (December–January 1987): 18–21 [H]; Black and Morris, *Israel's Secret Wars*, 127, 230–3; Cohen, "Israeli Military Intelligence," 100, 103–11; Raymond Cohen, "Threat Assessment in Military Intelligence," *Intelligence and National Security* 4, no. 4 (1989): 735–64; Yoel Ben-Porath, *Neila* (Tel-Aviv: Idanim, 1991), 45, 172 n. 1 [H]; Granot, *The Intelligence Corps*, 34, 65–7, 77.

5. Granot, *The Intelligence Corps*, 32–3, 103; Black and Morris, *Israel's Secret Wars*, 193, 227; Cohen, "Israeli Military Intelligence," 101–2; Meir Amit, *Rosh be-Rosh* [Banging Heads] (Or Yehouda: Hed Artzi, 1999), 98–100 [H].

6. Ben-Porath, *Neila*, 55, 70, 129–30, 140, 164–5.

7. Yoel Ben-Porath, "Intelligence Assessments: Why Do They Collapse?" *Maara-chot* 289–290 (October 1983): 29–38 [H]; see also Zvi Lanir, *Fundamental Surprise: Intelligence in Crisis* (Tel-Aviv: Hakibutz Hameuchad, 1983), 113 [H].

8. Arye Shalev, director of the research branch, speaking before a closed session of the Cabinet on October 3, 1973, three days before the Syrian and Egyptian armies attacked. Quoted in Moshe Maoz, *Asad, The Sphinx of Damascus: A Political Biography* (London: Weidenfeld and Nicolson, 1988), 89. For examples of intelligence assessments formulated as representations of enemy leaders and their ways of thinking, see Uri Bar-Yosef, *The Sentinel Who Fell Asleep: The Yom Kippur Surprise and Its Origins* (Tel-Aviv: Zemora-Bitan, 2001), 45, 47, 102, 163–4, 173 [H].

9. Black and Morris, *Israel's Secret Wars*, 536–7; Aviezer Ya'ari, *On the Road from Merhavia: Story of an Israeli Intelligence Officer* (Tel-Aviv: Zemora-Bitan, 2003), 139–46 [H].

10. Ben-Porath, *Neila*, 159.

11. Ehud Barak, "Issues in the Operation of Intelligence," in Ofer and Kover, *Intelligence and National Security*, 492 [H]; Ya'ari, *On the Road from Merhavia*, 150, 182; Black and Morris, *Israel's Secret Wars*, 316–17, 549; Cohen, "Threat Assessment in Military Intelligence," 737–9.

12. Yoram Peri, *Between Battles and Ballots: Israeli Military in Politics* (Cambridge: Cambridge University Press, 1983), 167.

13. One such journalist is Amir Oren of *Haaretz*. His articles typically open with formulas such as "Sources in the intelligence branch assess that..." or "The intelligence assessment is..." or "One hundred percent reliability, a member of the intelligence community said this week, putting a quality tag on the intelligence material brought by his colleagues..." Amir Oren, "By Order of the Rabbi," *Haaretz*, February 11, 2001, 16 [H]; idem, "Ceasefire," *Haaretz*, June 4, 2001, online archive http://www.haaretz.co.il/hasite/pages/arch (no. 726804) [H]; idem, "After Iraq, Palestine," *Haaretz*, February 21, 2003. The position of the research branch on this issue was summarized by one of its former commanders: "The principal points of the intelligence assessment should be passed to the media, so it would present them to the public. The public must know the truth; it is an important moral we drew from the Yom Kippur fiasco." Amos Gilad, quoted in Zeev Schiff, "A New Challenge for Mr. Intelligence," *Haaretz*, July 20, 2001, 17 [H]. In another place, the same officer expressed his dissatisfaction with the Israeli media, which "serves the terrorists." Quoted in Sarah Leibovitz-Dar, "The Chief Expounder," *Haaretz*, February 14, 2003, magazine section, 26–30 [H].

14. The most famous such scandal was the disagreement between the commander of military intelligence and the defense minister, Ariel Sharon, over the scenario the latter painted in order to justify extending the invasion of Lebanon in 1982 beyond previous and more limited plans. Ehud Yaari and Zeev Schiff, *A War of Deceit* (Jerusalem: Schoken, 1984), 24, 99–122 [H].

15. Cohen, "Threat Assessment in Military Intelligence," 741–9.

16. Amos Gilboa, "Syria and Israel's Security," in *Syria and Israel's Security*, ed. Avner Yaniv, Moshe Maoz, and Avi Kover (Tel-Aviv: Maarachot, 1991), 18 [H].

17. Cohen, "Threat Assessment in Military Intelligence," 736.

18. Amit, *Rosh be-Rosh*, 98–100; Black and Morris, *Israel's Secret Wars*, 200.

19. In the summer of 2004, an acrimonious debate erupted between members of the intelligence community and was conducted on the pages of Israeli newspapers. A former commander of military intelligence accused the former commander of the research branch (i.e., his former subordinate) of knowingly misrepresenting to the cabinet the official assessment of military intelligence about the intentions of the Palestinians on the eve of the Al-Aksa Intifada. Instead of giving a balanced assessment representing the varied views of intelligence researchers, so it was claimed, he presented only his own personal assessment, according to which Arafat was not really interested in peace and his participation in the Camp David talks was only a ploy. Later in this chapter, I discuss the intelligence discourse about Arafat, but for the moment, without presuming to adjudicate the dispute, I merely note that this accusation is symptomatic. The accuser charged that there "was a gap between, on the one hand, the written assessments, which are based on reliable information and are presented to the decision makers for their perusal, and on the other hand, the assessments conveyed to the leaders in the course of cabinet meetings." That is, those who are positioned at the bottleneck of the intelligence process possess the power to determine what the decision makers are going to hear. At the same time, however, the accusation also makes clear the weakness and vulnerability of those who occupy the bottleneck of the intelligence process, as it is easy to attribute to their schemes or personal failures the responsibility for the total process by which the supply of assessments is adapted, as we saw, to the political demand. Akiva Eldar, "His Real Face," *Haaretz*, June 11, 2004, 12 [H]; Yoav Stern, "An Unfounded Conception," *Haaretz*, June 18, 2004, 4 [H]; Yoav Stern, "Hitler, Too, Promised Peace," *Haaretz*, June 18, 2004, 4 [H]; Bar-Yosef, *The Sentinel Who Fell Asleep*, 154.

20. Oron, "Political Intelligence Research," 304.

21. Granot, *The Intelligence Corps*, 46–7.

22. The Shiloah Institute, however, is not the only academic research center to be shaped as a protected liminal space. About ten years after it was established, another such institute – the Yoffe Center for Strategic Studies – was created at Tel-Aviv University. It too is populated by former military intelligence officers and is in close contact with the research branch. Haifa University and the Hebrew University, as well, boast similar institutes, and in recent years the Interdisciplinary Center in Hertzeliya has established an institute for terrorism research where former intelligence officers and former military governors work. Nonetheless, the Shiloah Institute was the first to be shaped in this way, and its researchers have enjoyed more prestige and publicity than the others. For this reason, it (and its successor, the Dayan Center) are the focus of this chapter.

23. Shimon Shamir, "Establishment of a Research Institute alongside the Department for Middle East and Africa, 12.2.1965," quoted in Roni Eshel, "History of Tel-Aviv University" (unpublished manuscript, Tel-Aviv University Archive), chap. 8, p. 14 [H]; "The Shiloah Institute for the Study of the Middle East and Africa," *Ha-universita: Tel-Aviv University Monthly* 7 (June-July 1972): 3 [H]; Hagai Eshed, *Reuven Shiloh: A Mossad of One Man* (Tel-Aviv: Idanim, 1985), 21 [H]; Shlomo Dov Goitein, "Congratulatory Letter to the Israeli Oriental Society on Its

30-Year Anniversary," *Hamizrah Hachadash* 28, nos. 3–4 (1979): 173–4 [H]. Yitzhak Oron, "Preface," *Middle East Record*, 5 (1964–1965): vii–viii, xxiv–xxix; "List of Research Grants, 1964–1969," Tel-Aviv University Archive; *Bulletin of the Faculty of Humanities*, Tel-Aviv University, 1965–1967 [H].

24. *Bulletin of the Faculty of Humanities*, Tel-Aviv University, 1965–1967.

25. Ibid.

26. Shimon Shamir, ed., *The Decline of Nasserism, 1965–1970: The Decline of a Messianic Movement* (Tel-Aviv: Shiloah Institute, 1978) [H]. In response to a scathing attack on the book, Shamir explained that "at issue is a volume dedicated to the memory of... the deputy commander of military intelligence... and the initiative for its compilation came from the deceased's former unit. Many of the authors in this volume contributed to it papers they prepared for this unit as well as other governmental research agencies. Even among the papers of the few historians included in the volume... there are some that were written for the defense establishment and according to its specifications (for example, Professor Rabinovich's survey of the Yemen war). The same is true for the papers that were prepared in university research institutes. They were mostly prepared in the framework of projects connected to the defense establishment or of a similar nature." Shimon Shamir, "Letter to the Editor: The Decline of Nasserism," *Haaretz*, June 22, 1979, literary supplement [H]. A similar composition of contributors can be found also in Itamar Rabinovich and Haim Shaked, eds., *The Middle East and the United States* (Tel-Aviv: Am-Oved, 1980) [H]. Other universities followed in the footsteps of Tel-Aviv and created institutes and programs based on a special relationship with the army or with government ministries. Haifa University – where Middle East experts and former intelligence officers have held the positions of rector, deputy rector, dean of humanities, and chair of political science department – went even further and took it upon itself to create a master's program especially for the graduates of the army's national security college, something that even Tel-Aviv University refused to do. Ya'ari, *On the Road from Merhavia*, 153–4.

27. Ya'ari, *On the Road from Merhavia*, 178; Ben-Porath, *Neila*, 93; Ze'ev Schiff and Eitan Haber, *Lexicon of Israeli Security* (Jerusalem: Zemorah u-Bitan, 1976), 20 [H].

28. Haim Shaked, ed., *Middle East Contemporary Survey, 1976–1977*, vol. 1 (New York: Holmes and Meier, 1978); "The Shiloah Institute for the Study of the Middle East and Africa," 3.

29. "The Shiloah Institute for the Study of the Middle East and Africa," 3; Granot, *The Intelligence Corps*, 91.

30. *Bulletin of the Faculty of Humanities*. Tel-Aviv University, 1971, 40–56 [H].

31. "Beginning in the advanced stages of their BA studies, the opportunity is granted to excellent students to work at the Shiloah Institute and to specialize in their areas of interest. Afterwards, they are absorbed in the academic community, or in the institute itself, or in the service of public and governmental institutions that need experts on contemporary issues." "The Shiloah Institute for the Study of the Middle East and Africa," 3.

32. Tables available from the author.

33. On the classified materials collected in the information center, see Eshel, "History of Tel-Aviv University," 14; "The Shiloah Institute for the Study of the Middle East and Africa," 3; *Bulletin of the Faculty of Humanities*, Tel-Aviv University, 1969, 146. Works using the Jordanian police archive captured in the 1967 war are Eliezer Be'eri, *The Palestinians under Jordanian Rule* (Jerusalem: Magnes, 1978), 7 [H]; Amnon Cohen, *Parties in the West Bank under Jordanian Rule, 1948–1967* (Jerusalem: Magnes, 1980), 2–3 [H]; Asher Susser, *Between Jordan and Palestine: A Political Biography of Watzfi al-Tel* (Tel-Aviv: Hakibutz Hameuchad, 1983), 216 [H]. Works using Syrian, Egyptian or Iraqi documents similarly captured are Itamar Rabinovich, *Syria under the Ba'th, 1963–66: The Army-Party Symbiosis* (Jerusalem: Israel Universities Press, 1972), ix–xiii; Uriel Dann, *Iraq under Qassem: A Political History* (Jerusalem: Israel Universities Press, 1968), 381; Yehoshafat Harkabi, *The Position of the Arabs in the Israeli-Arab Conflict* (Tel-Aviv: Dvir, 1969), 9, 491–5 [H]; Maoz, *Asad*, xiii.

34. Thus, the head of the Jordanian desk in the research branch of military intelligence delivered a lecture to institute personnel based on "personal knowledge I have accumulated for 20 years." Zeev Bar-Lavi, *The Hashemite Regime, 1949–1967, and Its Standing in the West Bank,* Skirot, no. 80 (Tel-Aviv: Shiloah Institute, 1981) [H]. Another institute researcher reported that some of the evidence in her book was based on interviews with Mossad personnel, who asked "to remain incognito." Ofra Benjo, *The Kurdish Rebellion against Iraq* (Tel-Aviv: Dayan Center, 1990), 12, 224–5 [H].

35. One researcher reported that he used summaries of Arab newspapers prepared by military intelligence. Dan Schuftan, *A New Phase of Jordan-PLO Relations*, Machbarot Heker, no. 13 (Ramat Efal: Yad Tabenkin, 1984) [H]. Another cites documents he obtained "while in office" (he was an adviser to the military government in the occupied territories). Menahem Milson, *Jordan and the West Bank,* Policy-Directed Publications no. 10 (Jerusalem: Davis Institute, January 1984) [H].

36. Vered Levi-Barzilay, "How Do You Say 'Doctor' in Arabic," *Haaretz*, July 13, 2001, magazine section, online archive http://www.haaretz.co.il/hasite/pages/arch (no. 737937) [H].

37. This social order is also systematically manifested in the propensity to study Arabic in high school. Although high school students in Tel-Aviv typically avoid the study of Arabic, those in the dormitory towns around Tel-Aviv – who are more likely to be of lower-class and of *mizrahi* origins – avidly embrace it. The explicit purpose of the study of Arabic is to allow students "to continue working on this issue also during their army service." The Education and Defense ministries have formed a joint agency entrusted with encouraging the teaching of Arabic and assigning Arabic speakers to relevant army units upon their mobilization. Anat Shinkman, "Arabic Study Is Losing Popularity," *Yediot Aharonot*, May 3, 1991, Tel-Aviv supplement, 16 [H]. Although in the dormitory towns, the study of Arabic seems to be part of a trajectory of upward mobility, among upper-class Tel-Aviv students, it seems to signify downward mobility. Those who specialized in Arabic in high school or are fluent in Arabic from home (i.e., of *mizrahi* origins) are typically recruited into the information-gathering unit of military intelligence, doing "apprentice" jobs such as translating Arabic newspapers and monitoring Arabic radio transmissions. Movement

to the more prestigious research division is almost completely impossible for them, as the two divisions constitute virtually segregated occupational blocks. No surprise, therefore, that even fewer manage to make it into the Shiloah Institute. In this sense, the status of apprentice, the epistemological superiority of distance over proximity, and the social production of ignorance, that same trap into which the Arabists refused to enter (but into which, as we saw, the new *mista'ravim* were placed), have today become part of the social definition of what it means to be *mizrahi* in Israeli society.

38. Oron, "Political Intelligence Research," 302–3; Ludwig Wittgenstein, *Philosophical Investigations*, pt. 1 (Oxford: Basil Blackwell, 1958). Another way of acquiring these skills is to participate in simulations, war games, etc., where one is entrusted with the task of representing the enemy leader. In June 2002, for example, the School for Public Policy and Government at Tel-Aviv University organized such a simulation game. The king of Jordan and other Arab leaders were represented by experts from the Dayan Center, Arafat was played by a former commander of military intelligence, and so on. Amnon Barzilay, "In the Last Moment, the Palestinian Authority Was Eliminated, and Arafat as Well," *Haaretz*, June 21, 2002, 18 [H].

39. Oron, "Political Intelligence Research," 293–4, 297.

40. "The Shiloah Institute for the Study of the Middle East and Africa," 3.

41. Yehoshafat Harkabi, "For a National Soul-Searching," *Ma'ariv*, April 19, 1974, op-ed section, 18 [H]; Eli Eyal, "The Orientalists' Polemics after the Agranat Report," *Ma'ariv*, April 26, 1974, magazine section, 12–13 [H]; Moshe Maoz, ed., *The Goals of the Arab Struggle against Israel in the Wake of the Yom Kippur War* (Jerusalem: Mount Scopus Center for Research on the Arabs of Eretz Israel and Israeli–Arab Relations, 1974), 25 [H].

42. Yehoshafat Harkabi, *Basic Aspects of the Israeli-Arab Conflict* (Tel-Aviv: IDF Education Corps, 1971), 11 [H]; Yehoshafat Harkabi, *Arab Attitudes to Israel* (New York: Hart Publishing Co., 1972), xvi–xix.

43. Yehoshafat Harkabi, "Strategic Studies – Also in Israel?" *Maarachot* 165 (March 1962): 4–8 [H].

44. Harkabi, "For a National Soul-Searching," 18.

45. See, for example, Yehoshafat Harkabi, *The Position of the Palestinians in the Israeli Arab Conflict and Their National Covenant* (Jerusalem: Hasbara Center, 1968); Yehoshafat Harkabi, *The Problem of the Palestinians* (Jerusalem: Israeli Academic Committee on the Middle East, 1973); Yehoshafat Harkabi, *Time Bomb in the Middle East* (New York: Friendship Press, 1969); Yehoshafat Harkabi, "We Must Learn to Understand the Substance of the Arab Case," *The New Middle East* 2 (November 1968): 26–30; Yehoshafat Harkabi, *How Was the Arab Position Explained in the Egyptian Army* (Tel-Aviv: IDF Education Corps, 1967) [H]; Yehoshafat Harkabi, *The Palestinian Covenant and Its Significance: Explanations and Consequences* (Jerusalem: Hasbara Center, 1969) [H]; Yehoshafat Harkabi, *The Fatah in Arab Strategy* (Tel-Aviv: Maarachot, 1969) [H].

46. Harkabi, *The Palestinian Covenant*, 10.

47. Ibid., 9–11, 13.

48. Throughout this period, intelligence and *hasbara* remained intimately connected with one another. During the Yom Kippur war, the former commander of

military intelligence and the former commander of the research branch received special emergency appointments to coordinate Israeli *hasbara* abroad. Israel's first and only minister of *hasbara*, appointed in 1974, was the former commander of military intelligence. Two of the directors of the *hasbara* department of the Foreign Office in the 1970s and 1980s were former military intelligence research officers. Yeger, *History of Israel's System for Foreign Hasbara*, 105.

49. Shimon Shamir, interviewed in Eyal, "The Orientalists' Polemics after the Agranat Report," 12–13. They reminded the interviewer that after the Six-Day War Harkabi wrote a famous article in which he argued that "Arab society lacks social cohesion . . . that an Arab army unit under fire falls apart," and that it was this sort of literature, rather than their own studies, that was "disseminated in tens of thousands of copies to the IDF and to schools." Even the prime minister, they said, used to cite Harkabi. "It is ridiculous to see people who were an integral part of the dominant conception trying to absolve themselves and become admonishing prophets." Ibid., 37.

50. Itamar Rabinovich, ibid., 13, 37.

51. Yehoshafat Hrakabi, "For a Personal Soul-Searching," *Ma'ariv*, May 3, 1974, op-ed section, 17 [H].

52. Harkabi, "For a National Soul-Searching," 18; Shamir, in Eyal, "The Orientalists' Polemics after the Agranat Report," 12.

53. Bar-Yosef, *The Sentinel Who Fell Asleep*, 102–3.

54. Zvi Al-Peleg, "Intentions – and Deeds," *Yediot Aharonot*, May 12, 1974 [H].

55. The story is recounted in Black and Morris, *Israel's Secret Wars*, 323–6.

56. Shamir was dean of humanities and later ambassador to Egypt. Rabinovich was dean of humanities and rector of Tel-Aviv University and was appointed directly by Rabin to head the Israeli delegation negotiating with the Syrians. Later, he became ambassador to the United States. Itamar Rabinovich, *The Brink of Peace: The Israeli-Syrian Negotiations* (Princeton, NJ: Princeton University Press, 1998), 54, 64–6.

57. Harkabi, *The Palestinian Covenant*, 6, 11–12. 15–16.

58. Shlomo Gazit, *The Carrot and the Stick: The Israeli Military Government in the West Bank* (Tel-Aviv: Zemorah u-Bitan, 1985), 63–6, 73, 76, 126, 154 [H]; Shlomo Gazit, *Fools in a Trap: Thirty Years of Israeli Policy in the Occupied Territories* (Tel-Aviv: Zemorah u-Bitan, 1999), 46–7, 55 n. 4, 61, 71, 82–3, 86 n. 3 [H]; Amnon Cohen, "David Farhi: An Obituary," *Ha-Mizrah Ha-Hadash* 28 (1979): 1–2 [H]; Pinhas Inbari, *A Triangle on the Jordan River* (Jerusalem: Kaneh, 1982), 188–9 [H]; "Colleagues Speak about the Late Yosef Luntz," in *The Palestinian National Movement: From Confrontation to Acceptance?*, eds. B. Z. Keidar and Menahem Milson (Tel-Aviv: The Defense Ministry, 1999), 411–12 [H]. To interpret the significance of military intelligence's avoidance of the territories, one should know that already on the 4th day of the Six-Day War, the research branch of military intelligence presented the Defense Minister, Dayan, with an assessment regarding the future of the territories. The recommendation of the research branch was to solve the problem of the refugees by creating a Palestinian state in the territories. Such a state would have purified the refugee/infiltrator hybrid, and thus would have integrated it within the jurisdiction of the network of intelligence expertise. When this did not happen, the research officers

considered themselves exempt from dealing with the refugees. Reuven Pedhatzur, *The Victory of Confusion: The Policy of the Israeli Government in the Territories after the Six-Day War* (Tel-Aviv: Bitan, 1996), 39–41 [H].

59. David Farhi, "From the Writings and Speeches of the Late David Farhi," in *Ten Years of Israeli Rule in the West Bank, 1967–1977*, ed. Rafi Israeli (Jerusalem: Magnes, 1981), 145–206 [H]. The interview was conducted in 1977.

60. Farhi, "From the Writings and Speeches," 155, 165, 192; David Farhi, "The Residents of the Territories and Their Political Positions," in *Panel Discussions on Historical Affairs and Basic Problems,* no. 17 (Ramat Efal: Yad Tabenkin, 1976), 15, 22. On Dayan's policies and their critics, see Shabtai Teveth, *Curse of the Blessing* (Jerusalem: Schoken, 1970), 5, 28, 64, 134, 165, 289 [H]; Zvi al-Peleg, "The Forces Operating in the Territories," in *In the Eye of the Political Storm,* no. 36 (Ramat Efal: Yad Tabenkin, 1983), 23–38 [H]; Zvi al-Peleg, "The Open Bridges Must Be Closed," *Yediot Aharonot,* May 20, 1974, op-ed section, 11 [H]; Inbari, *Triangle on the Jordan River,* 79. When the decision maker was replaced, a few years later, the interpretation changed as well. There was an obvious correspondence, the correspondence between supply and demand, between Milson's conception – according to which there existed an authentic moderate Palestinian nationalism that rejected the PLO and that could be cultivated through the "village associations" he created – and the policies of his masters, Begin and Sharon, which involved massive confiscation of Palestinian lands and a massive settlement drive, a military campaign to push the PLO out of the territories, "normalization" in the form of a civil administration in the territories, and an ambiguous autonomy program about which they negotiated with the Americans and the Egyptians. Milson's conception relied on literal interpretation once more. He did not consider vows of allegiance to the PLO to be merely a "tactical" move and therefore believed that the moderates must be encouraged to speak while the extremists must be censored or even punished. Moshe Maoz, *The Palestinian Leadership in the West Bank* (Tel-Aviv: Reshafim, 1985), 199–222 [H]; Menahem Milson, "How to Make Peace with the Palestinians," *Commentary* 7, no. 5 (1981): 25–35.

61. Yoram Ben-Porath, Emmanuel Marx, and Shimon Shamir, *A Refugee Camp on the Mountain Slope* (Tel-Aviv: Shiloah Institute, 1974), 2–3, 71, 99–100, 106, 110, 112, 127 [H].

62. Yehoshafat Harkabi, ed., *Arabia and Israel: A Collection of Translations from Arabic* 1, no. 1 (1974): 1 [H]; Yeger, *History of Israel's System for Foreign Hasbara,* 105; The Foreign Office, Department of Instruction, *The Israeli-Arab Conflict: An Anthology of Documents and Selected Articles* (Jerusalem: 1985) [H]; David Niv, ed., *Take with You: A Guide to the Problems of the Israeli-Arab Conflict* (Jerusalem: Department of Culture and Education in the Diaspora, World Zionist Federation, 1984) [H]. See also the monthly *Flashlight on the Middle East* [*Zrakor La-Mizrah Ha-Tichon*] published by the monitoring department of the Hasbara Center and distributed to policymakers and influential commentators around the world. Not only were the operatives at the department of monitoring using the writings of Israeli orientalists, but their very choice of topics and how they dealt with them directly followed the patterns that Harkabi established. The October 1989 issue of *Flashlight on the Middle East*, for example, focused on the PLO and analyzed the question of "the consistency in its

declarations," that is, the extent to which the recent decisions of the Palestinian National Council really deviated from the Palestinian Covenant. The commentators interviewed or mentioned came from both the Shiloah Institute and the Truman Institute. See Hasbara Center, Department of Monitoring, "Topics in Focus: The PLO between the Geneva Declaration (12.14.1988) and the Fifth Convention of the Fatah (8.8.1989)," *Flashlight on the Middle East* 13 (October 1989): 1–15 [H]; Harry S. Truman Research Institute for the Advancement of Peace, *Annual Report: Activities during 1989* (Jerusalem: Hebrew University, Spring 1990), 38–40.

63. Yehoshua Porath, "Palestinian Historiography," *Jerusalem Quarterly* 5 (Fall 1977): 95–104; idem, "On the Writing of Arab History by Israeli Scholars," *Jerusalem Quarterly* 32 (Summer 1984): 28–35; Martin Kramer, "Islam Is the Power of the Future," in *Islam and Democracy in the Arab World*, ed. Meir Litwak (Tel-Aviv: Dayan Center, 1997), 24–43 [H]; Emmanuel Sivan, "Listening to Radical Islam," in *Intelligence for Peace*, ed. Hezi Carmel (Tel-Aviv: Miskal, 1998), 225–49 [H]. Reiter, who is a researcher at the Truman Institute, wrote a study that is also used by the Foreign Office as a policy paper, about the Islamic literature denying the Jewish origins of Jerusalem. Nadav Shragai, "At the 4000 Year Anniversary of the Al-Aksa Mosque," *Haaretz*, May 11, 2004, online archive http://www.haaretz.co.il/hasite/pages/arch (no. 1092866) [H].

64. Harkabi, *Basic Aspects of the Israeli-Arab Conflict*, 15.

65. In Maoz, *Goals of the Arab Struggle*, 6.

66. Ibid., 20.

67. Amnon Cohen, ibid, 25, 60.

68. Ibid., 43–6.

69. Ibid., 27.

70. Ibid., 51–2.

71. This is precisely the concept of "position" or "attitude" that Harkabi employed. Another participant in the debate argued that the Arab position in the conflict has never changed. The Arabs are obsessed with the idea of pan-Arab nationalism, and only if the Jews agree to live in a canton will there be peace. Porath responded that this assessment might be true for the Palestinians, for whom hostility toward Israel is an existential issue, but not for the Egyptians. The more they emphasize an Egyptian identity that is separate from Arabness, the more their attitude to Israel will become moderate. It is possible to see from this exchange that the debate revolves around, not the intention of this or that human being, but something called the "Arab position" (or Palestinian or Egyptian), which is a sort of collective intention or idea that organizes all that the Arabs say and do with respect to Israel. Other participants in the debate sought to focus attention on the fact that what the Israelis do also plays a role in shaping the Arab attitude, but they were ignored. Ibid., 27–8, 35–7.

72. Sharet, *Political Diary*, 129–30; Bar-Yosef, *The Sentinel Who Fell Asleep*, 41, 121. On accounts, see Harold Grafinkel, "What Is Ethnomethodology?" in his *Studies in Ethnomethodology* (Englewood Cliffs, NJ: Prentice-Hall, 1967), 1–34.

73. Harkabi, *Basic Aspects of the Israeli-Arab Conflict*, 15. Shamir's attempt to interview the refugees and represent them was discontinued. Instead, a Palestinian desk was added to the other country desks at the Dayan Center (just as, in military

intelligence, Desk 4 was created to deal with the Palestinian organizations). Asher Susser, who specialized in the Jordanian leadership and in analyzing PLO documents and declarations, was appointed as its head. The compromise between the two did not mean that they liked each other or cooperated with each other. The antagonism between the Middle East experts in Tel-Aviv and Jerusalem is well known. Only five years later, Emmanuel Sivan wrote a scathing critique of the Shiloah Institute and bemoaned the "heavy mortgage that orientalist research pays to the mode of research in military intelligence." Despite such enmity, it is significant that both Shamir and Sivan similarly distinguished between "those who possess the skill for synthetic writing and those pedants who are mired in little details and are not able to see the whole picture" and agreed that Middle East experts should resemble the first and not the second. The difference between them was not really one of worldview or training but of position within the network of intelligence expertise. Shamir was closer to the center, while Sivan was more marginal. This explains why Shamir was also willing to pay tribute to the pedants and to those who collected the information, whose work provided, he said, "the material without which there are no knowledge, no understanding and no writing of history." Their work, after all, was the infrastructure upon which rested the research conducted at the Shiloah Institute. Emmanuel Sivan, "The Annual Survey of the Shiloah Institute," *Ha-Mizrah Ha-Hadash* 28 (1979): 300 [H]; Shamir, "Letter to the Editor: The Decline of Nasserism."

74. Harkabi, "For a National Soul-Searching." See also Yehoshafat Harkabi and Matti Steinberg, *The Palestinian Covenant in the Test of Time and Practice: Explanations and Consequences* (Jerusalem: Hasbara Center, 1988), 6–9 [H].

75. Harkabi's most loyal student and follower, Matti Steinberg, has managed in this way to create for himself a status not unlike that of the researchers of the Shiloah Institute: He is a respected and well-known commentator, frequently invited to contribute to newspapers; he was appointed as a special adviser on Palestinian affairs to the chief of the GSS; and he was even invited to participate in the work of the governmental agency in charge of preparing the future peace agreements with the Palestinians, as an expert on the Palestinian organizations and leadership. Eldar, "His True Face," 12.

76. The Syrian regime and President Asad are covered by Itamar Rabinovitz, Moshe Maoz, Avner Yaniv, and Eyal Zisser. The Egyptian regime and the careers of Nasser, Sadat, and Mubarak are covered by Shimon Shamir and Ami Ayalon. The Iraqi regime and its various leaders were the province of the late Uriel Dann, Amatsia Baram, and Ofra Benjo. The Jordanian regime and King Hussein are written about by Asher Susser and Uriel Dann. David Menashri specializes in the Iranian regime, while Gabriel Ben-Dor generalizes about the qualities that Arab regimes share and about the relations between the regimes. See Ami Ayalon, ed., *Regime and Opposition in Egypt under Sadat* (Tel-Aviv: Hakibutz Ha-Meuchad, 1983) [H]; Amatsia Baram, *Culture, History, and Ideology in the Formation of Ba'thist Iraq, 1968–89* (New York: St. Martin's Press, 1991); Gabriel Ben-Dor, *State, Society, and Military Elites in the Middle East: An Essay in Comparative Political Sociology,* Occasional Papers of the Dayan Center no. 88 (1984); Benjo, *Saddam's Iraq*; Dann, *Iraq under Qassam*; Uriel Dann, *King Hussein and the Challenge of Arab Radicalism: Jordan, 1955–1967* (New York:

Oxford University Press, 1989); Haggai Erlikh, *Ras Alula and the Scramble for Africa: A Political Biography: Ethiopia and Eritrea, 1875–1897* (Lawrenceville, NJ: Red Sea Press, 1996); Yoseph Kostiner, *South Yemen's Revolutionary Strategy, 1970–1985: From Insurgency to Bloc Politics* (Boulder, CO: Westview Press, 1990); Maoz, *Asad*; Moshe Maoz and Avner Yaniv, eds., *Syria under Assad: Domestic Constraints and Regional Risks* (London: Croom Helm, 1986); David Menashri, *Iran in Revolution* (Tel-Aviv: Ha-Kibutz Ha-Meuchad, 1988) [H]; Rabinovich, *Syria under the Ba'th*; Asher Susser, *Between Jordan and Palestine*; Shamir, *The Decline of Nasserism*; Shimon Shamir, *Egypt under Sadat* (Tel-Aviv: Dvir, 1978) [H]; Eyal Zisser, *The Face of Syria: Society, Regime and State* (Tel-Aviv: Ha-Kibutz Ha-Meuchad, 2003) [H].

77. Benjo, *Saddam's Iraq*, 9.

78. For examples, see Shamir, *Egypt under Sadat*, 119–26; Benjo, *Saddam's Iraq*, 93; Rabinovich, *Syria under the Ba'th*, 82 n. 15.

79. Shamir, *Egypt under Sadat*, 117. See also Benjo, *Saddam's Iraq*, 160.

80. Shamir, *Egypt under Sadat*, 12.

81. Gilboa, "Syria and Israel's Security," 14. This is also how the Israeli experts analyzed the PLO. They distinguished within it a pragmatic, realistic current, for whom the covenant was only a starting point, and arrayed against it a radical current motivated by ideology and adhering to the letter of the covenant. See Matti Steinberg, *From One Pole to the Other: Currents in Palestinian National Thought,* Policy Paper no. 25 (Jerusalem: Davis Institute, 1988) [H]; Matti Steinberg, "Arafat's PLO: Parameters of Pragmatism," *Israeli Democracy* (Spring 1989): 11–15.

82. Benjo, *Saddam's Iraq*, 163.

83. Hagai Ram, private communication, March 28, 2000.

84. Al-Sayid Yaseen, quoted in Benjo, *Saddam's Iraq*, 9, 68–70, 247–8, 253.

85. This property distinguishes, nonetheless, the discourse of commentary from a "deep" psychological analysis of the "distorted" personality of the Arab leader. Such an analysis is outside the rules of discourse. Thus, when a few psychologists endeavored to write a report about Saddam Hussein's personality and predicted on the basis of this analysis that he would be willing to launch missiles against Israel, the control department of military intelligence rejected their analysis outright: "The attempt to deduce how Saddam will deal with questions of strategy from his personality characteristics . . . is essentially problematic. . . . The control department does not believe that it is possible to learn from the makeup of Saddam's personality . . . when, or if at all, will Israel's deterrent image become less significant in his assessment . . . in this regard, the control department suggests to accept as reliable many statements made by Iraqi leaders from April onwards." Hussein, of course, eventually did launch missiles against Israel. Ronen Bergman and Ron Leshem, "How We (Almost) Cracked Saddam," *Yediot Aharaonot*, January 5, 2000, magazine section, 14–21, 86 [H].

86. Eyal Zisser, *Syria: The Question of Succession: Towards Decision: Data and Analysis* (Tel-Aviv: Dayan Center, June 1993) [H]; Eyal Zisser, *Syria's Asad: The Leader and His Image: Data and Analysis* (Tel-Aviv: Dayan Center, October 1993) [H]; Eyal Zisser, interview with IDF Radio, March 27, 2000 [H]; Maoz, *Asad*, 42; Rabinovich, *The Brink of Peace*, 27–8, 50–3, 77, 80–1.

87. Rabinovich, *The Brink of Peace*, 63, 80.

88. Asher Susser, "The Intifada and the Palestinian National Movement: The Historical Context," in *In the Eye of the Conflict: The Intifada*, ed. Asher Susser and Gad Gilbar (Tel-Aviv: Ha-Kibutz Ha-Meuchad, 1992), 208–9 [H]. Susser is also quoted to the same effect, along with Yehoshua Prath, in the Hasbara Center, "The PLO between the Geneva Declaration," 3–5.

89. Benjamin Ze'ev Begin, "The Years of Hope," *Haaretz*, September 6, 2002, magazine section, 32–8 [H].

90. Harkabi and Steinberg, *The Palestinian Covenant*, 8–9. See also Matti Steinberg, "The PLO Solution: The Meaning of a Three-Way Formula," in *Is There a Solution to the Palestinian Problem?* ed. Aluph Hareven (Jerusalem: Van-Leer, 1982), 151–71 [H]; Matti Steinberg, "Knowing How to Read the Demographic Clock," *Haaretz*, July 27, 2004, online archive http://www.haaretz.co.il/hasite/pages/arch (no. 1112876) [H].

91. Quoted in Sarah Leibovitz-Dar, "Ehud Ya'ari Said," *Haaretz*, November 10, 2000, magazine section, online archive http://www.haaretz.co.il/hasite/pages/arch (no. 668085) [H]. Essentially the same assessment was expounded by Ze'ev Schiff, "Cards of Fire and Negotiation," *Haaretz*, May 25, 2001, op-ed section, 17 [H], and by Amos Gilad, Israel's Coordinator of Policy in the Occupied Territories, quoted in Uzi Benziman, "The Noise That Drowns out the Main Thing," *Haaretz*, July 19, 2002, 15 [H]. See also Schiff, "A New Challenge," 17. It was public knowledge, on the other hand, that the assessment of the GSS – this notorious organization that does not, and cannot, avoid coming into contact with the hybrids and therefore suffers from the same pollution as the Arabists – was different. The GSS made known its opinion that the assessment of military intelligence was wrong and that Arafat did not control the situation and was not in a position to stop the violence. Ze'ev Schiff, "The GSS Is Not Retreating from Its Assessment," *Haaretz*, July 15, 2001, 7 [H].

92. Quoted in Uzi Benziman, "Arafat's Pressurized Suit," *Haaretz*, January 25, 2002, online archive http://www.haaretz.co.il/hasite/pages/arch (no. 790079) [H]. See also Begin, "Years of Hope," 33. Quite appropriately, Benziman asks, tongue in cheek, "Where did he get this fascinating information, and why did his predecessor withhold it from the public and from the members of the Parliamentary Foreign and Security Affairs Committee?"

93. A similar analysis was voiced by the coordinator of policy in the Occupied Territories, formerly a commander of the research branch of military intelligence: "Mentally, Arafat feels at his best, when he is surrounded by a reality of flames, fire, suffering and blood." Leibovitz-Dar, "The Chief Expounder," 30. There were many, including some experts on Arab affairs, who disagreed with this analysis, but it was supported by the experts of the Dayan Center: "Ya'ari is a serious commentator, responsible, who gives his best judgment. Nobody can give more than what he has. Generally, I agree with his assessments. He did not demonize Arafat. He presented reality. Arafat possesses the ability to calm what is going on in the field." Shimon Shamir, quoted in Leibovitz-Dar, "Ehud Ya'ari."

94. Ephraim Lavie, quoted in Stern, "An Unfounded Conception," 4. At the end of the day, the debate over whether Arafat was interested in a peace accord with Israel or was just dissembling in order to achieve his real goal, the destruction of Israel, is futile. This debate was, and is, completely internal to the network of intelligence expertise. It revolves around the same category of "intention" that was discussed here,

and it cannot provide a useful template for understanding Israeli policy after the failure of the Camp David talks. In fact, Israeli policy – which left Arafat nominally in his leadership position as president of the Palestinian Authority but destroyed everything around him, including the trappings and instruments of that position – reflected a sort of compromise between the two sides to the debate. On the other hand, the debate could never include what the network of intelligence expertise itself excluded, namely, the refugees, the ordinary residents, the local activists. The various parties to this debate did not refer to this excluded group, unless by a term that expressed indeed the fact that they were outside the rules of discourse – "the Arab street." This debate was internal to the network of intelligence expertise also in another sense: it touched on the degree of legitimacy of the alternative interpretation for the utility of this form of expertise, namely, *hasbara*. Those who criticized the prevailing theory thought that it was driven, at least in part, by propaganda concerns, and they thought that "it is absolutely not the role of the research branch to undertake any kind of *hasbara* activity." The other side was not so sure: "the reason why [military intelligence also engaged in *hasbara*] is that the official *hasbara* of the State of Israel is so clumsy. People were frustrated because we have in our hands all the proofs, but they are not communicated further. Maybe in this situation there is no other choice." Quoted in Stern, "An Unfounded Conception," 4; Stern, "Hitler, Too, Promised Peace," 4.

95. This is not really a thought experiment. Both arguments can be found in Oren, "Ceasefire," and in Ehud Ya'ari, "I Was Right," *Haaretz*, February 1, 2002, magazine section, online archive http://www.haaretz.co.il/hasite/pages/arch (no. 791857) [H].

96. Dani Rubinstein, "The Road Winding Down to Camp David: Introduction," in Rubinstein, *Camp David*, 47–8. See also Aluph Ben, "Now Everybody Knows: They Are Guilty," *Haaretz*, July 27, 2001, 15 [H]. The book was published as Ronen Bergman, *Permission Granted: Where Did We Go Wrong? How the Palestinian Authority Became an Assembly Line for Corruption and Terrorism* (Tel-Aviv: Hemed, 2002) [H]. The extent to which intelligence and *hasbara* have now become inseparable is evidenced by the fact that the most important *hasbara* positions are filled with former intelligence research officers. One former commander of the research branch of military intelligence was appointed to lead the Israeli delegation to the Israeli-Palestinian Joint Committee for the Prevention of Incitement, namely, the committee dealing with all the mutual accusations (mostly from the Israeli side) about the contents of textbooks and television and radio programs. Another former commander of the research branch was appointed as the "national expounder," the face of Israeli *hasbara*, in December 2002. Aviv Lavie, "Late Incitement," *Haaretz*, July 18, 2003, magazine section, 18–22 [H]; Leibovitz-Dar, "The Chief Expounder," 26.

CONCLUSION

1. Avi Shoshani, "Peace Will Come from the East," *Haaretz*, August 21, 2002, online archive http://www.haaretz.co.il/hasite/pages/arch (no. 921831) [H].

2. Yair Dalal, Israeli musician, quoted in Shiri Lev-Ari, "Know Thy Neighbor," *Haaretz*, February 26, 2003, online archive http://www.haaretz.co.il/hasite/pages/ arch (no. 973539) [H]. See also a large number of poems, stories, and essays that were

published in the literary journal *Ha-Kivun Mizrah* (Direction East). Not everybody who writes in this journal seeks to reinvent or reenchant the Orient, and certainly not all of them make use of images taken from European romantic orientalism, but there is no doubt that this is one of the main cultural options open for those who wish to "return to their roots": "Where are you, my smiling grandfather? / pouring from Aladdin's jug / tea of dreams with na'na' [mint] . . . up the narrow street / in the city Makhnas that is in Morocco / Arab and Jewish women / sat around huge tin ewers / and did their weekly laundry . . . where in the world can you find / children laughing in this way?" Dudu Eyal (Sayyag), "I Dream in Moroccan," *Ha-Kivun Mizrah* 3 (October 2001): 6 [H].

3. Aviv Lavie, "When Avri Ran Gets Angry," *Haaretz*, March 19, 2004, magazine section, 50–4 [H]; Gideon Aran, "Gush Emunim, Mormons and Jonestown: The Jewish West Bank Settlements in Comparative Historical Perspective" (paper presented at the Institute for Social and Economic Policy and Research, Columbia University, New York, November 7, 2002).

4. Professor David Der'i, quoted in Herzog, *Political Ethnicity*, 180.

Abu-Gosh, Subhi. "The Integration of the *Hamula* in the Local Council of an Arab Village." In *Arab Society in Israel: Changes and Trends*. Jerusalem: Office of the Adviser on Arab Affairs to the Prime Minister, 1969. [H]

————. "The Politics of an Arab Village in Israel." Ph.D. diss., Princeton University, 1966.

Almog, Oz. *The Sabra: A Profile*. Tel-Aviv: Am Oved, 1997. [H]

Almog, Shmuel. "The 'Land to Its Workers' and the Conversion of the Fellahin." In *The Nation and Its History*, edited by Shmuel Ettinger. Jerusalem: Zalman Shazar Center, 1984). [H]

Al-Peleg, Zvi. *The Forces Operating in the Territories*. In the Eye of the Political Storm no. 36. Ramat Efal: Yad Tabenkin, 1983. [H]

————. "Intentions – and Deeds." *Yediot Aharonot*, May 12, 1974, 11. [H]

————. "The Open Bridges Must Be Closed." *Yediot Aharonot*, May 20, 1974, op-ed section, 11. [H]

Amiran, David H. K., and Arye Shachar. *Development Towns in Israel*. Jerusalem: Hebrew University of Jerusalem, 1969.

Amit, Meir. *Rosh be-Rosh* [Banging Heads]. Or Yehouda: Hed Artzi, 1999. [H]

Amit-Kokhavi, Hana. "To Know and Understand Our Neighbors: On the Translation of Arab Literature into Hebrew, 1868–2002." *Ha-Mizrah Ha-Hadash* 43 (2002): 209–27. [H]

Amster, S. *The Face of the Orient: The Problems of Arab Federation, the Great Powers, and Zionism*. Jerusalem: Ahiassaf, 1945. [H]

Anden, Ariela, and Arnon Sofer. *New Neighborhood Model in Arab Villages in the North*. Haifa: University of Haifa Press, 1986. [H]

Aran, Gideon. "Gush Emunim, Mormons and Jonestown: The Jewish West Bank Settlements in Comparative Historical Perspective." Paper presented at the Institute for Social and Economic Policy and Research, Columbia University, November 7, 2003.

Ar'el, Moshe. "The Armistice Stage and Its Importance in the History of the State." In *The Foreign Office: The First Fifty Years*, edited by Moshe Yeger, Arye Oded, and Yosef Guvrin. Jerusalem: Keter, 2002. [H]

Arnon, Isaac, and Michal Raviv.*From Fellah to Farmer: A Study of Change in Arab Villages*. Rehovot: Settlement Study Center, 1980.

Aronoff, Myron. *Frontiertown: The Politics of Community Building in Israel*. Manchester: Manchester University Press, 1974.

Asad, Talal. "Anthropological Texts and Ideological Problems: An Analysis of Cohen on Arab Villages in Israel." *Economy and Society* 4 (1975): 251–81.

———, ed. *Anthropology and the Colonial Encounter*. London: Ithaca Press, 1973.

Ashkenazi, Tuvia. *The Near East*. Jerusalem: Kedem, 1932. [H]

Assaf, Michael. *The Arab Movement in the Land of Israel and Its Origins*. Tel-Aviv: Hotzat Ha-Mishmeret Ha-Tzeira, 1947. [H]

———. "The Bad Legend of the Military Government." *Be-Terem*, May 15, 1953. [H]

———. *Zionism, Socialism, and the Arab Question*. Tel-Aviv: Ha-Poel Ha-Tzair, 1938. [H]

Avitzur, M. *Taiybe*. Ramat-Gan: Bar-Ilan University, 1976. [H]

———. "Taiybe: Processes of Change." *Welfare and Society* [Hevra u-Revahah] 1, no. 1 (1978): 22–30. [H]

Ayalon, Ami, ed. *Regime and Opposition in Egypt under Sadat*. Tel-Aviv: Hakibutz Ha-Meuchad, 1983. [H]

Baer, Gabriel. "Review of Abner Cohen's *Arab Border Villages in Israel*." *Ha-Mizrah Ha-Hadash* 15 (1965): 308–10. [H]

———. *The Village Mukhtar in Palestine*. Jerusalem: Magnes, 1979. [H]

Bailey, Yitzhak. "Whither Leads Our Road with the Bedouin?" In *Israeli Arabs: Where Are They Heading? Debate of the Political Circle-Efal with the Participation of Yitzhak Bailey, Elie Rekhess, and Arnon Sofer, April 16, 1994*. Ramat Efal: Yad Tabenkin, 1996: 5–10. [H]

Bambji-Sasportas, Haya. "Whose Voice Is Heard/Whose Voice Is Silenced: The Construction of the Discourse on the 'Palestinian Refugee Problem' in the Israeli Establishment, 1948–1952." Master's thesis, Ben-Gurion University, 2000. [H]

Barak, Ehud. "Issues in the Operation of Intelligence." In *Intelligence and National Security*, edited by Zvi Ofer and Avi Kover. Tel-Aviv: Maarchot, 1987. [H]

Baram, Amatsia. *Culture, History, and Ideology in the Formation of Ba'thist Iraq, 1968–1989*. New York: St. Martin's Press, 1991.

Bar-Gal, Yoram, and Arnon Sofer. "Changes in the Minority Villages in the Galilee." *Horizons in Geography* [Ofakim Be-Geografia], Haifa University, 1976. [H]

———. *Geographical Changes in the Traditional Arab Villages in Northern Israel*. Durham: University of Durham Press, 1981.

Bar-Lavi, Zeev. *The Hashemite Regime, 1949–1967, and Its Standing in the West Bank*. Skirot, no. 80. Tel-Aviv: Shiloah Institute, 1981. [H]

Bar-Yosef, Uri. *The Sentinel Who Fell Asleep: The Yom-Kippur Surprise and Its Origins*. Tel-Aviv: Zemora-Bitan, 2001. [H]

Barzilay, Amnon. "In the Last Moment, the Palestinian Authority Was Eliminated, and Arafat as Well." *Haaretz*, June 21, 2002, 18. [H]

Bastouni, Rustom. "The Arab Society in Israel." *Ha-Mizrah Ha-Hadash* 15 (1965): 1–6. [H]

Be'eri, Eliezer. "Arab National Consciousness." *Ha-Shomer Ha–Tzair* 15, nos. 16–17, 19 (1943): 4, 7, 12. [H]

———. *The Arabs: A Bibliographical Survey.* Jerusalem: The Jewish Agency, 1944. [H]

———. *The Palestinians under Jordanian Rule.* Jerusalem: Magnes, 1978. [H]

Begin, Benjamin Ze'ev. "The Years of Hope." *Haaretz*, September 6, 2002, magazine section, 32–8. [H]

Beinin, Joel. "Know Thy Enemies, Know Thy Allies: The Orientalists of *Ha-Shomer Ha-Tzair.*" In *Jewish-Arab Relations in Mandatory Palestine*, edited by Ilan Pappe. Givat-Haviva: Institute for Peace Studies, 1995. [H]

Ben, Aluph. "Now Everybody Knows: They Are Guilty." *Haaretz*, July 27, 2001, 15. [H]

Ben-Avi, Itamar. "Only Clear Words." *Doar Ha-Yom*, August 8, 1918, 1. [H]

Ben-David, Yosef. "Ethnic Differences or Social Change?" *Megamot* 3 (January 1952): 171–83. [H]

Ben-Dor, Gabriel. *The Druze in Israel: A Political Study.* Jerusalem: Magnes, 1979. [H]

———. "State, Society, and Military Elites in The Middle East: An Essay in Comparative Political Sociology." *Occasional Papers of the Dayan Center* 88 (1984).

Ben-Eliezer, Uri. *The Making of Israeli Militarism, 1936–1956.* Tel-Aviv: Dvir, 1995. [H]

Ben-Gurion, David. *Letters of David Ben-Gurion*, vol. 1 (1904–1919). Edited by Yehouda Erez. Tel-Aviv: Am-Oved, 1971. [H]

———. *Our Neighbors and Us.* Tel-Aviv: Davar, 1931. [H]

Ben-Gurion, David, and Yitzhak Ben-Tzvi. *Eretz Israel: Past and Present.* Jerusalem: Yad ben-Tzvi, 1980 [1918]. [H]

Benjo, Ofra. *The Kurdish Rebellion against Iraq.* Tel-Aviv: Dayan Center, 1990. [H]

———. *Saddam's Iraq: Political Discourse and the Language of Power.* Tel-Aviv: Kav Adom, 1996. [H]

Bennet, James, "Between Two Homes and Two Peoples, a Soldier Wanders," *New York Times*, November 9, 2003, A1, A10.

Benor, Yehouda Leib. "Arab Education in Israel." *Ha-Mizrah Ha-Hadash* 3 (Autumn 1951): 1–8. [H]

Ben-Pazi, Shmaryahu. "The Impact of Agricultural Seasons on the Fighting between the Communities." Paper presented at the annual meeting of the Association for Israel Studies, San Diego, CA, May 2003.

Ben-Porath, Yoel. "Intelligence Assessments: Why Do They Collapse?" *Maarachot* 289–90 (October 1983): 29–38. [H]

———. *Neila.* Tel-Aviv: Idanim, 1991. [H]

Ben-Porath, Yoram, Emmanuel Marx, and Shimon Shamir. *A Refugee Camp on the Mountain Slope.* Tel-Aviv: Shiloah Institute, 1974. [H]

Ben-Tzvi, Yitzhak. *The Muslim World and the Arab World.* Jerusalem: Keren Kayemet, 1936. [H]

———. *The Populace of Our Land.* Warsaw: Beit Ha-Noar, 1932. [H]

Ben-Ze'ev, Efrat. "The Palestinian Village of Ijzim during the 1948 War: Forming an Anthropological History through Villagers' accounts and Army Documents." *Ha-Mizrah Ha-Hadash* 43 (2002): 65–82. [H]

Ben-Zeev, Yosef. "Intelligence during the 1956 War." *Maarachot* 306–7 (December-January 1987): 18–21. [H]

Benziman, Uzi. "Arafat's Pressurized Suit." *Haaretz*, January 25, 2002. Online archive http://www.haaretz.co.il/hasite/pages/arch (no. 790079). [H]

———. "The Noise That Drowns Out the Main Thing." *Haaretz*, July 19, 2002, 15. [H]

Bergman, Ronen. *Permission Granted: Where Did We Go Wrong? How the Palestinian Authority Became an Assembly Line for Corruption and Terrorism.* Tel-Aviv: Hemed, 2002. [H]

Bergman, Ronen, and Ron Leshem. "How We (Almost) Cracked Saddam." *Yediot Aharaonot*, January 5, 2000, magazine section, 14–21, 86. [H]

Berlovitz, Yaffah. *Inventing a Land, Inventing a People: The Literature of the First Aliya.* Tel-Aviv: Hakibutz Hameuchad, 1996. [H]

Bhabha, Homi K. *The Location of Culture.* London: Routledge, 1994.

Black, Ian, and Benny Morris. *Israel's Secret Wars: The Untold Story of Israeli Intelligence.* London: Hannish Hamilton, 1991.

Boimel, Yair. "The Military Government and the Process of Its Abolition, 1958–1968." *Ha-Mizrah Ha-Hadash* 43 (2002): 133–56. [H]

Bourdieu, Pierre. *Distinction: A Social Critique of the Judgment of Taste.* Cambridge, MA: Harvard University Press, 1984.

———. "Legitimation and Structured Interests in Weber's Sociology of Religion." In *Max Weber, Rationality and Modernity*, edited by Scott Lash and S. Whimster. London: Allen and Unwin, 1987.

———. *The Logic of Practice.* Stanford: Stanford University Press, 1991.

———. *Pascalian Meditations.* Stanford: Stanford University Press, 2000.

Boyarin, Daniel. "The Colonial Drag: Zionism, Gender, and Mimicry." In *The Pre-Occupation of Post-Colonial Studies*, edited by Fawzia Afzal-Khan and Kalpana Seshadri-Crooks. Durham: Duke University Press, 2000.

Brauer, Erich. *The Jews of Kurdistan: An Ethnological Study.* Jerusalem: Eretz Israel Institute of Folklore and Ethnology, 1948.

Brawer, Moshe. "The Internal Structure of the Traditional Arab Village." In *The Arab Settlement in Israel: Geographical Processes*, edited by David Grossman and Avinoam Meir. Ramat-Gan: Bar-Ilan University, 1994. [H]

Brodnitz, Michael, and Daniel Dominsky. "Industrialization in the Arab Village in Israel." *Rev'on Lekalkala (Economic Quarterly)* 33, no. 128 (1986): 533–46. [H]

Burla, Yehuda. "The Sepharadim and Our National Revival." *Mizrah u-Ma'arav* 1 (October 1919): 163–71. [H]

Canguilhem, Georges. *On the Normal and the Pathological.* Dordrecht: D. Reidel, 1978.

Center for Research on Settlement. *Development Towns and Their Hinterland.* Settlement and Development no. 11–12 (1968). [H]

Cohen, Abner. *Arab Border Villages in Israel.* Manchester: Manchester University Press, 1965.

Cohen, Amnon. "David Farhi: An Obituary." *Ha-Mizrah Ha-Hadash* 28 (1979): 1–2. [H]

———. *Parties in the West Bank under Jordanian Rule, 1948–1967.* Jerusalem: Magnes, 1980. [H]

Cohen, Gamliel. *The First Mista'aravim.* Tel-Aviv: Ministry of Defense, 2002. [H]

Cohen, Haim. "Jewish Theosophists in Basra: Symptom of the Struggles of the *Haskala* Generation." *Ha-Mizrah Ha-Hadash* 15 (1965): 401–7. [H]

Cohen, Hillel. "The Internal Refugees in the State of Israel: The Struggle for Identity." *Ha-Mizrah Ha-Hadash* 43 (2002): 83–102. [H]

Cohen, Ra'nan. *Entangled in the Web of Loyalties: Society and Politics in the Arab Sector.* Tel-Aviv: Am-Oved, 1990. [H]

———. *Kiss of the Tzabar: A Life Story.* Tel-Aviv: Yediot Aharonot, 2002. [H]

Cohen, Raymond. "Israeli Military Intelligence before the 1956 Sinai Campaign." *Intelligence and National Security* 3, no. 1 (1988): 100–41.

———. "Threat Assessment in Military Intelligence." *Intelligence and National Security* 4, no. 4 (1989): 735–64.

Cordova, Abraham. *Hasolel.* Unpublished manuscript.

———. "The Institutionalization of a Cultural Center in Palestine: The Case of the Writers Association." *Jewish Social Studies* 42 (Winter 1980): 37–62.

Cordova, Abraham, and Hanna Herzog. "The Editorial Board of Davar between Ideology and Politics, 1925–1938." *Rivon Le-Mehkar Hevrati* 20, no. 2 (1980): 5–30. [H]

Danin, Ezra. *Zionist without Conditions.* Jerusalem: Kidum, 1987.

Dann, Uriel. *Iraq under Qassem: A Political History.* Jerusalem: Israel Universities Press, 1968.

———. *King Hussein and the Challenge of Arab Radicalism: Jordan, 1955–1967.* New York: Oxford University Press. 1989.

Dayan, Moshe. *Living with the Bible.* Tel-Aviv: Yediot Aharonot, 1978. [H]

Deshen, Shlomo. "A Case of Breakdown of Modernization in an Israeli Immigrant Community." *Jewish Journal of Sociology* 7, no. 1 (1965): 63–91.

———. "Conflict and Social Change: The Case of an Israeli Village." *Sociologia Ruralis* 6 (1966): 31–51.

———. *Immigrant Voters in Israel: Parties and Congregations in a Local Election Campaign.* Manchester: Manchester University Press, 1970.

Dinur, Ben-Tzion, ed. *History of the Haganah.* Tel-Aviv: Maarachot, 1954. [H]

Doron, Gideon. "Israeli Intelligence: Tactics, Strategy, and Prediction." *International Journal of Intelligence and Counter-intelligence* 2 (Fall 1988): 305–20.

Dotan, Alexander. *The Arab War against Israel (as the Arabs Saw It).* Tel-Aviv: Tversky, 1951.

Douglas, Mary. *Purity and Danger.* London: Routledge, 1966.

Efrat, Elisha. *Development Towns in Israel: Past or Future.* Tel-Aviv: Ahiasaf, 1987. [H]

———. "Um-al-Fahem: A City?" *Haaretz*, October 25, 1984, 9. [H]

Efrat, Zvi. "The Plan: Drafting the Israeli National Space." In *A Civilian Occupation: The Politics of Israeli Architecture*, edited by Rafi Segal and Eyal Weizman. New York: Verso, 2003.

Eisenstadt, Shmuel N. *The Absorption of Immigrants.* Glencoe, IL: The Free Press, 1955.

―――. *Introduction to the Study of the Sociological Structure of the Oriental Ethnicities.* Jerusalem, 1948. [H]

Eldar, Akiva. "His Real Face." *Haaretz*, June 11, 2004, 12. [H]

Elishar, Eliahu. *Living with Palestinians.* Jerusalem: Va'ad Edat Ha-Sepharadim, 1975. [H]

Erlikh, Haggai. *Ras Alula and the Scramble for Africa: A Political Biography: Ethiopia and Eritrea, 1875–1897.* Lawrenceville, NJ: Red Sea Press, 1996.

Eshed, Hagai. *Reuven Shiloh: A Mossad of One Man.* Tel-Aviv: Idanim, 1985. [H]

Even-Zohar, Itamar. "The Emergence and Crystallization of a Native, Local Hebrew Culture in Palestine, 1882–1948." *Katedra* 16 (July 1980): 165–89. [H]

Eyal (Sayyag), Dudu. "I Dream in Moroccan." *Ha-Kivun Mizrah* 3 (October 2001): 6. [H]

Eyal, Eli. "The Debate among Orientalists after the Agranat Report." *Ma'ariv*, April 26, 1974, magazine section: 12–13, 37. [H]

Eyni, Yom-Tov. "Professional Aspects of Mizrahanut in Israel." Master's thesis, Tel-Aviv University, 1975. [H]

Fallah, Salman. "Kafr Summayya': A Druze Village in Upper Galilee." *Israel Exploration Journal* 18, no. 1 (1968): 27–44.

Farhi, David. "From the Writings and Speeches of the Late David Farhi." In *Ten Years of Israeli Rule in the West Bank, 1967–1977*, edited by Rafi Israeli. Jerusalem: Magnes, 1981. [H]

―――. *The Residents of the Territories and Their Political Positions.* Panel Discussions on Historical Affairs and Basic Problems no. 17. Ramat Efal: Yad Tabenkin, 1976.

Ferguson, James. *The Anti-Politics Machine.* New York: Cambridge University Press, 1990.

Foreign Office, Department of Instruction. *The Israeli-Arab Conflict: An Anthology of Documents and Selected Articles.* Jerusalem: Foreign Office, Department of Instruction, 1985. [H]

Foucault, Michel. *The Archeology of Knowledge.* London: Tavistock, 1972.

―――. *Madness and Civilization.* New York: Vintage Books, 1965.

―――. "Preface to Transgression." In *Essential Works of Michel Foucault, 1954–1984,* vol.2 , edited by Paul Rabinow. New York: The New Press, 1998.

―――. "The Subject and Power." In *Michel Foucault: Beyond Structuralism and Hermeneutics*, edited by Hubert L. Dreyfus and Paul Rabinow. Chicago: Chicago University Press, 1982.

―――. "Technologies of the Self." In *Technologies of the Self*, edited by Luther H. Martin, Huck Gutman, and Patrick H. Hutton. London: Tavistock, 1988.

Frankenstein, Carl. *The Abandonment of Youth.* Jerusalem, 1947. [H]

―――. "About the Concept Primitive." *Megamot* 2 (October 1951): 339–59. [H]

―――. "About the Problem of Ethnic Differences." *Megamot* 2 (July 1951): 261–76. [H]

―――. "Summary of the Debate about the Problem of Ethnic Differences." *Megamot* 3 (October 1952): 319–29. [H]

Frankenstein, Carl, and Gina Orther. "A Method to Improve the Powers of Abstraction in Children of Immigrants from Oriental Countries." *Megamot* 2 (1951): 261–76. [H]

Gabay, Moshe. *Kedma Mizracha, 1936–1939.* Givat Haviva: Institute for Arab Studies, 1984. [H]

Garfinkel, Harold. "What Is Ethnomethodology?" In *Studies in Ethnomethodology.* Englewood Cliffs, NJ: Prentice-Hall, 1968.

Gazit, Shlomo. *The Carrot and the Stick: The Israeli Military Government in the West Bank.* Tel-Aviv: Zemorah u-Bitan, 1985. [H]

———. *Fools in a Trap: Thirty Years of Israeli Policy in the Occupied Territories.* Tel-Aviv: Zemorah u-Bitan, 1999. [H]

Gelber, Yoav. "The Formation of Military Intelligence." *Marachot* 294–5 (July 1984): 20–31. [H]

———. *Roots of the Lily: Intelligence in the Yishuv, 1918–1947.* Tel-Aviv: Defense Ministry, 1992. [H]

———. *Seeds of a Regular Hebrew Army.* Jerusalem: Yad Ben-Tzvi, 1986. [H]

Gelblum, Arie. "A Journey among Israeli Arabs: The Political Truth and the General Elections." *Ha'aretz,* 1949. [H]

Gerber, Haim. "Zionism, Orientalism and the Palestinians." *Ha-Mizrah Ha-Hadash* 43 (2002): 27–47. [H]

Gieryn, Thomas F. "Boundary Work and the Demarcation of Science from Non-Science: Strains and Interests in Professional Ideologies of Scientists." *American Sociological Review* 48 (December 1983): 781–95.

Gilboa, Amos. "Syria and Israel's Security." In *Syria and Israel's Security,* edited by Avner Yaniv, Moshe Maoz, and Avi Kover. Tel-Aviv: Maarachot, 1991. [H]

Ginat, Yosef. *Changes in Family Structure in the Arab Village.* Ramat-Aviv: Tel-Aviv University, 1976. [H]

Gitlis, Baruch. *The Ugly Military Governor: The Truth about the Military Government.* Jerusalem: Ogdan, 1967. [H]

Goitein, Shlomo Dov. "About a Jewish-Arab Symbiosis." *Molad* 2 (February 1949): 259–66. [H]

———. "The Arab Schools in Israel Revisited." *Middle Eastern Affairs* 3 (October 1952): 272–5.

———. "Congratulatory Letter to the Israeli Oriental Society on Its Thirty-Year

———. *Hebrew Instruction in the Land of Israel.* Tel-Aviv: Yavne, 1945. [H]

———. *Jews and Arabs: Their Contacts through the Ages.* New York: Schocken Books, 1955.

———. "The New Orient." *Ha-Mizrah Ha-Hadash* 1 (1949): 1–2. [H]

———. "Oriental Studies in the Hebrew University." *Davar,* October 4, 1936, 14. [H]

Anniversary." *Hamizrah Hachadash* 28, nos. 3–4 (1979): 173–4. [H]

———. *Teaching the Bible.* Tel-Aviv: Yavne, 1957. [H]

Golan, Arnon. *Spatial Change as Consequence of War: The Formerly Arab Lands in the State of Israel, 1948–1950.* Sde Boker: Ben-Gurion University, 2001. [H]

Golany, Gideon. "Geography of the Traditional Arab Village of the Village Taiybe Model." Master's thesis, University of Haifa, 1967. [H]

Goldstein, Ya'acov. *The Group of the Shepherds, 1907–1917.* Tel-Aviv: Ministry of Defense, 1993. [H]

Gonen, Amiram. "The Geography of Electoral Competition between Labor and Likud in the Jewish Cities of Israel, 1965–1981." *Medina, Mimshal u-Yehasim Bein-Leumyim* 19–20 (1982): 63–87. [H]

Gordon, Colin. "*Histoire de la folie*: An unknown book by Michel Foucault." *History of the Human Sciences* 3 (1990): 3–26.

Goren, Tamir. "Changes in the Design of the Urban Space of the Arabs of Haifa during the Israeli War of Independence." *Middle Eastern Studies* 35 (January 1999): 115–33.

Gormazano Goren, Yitzhak. "Preface." *Ha-kivun Mizrah* 3 (October 2001): 1. [H]

Granot, Oded. *The Intelligence Corps.* Vol. 5 of *The IDF: Encyclopedia of Military and Security.* Edited by Yaacov Eerz and Ilan Kfir. Tel-Aviv: Revivim, 1981. [H]

Grinberg, Lev. *Public Activists of the Histadrut and Municipalities: The Ethnic Dimension.* Jerusalem Institute for Israel Research 33 (1989). [H]

Grol, Meshulam. "On Human Dignity." *Megamot* 3 (October 1951): 50–64. [H]

Grossman, David. *Present Absentees.* Tel-Aviv: Ha-Kibutz Ha-Meuchad, 1992. [H]

Grunwald, K. "The Jewish Bankers in Iraq." *Ha-Mizrah Ha-Hadash* 11 (1961): 159–65. [H]

HaCohen, Dvora. *Immigrants in a Storm: the Great Aliya and Its Absorption in Israel, 1948–1953.* Jerusalem: Yad Ben-Tzvi, 1994. [H]

———. *The One Million Plan: David Ben-Gurion's Plan for Mass Immigration in the Years 1942–1945.* Tel-Aviv: Defense Ministry, 1994. [H]

Halperin, Liora R. "The 'Pioneering Work' of Zionist Arabic Study during the Mandate Period: Zionism in Conversation with Orientalism." Senior thesis, Harvard University, 2005.

Harkabi, Yehoshafat. *Arab Attitudes to Israel.* New York: Hart Publishing Co., 1972.

———, ed. *Arabia and Israel: A Collection of Translations from Arabic* 1, no. 1 (1974): 1. [H]

———. *Basic Aspects of the Israeli-Arab Conflict.* Tel-Aviv: IDF Education Corps, 1971. [H]

———. *The Fatah in Arab Strategy.* Tel-Aviv: Maarachot, 1969. [H]

———. "For a National Soul-Searching." *Ma'ariv*, April 19, 1974, op-ed section, 18. [H]

———. "For a Personal Soul-Searching." *Ma'ariv*, May 3, 1974, op-ed section, 17. [H]

———. *How Was the Arab Position Explained in the Egyptian Army.* Tel-Aviv: IDF Education Corps, 1967. [H]

———. *The Palestinian Covenant and Its Significance: Explanations and Consequences.* Jerusalem: Hasbara Center, 1969. [H]

———. *Personal Testimony: The Affair from My Point of View.* Tel-Aviv: Ramot, 1994. [H]

———. *The Position of the Arabs in the Israeli-Arab Conflict.* Tel-Aviv: Dvir, 1969. [H]

————. *The Position of the Palestinians in the Israeli-Arab Conflict and Their National Covenant.* Jerusalem: Hasbara Center, 1968.

————. *The Problem of the Palestinians.* Jerusalem: Israeli Academic Committee on the Middle East, 1973.

————. "Strategic Studies – also in Israel?" *Maarachot* 165, March 1962, 4–8. [H]

————. *Time Bomb in the Middle East.* New York: Friendship Press, 1969.

————. "We Must Learn to Understand the Substance of the Arab Case." *The New Middle East* 2 (November 1968): 26–30.

Harkabi, Yehoshafat, and Matti Steinberg. *The Palestinian Covenant in the Test of Time and Practice: Explanations and Consequences.* Jerusalem: Hasbara Center, 1988. [H]

Harry S. Truman Research Institute for the Advancement of Peace. *Annual Report, Activities during 1989.* Jerusalem: Hebrew University of Jerusalem, 1990.

Hasbara Center, Department of Monitoring. "Topics in Focus: The PLO between the Geneva Declaration (12.14.1988) to the Fifth Convention of the Fatah (8.8.1989)." *Flashlight on the Middle East* 13 (October 1989): 1–15. [H]

Heller, Yosef. *From Covenant of Peace to Ichud: Yehouda Leib Magnes and the Struggle for a Bi-National State.* Jerusalem: Magnes, 2004. [H]

Herman, Tamar. "From Brit Shalom to Peace Now: The Pragmatic Pacificism of the Peace Camp in Israel." Ph.D. diss., Tel-Aviv University, 1989. [H]

Herzog, Hanna. "The Concepts 'Old Yishuv' and 'New Yishuv': A Sociological Approach." *Katedra* 32 (1984): 99–108. [H]

————. "Penetrating the System: The Politics of Collective Identities." In *The Elections in Israel: 1992,* edited by Asher Arian and Michal Shamir. Albany: SUNY Press, 1995.

————. *Political Ethnicity: Image versus Reality: A Historical-Sociological Analysis of the "Ethnic" Lists to the Convention of Delegates and the Knesset, 1920–1984.* Ramat Efal: Yad Tabenkin, 1986. [H]

Heschel, Susannah. *Abraham Geiger and the Jewish Jesus.* Chicago: University of Chicago Press, 1998.

Hever, Hannan, Yehouda Shenhav, and Pnina Motzafi-Haller. *Mizrahi Perspectives on Society and Culture in Israel: A Report on Israeli Patterns of Representation.* Jerusalem: Van-Leer Institute, 1999. [H]

Heyd, Uriel. *The Modern Middle East as a Topic of Research and Instruction.* Jerusalem: Magnes, 1953. [H]

Hirschberg, H. Z. "About the Ethnicities of Israel in the Muslim Orient." Foreward to *The Ethnicities in Israel,* by Hannah Helena Tehon. Jerusalem: Reuvan, 1957. [H]

————. "Editor's Note." In *Zakhor le-Avraham: A Collection of Articles in Memory of Avraham Elmaliah,* edited by H. Z. Hirschberg. Jerusalem: Committee of the Maghrebi Community, 1972. [H]

————. "Problems of the Shari'a in the State of Israel." *Ha-Mizrah Ha-Hadash* 1 (January 1950): 97–108. [H]

Hissin, Haim. *Writings of One of the Biluyim.* Jerusalem: Yad Ben-Tzvi, 1990. [H]

Horowitz, Dan, and Moshe Lissak. *Origins of the Israeli Polity: Palestine under the Mandate.* Chicago: Chicago University Press, 1978.

Hourani, Albert. *The Emergence of the Modern Middle East.* Berkeley: University of California Press, 1981.

Husayn, Taha. *The Future of Culture in Egypt.* Washington, DC: American Council of Learned Societies, 1954.

Inbari, Pinhas. *The Palestinian Option: The PLO Facing the Zionist Challenge.* Jerusalem: Carmel, 1989. [H]

———. *A Triangle on the Jordan River.* Jerusalem: Kaneh, 1982. [H]

Institute for Land Use Research. *Land Expropriation for Public Uses.* Vol 4. Jerusalem: Israel Land Authority, 1976. [H]

Israeli, Raphael. *Arabs in Israel: Friends or Foes?* Jerusalem: Ariel Center for Policy Studies, 2002. [H]

Jabotinsky, Zeev. "The Jews of the Orient." *Mizrah u-Ma'arv* 1 (September 1919): 59–60. [H]

Kalmar, Ivan Davidson, and Derek Penslar. "Orientalism and the Jews: An Introduction." In *Orientalism and the Jews,* edited by Ivan Davidson Kalmar and Derek Penslar. Waltham, MA: Brandies University Press, 2005.

Kanaana, Sharif. *Socio-Cultural and Psychological Adjustment of the Arab Minority in Israel.* San Francisco: R&E Research Association, 1976.

Kashua, Sayid. *And It Was Morning.* Jerusalem: Keter, 2004. [H]

———. *Arabs Dancing.* Tel-Aviv: Modan, 2002. [H]

Katzenelson, Berl. "The Real Content of the Arab National Movement." In *Writings,* vol.3. Tel-Aviv: Mapai, 1948. [H]

Keidar, Aharon. "The History of Brit Shalom in the Years 1925–1928." In *Research Chapters in the History of Zionism,* edited by Yehouda Bauer, Moshe Davies, and Israel Kulat. Jerusalem: The Zionist Library, 1976. [H]

Keidar, B. Z., and Menahem Milson, eds. *The Palestinian National Movement: From Confrontation to Acceptance?* Tel-Aviv: Defense Ministry, 1999. [H]

Kemp, Adriana. "Dangerous Populations: State Territoriality and the Constitution of National Minorities." Paper presented at the Boundaries and Belonging Conference, University of Washington, Seattle, 2000.

———. "'The Migration of Peoples' or 'the Great Fire': State Control and Resistance in the Israeli Frontier." In *Mizrahim in Israel: A Critical Observation into Israel's Ethnicity,* edited by Hanan Hever, Yehouda Shenhav, and Pnina Motzafi-Haller. Jerusalem: Van Leer, 2002. [H]

———. "Talking Borders: The Construction of a Political Territory in Israel, 1949–1957." Ph.D. diss., Tel-Aviv University, 1997. [H]

Khazzoom, Aziza. "The Origins of Ethnic Inequality among Jews in Israel." Ph.D. diss., University of California, Berkeley, 1998.

———. "Occidental Culture, Ethnic Stigmatization and Social Closure: The Background for Ethnic Inequality in Israel." *Israeli Sociology* 1, no. 2 (1999): 385–428. [H]

———. "The Great Chain of Orientalism: Jewish Identity, Stigma Management and Ethnic Exclusion in Israel." *American Sociological Review* 68 (August 2003): 481–501.

———. "Did the Israeli State Engineer Segregation? On the Placement of Jewish Immigrants in Development Towns in the 1950's." *Social Forces* 84, no.1 (2005): 117–36.

Kimmerling, Baruch. *Zionism and Territory*. Berkeley, CA: Institute for International Studies, 1983.

Kislev, Ran. *The Land Expropriation Affair*. Givat Haviva: Center for Arab Studies, 1976. [H]

Kloisner, Yosef. "The Eternal Value of the Period of Sepharad." *Mizrah u-Ma'arav* 1 (September 1920): 307–11. [H]

Kohn, Hans. *History of the Arab National Movement*. Tel-Aviv: Ha-Poel Ha-Tzair, 1926.

Kopelevitz, Emanuel. "Changes in the Arab Village in Israel." *Kama* 4 (1952): 203–23. [H]

Kostiner, Yoseph. *South Yemen's Revolutionary Strategy, 1970–1985: From Insurgency to Bloc Politics*. Boulder, CO: Westview Press, 1990.

Kramer, Martin. Introduction to *The Jewish Discovery of Islam: Studies in Honor of Bernard Lewis*, edited by Martin Kramer. Tel-Aviv: Dayan Center, 1999.

———. "Islam Is the Power of the Future." In *Islam and Democracy in the Arab World*, edited by Meir Litwak. Tel-Aviv: The Dayan Center, 1997. [H]

Kramer, Yoel. "Goitein and His Mediterranean Society." *Zemanim* 33–34 (1990): 4–17. [H]

Landau, Ya'akov. *The Arabs in Israel*. London: Oxford University Press, 1969.

Lanir, Zvi. *Fundamental Surprise: Intelligence in Crisis*. Tel-Aviv: Hakibutz Hameuchad, 1983. [H]

Latour, Bruno. *Science in Action*. Cambridge, MA.: Harvard University Press, 1987.

———. *We Have Never been Modern*. Cambridge, MA.: Harvard University Press, 1993.

Lavie, Aviv. "Late Incitement." *Haaretz*, July 18, 2003, magazine section, 18–22. [H]

———. "When Avri Ran Gets Angry." *Haaretz*, March 19, 2004, magazine section, 50–4. [H]

Layish, Aharon. "Changes in the Arab Society in Israel." In *Arab Society in Israel: Changes and Trends*. Jerusalem: Office of the Adviser on Arab Affairs to the Prime Minister, 1969. [H]

———. "Trends after the Six-Day War." In *The Arabs in Israel*, edited by Aharon Layish. Jerusalem: Magnes, 1981. [H]

Lazar, Hadara. *In and Out of Palestine*. Jerusalem: Keter, 2003. [H]

Lazarus-Yafeh, Hava. "The Transplantation of Islamic Studies from Europe to the Yishuv and Israel," In *The Jewish Discovery of Islam: Studies in Honor of Bernard Lewis*, edited by Martin Kramer. Tel-Aviv: Dayan Center, 1999.

Leibowitz-Dar, Sarah. "The Chief Expounder." *Haaretz*, February 14, 2003, magazine section, 26–30. [H]

———. "Ehud Ya'ari Said." *Haaretz*, November 10, 2000, magazine section. Online archive http://www.haaretz.co.il/hasite/pages/arch (no. 668085). [H]

————. "Political Asylum? For an Israeli?" *Haaretz*, July 25, 2003, magazine section, 22–8. [H]

Lephen, Asa. "The Shai: The Paramilitary Intelligence Service." In *Intelligence and National Security*, edited by Avi Kover and Zvi Ofer. Tel-Aviv: Marachot, 1987. [H]

————. *The Shai: The Roots of the Israeli Intelligence Community*. Tel-Aviv: Ministry of Defense, 1997. [H]

Lev-Ari, Shiri. "Know Thy Neighbor." *Haaretz*, February 26, 2003. Online archive http://www.haaretz.co.il/hasite/pages/arch (no. 973539). [H]

Levi-Barzilay, Vered. "How Do You Say 'Doctor' in Arabic?" *Haaretz*, July 13, 2001, magazine section. Online archive http://www.haaretz.co.il/hasite/pages/arch (no. 737937). [H]

Lewin, Michael. "Notes on Trends in the Emergence and Crystallization of a Local Art and Architecture in Palestine." *Katedra* 16 (July 1980): 194–204. [H]

Lewis, Bernard. "The Pro-Islamic Jews." In *Islam in History*. Chicago: Open Court, 1993.

Lin, Amnon. *Before the Storm: The Relations of Jews and Arabs in the State of Israel between Hopes and Disappointments*. Tel-Aviv: Karni, 1999. [H]

Lissak, Moshe. *The Great Aliya of the 1950s: The Failure of the Melting Pot*. Jerusalem: Bialik Institute, 1999. [H]

Livne, Neri. "The Legend of Nimrod." *Haaretz*, February 23, 2002, magazine section. Online archive http://www.haaretz.co.il/hasite/pages/arch (no. 796579). [H]

Lockard, Joe. "Somewhere between Arab and Jew: Ethnic Re-Identification in Modern Hebrew Literature." *Middle Eastern Literature* 5, no. 1 (2002): 49–62.

Lustick, Ian. *Arabs in the Jewish State*. Haifa: Mifras, 1985. [H]

Manor, Dalia. "Biblical Zionism in Bezalel Art." *Israel Studies* 6 (Spring 2001): 55–75.

————. "Orientalism and Israeli Art: The Case of Betzalel." Paper presented at the Association for Israel Studies Conference, Vail, CO, 2002.

Maoz, Moshe. *Asad: The Sphinx of Damascus: A Political Biography*. London: Weidenfeld and Nicholson, 1988.

————, ed. *The Goals of the Arab Struggle against Israel in the Wake of the Yom Kippur War*. Jerusalem: Mount Scopus Center for Research on the Arabs of Eretz Israel and Israeli-Arab Relations, 1974. [H]

————. "Local Government in the Arab Settlements in Israel." *Ha-Mizrah Ha-Hadash* 12 (1962): 233–40. [H]

————. *The Palestinian Leadership in the West Bank*. Tel-Aviv: Reshafim, 1985. [H]

Maoz, Moshe, and Avner Yaniv, eds. *Syria under Asad: Domestic Constraints and Regional Risks*. London: Croom Helm, 1986.

Marx, Emmanuel. "On the Anthropological Study of Nations." In *A Composite Portrait of Israel*, edited by Emmanuel Marx. New York: Academic Press, 1980.

————. *The Social Context of Violent Behavior: A Social Anthropological Study in an Israeli Immigrant Town*. London: Routledge and Kegan Paul, 1976.

————. "The Social World of Refugees: A Conceptual Framework." Unpublished manuscript. Revised version of the Refugee Studies Program Second Annual Colson Lecture, Oxford, March 7, 1990.

Masalha, Nur. *Expulsion of the Palestinians: The Concept of Transfer in Zionist Political Thought, 1882–1948.* Washington, DC: Institute for Palestine Studies, 1992.

Menashri, David. *Iran in Revolution.* Tel-Aviv: Ha-Kibutz Ha-Meuchad, 1988. [H]

Meyuchas, Yosef. *The Fellahin: The Life of the Fellahin in Comparison with the Life of the Jews in Biblical and Talmudic times.* Tel-Aviv: Davar, 1937. [H]

Milson, Menahem. "The Beginning of Islamic and Arabic Studies in the Hebrew University." In *The History of the Hebrew University in Jerusalem: Origins and Beginnings,* edited by Shaul Katz and Michael Heyd. Jerusalem: Magnes, 1997. [H]

———. "How to Make Peace with the Palestinians." *Commentary* 7, no. 5 (1981): 25–35.

———. *Jordan and the West Bank.* Policy-Directed Publication no. 10. Jerusalem: Davis Institute, January 1984. [H]

Ministry of Labor, Authority for Manpower Planning. *Development Towns in Israel: First Report about Twenty-one Towns.* Jerusalem: Ministry of Labor, Authority for Manpower Planning, 1964. [H]

Mishory, Alec. *Lo and Behold: Zionist Icons and Visual Symbols in Israeli Culture.* Tel-Aviv: Am Oved, 2000. [H]

Mitchell, Timothy. "The Limits of the State: Beyond Statist Approaches and Their Critics." *American Political Science Review* 85 (March 1991): 77–96.

Morris, Benny. *The Birth of the Palestinian Refugee Problem, 1947–1949.* Tel-Aviv: Am-Oved, 1991. [H]

———. "The Expulsions during the Hiram Operation: Mending an Error." In *Jews and Arabs in Palestine/Israel, 1936–1956.* Tel-Aviv: Am Oved, 2000. [H]

———. "A Form of Migration in which Both Free Will and Coercion Are Entangled: About the Transfer of Majdal's Remaining Inhabitants to Gaza, 1950." In *Jews and Arabs in Palestine/Israel, 1936–1956.* Tel-Aviv: Am Oved, 2000. [H]

———. *Israel's Border Wars, 1949–1956: Arab Infiltration, Israeli Retaliation, and the Countdown to the Suez War.* Oxford: Clarendon Press, 1993.

Morris, Benny, and Ehud Barak. "The Camp David Summit and Its Aftermath." In *Camp David 2000: What Really Happened There?* edited by Danny Rubinstein. Tel-Aviv: Hemed, 2003. [H]

Nakhleh, Khalil. "The Direction of Two-Level Conflict in Two Arab Villages in Israel." *American Ethnologist* 23 (1975): 497–516.

———. "The Shifting Patterns of Conflict in Selected Arab Villages in Israel." Ph.D. diss., Princeton University, 1973.

Niv, David, ed. *Take with You: A Guide to the Problems of the Israeli-Arab Conflict.* Jerusalem: Department of Culture and Education in the Diaspora, World Zionist Federation, 1984. [H]

Nordau, Max. "The Arabs and Us." *Ha-Olam,* June 17, 1937. [H]

Nuriely, Benny. "Strangers in the National Space." Master's thesis, Tel-Aviv University, 2004. [H]

Oren, Amir. "After Iraq, Palestine." *Haaretz,* February 21, 2003, 12. [H]

———. "By Order of the Rabbi." *Haaretz,* February 11, 2001, 16. [H]

———. "Ceasefire." *Haaretz,* June 4, 2001. Online archive http://www.haaretz.co .il/hasite/pages/arch (no. 726804). [H]

Oron, Yitzhak. "Political Intelligence Research: Personal Accents." In *Intelligence and National Security*, edited by Zvi Ofer and Avi Kover. Tel-Aviv: Maarachot, 1987. [H]

―――. "Preface." *Middle East Record* 5 (1964–1965): vii–viii, xxiv–xxix.

Ozacky-Lazar, Sarah. *From a Hebrew Histadrut to a General Histadrut: The Integration of Arabs in the Organization, 1948–1966*. Tel-Aviv: Lavon Institute for the Study of the Labor Movement, 1998. [H]

―――. "From a Hebrew Trade Union to an Israeli Trade Union: The Integration of Arabs in the *Histadrut*, 1948–1966." *Studies in Israel's Revival* 10 (2000): 389–97. [H]

―――. "The Military Government as an Apparatus of Control of the Arab Citizens in Israel: The First Decade, 1948–1958." *Ha-Mizrah Ha-Hadash* 43 (2002): 103–32. [H]

Oz, Amos. *A Story about Love and Darkness*. Jerusalem: Keter, 2002. [H]

Palmon, Yehoshua. "To Enter the Enemy's Mind: A Personal Point of View." In *Intelligence and National Security*, edited by Avi Kover and Zvi Ofer. Tel-Aviv: Maarachot, 1987. [H]

Pedhatzur, Reuven. *The Victory of Confusion: The Policy of the Israeli Government in the Territories after the Six-Day War*. Tel-Aviv: Bitan, 1996. [H]

Peled, A. "Intelligence and the Intelligence Officer." *Maarachot* 80 (1954): 50–3. [H]

Peled, Alisa Rubin. *Debating Islam in the Jewish State: The Development of Policy toward Islamic Institutions in Israel*. Albany: SUNY Press, 2001.

Peri, Yoram. *Between Battles and Ballots: Israeli Military in Politics*. Cambridge: Cambridge University Press, 1983.

Piterberg, Gabriel. "The Nation and Its Story-tellers: National Historiography and Orientalism." *Teoria ve-Bikoret* [Theory and Criticism] 6 (Spring 1995): 81–103. [H]

Porath, Yehoshua. "On the Writing of Arab History by Israeli Scholars." *Jerusalem Quarterly* 32 (Summer 1984): 28–35.

―――. *The Palestinian Arab National Movement: From Riots to Rebellion, 1929–1939*. London: F. Cass, 1977.

―――. "Palestinian Historiography." *Jerusalem Quarterly* 5 (Fall 1977): 95–104.

Rabin, Yitzhak. *My Father's House*. Tel-Aviv: Hakibutz Hameuchad, 1974. [H]

Rabinovich, Itamar. *Syria under the Ba'th, 1963–66: The Army-Party Symbiosis*. Jerusalem: Israel Universities Press, 1972.

―――. *The Brink of Peace: The Israeli-Syrian Negotiations*. Princeton, NJ: Princeton University Press, 1998.

Rabinovich, Itamar, and Haim Shaked, eds. *The Middle East and the United States*. Tel-Aviv: Am-Oved, 1980. [H]

Rabinowitz, Dan. *Anthropology and the Palestinians*. Ra'nana: Institute for Israeli Arab Studies, 1998. [H]

Raz-Krakozkin, Amnon. "Orientalism, Judaism Studies and Israeli Society: A Few Notes." *Jama'a* 3, no. 1 (1999): 34–61. [H]

Rekhess, Elie. *The Arab Village: A Revitalized National-Political Center*. Tel Aviv: Shiloah Center, 1985. [H]

———. "Initial Israeli Policy Guidelines towards the Arab Minority, 1948–1949." In *New Perspective on Israeli History: The Early Years of the State*, edited by Laurence J. Silberstein. New York: NYU Press, 1991.

———. "The Intelligentsia." In *The Arabs in Israel*, edited by Aharon Layish. Jerusalem: Magnes, 1981. [H]

———. "Israeli Arabs after the Oslo Agreements." In *Israeli Arabs: Where Are They Heading? Debate of the Political Circle-Efal with the Participation of Yitzhak Bailey, Elie Rekhess, and Arnon Sofer, April 16, 1994.* Ramat Efal: Yad Tabenkin, 1996. [H]

Reuveni, Yaacov. *The Mandatory Government in Palestine, 1920–1948: A Political-Historical Analysis.* Ramat Gan: Bar-Ilan University, 1993. [H]

Rivlin, Yoel Yosef. "Professor Yosef Horowitz." *Moznaim* 49–50 (1931): 15–17. [H]

Rosch, Eleanor. "Principles of Categorization." In *Cognition and Categorization*, edited by Eleanor Rosch and B. B. Lloyd. Hillside, NJ: Lawrence Erlbaum Associates, 1978.

Rose, Nikolas. "Engineering the Human Soul: Analyzing Psychological Expertise." *Science in Context* 5, no. 2 (1992): 351–69.

Rosenfeld, Henry. "Change, Barriers to Change, and Contradictions in the Village Family." In *The Arabs in Israel*, edited by Aharon Layish. Jerusalem: Magnes, 1981. [H]

———. *They Were Fellahs.* Tel-Aviv: Hakibutz Hameuchad, 1964. [H]

Rotbard, Sharon. "Wall and Tower." In *A Civilian Occupation: The Politics of Israeli Architecture*, edited by Rafi Segal and Eyal Weizman. New York: Verso, 2003.

Rotensstreich, Nathan. "An Absolute Yardstick." *Megamot* 2 (October 1951): 327–38. [H]

Rubinstein, Dani. "The Road Winding Down to Camp David: Introduction." In *Camp David 2000: What Really Happened There?* edited by Danny Rubinstein. Tel-Aviv: Hemed, 2003. [H]

Sade, Yoram. "The Academic Group in Brit Shalom and Its Successors: Political and Ideological Behavior in Light of Their Self Image." Master's thesis, Tel-Aviv University, 1976. [H]

Said, Edward. *Covering Islam.* New York: Pantheon Books, 1981.

———. *Orientalism.* London: Penguin, 1978.

Salomon, Hezi. "The Influence of the Intelligence Services of the Yishuv on Ben-Gurion's Assessment of the Situation, 1946–1947." *Marachot* 309 (July–August 1987): 28–36. [H]

Schiff, Zeev. "Cards of Fire and Negotiation." *Haaretz*, May 25, 2001, op-ed section, 17. [H]

———. "The GSS Is Not Retreating from Its Assessment." *Haaretz*, July 15, 2001, 7. [H]

———. "A New Challenge for Mr. Intelligence." *Haaretz*, July 20, 2001, 17. [H]

Schiff, Zeev, and Eitan Haber. *Lexicon of Israeli Security.* Jerusalem: Zemorah u-Bitan, 1976. [H]

Schnell, Yitzhak. "Changes in the Arab Village in Israel: Urbanization under Conditions of Marginality." In *The Arab Settlement in Israel: Geographical Processes*, edited by David Grossman and Avinoam Meir. Ramat-Gan: Bar-Ilan University, 1994. [H]

Schuftan, Dan. *A New Phase of Jordan-PLO Relations.* Machbarot Heker, no. 13. Ramat Efal: Yad Tabenkin, 1984. [H]

Segal, Rafi, and Eyal Weizman. "The Mountain: Principles of Building in Heights." In *A Civilian Occupation: The Politics of Israeli Architecture,* edited by Rafi Segal and Eyal Weizman. New York: Verso, 2003.

Segev, Tom. *1949: The First Israelis.* Jerusalem: Domino, 1984. [H]

———. *One Palestine, Complete.* New York: Metropolitan Books, 1999.

Semyonov, Moshe, and Noah Levin-Epstein. *Hewers of Wood and Drawers of Water: Non-Citizen Arabs in the Israeli Labor Market.* Ithaca, NY: ILR Press, 1987.

Shabtai, Jacob. *Past Perfect.* Tel-Aviv: Hakibutz Hameuchad, 1984. [H]

Shafir, Gershon. *Land, Labor, and the Origins of the Israeli-Palestinian Conflict, 1882–1914.* Cambridge: Cambridge University Press, 1989.

Shaked, Haim, ed. *Middle East Contemporary Survey, 1976–1977.* Vol. 1. New York: Holmes and Meier, 1978.

Shamir, Shimon. "Changes in the Village Leadership of Ar-Rama." *Ha-Mizrah Ha-Hadash* 11 (1961): 241–57. [H]

———. "Changes in Village Leadership." *New Outlook* 5, no. 3 (1962): 93–112.

———, ed. *The Decline of Nasserism, 1965–1970: The Decline of a Messianic Movement.* Tel-Aviv: Shiloah Institute, 1978. [H]

———. *Egypt under Sa'adat.* Tel-Aviv: Dvir, 1978. [H]

———. "Letter to the Editor: The Decline of Nasserism." *Haaretz,* June 22, 1979, literary supplement, 18. [H]

———. "The Palestinians Are a Nation." *New Outlook* 12, nos. 6–8 (1969): 191–7.

Shapira, Anita. *Yigal Alon: The Springtime of His Life.* Tel-Aviv: Hakibutz Hameuchad, 2004. [H]

———. *Walking into the Horizon.* Tel-Aviv: Am Oved, 1988. [H]

Shapira, Yonthan. *Democracy in Israel.* Ramat-Gan: Massada, 1977. [H]

Sharet, Moshe. *Personal Diary, 1953/54.* Vol. 1. Tel-Aviv: Ma'ariv, 1978. [H]

———. *Political Diary, 1936.* Edited by Ahuvia Malkin. Tel-Aviv: Am Oved, 1968. [H]

Sharon, Arye. *Physical Planning in Israel.* Jerusalem: Prime Minister's Office, 1949. [H]

Shenhav, Yehouda. *The Arab-Jews: Nationalism, Religion and Ethnicity.* Tel-Aviv: Am-Oved, 2003. [H]

Shidlowsky, Benjamin, ed. *The Arab and Druze Settlements in Israel.* Jerusalem: Office of the Adviser on Arab Affairs, 1969. [H]

———. "Changes in the Development of the Arab Village in Israel." *Ha-Mizrah Ha-Hadash* 15 (1965): 26. [H]

Shimoni, Yaacov. *The Arabs of the Land of Israel.* Tel-Aviv: Am Oved, 1947. [H]

Shinkman, Anat. "Arabic Study Is Losing Popularity." *Yediot Aharonot,* May 3, 1991, Tel-Aviv supplement, 16. [H]

Shohat, Ella. *The Mizrahi Revolution: Three Essays on Zionism and the Mizrahim.* Jerusalem: Center for Alternative Information, 1999. [H]

———. "Sepharadim in Israel: Zionism from the Standpoint of Its Jewish Victims." In *Dangerous Liaisons: Gender, Nation and Postcolonial Perspectives,* edited by

Anne McClintock, Aamir Mufti, and Ella Shohat. Minneapolis: University of Minnesota Press, 1997.

Shokeid, Moshe. *The Dual Heritage: Immigrants from the Atlas Mountains in an Israeli Village.* Manchester: Manchester University Press, 1971.

Shoshani, Avi. "Peace Will Come from the East." *Haaretz*, August 21, 2002. Online archive http://www.haaretz.co.il/hasite/pages/arch (no. 921831). [H]

Shragai, Nadav. "At the 4000 Years Anniversary of the Al-Aksa Mosque." *Haaretz*, May 11, 2004. [H]

Shtendel, Ori. *Minorities.* Jerusalem: Hasbara Center, 1972. [H]

———. *Minorities in Israel.* Jerusalem: Merkaz Ha-Hasbara, 1970. [H]

Simon, E. E. "About the Double Meaning of the Concept Primitive." *Megamot* 2 (July 1951): 277–84. [H];

Sivan, Emmanuel. "The Annual Survey of the Shiloah Institute." *Ha-Mizrah Ha-Hadash* 28 (1979): 300. [H]

———. "The Decline of Nasserism or the Decline of Orientalism?" *Haaretz*, June 15, 1979, 23. [H]

———. "Edward Said and His Arab Reviewers." *Jerusalem Quarterly* 35 (Spring 1985): 11–23.

———. "Listening to Radical Islam." In *Intelligence for Peace*, edited by Hezi Carmel. Tel-Aviv: Miskal, 1998. [H]

Smilanski, Moshe. *Jewish Colonization and the Fellah.* Tel-Aviv: Mishar u-Ta'asia, 1930. [H]

———. *Sons of Arabia: Stories and Drawings from the Lives of the Arabs in Palestine.* Odessa: Haylprin, 1911. [H]

Smooha, Sammy. *Arabs and Jews in Israel.* London: Westview Press, 1989.

———. "Existing and Alternative Policies towards Arabs in Israel." *Megamot* 16, 7 (September 1980): 7–36. [H]

Smooha, Sammy, and Ora Cibulski. *Social Research on Arabs in Israel 1948–1982: Trends and an Annotated Bibliography.* Vols. 1–2. Haifa: University of Haifa, Jewish-Arab Center, 1989.

Sofer, Arnon. "Israeli Arabs: Facts and Trends." In *Israeli Arabs: Where Are They Heading? Debate of the Political Circle-Efal with the Participation of Yitzhak Bailey, Elie Rekhess, and Arnon Sofer, April 16, 1994.* Ramat Efal: Yad Tabenkin, 1996: 16–37. [H]

Solovitshik, M. *Treasures of the Bible.* Berlin: Dvir, 1925. [H]

Stavski, Moshe. *The Arab Village.* Tel-Aviv: Am Oved, 1946. [H]

Steinberg, Matti. "Arafat's PLO: Parameters of Pragmatism." *Israeli Democracy* (Spring 1989): 11–15.

———. *From One Pole to the Other: Currents in Palestinian National Thought.* Policy Paper no. 25. Jerusalem: Davis Institute, 1988. [H]

———. "Knowing How to Read the Demographic Clock." *Haaretz*, July 27, 2004. Online archive http://www.haaretz.co.il/hasite/pages/arch (no. 1112876). [H]

———. "The PLO Solution: The Meaning of a Three-Way Formula." In *Is There a Solution to the Palestinian Problem?* edited by Aluph Hareven. Jerusalem: Van-Leer, 1982. [H]

Stern, Yoav. "Hitler, Too, Promised Peace." *Haaretz*, June 18, 2004, 4. [H]
———. "An Unfounded Conception." *Haaretz*, June 18, 2004, 4. [H]
Stoler, Ann Laura. *Race and the Education of Desire*. Durham, NC: Duke University Press, 1995.
Susser, Asher. *Between Jordan and Palestine: A Political Biography of Watzfi al-Tel*. Tel-Aviv: Hakibutz Hameuchad, 1983. [H]
———. "The *Intifada* and the Palestinian National Movement: The Historical Context." In *In the Eye of the Conflict: The Intifada*, edited by Asher Susser and Gad Gilbar. Tel-Aviv: Ha-Kibutz Ha-Meuchad, 1992. [H]
Tehon, Hannah Helena. *The Ethnicities in Israel*. Jerusalem: Reuvan, 1957. [H]
Tel-Aviv University. *Bulletins of the Faculty of Humanities, 1965–1971*. Ramat-Aviv: Tel-Aviv University, 1965–1971. [H]
———. *List of Research Grants, 1964–1969*. Ramat-Aviv: Tel-Aviv University, 1970.
———. "The Shiloah Institute for the Study of the Middle East and Africa." *Hauniversita: Tel-Aviv University Monthly* 7 (June–July 1972): 3. [H]
Teveth, Shabtai. *Curse of the Blessing*. Jerusalem: Schocken, 1970. [H]
———. *Moshe Dayan: A Biography*. Jersualem: Schocken, 1971. [H]
Tzfadia, Erez, and Oren Yiftachel. "Between National and Local: Political Mobilization among Mizrahim in Israel's 'Development Towns.'" *Cities* 21, no. 1 (2004): 41–55.
Ullendorf, Edward. "D. H. Baneth and Philological Precociousness." In *Studia Orientalia Memoriae D. H. Baneth Dedicata*, edited by Joshua Blau. Jerusalem: Magnes, 1979.
Ussishkin, S. *Occident in the Orient: History of the Crusaders in Palestine*. Tel-Aviv: Mitzpe, 1937. [H]
Waschitz, Yosef. *The Arabs in the Land of Israel: Economy and Society, Culture and Politics*. Merhavia: Ha-Kibbutz Ha-Meuhad, 1947. [H]
———. "On the Problems of the Arab Village in Israel."*Kama* 4 (1952): 187–202. [H]
Weber, Max. *Economy and Society*. Berkeley: University of California Press, 1978.
———. "Religious Rejections of the World and their Directions." In *From Max Weber*, edited by Hans H. Gerth and Charles Wright Mills. New York: Oxford University Press, 1948.
———. "Science as a Vocation." In *From Max Weber*, edited by Hans H. Gerth and Charles Wright Mills. New York: Oxford University Press, 1948.
———. *Sociology of Religion*. Boston: Beacon Press, 1963.
Weingrod, Alex. *Reluctant Pioneers: Village Development in Israel*. New York: Cornell University Press, 1966.
Weintraub, Dov. "A Study of New Farmers in Israel." *Sociologia Ruralis* 4 (1964): 3–51.
Wittgenstein, Ludwig. *Philosophical Investigations*. Part 1. Oxford: Basil Blackwell, 1958.
Yaari, Aviezer. *On the Road from Merhavia: Story of an Israeli Intelligence Officer*. Tel-Aviv: Zemora-Bitan, 2003. [H]

Ya'ari, Ehud. "I Was Right." *Haaretz*, February 1, 2002, magazine section. Online archive http://www.haaretz.co.il/hasite/pages/arch (no. 791857). [H]

Ya'ari, Ehud, and Zeev Schiff. *A War of Deceit.* Jerusalem: Schoken, 1984. [H]

Yadin, Yigael. *The Absorption of Arab Refugees into Israel from the Security Point of View: Appreciation of the Situation.* Letter to David Horovitz, General Manager of the Ministry of the Treasury, September 1949. IDF Archive, 1.2.5/20/1951.

Yalan, Emmanuel. *The Modernization of Traditional Agricultural Villages: Minority Villages in Israel.* Rehovot: Settlement Study Center, 1972.

Yeger, Moshe. *The History of Israel's System for Foreign Hasbara.* Hetzelyia: Lahav, 1986. [H]

Yehoshua, A. B. *The Lover.* Jerusalem: Schoken, 1979. [H]

Yiftachel, Oren. "Social Control, Urban Planning and Ethno-Class Relations: Mizrahim in Israel's Development Towns." *International Journal of Urban and Regional Research* 24, no. 2 (2000): 417–34.

Zisser, Eyal. *The Face of Syria: Society, Regime and State.* Tel-Aviv: Ha-Kibutz Ha-Meuchad, 2003. [H]

———. *Syria: The Question of Succession: Towards Decision: Data and Analysis.* Tel-Aviv: Dayan Center, June 1993. [H]

———. *Syria's Asad: The Leader and His Image: Data and Analysis.* Tel-Aviv: Dayan Center, October 1993. [H]

Index